Receiving Erin's Children

Receiving

Erin's Children

Philadelphia, Liverpool, and the

Irish Famine Migration, 1845–1855

J. MATTHEW GALLMAN

The University of North Carolina Press   Chapel Hill and London

© 2000
The University of North Carolina Press
All rights reserved
Set in New Baskerville and Clarendon by
Tseng Information Systems
Manufactured in the United States of America
The paper in this book meets the guidelines for
permanence and durability of the Committee on
Production Guidelines for Book Longevity of the
Council on Library Resources.

Library of Congress Cataloging-in-Publication Data
Gallman, J. Matthew (James Matthew)
Receiving Erin's children : Philadelphia, Liverpool, and the Irish famine migration,
1845–1855 / J. Matthew Gallman.
    p.   cm.
Includes index.
ISBN 0-8078-2534-4 (cloth : alk. paper). — ISBN 0-8078-4845-x (pbk. : alk. paper)
1. Irish Americans—Pennsylvania—Philadelphia—History—19th century.   2. Immigrants—
Pennsylvania—Philadelphia—History—19th century.   3. Irish—England—Liverpool—
History—19th century.   4. Immigrants—England—Liverpool—History—19th century.
5. Philadelphia (Pa.)—Emigration and immigration—History—19th century.   6. Ireland—
Emigration and immigration—History—19th century.   7. Ireland—History—Famine, 1845–
1852.   8. Liverpool (England)—Emigration and immigration—History—19th century.
9. Philadelphia (Pa.)—Social conditions—19th century.   10. Liverpool (England)—Social
conditions—19th century.   I. Title.
F158.9.16G35   2000
942.7′53081—dc21   99-42768
                    CIP

04   03   02   01   00   5   4   3   2   1

For Robert E. Gallman (1926–1998)

Contents

Acknowledgments

I have been working on this project, on and off, for more than a decade, and I have been thinking about some of the underlying questions for at least twice that long. In that time I have accumulated many debts, both personal and professional.

This book grew out of several long-standing scholarly interests. This is not a traditional study of the Irish famine migrants; rather, it is a comparative analysis of how two of the most important host cities—Liverpool and Philadelphia—responded to emerging policy dilemmas in the midst of the Irish famine. As I explain more fully in the first chapter, I selected this project out of the conviction that some of the crucial questions in American history are best examined in a comparative context. This comparative perspective was central to my early graduate training at Brandeis University, and I owe a special thanks to Morton Keller and Steve Schuker who ran a particularly rigorous graduate seminar in comparative history. My fascination with the social history of Victorian England began long before I became a professional historian, when my family visited England and I spent a year as a fifth former preparing for the O level exams. I cultivated these interests in nineteenth-century England during my early years in graduate school and then set them aside until I began this project. Most recently I have been drawn, in both my scholarship and teaching, to the ways in which cities and national governments address a variety of social ills, particularly those affecting the materially disadvantaged. Although my conclusions on these topics have been shaped by the traditional process of reading and research, I would also like to acknowledge the important impact of Loyola College's Center for Values and Service—and all the marvelous friends and colleagues associated with the Center—in helping me place both my questions and my findings in a broader context.

This book would not have been possible without substantial material assistance from several sources. I began work with the support of a summer research fellowship from the Historical Society of Pennsylvania and the Library Company of Philadelphia. The National Endowment for the Humanities supported me through one summer of research and later provided me with a year-long Fellowship for College Teachers to draft the manuscript. Loyola College's Center for the Humanities—also funded by the National Endowment for the Humanities—awarded me a semester-long pretenure sabbatical, and Loyola's Faculty Development committee and the dean of Arts and Sciences funded three summers of travel and research as well as a year-long sabbatical. I only hope that this finished product justifies such generous support and provides further evidence that these national and campus-based programs are vital to ongoing scholarship, especially for faculty at liberal arts colleges with a strong commitment to teaching.

I did most of my research in Philadelphia and Liverpool, two marvelous cities to visit and study. While in Philadelphia, I received special assistance from the librarians and archivists at the Library Company of Philadelphia, the Historical Society of Pennsylvania, and the Philadelphia City Archives. I would also like to thank the librarians at the University of Pennsylvania and the Balch Institute for Ethnic Studies. Most of my research time in Liverpool was spent at the superb Liverpool Record Office and the Local History Library (both housed in the William Brown Library) and at the many fine libraries at the University of Liverpool. I would also like to thank the staffs at the Lancashire Record Office in Preston, the Merseyside Record Office, the Public Record Office in London, the Merseyside Maritime Museum, the Merseyside Police Station (where I found little information but was presented with a replica policeman's badge on my departure!), and the small Cathedral archives. I was able to maintain a productive research agenda while in Baltimore through the assistance of Loyola College's Center for the Humanities, which paid for numerous reels of microfilm; the dean of Arts and Sciences, who approved the purchase of a microfilm reader for my home use; the painstaking efforts of the Inter Library Loan department at the Loyola-Notre Dame Library; and the fine collection down the street at the Milton Eisenhower Library of Johns Hopkins University.

My personal debts in the writing of this book are too numerous to name. My colleagues and students during my twelve years at Loyola College helped create an ideal environment for teaching, writing, and living. My new colleagues at Gettysburg College have done the same as I have put the finishing touches on this manuscript. I would like to offer a special thanks to Barbara Vann and Tom Pegram for their years of friendship and words of counsel on this project. During my visits to Merseyside I enjoyed the good cheer and companionship of Father Denis Marmion and the folks at Our Lady's Church and Presbytery in Birkenhead. Many scholars at the University of Liverpool shared ideas and friendship during my visits. I am especially indebted to Paul Laxton for being such a gracious host and diligent correspondent. I would also like to thank John Belchem, Patrick Buckland, Gerry Kearns, Roger Swift, and Michael Tadman for their warm hospitality. I am grateful to Margaret Proctor and Gordon Read for taking the time to point me to useful sources. During my summer as a Historical Society of Pennsylvania–Library Company of Philadelphia research fellow in Philadelphia I enjoyed the company of a diverse group of fellow researchers and the unflagging enthusiasm of the Library Company's Jim Green, who has remained a good colleague and valuable resource. In subsequent visits to Philadelphia I took advantage of the hospitality of my old and dear friends C. Dallett Hemphill and John Hill.

It is the nature of such a comparative project that I was routinely wandering onto unfamiliar terrain, learning from scholars who had long been in the field ahead of me. Many people took time out to meet with me, answer a letter or E-mail, or read a chapter or conference paper. In addition to the British scholars noted above, I would like to thank Howard Wach, Patricia Seleski, Susan Tananbaum, Priscilla Clement, Charles Rosenberg, Eric Monkkonen, Judith Hunter, Deidre Mageean, W. J. Lowe, and the late Dennis Clark for words of support or advice. I also owe a particular word of thanks to my two readers for the University of North Carolina Press, Roger Lane and Jon Gjerde, and to my editor, Lewis Bateman.

In truth, these occasional exchanges with scholars in the field (some of which were so modest and so long ago that they have probably been forgotten by the "acknowledgee") barely scratch the surface of my scholarly debts. In the chapters that follow I have tried to make some sense of a wide range of topics as they affected life in mid-nineteenth–century England and the United States. Each topical chapter combines my own interpretation of original sources with a broad synthesis of the relevant scholarship. Thus, many of my most substantial intellectual debts are acknowledged in the endnotes to each chapter. I hope that these notes properly convey my deep admiration for the many scholars from whose work I have learned.

I conclude these acknowledgments, much as I did in another book nearly a decade ago, by thanking three men who offered advice on this manuscript and who have been central to my thinking about the discipline of history and about the profession of historian. Morton Keller and Stanley Engerman each read early drafts of this book and offered characteristically wise counsel on matters large and small. I am truly fortunate to have had both of these wonderful scholars as mentors and advisers. If I could have answered all of their suggestions I am sure that the result would have been much stronger. My deepest personal and intellectual debts are to my father, Robert E. Gallman. We talked about this project and he read drafts of most of the chapters, and in that immediate sense the book is better from his efforts. But in a much larger sense this book is simply the most recent product of a lifetime of learning from my father. The ideas that follow really owe more to other scholars I have acknowledged above, but the fact that I have written it at all owes everything to his example. Robert Gallman's life and his career are a model that I can only hope to emulate. I wish that he had lived long enough to see this book into print. It is with great pride that I dedicate it to his memory.

I write these words at the end of a very challenging year. I would like to close by thanking my sisters, Anita Cotuna and Eve Potgieter, and my brothers-in-law Theo Cotuna and Kurt Potgieter, and my mother, Jane Gallman, for many, many things.

Gettysburg, Pennsylvania

Receiving Erin's Children

1. Immigrants and Hosts

INTRODUCTION: THE IRISH FAMINE MIGRANTS

In July 1847 eighteen-year-old Ann Murphy left home for Belfast on a journey that would eventually lead her to Philadelphia. She carried with her a steerage ticket for passage from Liverpool to Philadelphia on the *Susquehanna,* one of the packet ships owned by Philadelphia's H & A Cope Company. Theodore Wilson, an Irishman living in Philadelphia, had purchased the ticket at the Cope Company's Walnut Street offices on January 22. Before mailing the ticket, Wilson had scrawled a few hasty words of advice on the back:

> [Tell] her to pay particular attention to the following directions I am going to give her, when she has got her sea store and clothes packed up as small bulk as possibel she can get to Belfast by the best conveyance and get put on board the steamer for Liverpool in Belfast and on board the boat she must be very careful of herself and things and form no acquaintance with any body, and take care of any body medling with her things when she arrives in Liverpool and she can find one of the Steam Boat porters to take her to the office of [Harnden and Company?].[1]

The following February, Margaret McKee and her friend Catherine Ronaghan arrived at the Liverpool docks with steerage tickets—also for the *Susquehanna*—purchased in Philadelphia by Margaret's brother Michael. Michael's written advice and warnings picked up where Theodore Wilson's had left off: "Inquire for Copes office and show them this and you will get your passage. be there on the eighth of the month that you are going to come bring herrings plenty with you that is the mainstay on board of ship . . . when you come on the ship . . . be wise and take care of yourselves for board of ship is an awful place and make no freedom with any person and no one will enterfere with yous keep to your selves when you land."[2]

Ann, Margaret, and Catherine were all part of the massive Irish migration during the potato famine. The history of the famine and migration has been told often, from many different perspectives, and needs no detailed retelling here.[3] In the fall of 1845 a deadly blight struck the potato crop in eastern Ireland. The next year the potato famine swept across the country. In 1847 the potato crop was small, although the yields were actually fairly strong, but 1848 saw another round of disaster. Four years of poor harvests took a tremendous toll, as a weakened citizenry fell easy victim to typhus, dysentery, and other deadly diseases. By some estimates, roughly a million Irish men and women—or about a ninth of the total population— succumbed to starvation and disease because of the famine.[4] Many others faced eviction or fled their homes in search of new lives. Between 1845 and 1855 an estimated 1.5 million Irish women and men sailed for the United States, landing largely in New York, Philadelphia, New Orleans, Boston, and Baltimore. Another 600,000 left Ireland for England, Canada, Australia, and other destinations.[5]

During the peak of the Irish famine migration the H & A Cope Company—which had five vessels in operation in 1848—was sending packet ships westward from Liverpool to Philadelphia on the twelfth of every month. The passenger lists ranged from as few as 150 to well over 300 steerage travelers per voyage, the vast majority coming originally from Ireland.[6] Between January 1847 and the end of 1849, Cope's Philadelphia offices sold more than 2,500 tickets for passage from Liverpool, primarily to Irish immigrants who mailed them home to friends and relatives. Perhaps a hundred or so of the small notes written on the back of tickets survive.[7] Taken together they describe a world of great opportunities, but a journey fraught with dangers and hardship. John Stott's message to John and Sarah Glehill and their four young daughters was typical: "we hope that you will brace your nerves and steel your face and be nothing daunted and you will soon join with us on this Great Continent. There will be dificultyes to meet with but then consider the object you have in view."[8] Often those difficulties would be from strangers, with familiar sounding brogues, who haunted the Liverpool and Philadelphia docks preying on migrants who carried all their possessions in their hands and their savings in their pockets. One correspondent warned Howard Berne that "Liverpool is full of Imposters if they can trick any person they can lay hold of . . . you will require to be very cautious & clever & no way shy without getting your rights."[9] Mary

Kon left home with explicit instructions to seek out a Mr. Lynch in Liverpool; if he did not appear she was to "inquire for the Constable and show him the card and he will dirrect you wher the house is." [10] Catherine Cardary directed Alice Cleland to a small court off of Carlton Street "opposit the cloureness dock liverpool," adding that "we think you would be safer there thane aney other plase when you lave the steem boat." [11]

Other notes offered advice on what food to pack to supplement the meager official rations and appropriate clothing for the voyage. "My advice to you" wrote Hugh Clark to Mary Clark, "is to keep off the Deck in the night and stormy times as it is dangeres[.] you will want [a] tin pan . . . in the shape of a bottil that will hold 4 qt for your fresh water[.] you will want some tin plats and some tin cups and a boiler[.] you need not get any new close [clothes] as it is not the fashins in america that thy hav at home." [12] Many other correspondents shared this last suggestion. Apparently clothing in Philadelphia was sufficiently inexpensive and distinctive that even the humblest migrant should expect to acquire a new wardrobe on arrival.

Those immigrants who were fortunate enough to have relatives or friends in the United States were generally told to hurry to a particular lodging house or tavern near the docks where a friendly face would await them. One woman was to "Inquire for William Rushworth" at the "English Tav[ern,] No 87 South Water Street Philadelphia." [13] Another correspondent told his nineteen-year-old brother that "when he lands in Philadelphia Enquire for 252 North Water Street and you will find your Friend to welcome you." [14] Catherine Whelan told her brother and sister to "come to Mrs. Weines[,] 159 Front Street between Spruce St and Dock St." [15] Some of the Philadelphians who mailed tickets promised to meet each of the Cope vessels until their relative arrived. Whatever their economic prospects, strangers were best off with a trustworthy human contact as a buffer against a potentially hostile new world.

The disaster that struck Ireland in the late 1840s had a very real agricultural basis. By some estimates the lost potato crop between 1846 and 1848 was enough to have fed almost five million people daily. Nonetheless, the Irish peasantry had ample reason to see human agency behind their troubles. Parliamentary debates about the Irish crisis moved within tight ideological constraints, shaped by a trio of powerful—and often painfully abstract—ruling principles: localism, laissez-faire economics, and "less eligibility." Landlords, encouraged by public policy, sometimes ruthlessly drove starving tenants from their homes; between 1846 and 1855 an estimated half-million people faced eviction. The public relief forthcoming from Parliament amounted to a tiny portion of the nation's resources, as policymakers clung to a faith in charitable assistance and local poor rates.[16] One historian has described the Great Famine as "the tragic outcome of three factors: an ecological accident that could not have been predicted, an ideology ill-geared to saving lives and, of course, mass poverty."[17] A similar confluence of factors—material conditions, intellectual assumptions, and the serendipity of events—shaped the experiences of the Irish migrants as they fled their homeland.

Proximity and shipping routes dictated that most emigrants headed for Liverpool. The first step in the journey would be overland to an Irish port, where crowded ferries made the crossing to the Merseyside city in twenty-four hours or more. Many would remain in the thriving port city, either by design, or because of limited resources, or simply because disease took its toll too quickly. Others soon boarded ships bound for North America. Along the way the weary, often sickly travelers were subject to all sorts of dangers. The passage across the Irish Sea was barely regulated. Ferry operators cared little for health and sanitation as they crammed as many deck passengers as they could onto each vessel. The migrants arrived in Liverpool seasick, exhausted, and ripe for plucking at the hands of an assortment of unscrupulous "runners," lodging house keepers, ticket brokers, and other crooks. The lucky ones had a place to sleep and prepaid passages in hand. However long they stayed, the migrants found themselves in a world of crowded housing, unsanitary streets, and ethnic tension. For those who set off for North America, the hardships were just beginning. Ships varied tremendously in size and condition, generally falling far short of their advertised specifications. A slowly evolving set of laws regulated the amount of sleeping space, the food and water to be allocated for each passenger, and the circumstances when a surgeon was required to be on board. But much of the most important legislation passed on both sides of the Atlantic came after the heaviest migration. On their arrival at an American port, passengers were liable to physical inspection, quarantine, and perhaps prohibitive bonds. As they disembarked, the exhausted immigrants were once again targets for competing armies of shady characters and diverse philanthropists. It is no wonder that the snippets of advice written on the back of the Cope tickets stressed packing food and clothing with care and trusting no one along the way.[18]

The famine migrants are at the center of this book, but it is not really their story. Rather, it is the story of the worlds that they entered and the ways in which their presence helped to change those worlds.[19] If the circumstances of their exodus and the nature of their journeys reflected the combined forces of historic chance, contemporary ideology, and material circumstances, so too did the evolution of their new homes. This book compares the histories of two important host cities—Liverpool and Philadelphia—during the famine years. It is an attempt to understand how the famine migration both illuminated and shaped circumstances and policies in each city and nation. In a broader sense, this study seeks to use the years of the famine migration to compare two societies at a crucial moment in their histories.

As for any historical study, the design of this book reflects several conscious decisions, each with its own underlying assumptions. The project has its genesis in a desire to examine nineteenth-century urban development, with a particular emphasis on the ways in which cities confronted the broad array of social challenges that accompanied increased size and population density. Having spent considerable time studying Northern cities during the American Civil War, I was drawn to the immediate antebellum decades as the occasion for many of the most crucial urban developments. I also brought to this project an interest in comparative history and a conviction that my examination of these urban questions should not be confined to a single nation. Clearly English and American cities faced many of the same challenges at roughly the same time. My goal was to construct a study that would allow for a profitable comparative analysis across the Atlantic.[20]

The decision to focus on the Irish famine migration proceeded logically from this scholarly agenda. Given my interest in examining how cities in both England and the United States faced numerous midcentury challenges—including poverty, disorder, and disease—the central task was to sharpen the focus as much as possible to enhance the value of the comparison. The famine migrants did not create these urban problems, but their arrival made the circumstances more dire in some cities, suggesting the possibility that cities in both countries may have been addressing similar problems at roughly the same time. But that having been said, I also did not want to let the tail wag the dog. My comparative focus is on the responses to a specific set of urban problems during the famine years, not merely on the direct responses to the Irish newcomers. In some cases the analysis indicates that the crucial institutional developments preceded the migration, and in other instances the immigrants did not prove to be the major shaping forces in one or both cities. In such situations the focus remains on the emerging responses to the specific constellation of problems, not merely on the institutions and policies as experienced by the Irish immigrants.

The final preparatory decision was to compare Liverpool and Philadelphia. There were certainly other reasonable candidates, including London, Manchester, and Glasgow on one side of the Atlantic and New York, Boston, and Quebec on the other. I quickly excluded London as an option, both because it was several times larger than any American city at midcentury and because the Irish community had been already so carefully examined by Lynn Hollen Lees. Among the remaining alternatives, I selected Philadelphia and Liverpool largely because they were similar in size (both demographically and geographically) and had similarly large Irish populations, allowing for some control over those crucial variables.[21] In selecting those two cities I was also opting for a relatively limited comparison, rather than, for instance, attempting an analysis of a half-dozen cities of different sizes and circumstances. This choice reflects a preference for depth over breadth. By limiting my research to two cities I have been able to address a wider range of topics in some detail, rather than restricting my attention to a single set of issues.[22]

LIVERPOOL AND PHILADELPHIA AT MIDCENTURY

Liverpool and Philadelphia played similar roles in their respective worlds.[23] Second in size and importance to the dominant metropolises of London and New York, they both enjoyed international prominence as major ports and commercial centers. Between 1831 and 1851 the borough of Liverpool's population jumped from 165,175 to 375,955. In the same two decades Philadelphia County's population more than kept pace, rising from 167,751 to 408,742.[24] Both cities, too, had large Irish populations dating from well before the potato famine. By midcentury nearly 72,000 Philadelphians (17.6 percent) and 84,000 Liverpudlians (22.3 percent) were Irish-born immigrants.[25] Philadelphia's population was otherwise more demographically diverse than its English counterpart, with nearly 50,000 (12 percent of the total population) non-Irish immigrants, including 22,750 (5.6 percent) Germans and 17,500 (4.3 percent) English natives. Over 10 percent of Liverpool's residents were non-Irish immigrants, but the vast majority of these were from neighboring Wales (20,262, 5.4 percent) and Scotland (14,059, 3.7 percent), with a mere 1.4 percent from other nations. Nearly 5 percent (19,761) of Philadelphians were African American, giving the city a racial diversity almost completely absent in Liverpool.[26]

A modern observer landing at either nineteenth-century port might well have been struck, at a visceral level, by the cities' similarities. With sanitation measures lagging far behind needs, a newcomer's senses would have been overwhelmed by the odors from scores of "nuisances," ranging from overflowing privies to foul-smelling slaughterhouses and rag-and-bone shops.[27] But contemporary travelers, arriving with different sensibilities, generally stressed each city's distinctive characteristics.

Americans landing in Liverpool marveled at the city's magnificent docks. Herman Melville's fictional Wellingborough Redburn "never tired of admiring" the "long China walls of masonry; vast piers of stone; and . . . succession of granite-rimmed docks." To Redburn the docks were like "the old Pyramids of Egypt," in sharp contrast to New York's "miserable wooden wharves." [28] Other travelers were equally impressed with the docks and with the view across the River Mersey to Birkenhead, which some observers compared to Brooklyn across the Hudson River from New York.[29]

Like other nineteenth-century cities, Liverpool boasted a wide assortment of monuments and impressive public buildings.[30] "A Stranger in Liverpool" reported back to the *Philadelphia Public Ledger* that "the public buildings of Liverpool are both numerous and beautiful" and that the Nelson monument was particularly noteworthy.[31] One Georgia diarist admired Liverpool's large granite railroad terminal and the new Northern Hospital. Nathaniel Bowe was impressed with the "rather nice dwelling places" in "the upper part of the City." Another observer, writing in *The Workingman's Friend and Family Instructor,* insisted that "the general appearance of Liverpool was more inviting than I had supposed. Its streets, though not so wide or regular as those of New York, are much cleaner, and better paved." But one suspects that that correspondent protested too much. More typical was a European traveler in the late 1850s who acknowledged that "the George's Hall which occupies a central site is a splendid and imposing edifice" but generally concluded that "Liverpool is a large and growing commercial emporium but with the exception of 2 or 3 public buildings of great magnificence there are but few objects that strike the stranger on his first arrival in the city." Even those travelers willing to praise a few buildings found much to criticize. The *Public Ledger*'s reporter wandered Liverpool's streets and claimed that "incredible as it may seem, [they] are much more filthy and irregular" than New York's. John Twiggs found "the buildings . . . very dingy, being very much smoked, clouds of this article always overhanging the city." After several weeks of rain, mud, and smoke, the Georgian was thrilled to see the last of the "miserable city." Soon after arriving to serve as U.S. consul to Liverpool, a melancholy Nathaniel Hawthorne wrote home that "Liverpool is a most detestable place as a residence that ever my lot was cast in—smoky, noisy, dirty, pestilential."[32]

Most visitors saved their harshest comments for Liverpool's legions of paupers. The *Ledger*'s "Stranger in Liverpool" reported:

I have seen more beggars in *one week* in Liverpool than I have ever seen in all my life. The streets are full of them; at every step you are arrested and often followed by the pitiful cries of distress and want. Poor, ragged and haggard wretches, with four and five barefooted and poorly clad children. The most of these distressed beings are Irish, and have been driven over the channel by the approach of starvation. Some of these poor creatures may be undeserving of charity, but most of them, I doubt not, are proper objects of Christian benevolence and kindness.[33]

Nathaniel Hawthorne quickly became fascinated by his new city's worst streets. "Almost every day," he recorded in his diary, "I take walks about Liverpool; preferring the darker and dingier streets, inhabited by the poorer classes. The scenes there are very picturesque in their way; at every two or three steps, a gin-shop; also [fil]thy in clothes and persons, ragged, pale, often afflicted with humors; women, nursing their babies on dirty bosoms; men haggard, drunken, care-worn, hopeless, but with a kind of patience, as if all this were the rule of their life." Later that week he declared: "The people are as numerous as maggots in cheese; you behold them, disgusting, and all moving about, as when you raise a plank or log that has long lain on the ground, and find many vivacious bugs and insects beneath it." The entire experience left the transplanted New Englander convinced that "it is worth while coming across the sea in order to feel one's heart warm towards his own country."[34]

Philadelphia fared better in the estimation of both American and foreign visitors. William Penn's carefully laid out grid of streets—with a large, open square marking each corner—gave Philadelphia a sense of order that stood in sharp contrast to Liverpool's bewildering web of streets and lanes, which wandered across the terrain more like those in Boston than in Philadelphia or even New York.[35] Philadelphians took pride in the city's broad, clean, well-paved streets and in a host of grand public buildings.[36] A Bostonian writing in a local paper called Philadelphia "a charming city to look at" with "handsome streets [and] wide sidewalks." [37]

Europeans touring American cities were sure to pass through Philadelphia and visit several important sites. W. I. Mann's experience was typical. In his brief stay the Liverpudlian stopped at Girard College Orphanage, which he found far "too good for the little orphan boys that we saw running about," and the Fairmount Waterworks, which he grudgingly acknowledged would be "a very pretty place in summer." Mann also shared the common observation that Philadelphia's streets were much cleaner than those in New York City. Anne Holt, a young Liverpool Unitarian, spent several days in Philadelphia in May 1851. On arriving she noted that her "first impression of Philadelphia is that it is a decidedly handsome city." She, too, toured the waterworks and Girard College, recording her admiration of both spectacles. Holt was also interested in visiting Philadelphia's House of Refuge to see how local officials treated the poor. Southerner Henry L. Cathell made his own pilgrimage to Girard College in 1856. But although impressed with much of his visit, Cathell returned from a rainy afternoon walk with the conviction that "There is but one description of the streets of this place[,] speaking of one you speak of all—viz—plain and straight— There are three predominant colours about the buildings—White, Red & Green—Homes built of brick that is red,—window sills . . . and front door trimmings of white marble & all woodwork painted white,—that is white— The blinds of windows, painted green—that is green." The sardonic Cathell had certainly resisted Philadelphia's charms, but his criticism hardly compares with the more scathing indictments of Liverpool's environment.[38]

❦

Although visitors passing through Liverpool and Philadelphia were most likely to note buildings, monuments, streets, and the like, the urban geography also presented a revealing map of each city's economic, demographic, and political life. Liverpool's tremendous docks spoke plainly of what one scholar described as the city's "single-minded devotion to furthering commerce." By midcentury steamers from Liverpool were a familiar sight in ports across the globe. This tradition of trade had often led the city to look toward America; Liverpool's merchants grew rich trading slaves and cotton across the Atlantic. Between 1820 and 1850 four-fifths of the raw cotton entering England came through the port. The opening of the Liverpool-Manchester railroad in 1830 buttressed the city's economic links to the industrial North, strengthening an already heavy trade in manufactured goods. Liverpool's emphasis on commerce and its modest manufacturing sector combined to shape a workforce dominated by casual laborers. Workers could find ample day labor unloading ships, carting goods, or performing similar unskilled tasks, but only a small portion of local laborers worked in manufacturing.[39]

Philadelphia, long a major trading port, had by the 1840s emerged as a leading industrial center even as it was losing ground commercially to New York City. The development of canals in the 1820s, and railroads in later decades, enabled Philadelphia manufacturers to look to the hinterlands for raw materials and markets. By 1850 Philadelphia County had 58,000 manufacturing workers. As manufacturing grew and railroad transportation developed, the districts surrounding the city blossomed into distinct communities, each with its own ethnic flavor. North of the city center, Kensington and Germantown were important textile centers attracting skilled immigrant workers. Germantown, for instance, became known as an important enclave for German stockingers. Several miles to the northwest, the borough of Manayunk—the self-styled "Manchester of America"—became home to British weavers and spinners. And as cotton and woolen textile industries boomed, Philadelphia's machine works prospered by supplying the new factories.[40] We should not, however, overstate the impact of Philadelphia's superior manufacturing base on its Irish newcomers. At midcentury Irish immigrants were far less likely to find skilled manufacturing work than their German and native-born brethren, clustering instead in day labor and other unskilled jobs, much like their counterparts in Liverpool.[41]

Although neither city had truly insular ethnic or racial "ghettos," both Liverpool and Philadelphia had become increasingly segmented along ethnic and class lines.[42] Neither Philadelphia nor Liverpool had developed streetcar lines by midcentury, but both cities had horse-drawn omnibus lines that enabled the wealthiest citizens to move away from the city centers. Philadelphia's African American community supported a small, vibrant elite with a complex network of churches, newspapers, and institutions. But most Philadelphia blacks were poor. Many crowded into congested neighborhoods in Moyamensing, just south of the city center, a district that was also home to large numbers of Irish poor. Irish immigrants dispersed throughout both cities, but clustered in poor neighborhoods near the waterfronts. Philadelphia's Irish were most concentrated in the industrial areas of Kensington and Southwark, north and south of the city. But unlike later immigrant groups, the Irish did not find a ready supply of deteriorating center city housing in which to settle.[43] In Liverpool, the populations in six wards adjoining the docks were roughly a quarter Irish-born in 1851, and two—Vauxhall and Exchange—were nearing half Irish-born.[44] Both cities had streets in these Irish neighborhoods that became notorious for their crowded, unsanitary conditions.[45]

Like their physical and economic characteristics, the political structures of Liverpool and Philadelphia had essential similarities, but also marked differences. Both cities had an elected Council and a separate elected Board of Guardians to address the needs of the poor.[46] The bureaucratic structure of each city was complicated by a variety of separate political sub-divisions. By midcentury the relatively compact city of Philadelphia was bordered by five built-up suburbs to the north and south. Philadelphia County included an additional twenty-three townships, boroughs, and districts. For most purposes these were distinct political units, with their own elected officeholders and police. But the outlying areas relied on the city for some services—water, for instance—and certain government bodies, such as the Board of Health and the Guardians of the Poor, had jurisdictions that went beyond the city boundaries. The 1854 Act of Consolidation solved many jurisdictional dilemmas by absorbing the entire county into the city of Philadelphia. The parish of Liverpool was divided into twelve wards. The borough of Liverpool, as extended in 1835, included the parish and an additional five extraparochial wards. The Council had jurisdiction over the entire borough, but Liverpool's Guardians of the Poor—charged with administering poor relief and running the workhouse—only addressed parochial concerns. (In this sense, then, the cities were mirror images of each other: Philadelphia's Council controlled a smaller area than the Guardians, whereas Liverpool's Council administered an area touching more than one Poor Law Union.) Both Councils oversaw a range of committees, often composed of Council members, that attended to various new urban functions including policing, health, and sanitation. As we shall see, these Council committees occasionally conflicted with the local Guardians, revealing organizational shortcomings that were periodically aggravated by the flow of Irish migrants.[47]

From the institution of its royal charter in 1207 until the 1830s the Corporation of Liverpool had been under the control of the city's freemen, a hereditary body that initially included most adult males but eventually evolved into a small, closed group. Since 1695 the Council had consisted of elected councillors—who served for life—and a mayor, selected from among the councillors. The Council occasionally ventured into municipal reform, but the councillors generally concentrated on supporting local commercial interests, which often meant emphasizing the Liverpool docks. The 1835 Municipal Reform Act reorganized the Council and opened up the franchise to local ratepayers. Still, access to the vote remained limited. In 1832 Liverpool had a registered electorate of only 11,283; twenty years later that figure had climbed to 17,433, or less than 5 percent of the total population.[48]

Philadelphia, in contrast, was never controlled by a small, self-perpetuating group comparable to Liverpool's freemen. Since 1776, nearly all adult male taxpayers had had access to the vote. In 1838 the new Pennsylvania constitution opened up the franchise to all white men aged twenty-one or over (in the process, it formally disenfranchised all black men as well as all women). In 1841 the mayor became an elected officer, rather than a Council appointee. In the 1849 local elections over 40,000 county residents (roughly 10 percent of the population) cast a vote, or more than twice as many as Liverpool's *registered* voters in 1852.[49]

Before the 1835 reforms, Liverpool's government had been dominated by Tory-Anglican interests. The reformed Council following the 1835 elections included fifty-eight Liberals among its sixty-four members. Although political debates continued to center on commercial questions and officeholders continued to be drawn from the city's elites, the Liberal Council pushed through a number of important reforms in its six years in power.[50] Before the 1840s Philadelphia's elections pitted Whigs against Democrats, with the traditionally wealthier Whigs controlling the Council and the Democrats (who claimed to speak for the masses) holding sway in the outlying districts. This two-party system fell into disarray with the rise of the nativist Know-Nothings.[51]

It may be possible to look beyond differing suffrage laws and discover fundamentally different assumptions about the roles and responsibilities of local government. Certainly officeholders in both cities struggled mightily with the problems posed by rising populations. But Liverpool's councillors consistently saw their charge as largely to protect commerce and to keep rates down. Consider, in contrast, the *Public Ledger*'s thoughts on "Municipal Government in Philadelphia," published in 1848:

The good government of a city is a simple, and yet a difficult object, being plain in its general principles, yet complex in its details. Watching and lighting by night, a good day police, clean streets, faithful public agents, a healthy atmosphere, property secure from depredations, and personal safety amply provided for by the dispersion of crowds and the suppression of mobs, violence and outrage, the arrest and punishment of thieves, the maintenance of public morals, and decorum in the streets and highways, and the construction of combustible buildings prevented, and in fine, the removal of all nuisances, and the prevention of all disorders and breaches of the peace, constitute the sum and substance of good municipal government.[52]

This is clearly the charge to a broadly elected local government, not to a small coterie of local commercial elites.

The social, cultural, and institutional life of Liverpool and Philadelphia was intrinsically linked to each city's ethnic makeup. Thus the sudden increase in poor, Irish Catholic immigrants had an important effect on the equilibrium in both cities. Whereas many of the earlier Irish migrants were Protestants, the famine immigrants were heavily Irish Catholic. In both cities these Catholic newcomers entered largely Protestant, often hostile, worlds, placing particular strains on local Catholics who struggled to provide their coreligionists with spiritual and benevolent support. In Liverpool, the dominance of the Established Church in public affairs only complicated matters.[53] The immigrants also entered worlds with complex associational patterns both in and out of the Church. Philadelphia's Irish developed a multitiered associational world, including elite clubs, literary societies for the upwardly bound, friendly societies for those who were closer to the edge, and volunteer fire companies, which attracted a range of classes, including many working-class immigrants. The Irish newcomers also became active participants in labor unions and political clubs.[54] Liverpool's Irish joined many of the same kinds of associations. But whereas Philadelphia's fire companies served as an important gathering point for Irish and German immigrants (as well as working-class nativists), the Irish in Liverpool congregated in an assortment of secret clubs.[55]

Both cities had been stung by sectarian conflict in the decade before the migration. Liverpool's reformed Council sparked controversy when its Liberal members expanded religious instruction in the heretofore Protestant corporation schools. The Tories used this issue as a lever to pry political control from Liberal hands. In Philadelphia, similar battles over the teaching of the Bible in schools culminated in bloody rioting between Irish Protestants and Catholics in 1844.[56] Sectarian conflicts continued to play an important role, both in and out of party politics, in the two cities throughout the famine years and beyond. Philadelphia's Irish Catholics typically voted Democratic, helping to stimulate a powerful Native American (nativist) movement in the early 1840s. A decade later the anti-immigrant Know-Nothings found strong support in Philadelphia, peaking with the 1854 mayoral election of Know-Nothing candidate Robert Taylor Conrad. In Liverpool, debates about the position of Catholics—locally, nationally, and in Ireland—continued to figure in Council discussions and church sermons, and sectarian street violence remained a source of persistent concern.[57]

URBAN DEVELOPMENT AND COMPARATIVE HISTORY

As their populations grew, Philadelphia and Liverpool shared a discouraging array of urban problems. Both cities had to feel their way in unfamiliar terrain, coping with the effects of rising population densities. This book employs a comparative approach to sort out how they responded to these challenges and, in a larger sense, to examine how fairly comparable cities in dissimilar political and cultural worlds developed through the crucial decades of the mid-nineteenth century. Most of these new urban problems were magnified by the thousands of poor Irish Catholic immigrants. The famine years and the famine migrants thus serve as a crucial analytic lens through which to study these developments. But although the Irish immigrants figure prominently in what follows, this is not really their story so much as it is a comparative study of urban development.

Chapter 2 considers each city's immediate reactions to the rising numbers of Irish immigrants. What was the public response to the flood of poor, often sickly, immigrants? Did policymakers act to stem the tide? How did philanthropic agencies respond to the new demands?

The next five chapters address specific social problems that plagued Liverpool and Philadelphia in the mid-nineteenth century. Chapter 3 asks how each city dealt, both publicly and privately, with the increase of the poor who crowded their streets. Who received assistance? In what form and under what conditions? Chapters 4 and 5 consider the interrelated problems of health and sanitation. In 1849 cholera swept through Europe, taking an enormous toll in Liverpool's poor neighborhoods. Although the disease proved less destructive in American cities, Philadelphia's preparations for the epidemic and its emergency measures on its arrival are nonetheless illuminating. Two summers earlier, typhus—labeled "Irish Fever"— had cut a swath through Liverpool's Irish community, including several Catholic priests among its victims. In 1853 Philadelphians battled an attack of yellow fever. These highly visible epidemics, along with the more routine health disamenities associated with urban life, prompted various legislative and institutional responses, ranging from quarantines to hospital construction. Meanwhile, the threat of disease helped spur innovative sanitation measures. Public officials in both cities were charged with cleaning streets, clearing nuisances, and inspecting dwellings. How did they balance the demands for improved sanitation against traditional views of private property and persistent concerns about excessive costs?

Chapters 6 and 7 shift the focus from environmental concerns to human conflicts. Chapter 6 considers the religious implications of the famine migration. How did the Catholic Church in each city respond to the new demands? How did the newcomers affect the sectarian tensions that had previously erupted? How did each city's institutions—poorhouses, schools, hospitals, orphanages—address religious differences? The final chapter focuses on disorder and the forces of order in each city. What can be learned by comparing patterns of crime, policing, and incarceration in a major English and a major American city?

In a recent study of nineteenth-century American cities, Mary Ryan examined the changing nature of "democracy and public life" in New York, San Francisco, and New Orleans through a close reading of a wide array of public encounters, ranging from formal public ceremonies and rituals, to spontaneous gatherings and riots, to scores of public meetings where true democracy was on display.[58] This study charts a different route over comparable historical, and evidentiary, terrain. Like Ryan, I have tried to come to an understanding of nineteenth-century civic life, relying on a variety of printed evidence including newspapers, annual reports, and government documents. But in this study the public *problem,* not the public place, is the organizing idea. Specifically, how did public officials and private citizens understand the proper responses to developing urban dilemmas? What were local assumptions about the appropriate role of government in addressing social problems? When should citizens expect solutions from pub-lic officials? which officials and at what level of government? When should the problems and their solutions remain the purview of individuals, volun-tary societies, and church groups?

The answers that each city selected to the problems posed by mid-nine-teenth–century growth would prove crucial to shaping future local devel-opments. In a larger sense, their approaches to urban policy-making re-flected broader assumptions about what properly constituted the "public good" and how those collective interests should be protected.[59] One task of this study will be to evaluate competing explanations for the policy devel-opments in Philadelphia and Liverpool, and—where appropriate—in the United States and England. In his study of the "evolution of the British welfare state," Derek Fraser identified seven historiographic models that have been used to explain his subject: (1) the *Whig model,* emphasizing the march of progress; (2) the *pragmatic model,* which sees welfare reform as a response to necessity in the wake of industrialization; (3) the *bureaucratic model,* which stresses the importance of legislation and administration and the dominant role of public officials; (4) the *ideological model,* countering the previous two interpretations by placing ideas at center stage; (5) the *conspiratorial model,* stressing the importance of coercion or larger political agendas; (6) the *capitalist model,* which sees reform as serving the economic interests of an evolving society; and (7) the *democratic model,* which argues that reform was a response to democratic demands.[60]

Fraser's seven models make a useful point of departure for this study. As he points out, no single model can adequately explain such a complex set of events. This observation is (at least) doubly true when we expand the discussion beyond welfare policy. Rather than treating these interpre-tations as adversarial stances, we should approach them as complementary pieces in a complex puzzle. As such, they are particularly useful in compar-ing two worlds with distinct histories and historiographies. For instance, British historians have expended a tremendous amount of energy debating the role of national bureaucrats in molding Victorian policies.[61] This de-bate is put in a different context if we set it beside Eric Monkkonen's analy-sis of American urban development, which emphasizes the importance of local decision-making in contrast to the traditional focus on technological and economic determinism.[62] We must consider how the models required to explain Liverpool's experience compare with those that we would use to explain Philadelphia's history.

This book's comparative approach is valuable in sorting out the relative importance of diverse forces shaping decision-making. But along with the potential benefits come a host of methodological challenges and ideological minefields. Their similar size and circumstances make Liverpool and Philadelphia a logical focus for a comparative investigation. Moreover, in many senses the two cities existed within the same intellectual universe. As we have seen, many migrants moved directly from one port to another. Newspapers in each city routinely reported news from the other, fresh from the latest packet ships. Doctors, sanitarians, and prison reformers had access to the same journals and theories. Philanthropists, temperance reformers, and abolitionists drew from the same ideological traditions, periodically crossing the Atlantic to share insights in lectures and face-to-face discussions. When the two cities behaved differently, it was not for want of information. On the other hand, these shared traits should not disguise crucial differences in local conditions. Even where they faced the same basic problems, the magnitude of the challenge was rarely equal. Generally, in fact, Liverpool encountered a much tougher road. In addition to the Irish immigrants who settled in Liverpool, a large proportion of those bound for distant ports spent days or weeks crowded into local cellars or lodging houses. Their numbers contributed to Liverpool's dramatic mid-century battles with poverty, deplorable housing, and disease. These unequal challenges provide an important context for any comparative analysis of developments in the two cities.

In addition to these methodological considerations, any comparative project—especially one involving the United States—must come to terms with the long-standing debate over national characteristics. Contemporary travelers to the United States commonly spoke of unique traits that they claimed lay behind American distinctiveness. Historians have periodically taken up the same challenge, offering either implicit or explicit discussions of characteristics that set America apart from other nations. Most controversial (and in my view problematic) are those scholars who describe an "American exceptionalism" that often includes an implicit, and sometimes explicit, claim of national superiority or divine protection. But surely a careful comparison of specific cities, or even nations, need not fall victim to such nationalistic assumptions. A balanced comparative investigation would weigh the importance of distinctive cultural, structural, or institutional characteristics in yielding different results in different settings. Some of these differences might have local, or entirely idiosyncratic, roots; other observed differences might point to distinctive national traits.[63]

While Fraser's seven models offer one avenue for comparing policy developments in Philadelphia and Liverpool, the vast literature on American exceptionalism provides a wealth of other models to be tested. If we jettison all notions of national superiority, we are left with a series of causal arguments hypothesizing links between different circumstances and distinctive national characteristics. The range of arguments fall, once again, into seven categories.

When traveling through America in the early 1830s, Alexis de Tocqueville took pains to identify the sources of what he saw as the distinct American identity.[64] Many of his observations emphasized the importance of American democracy. We need not embrace all of Tocqueville's ideas to identify *political structure* as a first category. As we have seen, although the Reform Act of 1835 dramatically altered the English political system, voter access remained much broader in Philadelphia than in Liverpool. Perhaps the suffrage laws and the political culture combined to create significantly different relationships between citizens and elected officials in the two cities.

A second source of distinctive experiences may be found in differing national commitments to *localism*. As we examine responses to social problems, we must be conscious of the relationships—both attitudinally and constitutionally—between the municipal government and the national (or state) government. Whom did citizens turn to in moments of crisis? Where did the necessary powers to reform lie? One school of English historians has stressed the importance of Victorian reform in spurring the rise of a national administrative state. Others have found persistent localism flourishing beneath a thin veneer of national bureaucracy.[65] How might a comparison with the American experience inform this discussion?

In one of his most famous observations, Tocqueville noted that "Americans of all ages, all stations in life, and all types of dispositions are forever forming associations." This passion for *voluntarism* is a third fruitful avenue for comparative investigation. Philadelphians certainly fit Tocqueville's image of a people constantly bustling around forming associations. Sam Bass Warner portrayed the city's set of organizations as a cornerstone to "the private city's" culture. Across the Atlantic, Margaret Simey's history of Liverpool charities emphasized that city's unusual reputation for philanthropy. The famine migration provides an excellent laboratory for comparing voluntarism in these two societies.[66]

The classic statement of American distinctiveness was framed by Frederick Jackson Turner, who stressed the importance of the *frontier*.[67] In the 1840s, a half century before Turner wrote, Americans could still speak confidently of vast unsettled lands ready to absorb strong-backed newcomers. While English policymakers worried about how to assimilate thousands of hungry Irish immigrants, many Americans saw the problem as purely one of transportation: How can we move the new workers to areas where they are most needed? We may also reframe this issue as one of geography rather than territory. Perhaps America's experience was distinctive because it was so far removed from Europe. Here, too, the Irish provide a good case in point. The East Coast cities were far better equipped to insulate themselves from unwanted migrants than was Liverpool or even Glasgow.

In his description of antebellum America, Daniel J. Boorstin wrote admiringly of the *booster* spirit that transformed small western towns into thriving communities.[68] This, too, may be a good starting point for comparative analysis. Although far from the "upstart" towns of Boorstin's analysis, both Liverpool and Philadelphia faced intense competition from other cities. Thus, policymakers and editorialists responded to reputation, as well as objective reality, in advocating reforms. We must consider how differing reputations might have led boosters in the two cities down distinctive paths.

One factor that molded Philadelphia's policy-making was its distressing reputation as a haven for violent gangs. Some scholars have posited an unusual level of *violence* in American culture. Clearly Philadelphia in the 1840s suffered through much disorder.[69] This history, and the resulting efforts to preserve the peace, may prove to be a sixth characteristic setting the United States apart from England.

Finally, any comparative study addressing immigration must consider the *demographic diversity* that was already apparent in American cities. In his study of evolving city services in Cincinnati, Alan I. Marcus argues for the importance of the popular reaction to "strangers" as a driving force promoting change. At midcentury Philadelphia was ethnically and racially much more diverse than Liverpool. Moreover, we must consider whether the Irish immigrants were deemed equally "foreign" on English and American soil. On the one hand, since the 1801 Act of Union, England and Ireland had been joined as Great Britain under parliamentary rule. On the other hand, although both the United States and England were predominantly Protestant, the United States did not have an Established Church, the presence of which perhaps underscored the "otherness" of England's Irish Catholics. We must ask how these differing preconditions might have dictated distinctive reactions to the waves of strangers.[70]

Each of the following chapters focuses on a specific set of historic events and issues as experienced in both Liverpool and Philadelphia. Some of the comparative analysis will be contained within a particular topic. For instance, how did the police force in each city answer the new challenges to social order? And how were those challenges distinctive in each city? But as we consider the specific aspects of each topic, we must remain mindful of the larger competing models used to explain midcentury policy development as well as the characteristics that have been offered as sources of American distinctiveness. Some interpretations and perspectives will reemerge in several chapters, others will only come into play in discussing a single issue. The task is not so much to select a single dominant interpretation as it is to weigh the forces—material, structural, cultural, and ideological—at work in each city, and to come to some larger understanding of how these forces shaped each society's responses to their shared challenges. Where those distinctive characteristics go beyond local circumstances—the role of the federal government or the availability of western lands, for instance—it will be possible to suggest larger national differences (without any specific contention that either England or the United States was further removed from international norms).[71]

The emphasis on a limited-time period—roughly 1845 to 1855—has virtues in controlling for interpretive variables. Philadelphia and Liverpool were not merely addressing similar issues, they were often dealing with the same people (and the same epidemics). Moreover, insofar as information and ideas traveled rapidly across the Atlantic, policymakers in both countries had access to the same constellation of opinions at roughly the same time.

The focus on the impact of a particular exogenous event—the potato famine—also forces an examination of chronology and historic contingency. Time and again we will see that Liverpool and Philadelphia went through roughly similar evolutions during the mid-nineteenth century. If we were to paint with a fairly broad brush, we would note merely that the two cities shared many general patterns of urban development. But by focusing on a few key years we see the importance of chronological timing. What was the state of ideas and institutions at that moment when the famine migrants first began arriving in large numbers? Were the Irish immigrants an *impetus* for reforms, or did their presence in fact slow—or divert—processes that were already under way? Episodes and decisions that immediately preceded the migration might have made all the difference in determining how the host cities would absorb the new arrivals. Philadelphia, for instance, had barely recovered from disturbing nativist riots a few years before the famine began. Liverpool had only recently passed revolutionary sanitary legislation. Both events established preconditions that would shape the way in which each city would respond to the famine migration's challenges. Our comparative analysis must weave an analysis of historic contingency into the broader discussion of ideology, institutional structure, and material conditions.[72]

Needless to say, our examination of this wide range of variables will not necessarily yield one simple conclusion. Even the events and decisions surrounding a single issue in a single community will reflect the impact of a multitude of forces. Although a monocausal conclusion might be viscerally satisfying, it would almost certainly do an injustice to the historical evidence. This study of a range of issues as they developed in two major nineteenth-century cities will provide some support for most of the competing interpretations summarized above. And the array of "independent variables" underlying the comparative analysis will not allow for the sort of absolute, definitive conclusions that one might reach in a cleaner, more controlled "laboratory." Nonetheless, several dominant patterns will emerge, pointing toward larger comparative conclusions. First, although the two city government bureaucracies were fairly similar and both were rhetorically committed to local autonomy, the differences in national governments were crucial in shaping local events, with parliamentary decisions and committees regularly playing an important role in Liverpool's development. Second, Philadelphians demonstrated a broader range of voluntaristic responses to social problems and a deeper commitment to protecting private property. Third, the vast Atlantic Ocean and the availability of western lands gave the Americans a broader range of options for limiting the flow of immigrants and for finding distant homes for unwanted newcomers, thus shaping differing national experiences. And fourth, the more demographically diverse American city struggled more profoundly with various notions of "otherness," yielding political attacks on immigrants, evangelical efforts to "Americanize" Catholic newcomers, and a wide variety of racial and ethnic street violence.

Each of these comparative differences is a matter of degree and not absolute rule. For instance, it is only in comparison with Philadelphia that Liverpool seems relatively less voluntaristic and more peaceful. In some arenas the arrival of the Irish famine migrants served to test and illuminate policies and institutions that were already in place; on other occasions their arrival was at least partially responsible for generating specific responses. And while the host cities responded to their new arrivals, the immigrants themselves adapted to their new environments and cultures. In this sense the Irish famine immigrants in each city were both shaping and being shaped by their new homes.

2. Migration and Reception

INTRODUCTION: IMMIGRATION AND URBAN POLITICAL DISCOURSE

From their first days in Liverpool and Philadelphia, the thousands of famine migrants were central to the social challenges—poverty, disease, poor sanitation, sectarian conflict, and crime—that define this book. But even before the Irish newcomers became part of the world of poor, unskilled city dwellers, they posed crucial problems for policymakers and philanthropists alike. Most immediate were those concerning the migration itself. What regulations should be placed on the immigrant ships as they crossed the Irish Sea and the Atlantic? Should the cities restrict access to their ports? In both Liverpool and Philadelphia a variety of local forces mobilized to protect the city from the Irish immigrants or to protect the immigrants from the city. Self-styled "emigrants' friends" set about advising prospective migrants on the dangers that lay before them. Others sought to erect barriers to keep out the immigrants who were most likely to become a drain on local resources.

These responses to the Irish immigrants were important concerns in each city, but it would be incorrect to see the migrants as driving all public policy discourse. This chapter begins with a brief sketch of the chief political concerns in each city, providing a larger context for the public responses to the famine migrants. With this political perspective in mind, we will then turn to the public and private responses to the Irish newcomers.

As we have seen, the two cities had similar populations but distinct economies and political systems. In Liverpool, two issues—the dock-rating controversy and the Rivington Pike scheme—monopolized the attention of politicians during the late 1840s. The former debate centered on whether the docks should be subject to taxation. Advocates of dock rating argued that the independent dock estate should pay its share of local costs, including the rising burden of poor relief. Opponents claimed that taxing the docks would inhibit commerce, the lifeblood of the city. The battle between Pikists and anti-Pikists was over competing proposals for supplying the city with water. Proponents of the Rivington Pike scheme supported an elaborate plan to pump water in from a distant source. Its opponents insisted that there were cheaper alternatives closer to home. The power of these two issues was perhaps best reflected in the 1848 electoral defeat of popular Liberal William Rathbone, who lost his seat on the Council after advocating the Rivington Pike scheme and opposing dock rating—two unpopular stances. While these debates monopolized the attention of politicians and cost-conscious voters, local officials also worried about Liverpool's disturbing reputation as the nation's unhealthiest city.[1]

Philadelphia's midcentury political debates are best captured in the 1849 elections, in which an Independent People's Ticket challenged the dominant Whigs, winning the mayoral election by a small margin. This independent combination of Democrats, anti-immigrant nativists, and some renegade Whigs ran on a multitiered reform platform. First, they claimed that the City Council had become the private preserve of a handful of Whigs who had placed friends and relatives in the city's key appointed offices. They also complained of recent maneuverings that had left the county's upper districts with their own new water sources, costing the city revenue. But they were most emphatic in denouncing Philadelphia's recent pattern of rioting, which had seriously tarnished the city's reputation.[2] All of these issues—leadership, competing jurisdictions, nativism, and, most dramatically, street disorder—were part of Philadelphia's political landscape at midcentury. But these squabbles aside, in the late 1840s Philadelphians were fond of trumpeting the city's rapid growth and economic improvements, often setting local achievements alongside New York City's record.[3] Only the persistent reports of disorder in some districts seemed to mar this air of self-satisfaction.

Although the specific issues were unique to each city, politicians in Philadelphia and Liverpool shared a basic concern for balancing the increasing demand for urban services—utilities, sanitation, poor relief—with a powerful pressure to keep taxes in check, particularly when the taxes were perceived as going toward the wasteful support of unwelcome outsiders. Ratepayers were also ever vigilant to block perceived waste or unfair burdens. For instance, a December 1849 editorial in the *Liverpool Standard* (reprinted approvingly by the *Mercury*) questioned the value of the new Industrial School, which it characterized as "a mere hobby of the Poor-law Commissioners, unwisely sanctioned at our cost by a portion of the Select Vestry." Concern for costs proved a critical factor in Liverpool's responses to the famine migrants. Philadelphians were equally alert to any untoward public expenditures. The Independent People's Ticket emphasized a claim that taxes had tripled with only negligible benefits. In October 1849 the grand jury for the August court of quarter sessions reported on the state of Philadelphia institutions and then went on to call for a rethinking of local tax assessments. Sounding much like those Liverpudlians who objected to the dock estate, the grand jury suggested broadening the tax base to cover rising costs, pointing out that many properties—churches, schools, and other corporate bodies—were exempt from taxation.[4]

The political discourse in each city at midcentury created an important backdrop to the local policy debates over the famine migrants. These debates also suggest some comparisons of the two urban political structures. The *range* of issues debated in each city was similar, suggesting the shared challenges of urban growth. Government officials in Liverpool and Philadelphia worried about providing essential services while limiting costs and contending with increasingly unwieldy jurisdictional and bureaucratic dilemmas. Both cities paid particular attention to problems that hurt their international reputation: Liverpool's unsanitary streets and Philadelphia's violent gangs. Such urban boosterism calls to mind Daniel Boorstin's portrait of city building in western America. Beneath these broad similarities there were clear political differences, pointing to several aspects of national distinctiveness.

First, Liverpool's heavy emphasis on commercial concerns reflects the traditional assumption that local government's first priority should be the economic health of the borough. The 1835 electoral reforms, which had given the middle classes a larger voice, and the short-lived dominance of local Liberals had not shaken what one historian termed local "apathy" about broader municipal reforms.[5] Even where Philadelphia's social reforms were every bit as modest as those in Liverpool, the nature of partisan discourse reflected the Jacksonian legacy of broad political participation.

Political conflicts in the two cities were also shaped by their distinctive social and cultural divisions. Philadelphia's powerful nativist movement reflected overlapping antagonisms toward immigrants and Roman Catholics. In the meantime, hostility toward both African Americans and abolitionists was behind other periodic outbursts of civic disorder. Liverpool's comparable conflicts took on a more explicitly sectarian aspect, as defenders of the Established Church battled Catholics and Dissenters.

National distinctiveness shaped local political discourse in a third crucial way: residents of Philadelphia and Liverpool had different understandings of the role of the national government in local affairs. Although Liverpool prided itself in the Corporation's relative political autonomy, the fact remained that by the late 1840s Parliament had claimed a clear voice in various local governmental affairs. National political reforms had redrawn the political landscape and parliamentary investigations had entered a wide array of economic and social arenas. Philadelphians might occasionally turn to the state legislature for an act of incorporation or some modest regulation, but neither state nor federal authorities possessed anywhere near the range of regulatory powers and economic inducements that were the mainstay of England's Chadwickian reforms.[6]

RESPONSES TO THE FAMINE

The immediate responses to the famine migration in Liverpool and Philadelphia illustrate their broadly shared political priorities while pointing to several areas of national distinctiveness. Philadelphia's physical distance from Ireland and the economic potential of the "frontier" helped shape the American response to the migrants in several ways. In the meantime, initial efforts at assisting, advising, and blocking the migrants suggest differing national assumptions about the major role of voluntary efforts and the potential for governmental solutions—at both the local and national levels.

English and American observers shared a concern for the suffering brought about by the Irish famine. But they responded to the disaster in different and revealing ways. Irish Poor Law resources and local charities proved woefully inadequate to meet the famine victims' needs. Despite appeals for assistance—including a widely publicized visit to Parliament by the aging Irish Catholic leader, Daniel O'Connell—the English government offered only modest aid. Under Prime Minister Robert Peel, the government distributed Indian corn from America and provided public works jobs for thousands of the laboring poor. But Whig prime minister Lord

John Russell, who replaced the Tory Peel in mid-1846, temporarily closed the food depots and canceled the public works projects. Worsening conditions the following year prompted a return to government assistance; still, many starving Irish remained reliant on private charity.[7]

Liverpool newspaper editors urged voluntary assistance to Ireland, and religious leaders called on their flocks to aid the famine victims. Liverpool Catholics gathered on January 21, 1847, to pass a series of resolutions encouraging fund-raising. But the local calls for aid to Ireland seem quite modest when set beside the despair across the Irish Sea. Meanwhile, ministers and priests sparred over the famine's larger meaning. Rev. Hugh M'Neile, the city's leading "anti-Popery" Protestant, published a sermon calling for aid to Ireland while reminding his audience that the famine was a punishment visited on Catholics, whose "idolatory" he termed "a sin against God's holy law."[8] Unitarian James Martineau rejected the notion that the famine was a product of divine will, preferring to blame political institutions and the "criminal neglect of their obligations by the proprietors of the soil." Local political conflicts and sectarian battles probably helped limit the flow of charitable donations from England to Ireland. As Kerby A. Miller notes, "No doubt, British responses in 1845–55 would have been far more generous had famine threatened England's home counties instead of Munster and Connaught." But Liverpool's benevolent energies were also absorbed by the famine's impact at home. The parishioners at St. Michael's Church in Toxteth Park, for instance, raised £82.14 for the famine victims but reserved half that money for the local District Provident Society because "the town of Liverpool had become the city of refuge to the starving Irish, . . . of 1080 persons who had received relief from the District Provident Society within the last few days, 765 were Irish."[9]

With local and English aid proving insufficient, the Irish famine victims turned to the United States for assistance. On February 17, 1847, Philadelphia mayor John Swift called a town meeting "to provide means to relieve the sufferings of Ireland." The day's speeches stressed Philadelphia's tradition of disinterested benevolence rather than any particular ties to Ireland. The Executive Committee reported that "men of all creeds and parties" were present; the famine required extraordinary public measures because "there were few ties of a social or domestic kind between the citizens of this country and those of the disturbed Kingdoms to give that particular and private interest which is the foundation of more enlarged and active sympathies." This citywide effort, combined with a smaller fund-raiser staged by the Society of Friends, netted over $75,000 in donations (including food and clothing). Meanwhile, the committee reported that Pennsylvania's Catholic churches had sent an additional $3,000 and the state's Episcopalians had raised over $6,000.[10]

Philadelphia's benevolent display was indeed impressive, far outstripping Liverpool's efforts.[11] But the greatest assistance came not from disinterested philanthropists but from Irish immigrants already in Philadelphia. Several banks ran regular newspaper ads offering to send immigrants' money home to relatives in Ireland. In early 1847 four local banks reported that in the previous twelve months they had drawn $311,200 in small bills, "'sold chiefly to working people, for remittances to their friends in Ireland.'" This clearly underestimated the private aid sent home up to that point. And there were still several years of famine ahead.[12]

THE MIGRANTS IN LIVERPOOL

As the port nearest to Ireland, Liverpool bore the brunt of the famine migration. For a shilling or less, Irish paupers could purchase passage to the Merseyside city. It is impossible to offer precise estimates of the flow of Irish paupers into Liverpool or to fully gauge the significance of those numbers. Some passengers were part of the normal flow of travelers bound for other destinations. Many paupers fleeing the famine arrived with tickets for North American ports, or at least with plans of further travel. Others returned—or were removed—to Ireland. But for thousands, intentionally or not, Liverpool became the final stop. In late 1846, as it became clear that the newcomers were an increasing problem, stipendiary magistrate Edward Rushton ordered a police count of arriving immigrants, with separate estimates of the number of paupers likely to become a burden on the city. He reported that between mid-January and mid-December 1847, 296,000 passengers arrived from Ireland. Of these, 130,000 went on to the United States and roughly 50,000 were there on normal business. "The remainder," Rushton reported, "[were] mere paupers, half-naked and starving, [who] landed for the most part during the winter, and becoming, immediately on landing, applicants for parochial relief." Frank Neal has estimated that over 250,000 migrants, including more than 94,000 paupers, landed the following year. Between 1849 and 1853 the parish authorities reported that 1,241,000 passengers arrived from Ireland, including about 375,000 deck passengers who were likely paupers. Overall, according to Neal, more than 586,000 Irish paupers landed in Liverpool between 1847 and 1853.[13]

The steamers that crossed the Irish Sea were notorious for their over-crowded, unsanitary conditions. The poorer passengers were often forced to huddle together on deck, with little protection from the elements. Peri-odically reports of specific outrages sparked calls for reform, but the ma-chinery of regulation moved slowly. In December 1848 Liverpudlians were horrified to discover that 72 of 206 deck passengers on the *Londonderry* had suffocated on the journey from Sligo when they crowded belowdecks for protection from the weather. It was not until the spring of 1849 that com-plaints from Liverpool finally prompted a parliamentary investigation. The resulting regulations addressed the worst conditions and, perhaps more im-portant to Liverpool officials, reduced the Irish Channel traffic by limiting overcrowding on the steamers.[14]

As Edward Rushton reported to Parliament, the most destitute Irish im-migrants became an immediate drain on local resources, overwhelming the city's poor relief apparatus and threatening its already precarious health and sanitation. Impoverished new arrivals turned to the parochial officers for aid, prompting the creation of an ad hoc system of emergency relief without the normal process of inspection. By late 1846 the Select Vestry reported that it was providing assistance, mainly soup and bread, to nearly 5,000 families a week, far exceeding the previous year's demands. In mid-January it was aiding as many as 20,000 Irish casual poor a day. Ratepayers objected to the resulting increase in poor relief costs, and cynics charged that the local poor were taking advantage of the free handouts earmarked for the starving arrivals.[15]

In January, Alfred Austin, the assistant Poor Law commissioner for Liv-erpool, instituted a new system of emergency poor relief aimed at reducing expenses. Austin divided the city into twenty-four relieving districts, each with a policeman acting as relieving officer. Paupers seeking assistance would apply in the morning and receive vouchers for bread and soup only after being visited by an officer. The Vestry reported an immediate drop in applicants under this new system, attributing the decline to reduced "imposition" by the poor. On February 1 over 22,000 Irish casual poor sought assistance; the following day—the first under Austin's plan—that figure plummeted to below 5,000. But the flood of new migrants con-tinued, and soon the Vestry was relieving over 10,000 Irish poor daily, de-spite new resolutions "that every able-bodied pauper should be required to give three hours work before he was relieved."[16]

The next step in the city's battle against the newcomers was a movement to return the Irish paupers to their homes. The original Poor Law rules of settlement allowed for the forcible removal of paupers to their county of origin. In August 1846 Parliament modified these laws with the Five Years' Residence Act, which made it illegal to remove outsiders who had been continuous residents for at least five years. In the past Liverpool had rarely removed Irish paupers, preferring to encourage the arrival of unskilled labor. But with the famine migration, many local government officials saw removals as the only solution. The Poor Law Removal Act that June simplified the removal process, and the following month the Select Vestry began shipping Irish paupers who applied for parochial relief back across the Irish Sea. The *Liverpool Mercury* applauded the new policies, urging local citizens to resist their charitable urges so that the destitute would be forced into parish hands and thus home to Ireland. Within a month the Vestry had removed 362 Irish immigrants from the fever hospitals and workhouses; another 1,210 left "voluntarily" after receiving outdoor relief. Meanwhile, Rushton resolved to use his power as a magistrate to force the issue, offering convicted beggars the choice of jail or removal. But he found that the Irish paupers consistently chose incarceration.[17] In the final three months of 1846 Liverpool removed 4,335 Irish people to Ireland; the next year this figure jumped to 14,637.[18] Between 1845 and 1854 Liverpool removed a total of 66,589 paupers, including 62,881 Irish.[19]

These removal figures, which far surpassed Liverpool's previous experience or that of any other British city, produced widespread concern about costs. It seemed to local citizens that the famine migration had presented a choice between two untenable options: pay to support thousands of destitute immigrants or pay to send them home. In December 1846 and again the following May, Liverpool appealed to the Home Office for some relief. But the city received little sympathy and no solutions. The government, it was told, could not restrict population movement within the United Kingdom, and the Poor Law commissioners were unwilling to accept the argument that the unusual circumstances required national financial solutions.[20]

The mounting costs also provoked sparring among Liverpool's various government authorities. Vestrymen complained that a heavy portion of the removal costs was in fact in the form of magistrates' fees, which effectively transferred funds from the parish to the Council. In November the Vestry argued that almsgiving was undercutting its efforts and called on the magistrates to act "for the suppression of vagrancy and mendacity," rather than sitting idly by while parochial authorities grappled with the problem. An irate Rushton countered that the magistrates were, in fact, doing their job and that the jails were overflowing with vagrants. All agreed that the situation required new solutions.[21]

In May 1849 the Liverpool authorities once again turned to the national government for relief. Rushton, speaking for both the Council's Finance Committee and the Select Vestry, wrote to Secretary of State Sir George Grey enumerating the problems associated with the Irish migrants. He warned that there was a physical and a moral danger from the "unchecked immigration of the most miserable of the Irish people into such towns as Liverpool."[22] Meanwhile, the Vestry sent a special committee to London to take its case directly to Sir George and other national officials. The Liverpool delegation succeeded in encouraging new regulation of steamer traffic (which had already been recommended by the aforementioned Parliamentary investigation), but its call for new rules governing removals met with resistance. And its appeal for financial assistance once again went unheeded. One MP suggested that Liverpool's current problems with Irish paupers were more than offset by the Irish commerce the city enjoyed. Mr. Baines, one member of the delegation, found the audience with Sir George "not very promising" and concluded that "we are thrown chiefly on our own resources. At any rate, the Jupiters of the Cabinet will not assist us, unless we put our own shoulders to the wheel; and if we exert our energies we may do something to help ourselves, providing the inhabitants will co-operate with us. If they will indulge their benevolent sympathies by relieving street beggars the case is hopeless." The *Liverpool Mercury* received this news with characteristic dismay, insisting that the city was being punished by a mere accident of geography and calling on Parliament to reform the "Inequalities of the English Poor Law."[23]

Liverpool's reactions to the Irish famine immigrants were characteristic of its responses to the various social problems that followed on their arrival. When the arriving paupers turned to the parish for aid, the parochial officers set aside established procedures and cobbled together emergency measures to meet the new demand. But the twin concerns of rising costs and fear of imposition led to the institution of new relief policies that retained some measure of inspection. In the meantime, local officials looked beyond their borders for solutions. The major problem, they concluded, was that there were insufficient checks on the flow of Irish migrants into

Liverpool and too many obstacles blocking their return. They turned to London for assistance—without much success. Finally, the reception and removal of Irish paupers underscored the jurisdictional divisions within Liverpool's government. The parish authorities had responsibility for relieving the poor and financing their removal. But in the former case they were forced to rely on police officers, under the Council's Watch Committee, and in the latter they had to work with the town magistrate. Each of these patterns—the revision of established procedures in response to a crisis, a passionate concern for costs, appeals to national authorities, and internal jurisdictional conflicts—recurred as Liverpool struggled with the intertwined problems of poverty, poor sanitation, disease, crime, and sectarian conflict.

THE MIGRANTS IN PHILADELPHIA

Throughout the famine migration Liverpool complained that it was the unfair victim of its location. Although the census data indicate that Philadelphia and Liverpool had fairly similar numbers of Irish-born residents at midcentury, Philadelphia—an ocean away—never witnessed a comparable flood of new arrivals. Still, the influx of immigrants from Ireland and Germany had a tremendous impact on North America's port cities. Between 1847 and 1853 roughly 1,085,000 Irish immigrants arrived in the United States. Over 150,000 immigrants entered the port of Philadelphia between 1840 and the end of 1855; roughly half of them were Irish. The bulk of these people arrived in the five or six years after 1847. In one week alone in April 1847, five ships delivered nearly 1,200 Irish immigrants. Roughly 9,000 immigrants arrived from Ireland and England in the first nine months of 1849. As in Liverpool, some moved on to new destinations and others died soon after landing. About half of the 72,000 Irish-born Philadelphians in 1850 had arrived in the previous five years. Some had journeyed south from New York, but most arrived directly in Philadelphia from Liverpool or an Irish port. Many more came in the next several years.[24]

Distance also affected the characteristics of the migrants to each city. The most destitute paupers could afford to travel only as far as Liverpool, raising the possibility that those who ventured on to North America arrived with more resources at their disposal. But we must not take this distinction too far. Both groups were predominantly unskilled laborers with few possessions.[25] Many relied on relatives in the United States for money or tickets. And even if those who set off for America were heartier than their brethren left behind in Liverpool, the transatlantic voyage took a heavy toll. In comparing the famine migrants to earlier Irish immigrants to the United States, Kerby A. Miller found that the later arrivals were "generally poorer, less skilled, and more in need of charity than their predecessors, [and] they were also much less able to fend for themselves abroad."[26]

The waves of Irish famine migrants did not dominate political discourse in Philadelphia as they did in Liverpool. Nonetheless, the arrival of the imposing transatlantic vessels each spring and summer attracted widespread public notice, revealing much about local conditions and assumptions. The *Public Ledger* regularly reported the arrival of new ships, paying the greatest attention to tales of disease and misery. One ship landed in June 1847 with nearly all of its 260 steerage passengers suffering from typhoid fever, dysentery, or measles. Eighteen passengers had died at sea. When the *Swatara* arrived that September, the *Ledger* reported that the 260 passengers had been en route for over six months, having twice been forced to turn back for repairs. Several passengers died during the journey, but more than a dozen gave birth.[27] In one of the most notorious episodes, the *Joseph Porter* arrived from Liverpool in early 1849 after having been at sea for nearly two months. For the last five weeks passengers had been restricted to a daily ration of one biscuit and a small amount of water. Most were emaciated; the Board of Health sent many directly to the City Hospital, where two children died the following day.[28] Tales of the greatest abuses engendered a series of laws—passed in both England and the United States— regulating ventilation, cleanliness, provisions, and general conditions on immigrant ships. Further regulations limited the number of passengers per square foot and required the presence of a superintendent of immigrants or a surgeon on larger vessels.[29]

Philadelphians were quick to recognize the potential threat posed by the famine migrants. In 1847 the *Catholic Herald* looked across the Atlantic and reported that "Liverpool and Glasgow are overrun with those poor creatures. In the former town as many as 100,000 have received out-door relief in a week. The pressure of local taxation on the rate-payers is likely to ruin many small housekeepers, and leave them without covering or shelter." [30] As the immigrant ships began arriving in the United States from Ireland and Germany, the *Ledger* warned that "the almshouses, hospitals and cellars of our cities are crowded with poor immigrants from Europe, without the means of procuring a loaf of bread." [31] Individual Philadelphians viewed the flood of Irish migrants with a combination of compassion, hostility, and skepticism. Retired shipping magnate Thomas P. Cope wrote in his diary: "Let them come, poor creatures, we must not flint our hearts against them, nor see them perish. They will be expensive & troublesome, but their offspring may make good citizens & we have in our extensive West room enough for all." Equally wealthy Sidney George Fisher drew other conclusions. "The emigration to this country is unparalleled," he wrote in May 1847. "They come in by thousands to New York, utterly destitute, many of them diseased, mere masses of rags & wretchedness. The almshouses, hospitals & poorhouses are crowded & they are dying by hundreds. . . . And here they come not only to work & eat, or die, but to vote. That is the danger & the evil." [32]

Fisher worried about the political implications of thousands of new lower-class voters, but most officials seemed more concerned about the costs accompanying the onslaught of diseased paupers. One response was to follow New York's lead and impose head taxes on new arrivals, with the funds earmarked to aid the immigrants requiring assistance. [33] But this solution, passed by the Pennsylvania legislature, drew complaints from the Philadelphia Board of Trade, which claimed that such head taxes were illegal and drove commerce out of Philadelphia into cities with lower rates. In 1849 the U.S. Supreme Court struck down the state immigrant head taxes as unconstitutional, but the Court's decision left the door open for the states to require large bonds from shipowners as insurance against newcomers becoming financial liabilities. New York and Pennsylvania circumvented the Court's ruling by imposing $300 bonds on immigrants with the provision that the Guardians could "commute" this fee down to $1.50 for healthy adults in lieu of bond. In February the H & A Cope shipping line asked the Board of Guardians to reduce the commutation fee to $1.00 per immigrant. The board's Committee on Emigrants advised against this measure, but a minority opinion—following the logic of the Board of Trade— recommended in favor of the reduction on the grounds that the current figure put local commerce at a competitive disadvantage with other cities. [34]

Philadelphia also joined other American cities in trying to erect barriers to keep out those immigrants who posed the greatest health risk. As we shall see, both Liverpool and Philadelphia routinely established quarantines to protect their citizens from disease. But whereas Liverpool could do little more than isolate sick migrants in fever sheds or lazarettos, Philadelphia took advantage of its location to keep the most unwelcome visitors from its shores. The story of the *Provincialist* illuminates the complex dynamics of Philadelphia's quarantine policies.

In April 1848 the *Provincialist,* out of Londonderry, landed near Wilmington, Delaware, with three hundred Irish passengers, bound chiefly for Philadelphia. About forty migrants disembarked near Wilmington to seek employment at the Dupont powder works. Their companions boarded the steamer *Rappahannock* for the trip north to Philadelphia. But when they arrived at the South Street Wharf Dr. Dietrich, the port physician, refused to let the ship land, claiming that he suspected disease was on board. The *Rappahannock's* captain circumvented Dietrich's injunction by moving south and dropping his passengers off at the Washington Street Wharf.[35] Throughout the City of Brotherly Love the machinery of outrage eased into motion. The propertyless migrants became the responsibility of the Guardians of the Poor, who objected that Wilmington had collected head taxes that rightly should have been paid in Philadelphia. Meanwhile, the Board of Health took umbrage at the *Rappahannock's* captain for surreptitiously depositing sick foreigners on its shores. On April 24 subcommittees from both bodies met "to take measures to prevent the introduction of foreign emigrants arriving at other ports into this District."[36] The Washington Street Wharf was in Southwark, which was part of Philadelphia County—and thus in the jurisdiction of the Guardians of the Poor and the Board of Health—but not yet part of Philadelphia City. When they learned of the *Rappahannock's* arrival, the Southwark commissioners fired off angry resolutions promising to assist local officials in blocking further outrages. Southwark's citizens distributed a bizarre petition requesting that the commissioners establish a special local police force to block the landing of foreign immigrants from other states, with the provision that the local citizenry be summoned by bells to join the fray if need be. The *Public Ledger* ridiculed this "Declaration of War by Southwark against the World," likening it to the emperor of China walling out the Tartars.[37]

Meanwhile, bickering across the state line escalated. The *Wilmington Gazette* claimed that the ship had been properly inspected by the local port physician, who had found one active case of smallpox, but no outbreaks in the previous fifteen days, and thus allowed the ship to pass on.[38] The Philadelphia Board of Health remained unconvinced and announced its intention to enforce a little-known 1802 law allowing it to refuse admission to such interstate migrants until they had spent fifteen days in Delaware. One local assailed the measure, claiming that the Board of Health "already possesses too much power under the law actually in force" and was guilty of "high handed" efforts to drive away foreign commerce.[39]

When the case against the *Rappahannock's* captain came before Mayor John Swift, Dr. Dietrich testified that one passenger had exhibited early signs of typhus and another soon ended up in the smallpox hospital. Although Captain Mason had clearly ignored the port physician's orders, the mayor—perhaps yielding to commercial pressures—threw out the case because there was insufficient evidence of contagious disease on board. By this time the immigrants had dispersed throughout Philadelphia's poorest wards and become "a source of great excitement and alarm" to citizens concerned about smallpox rumors. Tensions grew when Philadelphians read reports that the Board of Health had refused to let the smallpox victims enter the almshouse, leaving the disease to spread through poor neighborhoods in the southeastern corner of the city.[40]

This episode, which attracted considerable attention for several weeks, underscored Philadelphia's multitiered political structure. Although the Guardians of the Poor and the Board of Health found common cause in this instance, these distinct—"quasi-independent"—bodies were routinely at odds over public policy. Like their Liverpool counterparts, the Guardians and the board often had competing agendas, confused by their overlapping jurisdictions and independent budgets.[41] Meanwhile, Southwark's independent action in the face of external intrusion reflected the decentralized government structure (and accompanying political culture) that continued to plague Philadelphia until the 1854 consolidation. And the conflict between Philadelphia and neighboring Delaware indicates a peculiarly American emphasis on localism and state autonomy. Finally, although various officials and institutions claimed a voice in this discussion, the common assumptions were clear. At each level Philadelphians acted to protect themselves from disease and unwanted costs by "walling out the tartars." This reaction supports a Turnerian interpretation of American distinctiveness: The physical distance between Philadelphia and Liverpool, more than any distinctive cultural or political characteristics, played a crucial role in determining assumptions about quarantines and immigration.

EMIGRANTS' FRIENDS: ADVICE AND ASSISTANCE

While Guardians and shippers debated immigrant taxes and quarantines, more benevolent voices on both sides of the Atlantic expressed concern that the new arrivals would be victimized by fraud.[42] The officers of Philadelphia's Temporary Home Association reported that "[t]he proprietors of the low Taverns in Front and Water streets, are ever on the alert for victims, and send their agents down the river, to board the passenger ships before they arrive at our wharves, each recommending his own establishment." These innocent travelers, they warned, would soon become "paupers or criminals . . . and must be supported by the public." Some agents were notorious for cheating Irish immigrants out of funds for passage to the interior or for fraudulent transatlantic tickets mailed home to waiting relatives.[43] The strongest warnings were reserved for unaccompanied girls. The Temporary Home Association told the tale of a young Irish girl who arrived in New York with her brother and then journeyed alone to Philadelphia because she had heard that there was work to be found. Soon her money and food ran out and she fell in with "some girls of doubtful appearance," who took her to a boarding house "where her character, her happiness, and her virtue were sacrificed for a shelter and a mouthful of food."[44]

While various private institutions in Liverpool and Philadelphia addressed the material and spiritual needs of the Irish immigrants,[45] other organizations dedicated themselves to providing more intangible assistance: advice on immigration. As we have seen, some Irish Philadelphians sent home letters or notes penned on the back of tickets providing prospective immigrants with guidance on the challenges to come, but many travelers remained at the mercy of the unsavory types who worked the docks in both cities. Concerns for the immigrants' well-being spawned a variety of organizations declaring themselves to be "Friends" of the migrants. Their actions, particularly when contrasted with the advice from family members, reveal much about priorities and assumptions in the host cities.[46]

In April 1843, before the heavy famine migration had begun, a group of concerned Philadelphia Catholics called a meeting of the "Friends of Ireland and of the Oppressed and Persecuted Emigrant" and formed the Irish

Emigrant Society, dedicated to providing prospective migrants and bewildered newcomers with reliable information on transportation as well as a modicum of protection against fraud. In addition to acting in Philadelphia, the society hoped to send information directly to Ireland through priests and American consuls.[47] But this early effort does not appear to have survived into the heavy famine migration. Several years later, when the numbers of famine immigrants mounted, Philadelphians became increasingly concerned with distributing information that would protect all parties. In March 1847 the *Public Ledger* bemoaned "the poor emigrants who arrive in such crowds upon our shores" with neither food nor job prospects. The answer, the *Ledger* concluded, was to establish "societies for the aid of distressed emigrants" dedicated to transporting the newcomers inland, where there were more employment opportunities.[48]

In March 1848 several dozen local men formed the Philadelphia Emigrant's Friend Society (PEFS) "for the purpose of securing emigrants from imposition upon their arrival here, and directing them to suitable places of accommodation, employment or desirable locations for settlement, &c." At this early stage the society spoke of building barracks in the city suburbs where immigrants could be employed in truck gardens until transportation west became available.[49] Soon, however, PEFS members settled into a more limited role as advisers and intermediaries.

In September 1848 the PEFS Executive Committee reviewed its early efforts to aid the immigrant, the city, and employers desiring laborers. The society's activities took several forms. First, having identified the web of "mercenary and selfish men" waiting to pounce on unsuspecting immigrants, it proceeded to warn the new arrivals. Although the PEFS made some progress in this area, it was frustrated by the sheer magnitude of the task and the justifiable skepticism of immigrants who "have no means of discriminating their real from their pretended friends." In fact, attempts to earn the newcomers' confidence were particularly challenging because "the stranger . . . , instructed by the experience of those who have gone before him, shuns what may prove a bait." Thus the "personal advice" of family members in many cases actually obstructed the society's work.[50]

The PEFS reported better success in acting as an employment agency, matching immigrants with prospective employers and assisting the new arrivals in making their way to the state's interior. In its first five months the society aided 1,260 immigrants, including 860 Irish-born (68 percent), in search of employment. The following year it assisted 2,400 immigrants and in 1850 nearly 4,000. The directors invited new arrivals to visit their offices—armed with "testimonials of character" if available—to describe their condition and seek assistance. On discovering that there were more available jobs than immigrants, the PEFS distributed public announcements requesting "that no foreigners might receive any charitable relief who did not show a written certificate from the office, that they were the proper objects of charity." The directors also wrote to the Guardians of the Poor, asking that no healthy persons be admitted to the almshouse who had not previously sought the society's employment assistance. This private, voluntary body thus hoped to establish itself as a quasi-official arbiter of the immigrants' character.[51]

The members of the Emigrant's Friend Society quickly determined that their effectiveness as advisers and arbiters was hampered by delayed access to the immigrants. By the time the Irish immigrants reached Philadelphia, it was too late to prepare them fully for what lay in store. The solution, the PEFS concluded, was to distribute a practical guide for prospective emigrants. To that end the society's secretary, Rev. D. R. Thomason, published a 124-page book of *Hints to Emigrants or to Those Who May Contemplate Emigrating to the United States*. Described as a counterpoint to competing pamphlets that offered an unrealistically optimistic portrait of life in America, *Hints to Emigrants* promised plainspoken and sound advice. Thomason's message distilled down to a few central points: Do not come if you are too fond of drink, a "political malcontent," or afraid of hard work. Moreover, he warned, immigrants should not expect to find jobs in the eastern seaboard cities. Rather, they should plan on venturing into the American interior, where ample opportunities awaited those with strong backs and good character.[52]

Like the Irish Emigrant Society before it, the PEFS recognized that its message could find an audience only with aid from across the Atlantic. This realization dovetailed with a parallel discussion in Liverpool, where Irish immigrants also regularly fell prey to fraud and vice. In March 1848 the *Liverpool Mercury* reprinted a lengthy letter from Ireland's *Nation* sent by an Irishman living in Liverpool. He warned potential emigrants of a detailed "system [of] plunder and barefaced robbery" in which migrants bound for America fell victim to "mancatchers" who systematically charged extortionate prices for tickets, provisions, lodgings, and even U.S. dollars. The letter concluded: "I would suggest that benevolent societies be at once established in all seaport towns, to counsel and give advice gratis to emigrants, to enable them to lay out their money economically." A few months later the *Mercury* ran an editorial decrying "frauds on emigrants" and calling for the creation of a joint stock company to provide sanitary lodgings. Such an organization could make contact with similar societies in the United States. That December the *Mercury* issued a more emphatic call for a voluntary Emigrants' Protection Society, with government sanction, to dispense information and provide lodging and washhouses. A year later the exasperated newspaper was still trying—unsuccessfully—to drum up support among local "societies of philanthropic men."[53]

Although Liverpudlians created various benevolent bodies to assist the immigrants, they never established an information-disseminating society along the lines of those founded in Philadelphia and New York. Some concerned Liverpool citizens did, however, embrace the opportunity to work with their American brethren. In its first report, the PEFS Executive Committee announced that "[t]he clergy of Liverpool of the various denominations have united their hearts and hands in the same labour of love" and helped the society identify a local agent. Soon emigrant agents in Liverpool were working with the Philadelphians in distributing *Hints to Emigrants* and guiding the migrants to reliable ticket brokers. The *Mercury* ran a series of lengthy articles offering advice to emigrants and quoting liberally from the American publications, particularly from Rev. Thomason's book. In October 1849 the newspaper printed several favorable notices of a new newspaper by Thomason on *The Emigrant and American Citizen,* "which," the *Mercury* declared, "teems with information." The recurring message followed the PEFS's familiar lines: do not go unless you are ready for hard work; do not trust strangers; seek out members of the emigrants' friends societies.[54]

The various people and agencies offering advice to the Philadelphia-bound Irish migrants shared certain basic assumptions. Self-styled "emigrants' friends" in Liverpool and Philadelphia joined Irish immigrants writing home to relatives in fearing that ill-prepared migrants were liable to fall victim to evildoers in both ports. All concerned recognized that unscrupulous "runners" waited to seduce immigrants into seedy lodging houses, and unethical ticket agents conspired to rob them of their modest savings. Both philanthropists and family members recognized the importance of protecting the immigrants' health and safety. All agreed that successful migrants would have to find employment wherever they settled.

The emigrants' friends in both cities tried to battle swindlers on their own turf by providing competing agents, cautionary broadsides, and reliable information. In their more ambitious moments they spoke of following New York's lead by registering runners and lodging houses. The Irish immigrants already in Philadelphia who mailed tickets to relatives and friends back home approached the problem differently. They advised their friends and relatives to avoid *all* strangers (rather than suggesting that certain benevolent groups could be trusted). These personal advisers circumvented the worst dangers by purchasing the tickets themselves and by arranging to meet the arriving steamer in Philadelphia or sending careful directions on where to go on arrival. And while reformers pushed to improve conditions on vessels crossing the Irish Sea and on transatlantic steamers, relatives wrote with detailed instructions on the best food and clothing to pack for the voyage. The migrants thus placed their faith in family ties and personal networks rather than in benevolent or legislative bodies.

As much as they worried about the migrants becoming victims, the emigrants' friends expressed more concern about the newcomers' economic futures. On both sides of the Atlantic observers perceived the famine migration—and immigration in general—as an important movement of labor. Some in Great Britain decried the loss of workers, but more joined the *Mercury* in seeing the United States (and other immigrant destinations) as a "great human safety valve" for some types of unskilled workers.[55] In the United States, differences of opinion were sharper. Conservatives like Sidney George Fisher viewed Irish and German immigrants as prospective voters as well as workers. The new arrivals were "the most ignorant & depraved of Europe, wholly ignorant of our government, our laws, our history; entirely unused to political privileges, unable even to comprehend them." They would, he feared, "add to the already swollen ranks of radicals & levellers, to increase the already dangerous power of agitation & demagogues, to degrade still more the already degraded & foul condition of our politics & public morals & opinion."[56] In addition to shifting the nation's political balance, many observers feared that these unemployed newcomers would become an unwelcome demand on public finances. The Emigrant's Friend Society, declaring that its enemies were "stimulated by the organs of party," fought this battle on two fronts. First, it insisted that it never encouraged anyone to emigrate. In fact, its messages were designed to discourage all but the most committed migrants. Second, it argued that the United States had a clear need for healthy workers, so long as they were directed to the appropriate locations. "All must agree," the society asserted, "that wealth, population and products must and do increase in proportion to the demands made for their consumption and use."[57]

As we compare events in the two cities, the failure of Liverpool's "benevolent gentlemen" to heed the *Mercury*'s call for a local organization to assist the emigrants seems telling. Five months after its founding, Philadelphia's Emigrant's Friend Society already boasted 150 dues-paying members (all male). Although its immigrant problems were much more severe, Liverpool never supported a comparable body. Two factors may have combined to explain this national distinction. First, midcentury Philadelphians endorsed a far greater range of private benevolent organizations than their Liverpool counterparts, indicating that Tocqueville was correct in claiming a distinctly American propensity toward voluntary societies.[58] And second, despite their benevolent rhetoric, these societies were particularly interested in protecting American ports from immigrants who were liable to become burdens on local taxpayers. No such friendly "advice" would have kept desperate migrants out of Liverpool. The Americans' more purely philanthropic goals—such as warning about frauds on the docks—were an important piece of the message, but perhaps not enough on their own to support such extensive publishing ventures.

In a few years the PEFS began casting around for new arenas. In June 1850 the Board of Directors resolved that immigrants were in desperate need of a bathhouse and a temporary boarding house as well as access to short-term employment. To this end it called on the Executive Committee "to seek a conference with the Managers of the Temporary Home Association on this subject; also, with the Guardians of the Poor, the Temperance Society, the House of Industry and the Societies of Naturalized Citizens." In doing so the Executive Committee revealed an interest in going beyond its role as adviser and intermediary and joining the ranks of the city's benevolent providers. But a year later these objectives remained unreached, and the society continued in those established roles.[59]

In the meantime, the Philadelphia Emigrant's Friend Society was conscious of parallel efforts in New York and other eastern seaboard cities.[60] In 1851 the Philadelphia members led the way in establishing the American Emigrants' Friend Society (AEFS), a national organization with branch offices in several port cities. Although ostensibly a nationwide body, the AEFS continued to be dominated by the Philadelphians who had run the original PEFS. One goal of the new organization was to take the sale of tickets out of the hands of individual agents working for particular shipping lines and replace this system with refundable tickets purchased through the society's offices.[61]

In 1851 the society took steps to expand its employment assistance program by petitioning the Pennsylvania legislature for funds to supplement immigrants' travel expenses to the interior. This money, it argued, should come from one-third of the head taxes that the immigrants were already paying. In pursuing public funds the AEFS was stepping on the toes of Philadelphia's Guardians of the Poor, the normal recipients of the head taxes. The membership reasoned that its efforts would ultimately save money by transporting potential paupers and criminals to other locations. But not surprisingly, the AEFS reported an "unfriendly feeling" emanating from the Guardians of the Poor, who figured to lose part of their budget. In fact, the Executive Committee complained that the Guardians had refused to make consultation with the society a condition of receiving public assistance; moreover, they had resisted providing the AEFS with access to the almshouse when jobs were available.[62] In 1854, as Philadelphia neared political consolidation, Rev. Thomason and two other Philadelphians visited New York and reported back on the success of that city's commissioners of emigration, funded by emigrants' fees, in reducing the most notorious forms of fraud and imposition. Once again the Philadelphia society petitioned the state legislature for access to the immigrants' head money to fund their activities, promising that such an approach would end up saving the government money, but in vain.[63]

In addition to regular quarrels with Philadelphia's Guardians of the Poor, the Emigrant's Friend Society faced resistance from various quarters. Some Philadelphians accused it of encouraging migration out of a hidden political agenda, or at least of thoughtlessly jeopardizing the national economy. Others thought that the society was going beyond its charge when it lobbied for reduced port fees for immigrants.[64] The effort to sink organizational roots in Liverpool encountered resistance from just those people whom the PEFS sought to defeat. In 1848 the society's new Liverpool agent, Eleazer Jones, warned about disgruntled passenger agents in his city. "I am afraid," Jones reported, "that they will become jealous, and will not take our passengers for the same rates as others." This concern led Jones to suggest that the society "should contract with Cope, Esq., and the owners of the New Line to take your paid passengers at certain rates, and then to advertise in the country that you will contract passage with any that wish to send for their friends or relations, and that they will be taken care of by your Agent in Liverpool." In fact, the Irish in Philadelphia continued to send tickets through Cope's Philadelphia office, but with no intervention from the PEFS. In the early 1850s a plan to send a delegation of Americans to England "was cheerfully accepted by the merchants of Liverpool" but foundered when unforeseen circumstances arose. The PEFS blamed the plan's collapse on the violent disruption of a public meeting in New York "by a mob-resistance organized by the emigrant boarding-house keepers and the runners."[65] Meanwhile, the Philadelphia society continued to make repeated but unsuccessful calls for an expanded public presence, financed by immigrant head money, along the lines of New York's commissioners of emigration. This difference between New York and Philadelphia was probably owing to the tremendous flood of immigrants into New York. But it also reflects the Board of Guardians' successful defense of its own prerogatives against usurpation by the privately run PEFS.

The PEFS's failed efforts to expand its role also provide a point of comparison with events in England. When it became clear that Irish migrants awaiting passage to America were routinely falling victim to extortion and fraud, government emigration officers in Liverpool recommended the establishment of an official emigrant depot where the newcomers could receive food and lodging for a small fee. John Bramley Moore, the mayor of Liverpool, supported the scheme enthusiastically; the dock committee went so far as to arrange an architectural plan for the proposed depot. But Lord Grey and the Colonial Office blocked the idea as an inappropriate government intrusion into free trade, declaring that even if the legal niceties could be worked out, the emigrant depot should be run by the Corporation of Liverpool and not the national government. A discouraged Bramley Moore insisted that the Corporation "represented 'those parties whose object and business it is to live upon these emigrants by plundering them'" and thus would never support such a scheme.[66]

One might reasonably read this episode as evidence of the true limits on the national government's role in local matters, particularly those concerning free trade. Nevertheless, it is striking that the plan originated with the Colonial Office's agents in Liverpool and was pushed forward by local elected officials. Although Lord Grey did not share the analysis, the underlying assumption behind the proposed emigrant depot was that the national government could and should take a hand in protecting the emigrants. Conversely, in Philadelphia the impetus for expanded efforts (also stalled) came from the private, philanthropic PEFS. In 1855, when the worst of the migration had passed, New York finally opened Castle Garden, an immigrant depot that was similar to the Liverpool plan. Established with state authorization, Castle Garden was financed by head taxes and run by the commissioners of emigration, who were volunteer state appointees with direct links to the emigrant aid societies. In Philadelphia, such efforts to weave together public and private interests had failed; in Liverpool, no such collaboration had been contemplated.[67]

We are left to speculate about how the immigrants themselves might have felt about the PEFS's overtures. Clearly many of its initiatives were well intentioned and probably had a positive effect. But the directors acknowledged that the new arrivals had no particular reason to trust the PEFS agents. Moreover, although the Emigrant's Friend Society helped thousands of migrants find employment, it exacted its own price by sitting in judgment of each applicant's character and cleanliness.

The family members and the philanthropists who sought to advise prospective Irish migrants viewed the same world but refracted through decidedly different lenses. The Irish migrants who had already settled in Philadelphia understood their crucial role as guides to those who followed. The emigrants' friends conceived of themselves as helping the friendless. This in itself created an important distinction. They also dispensed advice with local interests in mind. Thus the immigrants became not simply individuals in need but potential laborers or, conversely, likely drains on the city's resources. But despite these diverging agendas, both groups of advisers helped the Irish famine migrants navigate the treacherous waters between private fraud and public relief.

CONCLUSION

The initial responses to the famine migrants followed many of the patterns that would filter through other aspects of life in Liverpool and Philadelphia. These early reactions allow for some preliminary observations about where the two cities differed and where they were fundamentally similar.

The comparison must begin with the crucial difference in the flow of migrants. Although one may reasonably speak of comparable Irish immigrant populations in each city, Liverpool became the temporary home of tens of thousands of transient Irish paupers, who placed tremendous short-term strains on local resources. The arrival of immigrant ships attracted attention in Philadelphia, but those newcomers never dominated popular discourse as they occasionally did in Liverpool. The diverging responses to the new arrivals nevertheless are illuminating. Several of Derek Fraser's seven explanatory models can be applied to policy-making in each city. And some of the differences between Philadelphia and Liverpool point to the applicability of various explanations of American distinctiveness.

Perhaps most striking was the sometimes conflicting role of economic concerns affecting decisions in each city. Despite their differing political worlds, voters in both cities desired economic stability and low taxes. On the one hand, ratepayers worried that the famine migrants would become a public expense. On the other hand, quarantine advocates faced resistance from commercial interests who feared that restrictions would inhibit trade. Of course, the immigrants were not only potential drains, they also represented an influx of unskilled labor. Nevertheless, policymakers in Liverpool and Philadelphia shared a basic reaction to this ready supply of workers: they should go somewhere else. The difference in their responses speaks to one aspect of American distinctiveness. The English seemed perfectly content to send this excess population to foreign ports. The emigrants' friends in the United States followed a Turnerian logic. America's vast "frontier" (in this case, mostly the western portions of Pennsylvania and New York) offered ample opportunities for immigrants. The crucial problems were logistical: how to transport new workers to areas where they were needed. Certainly some Irish paupers facing removal disappeared into the English countryside, but this was not presented as a systematic solution in Liverpool as it was in Philadelphia.

Fraser's bureaucratic model, which emphasizes the importance of administrative agencies and officials, also helps to explain the responses of each city. Prior to the famine Philadelphia and Liverpool each had erected a rather complex apparatus for addressing urban problems. In both cities the authorities responsible for poor relief were separate from the committees that oversaw health, sanitation, and policing. The arrival of shiploads of poor, and often sick, immigrants demonstrated the tensions inherent in such a structure. Once again, Philadelphia's version suggests theories of national distinctiveness as well. When the steamer *Rappahannock* arrived from Wilmington, Philadelphians demonstrated their pervasive localism. Rather than turning to state or federal authorities for protection, the Board of Health braced to do battle with Delaware on its own. And the residents of Southwark—furious that diseased migrants had landed at the Washington Street Wharf—threatened to sever ties with other ports. When faced with the costs accompanying poor relief and removals, Liverpool's officials turned to Parliament for answers. The Philadelphians had no such assumptions about their federal government. (Of course, Parliament did not share Liverpool's assumptions about national intervention.)

How should we interpret the actions of the Emigrant's Friend Society? No doubt we could apply a Whig interpretive model, viewing these actions as a positive response to a new set of social dilemmas. But the PEFS also served as an instrument of capitalism, providing local and western employers with ready supplies of labor. One might also see the Emigrant's Friend Society as another mid-nineteenth–century organization bent on social control, trying to impose middle-class values on the migrants, suggesting the conspiratorial model. Even as it acted to assist the arriving immigrants, this organization of elite men reserved the right to evaluate their new clients' characters and regulate their access to public assistance.[68] Finally, and most significantly, the emigrants' friends' different experiences in Liverpool and Philadelphia indicate the power of voluntarism in the United States. Despite repeated calls for a comparable voluntary society in Liverpool, the best local benevolent individuals could muster was occasional cooperation with the highly organized groups in Philadelphia and New York.

3. Poverty, Philanthropy, and Poor Relief

INTRODUCTION: ATTITUDES AND ASSUMPTIONS

After considering the immediate responses to the Irish famine migration in Liverpool and Philadelphia in the previous chapter, we now turn to the immigrants' impact on broader attitudinal and institutional issues. The complexity of the comparison requires that we periodically separate topics that are deeply interwoven. Thus although this chapter will examine private benevolence and public poor relief, philanthropists and policymakers who worried about poverty and its implications found solutions in various aspects of urban life—ranging from health and housing to education and prison reform—that will be the focus of subsequent chapters.

Victorian reformers on both sides of the Atlantic shared fundamental ideas about the origins of poverty and the proper forms of poor relief. Nevertheless, philanthropists and politicians in Liverpool and Philadelphia addressed the problem in dissimilar ways, reflecting different benevolent networks and distinctive local assumptions about public policy. Specifically, Philadelphians responded to the demands by turning to a tradition of decentralized voluntarism: existing benevolent societies expanded their operations and numerous new private institutions formed to meet the perceived challenges. Liverpool also had its private responses, but when compared to Philadelphia the English city's governmental responses were much more noteworthy. This chapter begins with a brief discussion of contemporary ideas about both poverty and reform. Then it considers each city's public and private poor relief institutions; in particular, organizations dedicated to children's welfare. Finally, it examines the institutional responses to the famine migration itself.

Citizens in England and the United States agreed that society had a responsibility to attend to the needs of the poor. Whatever their personal failings, people were not supposed to starve on the streets. The important questions centered on who should assist the poor and how that should be accomplished. These concerns were magnified in the emerging nineteenth-century urban centers. Traditionally the poor in villages and small towns, especially the aged and infirm, had been taken in by family members. The community placed those without relatives in the homes of local families or in small almshouses. But such assistance only extended to paupers who were claimed by the village. Strangers to the community who fell on hard times were liable to "warning out," forced to move on before they became financial burdens. The responsibility for poor relief in both England and the United States had traditionally fallen to the local community; but that tradition relied on long-established familiarity. This practice faced troubling strains in the impersonal nineteenth-century cities.[1]

Besides differentiating between resident and alien paupers, Anglo-American policymakers historically took pains to distinguish between the worthy and the unworthy poor. The former included the young, the old, and the incapacitated—those who bore no responsibility for their condition. The unworthy poor were able-bodied men and women who, their critics insisted, had their own shortcomings to blame for their poverty. In many instances private charities restricted their efforts to aiding the community's most deserving poor, leaving outsiders and the unworthy at the mercy of government assistance.

The range of explanations for poverty mirrored contemporary attitudes toward the poor. Most observers agreed that intemperance lay at the root of the problem. Alcohol bred immorality, sloth, and despair. Some blamed drink on individual failings, calling for moral reform. One correspondent to the *Liverpool Mercury* attributed the destitution in the Vauxhall District to the moral and spiritual decay that accompanied intemperance. Although he joined local reformers in decrying the district's terrible sanitation and overcrowding, the author insisted that the solution must begin with reforming personal habits.[2]

Others sought to weave indictments of alcohol into broader criticisms of urban life. The hordes of poor children seemed to be particular evidence of social ills. In 1848 Philadelphia's *Public Ledger* noted recent "accounts of appalling distress among children" who were being sent to beg in the streets in Philadelphia, New York, and Boston. The *effects* of the problem were "the foundation of prisons, hospitals and almshouses; of criminal justice, and of charity; of the taxation which sustains each." The editorial concluded that intemperance "causes poverty and drives parents to send children out to beg." The suggested solution—following the lines of the Emigrant's Friend Society—was to close the grogshops and devote tax dollars to buying western farms that could take in institutionalized paupers.[3]

Although many continued to stress the importance of personal failings, some observers, such as Philadelphia's Mathew Carey, argued that poverty was intrinsically linked to the nineteenth-century labor system. The seasonality of work forced many unskilled laborers onto public relief during the winter. Manufacturing workers, often cut loose from the agrarian safety net, were subject to regular shutdowns in normal years and devastating unemployment during periodic depressions. In an age without unemployment insurance, illness or injury could plunge even the most stable skilled laborer into pauperism in a matter of months. Working women, Carey noted, were particular victims of a system that rarely offered them a living wage.[4] The *Ledger* blamed Philadelphia's rampant prostitution on a labor system that favored men while failing to pay women enough to live on.[5]

Despite rising urban poverty at home, Americans were quick to claim an advantage over the older English cities. In his novel *Redburn,* Herman Melville devoted lengthy passages to descriptions of Liverpool's poor. And while serving as U.S. consul in Liverpool, Nathaniel Hawthorne wandered the Merseyside city's darkest streets, filling his diary with grim accounts of impoverished beggars. In early 1847 the *Public Ledger* noted reports of poverty in Manchester and other English factory towns and drew links between poor housing, intemperance, and poverty in the English factory town. Such comments became commonplace in the eastern United States, where citizens worried that their cities would develop the disamenities that had long plagued Old World cities.[6]

Discussions of poor relief, like responses to most of Victorian society's social ills, were shaped by contemporary discussions of political economy. British disciples of Adam Smith embraced a liberalism grounded in self-help and free market principles. Applying these principles to social problems, Jeremy Bentham called for the test of utility: were public measures helping to promote the greatest happiness of the greatest number? Versions of Bentham's utilitarianism filtered through English society, disseminated most prominently by John Stuart Mill. Edwin Chadwick, the architect of Victorian England's most sweeping national reforms, became the bureaucratic embodiment of Benthamism.[7]

Across the Atlantic, America's republicanism evolved from the tenets of the Founding Fathers to a broader ideology that absorbed the democratic fervor of the Jacksonians. Although Americans persisted in their celebration of individual liberty and their suspicions of excessive power and central authority, earlier doubts about the unbridled masses yielded to the enthusiastic rhetoric of equalitarianism and democracy. In both worlds, emerging—and intermingling—political philosophies melded with the teachings of evangelical Protestants. Evangelical ministers attracted huge audiences to open-air revivals, where they preached the perfectibility of man, convincing thousands of converts that they had a personal responsibility to reform their world.[8]

These intellectual currents flowed from varied sources and seemed to move in different—although not necessarily contradictory—directions. The English enthusiasm for state-sponsored reform appeared to run counter to the emerging American faith in individualism. But political theorists and evangelicals on both sides of the Atlantic shared an essential optimism. The defining ideas of the early nineteenth century seemed to intersect at one point: the problems of the day could be solved by men and women of conviction. One of the most striking similarities between Victorian England and the United States was this undercurrent of optimism. Even where policies moved in opposite directions, public officials and private reformers believed that their efforts would yield solutions rather than simply a temporary easing of symptoms. This was certainly the case when they discussed poverty.

By midcentury Anglo-American policymakers had endured several generations of debate over the best form of public welfare. A tradition of outdoor relief (the distribution of food, fuel, and small amounts of money) had given way to increasing reliance on more regulated indoor relief in almshouses or workhouses. This new emphasis matched mounting concern over the costs of poor relief with a new faith in the power of institutions. In the United States in particular, reformers experimented with an array of prisons and asylums to rehabilitate society's outcasts and to care for the sick and insane. Such institutions, they believed, would save money while providing inmates with the discipline necessary to survive the rigors of industrializing society.[9] In both countries government officials faced with rising poor relief costs struggled to fashion systems that provided adequate assistance in sufficiently unattractive forms so that only the most needy would apply. Meanwhile, private charitable institutions addressed the needs of the worthy poor, with varying degrees of material assistance and moral exhortation.

Evangelical reformers in England and the United States saw personal salvation as the route out of poverty. Their charitable institutions stressed morality and temperance, distributing religious tracts and counsel along with material assistance. In the second quarter of the nineteenth century newly formed urban missions sought to bridge the gap between the wealthy and the poor, and between moral reform and poor relief, through personal visitation. Pioneered by Thomas Chalmers in Glasgow, these efforts stressed personal contact between rich and poor. In 1828 Joseph Tuckerman, a student of Unitarian William Ellery Channing, established America's first Ministry at Large in Boston. He divided the city into districts, with visitors establishing their ministries among the poor. Tuckerman's teachings were vital to the development of both Philadelphia's Union Benevolent Association (UBA) and Liverpool's Domestic Mission Society (DMS).[10]

PUBLIC POOR RELIEF BEFORE THE FAMINE

The English government had long acknowledged that poverty was a state concern and not merely the purview of Christian charity. In 1536 legislation authorized parishes to assist the "impotent poor" who were unable to beg, thus establishing the possibility of public relief while also distinguishing between the worthy poor and those able-bodied paupers who remained subject to vagrancy laws. Various measures in the late sixteenth century established the principle of requiring labor of the able-bodied poor. The Poor Law Act of 1601 codified British poor relief for the next two centuries. The Elizabethan Poor Law distinguished among three main categories of poor. The impotent poor were to be housed in almshouses, the able-bodied poor were to work (in what became workhouses), and those able-bodied poor who refused to work were to be punished in houses of correction. Later, the 1662 Law of Settlement addressed persistent conflicts between localities by defining the terms under which an individual could claim a legal settlement in a community. Communities fearing costly poor relief could elect to remove strangers to their home parish.[11]

Although the Privy Council was to direct the poor relief system, local administration was left to the parish overseers of the poor. The most important local deviation from the Elizabethan template was the continued use of outdoor relief for the able-bodied. By the late eighteenth century many parishes had implemented some form of "allowance system" to supplement low wages and assist unemployed workers. These measures prompted a widespread debate, which reached a crescendo in the decades after Waterloo, as rising poor relief costs became a source of increased controversy. Reformers—often guided by Malthusian theories of population growth or Adam Smith's and David Ricardo's writings on wages and the free market—called for a dramatic rethinking of the existing Poor Law, which, they argued, inadvertently contributed to the problem.

In the early 1830s a Royal Commission, led by the Benthamite Edwin Chadwick, launched a detailed investigation culminating in the 1834 Poor Law Report. This report, which became the basis of the 1834 New Poor Law, called for a reformed system based on three principles: "less eligibility," the workhouse test, and administrative centralization. The first tenet was that to discourage idleness the level of poor relief must fall below the material conditions of an able-bodied worker. Outdoor relief for the able-bodied was to be abandoned in favor of complete reliance on the less attractive workhouse. The whole system was to function through newly established Poor Law Unions under the direction of a national Poor Law Commission. Scholars of British welfare stress that the New Poor Law did not revolutionize poor relief practice as much as has long been supposed, and that in fact Chadwick never succeeded in his aim of imposing a coherent system on all localities. Local variation persisted, and in many cases the former overseers of the poor performed the same functions with respect to the new Poor Law Unions as they had previously performed under the Old Poor Law. Nevertheless, the New Poor Law did change the terms of discussion: its defenders celebrated reduced poor relief rates, and its detractors attacked the harsh workhouses. And despite local variation, the nationally based assistant Poor Law commissioners did attain an effective voice in parish affairs.[12]

Under the Old Poor Law, the duty of providing Liverpool's poor relief fell to the Select Vestry, which gave indoor relief and medical assistance in the parish workhouse. Through the 1820s and 1830s the Vestry stressed economy, only dispensing in-kind outdoor relief in emergencies. The Poor Law Report applauded Liverpool's parish relief system for its careful scrutiny of applicants and its use of forced "oakum-picking" in the workhouse. Liverpool resisted the imposition of the centrally administered New Poor Law, claiming its special status as a Local Act Union. In 1841 the parish of Liverpool finally converted into a Poor Law Union, but near the close of that year the Special General Vestry met and petitioned for special parliamentary dispensation, claiming that the new system was more cumbersome than the old—and generally successful—Select Vestry system. With Chadwick long gone, the Poor Law Commission granted Liverpool's request, sacrificing centralization for efficiency. In July 1842 the General Vestry elected twenty-one members to a newly reconvened Select Vestry, subject to the oversight of the national Poor Law commissioners. Fourteen of these men had served on the short-lived Board of Guardians, suggesting the broad continuities beneath these bureaucratic changes. The two local relieving officers remained on the job undisturbed through each transition.[13]

Liverpool's example is evidence that Chadwick's most ambitious goals did not fare well in the face of local resistance. But the fact that 1834 was no great watershed in Liverpool's poor relief history is also evidence that the city, more so than most rural areas, had already established a system that met with the Poor Law Commission's approval. After 1834 Poor Law officials monitored local proceedings, adding another aspect of central inspection to the emerging Victorian state. The connection to Parliament became more explicit in 1847, when the Poor Law Board, under parliamentary direction, replaced the Poor Law Commission and began sending Poor Law inspectors into the field. On occasion these national government officials clashed with local authorities. In August 1848, for instance, the Poor Law Board chastised Liverpool's Board of Guardians for promoting vagrancy by failing to be sufficiently vigilant in examining relief applicants. Angry Select Vestry members lashed back, charging that the fault lay not in faulty implementation but in ineffective national laws.[14]

Even before the heavy Irish famine migration, Liverpool authorities worried that the rise in local pauperism threatened to outstrip the city's commitment to indoor relief and the principle of less eligibility. In 1843 Rector Brooks charged that Liverpool's shabby, overcrowded workhouse was damaging the city's reputation. After much debate the Vestry voted to build a grand new workhouse with the assistance of government loans.

Although the Vestry later settled on a less ambitious expansion plan, by midcentury Liverpool boasted England's largest provincial workhouse, standing atop Brownlow Hill. Thus the parish was well prepared to withstand a heavy influx of new paupers.[15]

America's poor relief owed its origins to inherited English traditions. Lacking any national policies, the colonies developed various systems modeled on the 1601 English law. Colonial communities followed English practice by accepting public responsibility for the poor who could not be cared for in the homes of family members. As the colonies matured, they established laws of settlement and began differentiating between the worthy and unworthy poor, much as their English brethren had done. By the late eighteenth century most American communities relied on local overseers of the poor, who distributed relief funded by a separate poor tax. Although some larger cities—including Philadelphia—supported almshouses, most assistance came in the form of outdoor aid. Many communities kept down costs by auctioning off the labor of the poor to the highest bidder.[16]

By the early nineteenth century Americans had begun to join the English in questioning their poor relief system. Outdoor relief had become increasingly expensive, and overly generous aid to the poor ran counter to contemporary laissez-faire economic theory. Although Malthusian fears about excessive population growth failed to strike a chord in the New World, moral critiques of the able-bodied poor found eager audiences among those who trumpeted America's economic opportunities and preached the Protestant work ethic. Americans turned increasingly to poorhouses as an economical and efficient means of imposing discipline on able-bodied paupers.[17]

Although it had an almshouse from the 1720s, Philadelphia had long relied on outdoor relief and private benevolence to provide for its poor. In 1766 local Quakers received the authority to build a "Bettering House" to replace the old almshouse, but a generation later official poor relief reverted to government hands. As the nineteenth century began, Philadelphia's Board of Guardians oversaw outdoor relief in the city and the surrounding districts while the almshouse managers controlled indoor aid. As long as the city prospered, the Guardians concentrated on distributing fuel and clothing during harsh winters and providing medical assistance during epidemics. According to Priscilla Clement, the vast majority of Philadelphians receiving cash assistance between 1810 and 1829 were women, most of whom were single. The men, and many of the women, who received aid were old or infirm. Although they made up 8–9 percent of the city population, blacks received only 1–4 percent of cash relief during these decades. The city further minimized expenses by indenturing out pauper children and vigorously enforcing settlement laws, which excluded nonresidents.

By the late 1820s concerns for costs and questions about the morality of the poor had prompted Philadelphians to join in the call for welfare reform. In 1827 the Board of Guardians appointed a committee to inspect poor relief facilities in other East Coast cities, including Boston, New York, and Baltimore. The committee issued an attack on outdoor relief, charging that intemperance—particularly among immigrants—lay at the heart of the poverty problem and calling for forced labor for able-bodied paupers. In 1828 the state legislature responded by passing a new Poor Law ending all outdoor cash relief. Beginning in 1829 the Guardians of the Poor were to be full-time paid officials named by the city Councils and the district commissioners, rather than unpaid volunteers who served for one-year terms. Although the Guardians only provided cash assistance in unusual emergencies, in-kind relief—generally food and fuel—continued to support Philadelphia's laboring poor. In 1835 Philadelphia opened the huge new Blockley Almshouse to accommodate the increased demand for indoor relief. Housed on a 170-acre estate on the west bank of the Schuylkill, Blockley's four buildings became showcases for the supposed virtues of enforced discipline and social control.[18]

In the two decades after 1828 Philadelphia's frugal Board of Guardians concentrated on keeping poor rates down, even in the face of heavy demands.[19] In 1840 the Guardians began providing short-term cash assistance to some applicants, but the share of the population receiving direct aid remained well below previous levels. Meanwhile, more poor laborers were receiving in-kind assistance, while paupers were forced into Blockley Almshouse. Although Philadelphia's poor did not necessarily share their enthusiasm, travelers and local citizens commonly remarked on Blockley's impressive facilities. Harriet Martineau found it a "magnificent pauper asylum."[20] Still, the almshouse struggled through poor administration and disappointing results. In 1849 a grand jury found that despite policies requiring labor, many almshouse residents were sitting idle in defiance of the Guardians' orders. By the eve of the famine many Americans had begun to grow disillusioned with their poorhouses and asylums. Optimism about reform had turned to grim acceptance of warehousing. And despite contradictory rhetoric, some communities had begun to shift resources back to outdoor relief.[21]

❧

Through the first half of the nineteenth century, public poor relief in England and the United States shared many essential assumptions and characteristics. Both nations began the century with a commitment to public assistance, locally administered. Each differentiated among the poor, offering the most benign assistance to those who could demonstrate residency and those who were deemed least responsible for their fate. As costs grew and cynicism about able-bodied paupers mounted, reformers turned to institutional solutions that promised cost efficiency, discipline, and—perhaps most important—a strong incentive to stay off public relief. The most dramatic difference between the two countries was the role of the national government. In England, the impetus for reform came from London; the New Poor Law was overseen by national agents. True, localism continued to reign in many quarters. But the contrast with the United States was still stark. In America, the federal government had nothing to say about poor relief; even state legislatures typically responded to local appeals (as in that from Philadelphia in 1828) rather than initiating actions.

The contrast in national approach, and similarity in result, is best illustrated by comparing the Philadelphia Board of Guardians's 1827 report with Chadwick's 1834 Poor Law report. In the former case, elected representatives from one city went on a fact-finding tour of six eastern cities. In the latter case, an appointed national official orchestrated a far more ambitious survey of poor-relief practices nationwide. Although the origins and scale of these two surveys—separated by less than a decade—were very different, their essential recommendations about the utility of indoor relief were similar.

The institutional similarities between Philadelphia and Liverpool were also pronounced. Both had poor relief officials who existed apart from the city Councils. (And, as we have seen, the poor relief jurisdictions in neither city were coterminous with the city boundaries.) Taxpayers in each city railed against costly poor relief, prompting a shift away from outdoor aid to what was hoped would be cheaper institutional relief. Both Liverpool and Philadelphia opted to construct large new almshouses (or workhouses) shortly *before* the famine migration. Partly because of this shift in policy, both cities boasted reduced poor relief expenditures, even while poverty was commonly acknowledged to be on the rise.

Public poor relief did not evolve in a vacuum. In both England and the United States, policymakers proceeded with the knowledge that numerous private charities already existed to aid selected poor residents. Generally, these benevolent organizations focused on the needs of the worthy local poor, leaving strangers and the unworthy to public officials. Most charitable organizations were small, emphasizing a specific client group. In each country middle-class women took the lead as charitable organizers, visitors, and fund-raisers.[22] Often benevolent groups carried a spiritual message and were commonly affiliated with a particular church or faith. Others declared a nonsectarian (although often Protestant) orientation. A few rejected any encroachment by organized religion. The actual assistance came in many forms. Some organizations supported small asylums. Others ran "houses of industry," providing work for the unemployed. Various bodies offered emergency outdoor relief in the form of clothing, bread and soup, or winter fuel. Many charities reflected a special concern for the problems of poor women. Asylums were created to reform prostitutes or to protect poor women from urban vices. American houses of industry provided work for unemployed sewing women to shield them from the poorhouse.[23]

At the outset of the nineteenth century Liverpool and Philadelphia each had several long-established charities, largely dedicated to medical relief. After around 1815 organized benevolence expanded in response to rising urban poverty. By the 1830s private philanthropists had begun to fill the gaps created by changes in public relief. Both cities, too, supported urban missions along the lines of Tuckerman's Boston ministry to the poor.

Many of Liverpool's oldest charities and institutions provided medical relief to the worthy poor. The Ladies' Charity, founded in 1796, sent middle-class women into the homes of poor women in childbirth. In keeping with the moral and legal dictates of the moment, the Ladies' Charity only assisted married women who had an established residency, leaving all others at the mercy of the Poor Law authorities. Among the city's institutions aimed at moral reformation, the oldest was the Female Penitentiary, founded in 1811 to reform prostitutes. Poor immigrants could turn to the Strangers' Friend Society. Founded in 1789, this organization sent visitors into the homes of the poor before providing them with food, fuel, and blankets.[24] In 1830 the Liverpool Night Asylum for the Houseless Poor opened in Chapel Street to provide a night's lodging for poor strangers, sparing them the workhouse and reducing the problem of street begging.[25] Local Protestants responded in 1844 to the upsurge of visitors from abroad by opening the Liverpool Foreigners' Mission, which provided spiritual sustenance—although not material assistance—to travelers.[26]

By the second quarter of the century several new visiting organizations, each with its own agenda, had joined the Strangers' Friend Society in ministering to Liverpool's poor. The most important of these was the District Provident Society (DPS), founded in 1829 to provide moral guidance and modest material assistance. Its twenty-one district committees sent over two hundred visitors into the city's poor neighborhoods, where they waged their war against vice and indiscriminate giving seemingly as energetically as they fought poverty itself.[27] The Liverpool Charitable Society, run by the Established Church, sent agents into the homes of the sick and distressed to "promote the spiritual welfare of the poor." By 1847 the Charitable Society was providing food, clothing, and spiritual guidance to over two thousand Liverpool families.[28]

At the same time that the DPS was beginning to offer outdoor assistance, two new missions began sending religious emissaries into Liverpool's poor neighborhoods. An 1829 meeting of the Society for the Promotion of the Religious Instruction of the Poor launched the Liverpool City Mission. The City Mission's agents distributed religious tracts and staged open-air services, but they gave minimal material assistance. Although its organizers claimed no particular religious affiliation, Roman Catholic poor were understandably skeptical about the City Mission, which portrayed itself as "an evangelical alliance at work."[29]

In 1835 Liverpool Unitarian John Thom delivered a sermon calling for the creation of a local Ministry for the Poor along the lines pioneered by Chalmers in Glasgow and Tuckerman in Boston. A year later Thom's father-in-law, Mayor William Rathbone, chaired the meeting that established the Domestic Mission Society. Under the guidance of its first minister, Rev. John Johns, the DMS became a leading voice for moral and social reform. Like the City Mission, Johns avoided material assistance, preferring to emphasize personal contacts and moral guidance. Soon he became affiliated with the District Provident Society, providing the most needy with tickets redeemable through the DPS for in-kind assistance. Johns rejected all denominational ties, struggling to convince Roman Catholics that he was not in search of conversions. Johns and the subsequent Ministers to the Poor regularly acknowledged their debt to Tuckerman, "our revered American father." In keeping with the changing intellectual currents, the DMS ministers issued warnings about excessive unregulated charity, while stressing the importance of environmental concerns—bad sanitation, overcrowding, poor ventilation—in producing immorality and poverty.[30]

On the eve of the famine migration, Liverpool's Catholics were too poor themselves to support much organized benevolence. From the early nineteenth century the Catholic Benevolent Society had raised funds to be distributed to the needy through the local parish priests. But even in prosperous times the amount distributed was small, only £237 in 1840. Within a few years the Benevolent Society was moribund, awaiting rebirth in 1850. In the meantime, local priests continued to minister to the poor, supported by church collections, while donations funded the city's small Catholic Orphan Asylum.[31] The Society of Saint Vincent de Paul, founded in Paris in 1833, established a branch in Liverpool in 1845 with the dual purpose of helping the needy and "giving the almsgiver tender feelings towards the poor." [32]

The modest budgets of Liverpool's mid-nineteenth–century charities may have been owing to contemporary thinking on the evils of mendicancy, but they also reflected the city's small philanthropic base. After surveying the contributors to Liverpool charities (including medical, religious, and educational) in 1852, Abraham Hume concluded that 689 citizens had provided more than half of the support to local charities, with a mere 122 "gentlemen"—who each gave to numerous organizations—bearing a disproportionate share of the burden.[33]

The City of Brotherly Love had a well-deserved reputation for organized benevolence. Philadelphia Quakers in particular had been involved in colonial philanthropy, but by the early nineteenth century all local sects had taken a hand in private welfare. In many ways Philadelphia's long-established institutions and asylums were similar to Liverpool's benevolent network. Various medical charities ministered to the needs of specific clienteles; the nonsectarian Indigent Widows' and Single Women's Society provided a home for fifty to sixty-five single elderly women; and the Magdalen Society, like Liverpool's Female Penitentiary, took in a handful of prostitutes each year. And as in Liverpool, new Philadelphia charities emerged in the early nineteenth century. Following the War of 1812 Philadelphians grew concerned about mounting poverty, establishing eleven new charities, including five soup kitchens, between 1815 and 1830. With the prohibition of public outdoor cash relief in 1828, the worthy poor became even more reliant on private assistance. In the 1830s ten new charities helped meet this additional demand. But private donors joined public officials in questioning the utility and wisdom of cash assistance. Mathew Carey's city-wide charity fund-raiser in 1829 yielded only modest contributions, suggesting that local citizens shared the government's skepticism about the new poor.[34]

In 1841 the managers of the Union Benevolent Association, one of Philadelphia's most prominent charities, explained their understanding of the difference between public and private assistance:

> With a population of more than two hundred thousand souls, subjected to a large annual influx by foreign emigration, two classes of individuals, standing in need of assistance, are to be found in our midst. One comprising a numerous class—properly known to us as paupers—the other, composed of the unfortunate, but industrious poor. The former are the fit subjects of the Guardians of the Poor, and occupants of the Blockley Alms-House;—the latter, the peculiar objects of the Association with which we are connected. One class avails itself of the provision, appointed by law for its relief, and on which it habitually depends; the other never condescends to be the partakers of its bounties, unless compelled by dire necessity.

Founded in 1831, the UBA was modeled directly on Chalmers's work in Glasgow. Like Liverpool's District Provident Society, established two years earlier, the UBA had over two hundred visitors who brought food, clothing, fuel, and moral guidance to Philadelphians who had not yet fallen onto the public relief rolls. Unlike its English counterpart, the UBA relied almost exclusively on female visitors and had black families among its client base. The UBA joined the English organization in stressing morality and temperance while decrying the evil effects of indiscriminate giving.[35] In 1835, as Liverpool's Unitarians were forming the Domestic Mission Society, benevolent Philadelphians established the Home Missionary Association, also based on Dr. Tuckerman's teachings. Like the DMS, the Home Missionary Association's minister—Rev. John Street—offered moral counsel and food and fuel but little cash assistance.[36]

Philadelphians had a particular fondness for institutions that provided the able-bodied poor with work. The Female Society of Philadelphia for the Relief and Employment of the Poor was initially founded by Quakers in 1795 to assist women in finding jobs. In 1816 the society opened a small house of industry for women and children who could find no other occupation in the troubled economy. By the late 1830s the membership had voted to offer direct assistance only to the aged and infirm, requiring that all other applicants work at the house of industry. The Northern Association for the Relief and Employment of Poor Women, established in 1844, provided rooms where black and white poor women could do needlework for 25 cents a day.[37]

Philadelphia's expanding Catholic population, much more so than its Liverpool counterpart, supported steady institutional growth in the second quarter of the nineteenth century. By 1851 there were seven Catholic benevolent institutions in the city, including two orphan asylums and St. Joseph's Hospital. The Ladies' Catholic Benevolent Society, founded in the early 1830s, sent visitors into Philadelphia's tenements to provide the "deserving poor" with money, food, and clothing. By 1847—a year in which Liverpool's Catholic Benevolent Society lay moribund—its counterpart in Philadelphia was aiding over five hundred families, with the assistance of numerous parish sewing circles and clothing donations from several Catholic Dorcas societies. This difference presumably reflected some combination of greater wealth among Philadelphia's Catholics and a stronger local and national tradition of organized benevolence. Irish Catholic immigrants also received modest assistance from Philadelphia's Hibernia Society, a social and benevolent club established by the Friendly Sons of St. Patrick. In the mid-1840s the Hibernia Society was raising between $660 and $840 a year for the relief of the poor.[38]

Clement has noted that as Philadelphia's mix of public and private poor relief changed, and as the emphasis moved away from cash relief, the identity of the recipients also changed. The reduction of cash assistance hit poor white women the hardest. Public and private officials had always resisted providing cash relief to able-bodied men, and black women rarely received cash outdoor assistance. Clement argues that with the shift to more extensive in-kind outdoor relief, Philadelphia's poor women had to become adept at maneuvering in a complex private institutional system, surviving by piecing together assistance from several sources.[39]

Institutions addressing the needs of children revealed many of Victorian society's central goals and assumptions. Politicians and reformers groping for solutions to crime, intemperance, and immorality concluded that poor children represented the best hope for the future. Some emphasized introducing them to religion. Others concluded that some form of education, providing technical skills and personal discipline, was the answer. Often those who advocated new initiatives aimed at poor children stressed the ultimate fiscal gains: money spent today will save prison costs tomorrow.[40]

In 1845 Liverpool's Select Vestry opened the Kirkdale Industrial Schools, designed to save poor children from the "adult contamination" of the workhouse. By 1853 more children than adults received indoor relief from the Vestry.[41] Although most poor children in Liverpool ended up in public institutions, a handful found homes in private orphanages. The Blue Coat Hospital, founded in 1708, provided for children of the parish who had lost one or both parents and could produce a parents' marriage certificate and a baptismal record. In 1844 the Female Orphan Asylum was founded for locally born girls who had lost both parents and who could prove their legitimacy. Seven years later the Liverpool Asylum for Boys opened with the same provisions. Both orphanages—like the Blue Coat Hospital—were sponsored by leading Protestant clergy who promised that all children would be "educated in the principles of the Established Church." The three Protestant orphanages had a total capacity of about 650 children; Liverpool's Catholic Orphan Asylum housed an additional 40 to 50 annually.[42]

Early-nineteenth-century Philadelphia had two small private orphanages—one Protestant and one Catholic—with the remaining poor orphans housed in the almshouse. The Philadelphia Orphan Society provided homes for up to a hundred local boys and girls; the Catholic Society of St. Joseph's housed over a hundred girls. In 1822 female members of the Society of Friends opened the Shelter for Colored Orphans for about a dozen children. Local Catholics added the small St. John's Orphan Asylum for boys in 1829.[43] In 1820 the city had opened the Children's Asylum, the nation's second public orphanage. But with the completion of the Blockley Almshouse in 1835, the relatively benevolent children's asylum shut its doors and indigent children joined adults in the new institution. Whereas Liverpool provided substantial (and separate) public indoor relief to orphans, at midcentury, only 523 Philadelphia children, or just 11 percent of the city's institutionalized poor, received indoor assistance, and they were housed among adults. Three decades earlier that figure had been closer to 1,700 children.[44]

Many Philadelphians worried that poor children were liable to mature into costly criminals. In 1828 the Society of Friends established a house of refuge to protect young vagrants from prison. Although privately run, the home worked closely with local officials. The Guardians of the Poor and local magistrates were authorized to sentence children who had committed minor infractions to a year in the house of refuge. Once their sentence had expired, they were apprenticed to local families.[45]

The reports of the almshouse and the house of refuge never explicitly acknowledge the rising proportion of Irish inmates, although they seem to have been drafted with that point in mind. The Guardians of the Poor first noted ethnicity in their report of 1852, when the Irish had become over half of the population. Similarly, the managers of the house of refuge began reporting parentage—in addition to nativity—in 1853, apparently to underscore that many children born in Philadelphia were from Irish families.

On the eve of the famine migration the poor relief systems in Liverpool and Philadelphia were similar in both assumptions and structure. Each city government had turned away from outdoor relief in favor of less inviting indoor assistance. To that end, Liverpool in 1842 had resolved to build a large new workhouse, at a time when Philadelphia's grand Blockley Almshouse was only a decade old. The private benevolent worlds were also comparable. Each city supported a range of small institutions and asylums with similar clienteles and agendas. As public officials reduced outdoor relief, philanthropists in Liverpool and Philadelphia established benevolent societies organized around teams of agents who visited the poor in their homes, dispensing moral advice and modest material assistance. In the generation before the famine both cities developed new home missions patterned on the teachings of Joseph Tuckerman. It was also common for the distinction between public and private to blur. Liverpool's Council made annual donations to private local charities; Philadelphia officials routinely sent children to the privately run house of refuge.[46]

Some characteristics did separate the two cities. Philadelphia had nothing comparable to Liverpool's Night Asylum, providing incoming poor with a night off the streets. Presumably the almshouse, or perhaps the city jail, served this function.[47] On the other hand, Liverpool had nothing like Philadelphia's house of industry, perhaps indicating a distinctive Jacksonian American faith in the transformative power of labor. Philadelphia Catholics were able to sustain a citywide benevolent organization—the Ladies' Catholic Benevolent Society—whereas Liverpool's poorer Catholic Benevolent Society essentially closed its books for several years in the mid-1840s. Philadelphia also supported *more* small benevolent organizations and institutions, whereas Liverpool's largest charity—the District Provident

Society—was larger than Philadelphia's comparable Union Benevolent Association. Taken as a whole, Philadelphia's more extensive benevolent world was in keeping with the city's historic reputation and Tocqueville's claims about the American propensity for voluntary societies.

The two cities' policies toward children also seem to have pointed in opposite directions. Two institutions—Liverpool's Kirkdale School and Philadelphia's house of refuge—illustrate a fundamental difference between the two cities. Guardians in both places recognized that the almshouse was no place for juveniles.[48] In Liverpool the answer was to construct the Kirkdale Industrial Schools, which offered segregated training for 1,250 children. Philadelphia continued to take pauper youth into the newly constructed Blockley Almshouse while relying on the privately run house of refuge (and, later, Girard College) to provide training and discipline for over 500 orphans and delinquents.[49] This contrast once again indicates differing assumptions about the utility of government institutions, as opposed to private institutions, for addressing social ills.

THE FAMINE MIGRATION AND LIVERPOOL'S POOR RELIEF

The Irish famine migrants put these evolving welfare systems to the test. How would theories about the worthy and unworthy poor and divisions between public and private relief fare in the face of such tremendous numbers? Although Liverpool had to contend with a far heavier flow of paupers, a comparison of the two cities reveals fundamental differences.

As we have seen, in late 1846 Liverpool's Select Vestry reported that outdoor relief to the arriving Irish paupers threatened to overwhelm the city's resources. In January the city implemented Assistant Poor Law Commissioner Alfred Austin's emergency relief system, establishing twenty-four relieving officers charged with inspecting applicants before providing them with bread and soup. Meanwhile, the Vestry "removed" over 60,000 Irish paupers to Ireland between 1845 and 1854. The mounting costs of poor relief and removals prompted city officials to turn to Parliament—largely in vain—for financial assistance. In the first nine months of 1847 the parish spent nearly twice as much on outdoor relief (£52,296) as it had in the comparable period in 1846 (£26,880). Ratepayers complained of excessive poor relief costs, and skeptics insisted that parish authorities were still regularly duped by fraudulent appeals for assistance.[50]

The wholesale removal, and the threat of removal, of immigrants had a clear impact on the Irish demand for public assistance. In July 1847 the special Irish Relief Committee reported to the Vestry that its expenditures had declined because "[m]any were going back to Ireland, and others went up the country." Two months later the committee reported that in the previous week it had relieved 7,960 Irish paupers and sent 4,460 back to Ireland. By 1848 the number of Irish people receiving outdoor assistance had fallen to 3,500 a week, roughly a quarter of the parish total. For the next six years this figure continued to decline.[51]

As more and more migrants learned that seeking parish relief made them liable to removal, many turned to begging. Even the city's most benevolent citizens felt overwhelmed. In December 1846 diarist George Holt Sr. wrote: "During the last month & especially the last fortnight the whole town swarming with Irish paupers the Famine consequent to the failure of the Potatoe Crop inducing thousands on thousands to come over to this country beggin—quite beyond the powers of private charity and help—the best method therefore appears to be to give the best encouragement one can to the parochial authorities & assistance to the public institutions." The following week a frustrated Holt added that "Private charity can do nothing. It becomes dangerous to give at the House or the counting Ho[use]. One dole brings hundreds of others instantly depriving you of the power of Entrance or Egress into yr own premises—The Parish Authorities & benevolent Societies the best channels to act thro—But all is only a patching up to be re-presented in a more aggravated form hereafter!" In the months to come Holt repeatedly returned to this theme, insisting that no individual could hope to make the slightest dent in such human misery.[52]

Holt's sympathy for the Irish beggars was tempered by his conviction that many of them were dishonest—"borrowing children so as to increase their claims," for instance. Such charges became commonplace, as correspondents to the *Mercury* offered an endless string of anecdotes, generally involving beggars who were discovered to have had hidden wealth. These doubts prompted a campaign to eliminate "indiscriminate giving." The Select Vestry called on citizens to make their donations to the District Provident Society, the Charitable Society, or the Strangers' Friend Society, rather than giving alms directly to the poor. Magistrate Rushton, frustrated by a growing vagrancy problem, chastised Catholics who gave money to beggars outside of church instead of donating to the proper societies. Of course, this campaign was not intended only to eliminate dishonest beggars. By stopping unregulated almsgiving, Liverpool officials hoped to drive the Irish poor into the arms of the parochial authorities, who could return them to Ireland.[53]

With parochial authorities curbing emergency outdoor relief, increasing numbers of Irish poor ended up in the workhouse. In the year ending in March 1848, roughly 3,800 Irish, or 29 percent of the total admitted, entered Liverpool's workhouse. After a decline in 1848, the number of Irish workhouse inmates climbed steadily, approaching nearly half of the workhouse population. In the short term, the heavy influx of Irish paupers undercut Brownlow Hill's deterrent value. But by the mid-1850s the workhouse had returned to an emphasis on the principle of less eligibility. Meanwhile, the Select Vestry continued to debate the proposed new workhouse that had been in the planning stages since 1842. After much talk of a new 3,000-space building on the outskirts of town, the Vestry finally resolved to expand the capacity of the existing workhouse from roughly 1,700 to 2,200; another 1,200 spaces were available in the Industrial Schools. Although it was substantially smaller than the original proposal, proponents of the new plan pointed out that the expanded workhouse would meet local needs while saving money.[54] Thus, although Liverpool expanded its workhouse in the midst of the Irish migration, the earlier decision to build a new workhouse actually preceded the famine; in fact, the Vestry opted for a more conservative expansion plan in the midst of the famine migration.

Liverpool's commitment to separate facilities for children continued during the famine years. In 1845, its first year of operation, the Kirkdale Industrial Schools listed only 9 Irish-born children among 766 boys and girls. By 1847, 153 of 642 new arrivals were Irish. Soon this rise in Irish inmates attracted official concern. At the end of March the Select Vestry's Industrial Schools Committee requested a special report on "the number of Irish children sent from the workhouse to the Industrial schools." The following May the committee resolved to send children slated for indoor relief to the workhouse before transferring eligible applicants to the Industrial Schools. In 1848 the total admittance dropped to 235 boys and girls, including only 31 Irish-born, suggesting that the resistance to aiding Irish immigrants extended to children.[55]

The impact of the famine migration on Liverpool's private charitable institutions varied widely, reflecting their differing orientations. The private orphanages explicitly excluded outsiders, leaving poor Irish children in public hands.[56] The Ladies' Charity responded to increased demands and reduced funds by amending its eligibility requirements from mothers of one child who had been in residence for at least one year to mothers of two children who had been in residence for two years. Some observers worried that the new demands would crowd out donations to existing charities, particularly in tough economic times. In 1847 the managers of the Blue Coat Hospital reported that the "many extraordinary calls on the bounty of [the] townsmen" had reduced customary subscriptions. But in 1851 the managers of the Female Orphan Asylum noted that "the tide of benevolence, which untoward circumstances will sometimes cause to ebb, has copiously flowed in various channels, and in many instances watered and replenished the thirsty land where dearth appeared to threaten."[57]

Some private organizations did report heavy demands from the Irish poor. Over half of the Strangers' Friend Society's 1,800 cases in 1846–47 were Irish-born. In early 1847 the District Provident Society announced that it was trying to assist only local poor, while shifting the famine migrants onto parish relief. Still, at its annual meeting in May 1847 the DPS reported an increase in clients from 8,102 to 29,639, including nearly 19,000 Irish-born (an additional 4,000 people with no specified birthplace received informal aid). The next year the DPS visited 32,696 people, including 20,489 Irish. In its February 1849 meeting the society reported a decline to 18,756 relieved, with half Irish-born. In their 1849 report the officers called on charitable local citizens to distribute DPS tickets rather than cash, since cash—they claimed—promoted mendicancy, especially among the Irish poor.[58]

Liverpool's missions, although steering clear of substantial material assistance, also reported increased demands in the late 1840s. John Johns, the Domestic Mission Society's first minister, proved a particularly able observer of local poverty. In his 1846 report, Rev. Johns wrote approvingly that "the cause of the poor has been taken up of late by the higher classes, with increased and increasing sympathy." A year later he seemed almost stunned by twelve months of misery: "The immigration of hundreds of famished Irish families either resting here on their way to America, or hoping to procure a subsistence from English charity or labour" had created "a state of things, in the lower sections of our town, which I have seen nothing like before, and hope to see nothing like again." The extreme distress prompted Johns to suspend his normal routine in order to dispense assistance without prior investigation. In 1851 Francis Bishop, the DMS's new minister to the poor, noted the prevalence of professional Irish beggars but argued that many had little choice because they had been denied Parish relief. The Liverpool City Mission made a special point that the "fearful amount of destitution" accompanying the famine did not disrupt "the spiritual character of its aim and agency." The City Mission's total number of visits actually declined annually—from over 79,000 in 1844 to 55,417 in 1849—before beginning a rapid climb. In 1851 the mission, which continued to resist providing material assistance, added a Gaelic-speaking Protestant agent to speak directly to the impoverished newcomers. The following year the its twenty-six agents made nearly 91,000 visits.[59]

In addition to working with the established charitable organizations, Liverpool's religious community responded to the new demands with occasional collections following special charity sermons, sometimes splitting the proceeds between direct assistance to Ireland and aid to the DPS.[60] Each winter local Catholics staged an annual charity ball to fund the Female Orphan Asylum and "other Catholic charities in Liverpool." After several years of inactivity the Catholic Benevolent Society reemerged in November 1850, raising small amounts of money—through donations, charity sermons, and the annual ball—to be distributed to the "sick and destitute poor" by parish priests. Between 1851 and 1856 the society paid out, in steadily increasing amounts, between £230 and £382 annually. Thus, in the final years of the famine migration Liverpool Catholics once again played an organized role—albeit small—in assisting the worthy poor.[61]

The famine years saw increased cooperation between Liverpool's public authorities and private agencies. In early 1847 local citizens responded to the flood of starving immigrants by opening several soup kitchens, where nonpauper poor could buy soup at below cost. The parish relieving officers worked with the soup kitchens, providing Irish migrants with tickets good for meals. In his 1847 report to the DMS, John Johns credited the new soup kitchens with reducing the city's worst starvation. "What has Liverpool owed to that admirable institution!" he wrote. At the close of the year, with demand down, the Soup Committee agreed to turn the operation over to the Select Vestry while continuing to help in the day-to-day administration. The Vestry consented to sell soup to the poor without placing them on the parish rolls.[62] In mid-1848 the Night Asylum became the center of controversy when a move from the Vauxhall District to Soho Street triggered neighborhood resistance. The Select Vestry proposed to replace the privately administered asylum with a new Vagrant Ward attached to the Brownlow Hill workhouse. The Night Asylum administrators kept their doors open for another year, until they were sure that paupers seeking a night's lodging in the Vagrant Ward would not be subject to the workhouse labour test.[63] In each of these cases private philanthropic organizations initially cooperated with parish authorities and then turned their operations over to the local government in exchange for assurances that the nonpauper poor would not be placed on relief.

Liverpool's most energetic responses to the social ills of the late 1840s emphasized pauper education rather than poor relief. Those poor children who remained in their homes became the object of numerous "ragged schools" founded by evangelical Christians in the late 1840s to address the most basic educational needs of poor children. By 1851 Liverpool had eighteen ragged schools serving over 2,700 children. While the ragged schools brought the scriptures to Liverpool's working-class children, other reformers turned their attention to the "lower and more degraded horde of youthful beings, whose pressing necessities these institutions do not, and cannot reach." Building on efforts pioneered in Scotland, they founded Liverpool's Industrial Ragged Schools in 1849 to provide religious training, secular knowledge, employment skills, and food to young boys from the city's lowliest classes. By the early 1850s the local Industrial Ragged Schools taught over 300 students a year. But even these schools, aimed specifically at Liverpool's poorest children, tried to exclude Irish newcomers. In response to an abundance of Irish applicants, the managers reported that they "were compelled to take their stand on a principle of the poor-laws, and refuse all children who had not been a certain time resident of the town." By 1855 Irish-born children comprised only 54 of 299 Industrial Ragged School students.[64]

Except for the soup houses, which remained in private hands only for a short time, Liverpool relied almost exclusively on the parochial authorities and a handful of established charities to provide for the famine victims' material needs, as opposed to creating new private benevolent responses. The tragic story of the *Ocean Monarch* is an illuminating exception. In August 1848 this unusually impressive packet ship set off from Liverpool for Boston. It carried 398 passengers and crew, including 322 Irish migrants in steerage. Before sailing, the crew brought the steerage passengers up from belowdecks so their quarters could be checked for stowaways. Apparently one of the searchers left his candle behind. Only a few hours out of port the first-class passengers began to smell smoke, leading the captain to conclude that some of his Irish passengers had mistaken the ventilator for a chimney. Soon fire spread throughout the ship, sending passengers and crew into a panic.[65]

The ship's crew quickly judged the situation hopeless and set off for safety in the two lifeboats on board. The captain, recognizing that his crew had deserted him, leaped into the ocean, where he clung to a spar, calling to the others to follow his example. The most fortunate first- and second-class passengers found places in the departing lifeboats; the rest either joined the captain in the sea or gathered their possessions and awaited rescue. Belowdecks, in the cramped, smoke-filled steerage quarters, desperation must have filled the air. Most accounts make special mention of a group of Irish women who had taken to their beds with seasickness. When the fire broke out they ran—partially clothed—for the stairs but found their path to safety blocked by several gentlemen dragging steamer trunks.

When night fell, 222 of the *Ocean Monarch*'s passengers and crew had been saved by passing vessels. Many of the surviving Irish migrants sought refuge in Liverpool's poorest streets at the northern end of town. In that world of disease and destitution, the new arrivals stood out because of the drama of their ordeal and the seeming hopelessness of their plight. In Regent Street, local reporters found "squalid masses of human beings," many suffering from burns and all with tales of horror to tell.[66] As various investigators sorted out the events surrounding the *Ocean Monarch*'s sinking, Liverpool turned to the needy victims in its midst. Proud locals repeatedly remarked on the "spirit of humanity" that permeated the city. The *Albion* declared: "Our townsmen on occasions when so much suffering and sorrow are to be relieved, are always ready to do their utmost to mitigate calamities of this nature."[67]

What, in fact, did they do? And how did they do it? In the first hours after the rescue, dozens of sailors and citizens showered the victims with gifts of food and clothing.[68] Benevolent locals escorted the worst off to local police stations, where they received food and shelter.[69] The next day the survivors congregated at the offices of Harnden and Company, the passenger agents responsible for the *Ocean Monarch*. There they were offered free passage either to North America or back to Ireland. Almost as soon as news of the disaster reached Liverpool, a committee of leading citizens—chaired by the mayor—formed "for the purpose of giving a proper direction to public benevolence." On August 26 this group held a public meeting in the town hall, and in the days to come its members accepted donations at the adjoining Exchange Rooms.[70] Liverpudlians employed a wide array of fund-raising devices. Several groups staged concerts or amateur theatricals, church collections were dedicated to the cause, a sketch of the burning ship was raffled off at the Exchange Rooms, and James Henry Legg donated the proceeds from his lengthy (and quite horrendous) narrative poem to the "surviving sufferers." By September 6 the city's two subscription lists had received £6,600. The published lists of donors indicated that £100 had been received from Queen Victoria and Prince Albert, £50 from Harnden and Company, and £5 from Robert Peel.[71]

The committee went about its business with speed and gravity. In the first few days the members handed out clothing and other goods from a shed on Prince's Dock. As donations poured in, they arranged for additional funds to be waiting in Boston for the migrants who had elected to continue their journey. At each stage the gentlemen took great pains to investigate all recipients, guaranteeing that no funds went to fraudulent claimants. On completing its work, the committee issued a detailed report explaining its procedures. What began as a tragedy for several hundred passengers quickly became an occasion for citywide self-congratulation. The *Journal* announced that the "liberal subscription reflects honour upon the prompt benevolence of Liverpool." The *Albion*'s editors could not "remember any previous occasion which has to so large an extent enlisted the public sympathy and generosity." And one local pamphleteer was proud to report that "[t]he whole of the merchants of our 'good-old town' have subscribed largely." The *Journal*—sensitive to Irish criticisms of Liverpool— was particularly pleased by a statement "on behalf of the sufferers" that ran in the *Clonmel Chronicle*. The Irish paper saluted "the merchants of Liverpool for their noble and generous conduct to those of our countrymen who escaped from death," adding: "We only give expression to the universal feeling here, when we say, that the generosity of the Liverpool people on the late disastrous occasion, is honourable to humanity, and worthy of our warmest feelings of gratitude."[72]

The *Ocean Monarch* tragedy, with its limited scope and identifiable victims, stimulated a benevolent passion in Liverpool that thousands of more mundane Irish famine migrants never could. The survivors were also clearly the innocent victims of an act of God and thus more liable to attract public charity. The fund-raising frenzy contrasted dramatically with the previous year, when citizens spoke of rising tax rates, not the need for donations. The variety of activities—concerts, theatricals, engravings raffled off, sermons—had some antecedents in Liverpool's benevolent history, but these events were sufficiently unusual to attract widespread comment. The distinctiveness of this private benevolence contrasted with antebellum urban America, where all manner of fund-raising fairs, for abolitionist societies and charitable organizations, were far more commonplace. And though the range of emergency measures followed American patterns, the ultimate structure of the *Ocean Monarch* relief seemed distinctly English. Almost as soon as the survivors reached the shore, the benevolent responsibility devolved to a small coterie of public officials and town dignitaries. The victims were taken to police stations rather than to private buildings such as churches, warehouses, or concert halls. That first day a committee of local leaders formed "for the purpose of giving a proper direction to public benevolence." And subscribers to that benevolence were directed to the Exchange Rooms adjoining the town hall. Thus, although dozens—perhaps hundreds—of citizens took a hand in aiding the survivors, certain local leaders were deemed the appropriate helmsmen for their efforts.

PHILADELPHIA'S POOR RELIEF DURING THE FAMINE MIGRATION

Even as Liverpool's Irish paupers filled its streets, fascinating Nathaniel Hawthorne and leading George Holt to throw up his hands in despair, Philadelphians exhibited increased alarm over the rising poverty in their city.[73] The *Public Ledger* regularly ran poignant tales of starving emigrants in 1847.[74] Whereas Liverpudlians saw a mass of undifferentiated human misery, Philadelphians periodically referred—in editorials and letters—to particular beggars by description or location.[75] Some writers expressed complete sympathy for the poor newcomers, but increasingly Philadelphians joined Liverpudlians in complaining about the prevalence of street beggars. In February the court of quarter sessions instituted an attack on vagrancy, but the complaints persisted. In the following March the Council received a communication from local citizens "asking that measures shall be taken to prevent street begging." One correspondent echoed Liverpool's George Holt's suggestion that fraudulent beggars were borrowing children when they went into the streets.[76]

As in Liverpool, many Philadelphians concluded that indiscriminate giving lay at the root of the problem. A correspondent to the *Ledger* complained that the overly charitable "encourage laziness, and perhaps intemperance; they prevent them from making the necessary exertion for their comfortable support in sickness and cold, and thereby load our institutions for the deserving with a miserable, dirty, lazy population—paupers upon the city, when they might be made to become respectable inhabitants." The same writer—apparently without intended irony—noted that "the repeated demands, at the private dwellings, give almost sufficient employment for an extra servant to answer them." The *Ledger* later noted that donations on the streets excluded "oppressed and friendless females who live in the retired places of our city."[77]

Even with such unfamiliar demands on local benevolence, Philadelphians—who had historically claimed immunity from the blight of street begging—continued to perceive an important distinction between the Old World and the New. In August 1849 the *Public Ledger* described a *Frazer's Magazine* article on "the excessive destitution and unseen private charities of London." "The articles are worth attention," the Philadelphia paper noted, "for, however we may flatter ourselves or thank Heaven upon our exemption, *thus far,* from the awful miseries of Europe, we have quite enough to inspire apprehension, and to demand the most vigorous efforts, public and private, for cure, and more especially prevention." The *Ledger* went on to question the view that charity (in America) bred idleness. Rather, it "confess[ed] some fears about suffering too many for *want* of charities." Finally, the editorial returned to another familiar theme in insisting that as bad as things were in Philadelphia, they were much worse in New York City.[78]

In the late 1840s Philadelphia's Blockley Almshouse, like Liverpool's Brownlow Hill Workhouse, experienced a short-term increase in total inmates, as well as a steady growth in the percentage who were Irish-born. In a typical year the almshouse housed several hundred more people in the winter than during the summer or fall. In December 1845 it housed roughly 1,700 paupers. By December 1848 the daily population was approaching 2,200; the following March it reached 2,373.[79] The annual figures tell a similar story. In the year ending in May 1847 Blockley admitted 5,995 paupers, including 485 children. Four years later that figure had risen to 6,719, with 895 children. But in April 1849 the court of quarter sessions visited Blockley and concluded that the recent increases were in fact quite modest, reflecting chiefly population increases, a recent upsurge of disease in Moyamensing, and "the falling off of inmates in the vagrant cells of the County Prison."[80]

According to Clement, 57 percent of the almshouse inmates between

1843 and 1850 were foreign-born, mostly from Ireland. A "register of white male children" in the almshouse between January 1848 and February 1849 noted that 64 of 247 were born in the almshouse and 41 of the remaining 183 (22 percent) were born in Ireland (only nine other boys were born outside of North America). The resident physician reported that in 1848 the almshouse hospital treated 3,584 patients. Of these, only 239 were born in Philadelphia and 1,605 (45 percent) were Irish-born. Over half (2,520) of the 4,999 inmates with known places of birth who entered in the year ending in May 1851 were born in Ireland. (This total population figure included 369 black inmates and 145 inmates born in the almshouse.) The population of Liverpool's Brownlow Hill was approaching half Irish-born at roughly the same time. Although Philadelphia's Guardians of the Poor never indicated that the Irish migrants represented an increased indoor relief burden, they were aggressive in collecting the Emigrant's Tax on incoming vessels.[81]

*

In Philadelphia, as in Liverpool, many established charities experienced no direct effects of the famine migration. Most institutional reports did not acknowledge any shift in their client base. The Home Missionary Association's quarterly reports in 1848 and 1849, for example, did not mention rising immigrant demands. However, when the General Assembly of the Presbyterian Church met in Philadelphia in May 1849, its discussion of home missions included explicit reference to increased demands accompanying "the influx of foreigners" (presumably both Irish and German).[82] The Union Benevolent Association took greater notice of the immigrants. Through the 1840s UBA visitors regularly reported the number of "foreigners" they went to see, and periodically the association described the growing needs produced by the famine migration. In 1847 the UBA's 250 visitors assisted 1,184 families. In its annual report the association noted the twin challenges of rising prices and "extensive emigration." The following year the UBA reported 310 foreign families among 1,371 receiving assistance, and a few visitors specifically referred to the unusual demands from the Irish newcomers. In 1849 and 1850 the UBA aided only 850–900 families, but these reduced figures included 229 foreign families in 1849 and 321 in 1850. In 1851 the UBA's numbers jumped dramatically, as they visited 838 immigrant families and a total of 2,139 families. But even if we assume—as the anecdotal reports indicate—that most of these foreign families were from Ireland, the UBA's clients included a smaller proportion of Irish immigrants than those who ended up in the almshouse.[83] The Hibernia Society also took notice of the new arrivals, canceling the annual society dinner to free up additional money for its Charity Fund.[84]

The story of Philadelphia's charitable adjustment to the famine migration lay not so much in the actions of established organizations as in the explosion of new institutions that emerged in the late 1840s and early 1850s. Some declared a specific interest in aiding the Irish immigrants, others seemed simply to address the rising poverty problem. As a group, the private organizations founded in the decade after 1846 greatly expanded the services available to Philadelphia's poor, creating a sharp contrast with Liverpool's charitable history.

Some new bodies were formed under evangelical Protestant auspices. The General Colporteur Association, founded in 1846, sent agents to visit poor families, providing food and clothing along with religious tracts. In 1847 the Ladies Union City Mission of Philadelphia began bringing nondenominational Protestant teachings to "the dens of darkness, where intemperance and crime sit triumphant on the hearth-stone, and the foulest curses are familiar household words!" In 1846 evangelical Protestants and Quakers in Moyamensing had established the Christian Home Missionary Society. The society initially emphasized moral and religious training (and conversion) but in January 1847 turned its attention to clients' material needs by opening a house of industry and an adjoining soup house.[85]

In the next few months several other small groups established houses of industry, which offered poor women winter work in exchange for small wages. The Association for the Relief and Employment of Poor Women started a house for fifty women in Spring Garden in December 1846. The Northern Liberties House of Industry opened the following February. Stimulated by these successes in the eastern part of the city, the Western Association of Ladies for Relief and Employment of the Poor established a location on Schuylkill Street in early 1847. By its third winter the association was assisting over eighty poor women. "Many of these were strangers," the managers reported, "lately landed on our shores, and . . . were the most part friendless and homeless."[86] Each of these associations was founded by middle-class women to assist poor women who were too "respectable" to beg but "not ashamed to work." Often they furnished shelter and food for their clients' children, thus creating an atmosphere in which their small ventures into welfare could better succeed.[87]

A meeting of local women in March 1847 launched the Philadelphia Society for the Employment and Instruction of the Poor (PSEIP), dedicated to assisting those "females, whose habits and situation have precluded them from the sympathies and respect of the virtuous part of the community." The PSEIP's ambitious founders looked across the Atlantic for inspiration, promising to "combine all the benefits of ragged schools, cheap bath houses, lodging houses for the homeless, and other charitable institutions of similar kind, which have lately attracted so much attention in London." In keeping with contemporary concerns, the managers called for charitable assistance to carefully constructed philanthropies rather than the "indiscriminate alms-giving" that characterized too much benevolence.[88] In its first winter the PSEIP—which quickly went beyond its initial goal of assisting only women—aided more than 500 people. The next year it provided winter occupation for over 2,000 women and men, with more being turned away. And between January and April 1848 the PSEIP gave 800 families clothing, distributed soup to 2,000 Philadelphians per day, and sold coal at below cost to 300 families daily. In the years to come the society continued to expand its operations, offering the poor work, clothing, food, fuel, baths, and lodgings each winter in new quarters at Catherine and Seventh Streets. During the winter of 1849–50 the PSEIP provided 1,700 men and women with work, 600 with a night's lodging, and over 2,000 with regular outdoor relief. In 1853 it added a Dispensary, delivering medical assistance to 886 men and women that year.[89]

Although the PSEIP aided both black and native-born white Philadelphians, a large proportion of its clientele consisted of Irish immigrants. In 1852, 507 of the 886 visitors to the Dispensary, but only 76 of the 770 people receiving a night's lodging, were black. Of the 693 whites who received lodgings, at least 428 (62 percent) were Irish-born. Two years later the managers reported that 605 of 1,266 (48 percent) receiving assistance were from Ireland and only 31 were born in Philadelphia. These figures, the report argued, "indicate the true source of the great mass of pauperism which afflicts the community." The next year the total number assisted dropped to 1,073, with Irish immigrants (550) making up an increased proportion (51 percent).[90]

The Rosine Association combined the goals of the houses of industry and the Magdalen Society. Founded in March 1847 for "the reformation, employment, and instruction of females, whose habits and situation, have precluded them from the sympathies and respect of the virtuous part of the community," the Rosine Association sought to find other occupations for Philadelphia's prostitutes. In 1852, 65 of 223 inmates were "foreign." The next year 95 of 320 inmates were from Ireland, Germany, or England.[91]

As the 1840s drew to a close, the *Public Ledger* published an editorial praising the city's benevolence, especially its emphasis on houses of employment. "Philadelphia abounds in benevolent institutions," the paper wrote, "where shelter for the houseless, food for the hungry, clothing for the naked, are to be found, and what is more and better than all, *employment for the idle*. Who can doubt that Philadelphia, with all her keen sympathies and high claims to the fame of philanthropy, would earn still a higher one if she found employment for all the idle, as well as food for all the hungry?" Whether or not an explicit response to the Irish immigrants, this emphasis on employment for the poor increased dramatically in the late 1840s in the midst of the famine migration.[92]

Other new organizations responded even more directly to the immigrants. As we saw in Chapter 2, the Philadelphia Emigrant's Friend Society formed to provide prospective migrants with advice on the transatlantic trip as well as protection against the fraud and corruption that awaited them on the docks. The Temporary Home Association was founded in mid-1849 by Philadelphia women to help homeless women and children who were new to the city and liable to fall prey "to the arts of the vicious and designing." In addition to furnishing a night's lodging to friendless strangers—rather like the Liverpool Night Asylum—the organizers of the Temporary Home also served as an employment agency, matching poor women with prospective employers. Although providing no specific numbers on ethnicity, the associations's annual reports included regular anecdotes about the thousands of "daughters of Erin" who crowded into Philadelphia.[93]

Soup houses, which were so central to Liverpool's emergency relief system, had more modest counterparts in Philadelphia. In January 1847 the *Public Ledger* noted the European tradition of church-sponsored soup houses and pointed out that both England's Poor Law and poverty legislation in the United States left ample room for expanded private charitable efforts, particularly where there were no wealthy churches to fill the void. In this and later editorials the newspaper called on philanthropic Philadelphians to form committees and "to seek and register the poor, and furnish them with tickets" to exchange for soup. The *Catholic Herald* seconded the *Ledger*'s call for soup houses, emphasizing the European tradition of the Catholic soup house. In the next several years Philadelphians set up soup houses across the city and in the adjoining districts. Some opened alongside houses of industry, providing the poor with sustenance as well as wages; others appeared in Spring Garden, Southwark, Moyamensing, and

West Philadelphia. All were small in scale. The Spring Garden Soup Society reported feeding about 130 families daily in the winters of 1848 and 1849. In early 1849 the Moyamensing and Southwark soup kitchens wrote to the Board of Guardians seeking official assistance. But Philadelphia's government never went as far as Liverpool's in monitoring the actions of the local soup kitchens.[94]

Philadelphia's Catholic charities were especially active during the famine years. In their annual report for 1847 the managers of the First District of the Ladies Catholic Benevolent Society announced that they had assisted sixty-three families with clothes, food, fuel, and medical care, "nearly all of whom were newly arrived emigrants in the most abject state of destitution." The following winter members of St. Joseph's Catholic Church began raising money for the newly established St. Joseph's Society for the Relief of the Distressed Emigrants from Ireland. In the same year local Catholics opened St. Anne's Asylum for indigent women and St. Joseph's Hospital for the poor. In 1851 they began raising funds for the House of the Good Shepherd for Penitent Females and the Society of Saint Vincent de Paul introduced in-kind relief for the poor in St. Joseph's Parish.[95]

By the end of the 1840s, the capacity of Philadelphia's orphan asylums had expanded dramatically. The total population and the number of Irish immigrants in the house of refuge grew steadily, starting in the late 1840s. In 1845 only 5 of 120 (4 percent) inmates (with known birthplaces) were Irish-born; by 1853 those figures had climbed to 63 of 295 (21 percent), with another 56 of Irish parentage. Two years later 146 of 314 juvenile offenders had Irish parents. Between 1843 and 1847 the Philadelphia Orphan Society assisted between 58 and 67 children. In the next several years the orphanage population climbed steadily, hovering at around 110 children between 1851 and 1854.[96] The city's two Catholic orphanages faced greater challenges, expanding their capacities to meet the new demands. In 1851 the managers of St. Joseph's Female Orphanage called for increased donations "especially now in view of the numberless demands that are being made for admission." In the same year St. Johns Orphan Asylum for boys began constructing a new building in West Philadelphia. By the early 1850s the two Catholic orphanages could accommodate 350 children, far exceeding their capacity of a generation earlier.[97]

In 1848 Girard College for Orphans opened with grand fanfare. Established under the terms of financier Stephen Girard's will, the college offered technical, nonsectarian training for up to three hundred of Philadelphia's white male orphans "taken from a class not likely to have received that very early discipline, so necessary for the success of efforts directed towards their moral culture." The boys in Girard College were nearly all locally born, although many had Irish names and may have been the children of recent migrants. The following year the new Southern Home for Destitute Children began taking in nearly a hundred boys and girls. Meanwhile, the Shelter for Colored Orphans and the Orphan Asylum for boys and girls also expanded. In 1854 a group of women in Northern Liberties established the Northern Home for Friendless Children, providing a home for white children "midway between the Schools and the Asylums on the one hand, and the Almshouse and house of refuge on the other." The Northern Home's reports occasionally included biographical vignettes, some of which described Irish children. Thus, by the mid-1850s the total spaces available for orphaned children in private asylums had grown significantly as public officials cut back their indoor aid.[98]

CONCLUSION

Through the first half of the nineteenth century, Liverpool and Philadelphia had approached the fundamental problems of poverty in similar ways. Each city combined the efforts of public Guardians of the Poor with the work of various private philanthropic agencies. Before the Irish famine migration, public poor relief officials in both countries had come to agree that outdoor assistance promoted mendicancy and should be used only in extreme cases. Increasingly, they turned to institutional solutions grounded in the principle of less eligibility, by which only the most desperate would seek indoor relief. The charitable asylums found their clients among those who had not yet "fallen" onto the public rolls, thus dividing the task of poor relief between those assisted by private donations and those supported through taxation. Although some observers in both nations had begun to look more closely at the environmental sources of poverty, many people still saw moral failings—often accompanied by intemperance—as the root of the problem and organized their actions accordingly. In the second quarter of the century both cities had supported a growth in city missions, whose ministers and visitors combined moral exhortation with in-kind relief.

Beneath these broad similarities there were differences. Local variation notwithstanding, after 1832 England was well on the road to a national poor relief system; the U.S. Congress had no voice in such matters and individual statehouses were only modestly involved. Whereas Liverpool's parochial authorities provided substantial separate quarters for pauper children, Philadelphians relied on the privately run house of refuge and a growing array of orphanages. Catholics in both cities sought to assist their impoverished coreligionists, but Philadelphia's Catholics had the wherewithal to support more substantial—and enduring—institutions.

Various data indicate that citizens in both England and the United States were well aware of poor relief measures across the Atlantic. The American children's asylums attracted regular admiration from the English. After traveling through Boston, New York, and Philadelphia in the early 1850s, the Domestic Mission's Francis Bishop was particularly enthusiastic about their houses of refuge, noting that Liverpool could use such institutions because of the large number of Irish families with absent fathers. Liverpool traveler W. I. Mann called Girard College "too good for the little orphan boys that we saw running about." Unitarian Anne Holt praised both Girard College and the house of refuge during her tour of the "decidedly handsome city." In 1846 Liverpool's Gaol Committee noted the high cost of juvenile crime and called for the creation of a house of refuge along American lines.[99] American reformers admired the English soup houses, and the Philadelphia papers occasionally mentioned the rise in British ragged schools.[100] The Missions to the Poor are a particularly noteworthy example of this transatlantic cross-pollination.

Given their similar intellectual climates, it comes as no surprise that the rise in urban poverty accompanying the famine migration provoked parallel reactions in the two cities. Officials and citizens in both Liverpool and Philadelphia worried about the public cost of arriving paupers. In Liverpool the solution was forced removals, accompanied by periodic calls for national assistance. In the United States, port cities charged an Emigrant Tax to cover the anticipated costs, while the Emigrant's Friend Societies urged newcomers to move to the interior where opportunities were more plentiful. These differing responses point to two geographic aspects of what we might truly describe as American distinctiveness. First, America's great distance from Ireland allowed for immigrant policies that would have been logistically and politically infeasible for cities in Great Britain. (On the other hand, forced removals were much less expensive in English cities.)

Second, as long as a frontier of unsettled land stretched to the west, Americans were well prepared to welcome thousands of unskilled laborers to their shores (if not their cities).

With only modest outdoor relief available—and, in Liverpool, only at the price of possible removal—Irish paupers turned increasingly to begging in the streets. In both cities this prompted repeated jeremiads about the dangers of indiscriminate giving and fraudulent appeals. Citizens were urged to make their donations to established charities which could properly measure need. The charitable organizations that formed during the famine migration present the most striking contrast between the two cities. Liverpool's parochial authorities bore the brunt of the new demand, with some increased activity by the established charities. The city's chief new benevolent responses in the late 1840s came on two fronts: the soup houses and the ragged schools. The soup house organizers, working in concert with parish officials, addressed the migrants' immediate need for sustenance. The ragged schools—and the Industrial Ragged Schools—responded to the perceived moral and material needs of the city's poor juveniles, an emphasis that many observers found most morally justified and most fiscally sound. Philadelphians established soup houses of their own, although their efforts were smaller, more decentralized, and more independent from public authorities than those in Liverpool. Meanwhile, groups of women all over Philadelphia responded to rising demands by opening new houses of industry, a solution that had no parallel in Liverpool.

What do these differences indicate? Philadelphia's voluntary response to the rise in poverty was more extensive and more decentralized than that in Liverpool. This was the case despite the fact that the English city faced a much sterner test. Philadelphia's emphasis on houses of industry underscored the presumption that the worthy poor needed work, not simply alms. By turning to privately subsidized work relief, Philadelphians revealed their confidence that the economy could absorb the labors of its worthy poor. The fact that these houses generally ran only during the winter months fit neatly with Mathew Carey's view that employment patterns were seasonal, sending even upright workers—especially women—into periodic poverty.

Perhaps the explanation lies in George Holt's resignation over the overwhelming numbers of street beggars: such a problem surpassed individual energies and required government, or at least highly centralized private, solutions. Liverpool's new soup kitchens suggest a city responding to more pressing needs without the luxury of offering work in exchange for assistance. But the difference between the two cities also seems to point to a deeper American tradition of decentralized voluntarism, particularly in response to crisis. Philadelphia's houses of industry and its wide range of charitable organizations certainly fits that aspect of Tocqueville's understanding of American distinctiveness. Liverpool's reaction to the sinking of the *Ocean Monarch* indirectly supports this portrait of American distinctiveness. The poignancy of the victims' plight led Liverpudlians to undertake emergency measures that were most noteworthy because they were so unfamiliar. Even in this explosion of voluntarism they turned to civic leaders and structures for direction, suggesting a different understanding of the role and utility of government intervention and centralization.

TO THE FUTURE: CHARITY ORGANIZING SOCIETIES

The reliance on voluntarism presented its own set of problems, notably when even the most philanthropic-minded doubted that all among the faceless mass of poor were equally needy. A generation after the migration, Liverpool's William Rathbone Jr. published a small volume entitled *Social Duties Considered with Reference to the Organisation of Effort in Works of Benevolence and Public Utility*. Rathbone, one of Liverpool's most celebrated philanthropists, surveyed England's public relief and private charity and found the "state of our great towns, and especially of our seaports, is a scandal to our humanity, a blot on our civilization." He argued that the parish relief system persisted in "degrading" paupers, requiring improved approaches to charitable assistance. The Liverpool philanthropist's detailed proposal stressed two themes: first, "the voluntary benefactor should come into personal contact with his suffering brother" to the benefit of both parties; second, charitable efforts should be centrally organized to avoid inefficiency and overlap. As a model, Rathbone referred his readers to Liverpool's Central Relief Society (CRS), which had been formed in 1863 to coordinate the activities of the District Provident Society, the Strangers' Friend Society, and the Charitable Society. Two years later, in 1869, the London Society for Organizing Charitable Relief and Repressing Mendacity began its campaign against indiscriminate giving much as Rathbone had recommended.[101]

Rathbone's call for enhanced personal contact between the classes had a long history in both the United States and England. In his proposal for special ministries for the poor, Joseph Tuckerman had stressed that such ventures could not replace the need for "personal connection between the wise and the ignorant, the rich and the poor, the virtuous and the vicious." Moreover, the organizing charities movement that took hold in England in the late 1860s had clear parallels in the United States the following decade. Philadelphia's Society for Organizing Charitable Relief and Repressing Mendicancy, founded in 1879, shared much in common with Liverpool's smaller and older Central Relief Society. Both were dedicated to coordinating existing charitable efforts in order to reduce deception and duplication, so that unworthy mendicants would not profit "to the detriment of less clamorous but more deserving poor"; each relied on reports from visitors organized into ward committees.[102]

Despite their essential similarities, the two charity-organizing movements owed their origins to somewhat different—perhaps illuminatingly so—impulses. Liverpool's Central Relief Society had its antecedents in the Systematic Beneficence Society (SBS), which, according to an 1862 report, "originated with an honest effort, in the midst of the Irish famine, to enable Christian people to continue their usual scale of contributions under the pressure of diminished income, and under the demand of a fearful distress." Whereas the SBS had done little more than advocate widespread "systematic" giving, the CRS was dedicated to organizational efficiency from the outset. But although the organization certainly hoped to combat duplicate giving and mendicancy, the founders were initially most concerned with encouraging wider *donations,* proposing a ward committee structure with an eye toward increasing contact between the needy and potential donors.[103] Philadelphia's Society for Organizing Charitable Relief, like the other American Charity Organizing Societies, was much more concerned with combating indiscriminate giving, instilling moral authority, and applying a "scientific" principle to philanthropy. These bodies had intellectual links to the national military and benevolent efforts that emerged during the American Civil War (which Rathbone, in fact, indicated in a footnote), but their timing owed more to the labor unrest of the late 1870s.[104]

What does this glance into the third quarter of the century tell us? In the late 1820s and early 1830s both cities—and nations—adopted similar approaches to making public poor relief more "rational" and scientific. Between 1860 and 1880 cities in both England and the United States embarked on similarly parallel paths toward organizing private philanthropy. But note that Liverpool took this step much earlier than Philadelphia, supporting the thesis that Liverpudlians had less emphatic antipathy for centralized authority. And whereas Liverpool's CRS was formed partially to encourage greater charitable sympathy and thus expanded benevolence, Philadelphia's large decentralized charitable world survived the famine migration, the Civil War, and major economic downturns in the 1850s and 1870s before embracing the scientific charity movement in times of prosperity. This chronology provides further evidence that throughout the mid-nineteenth century the two nations—although operating in the same intellectual universe—differed substantially in both the scope of their charities and in their philosophical approach to philanthropy.[105]

4. Hospitals, Cholera, and Medical Care

INTRODUCTION: MEDICINE AND MORAL REFORM

By midcentury the world's largest cities were sadly familiar with the ongoing battle against filth and disease. In an era before widely accessible urban transportation, rising populations crowded into cramped neighborhoods, presenting officials and reformers with new tests. For decades medical reformers on both sides of the Atlantic had debated the origins and prevention of disease. Before the emergence of germ theory, doctors in competing camps fashioned theories combining empirical evidence with their own principles of morality. The contagionists stressed the importance of avoiding direct contact with the disease, whereas the environmentalists warned of the dangers of deadly "miasmas" emanating from stagnant water or decaying matter. In the popular mind, and in some medical writings, disease struck hardest at the morally suspect, with the intemperate most likely to fall victim. Assumptions about disease and concern for public health directed urban reformers down various paths, sometimes almost by chance producing salutary effects. Fear of epidemic disease prompted widespread sanitary reform as cities battled filthy streets and crowded housing.[1]

Discussions of public health turned on some of the most important policy problems of urban Victorian society. As in poor relief, private and public institutions divided up responsibility for assisting the sick, raising questions about the appropriate roles of private benevolence and government asylums. Fear of epidemic disease led to proposals for aggressive sanitary policies that set concern for the public good against the desire to protect private property and individual liberty. The threat of disease from abroad caused city and national governments to weigh the wisdom of quarantines. And as health concerns generated new government initiatives, cities developed expanded urban bureaucracies. In the last years of the 1840s two intertwined forces combined to accelerate these developments. First, the Irish famine migration exacerbated existing health problems in both Liverpool and Philadelphia. The poor migrants, often crowded into small hovels, prompted popular outcry about unsanitary conditions and dangerous disease environments. Second, Liverpool and Philadelphia—like all nineteenth-century port cities—faced periodic waves of epidemic disease. In 1847 typhus—or Irish fever—swept through the cities' poor wards. Two years later the spread of cholera created an international crisis, prompting an illuminating set of responses in both cities.[2]

In both their institutional structures before the famine and their emergency responses to the medical crises of the late 1840s, policymakers in Liverpool and Philadelphia worked within a shared intellectual climate. Much like contemporary discussions of poverty and poor relief, reformers on both sides of the Atlantic perceived disease as reflecting some combination of environmental problems and personal failings. And, once again like their reactions to the materially poor, they distinguished between patients who were fitting objects of private charity and sickly paupers whose fate fell properly into public hands. But there were also important attitudinal and structural differences between the two cities. The famine migration found Liverpool adjusting to a revolutionary new health bureaucracy, grounded in centralized local authority shaped by national legislation. Philadelphians—and Americans—had made no such organizational strides by the 1840s, but the City of Brotherly Love had a more substantial tradition of private and public hospitals. The famine years would underscore both these broad similarities and each city's distinctive characteristics, once again demonstrating Liverpool's heavier reliance on government solutions as opposed to Philadelphia's persistent voluntarism.

INSTITUTIONAL CARE

In the first half of the nineteenth century hospitals were reserved largely for poorer patients who could not afford private medical care in their own homes. The working poor in most cities relied on public dispensaries for outdoor medical assistance or privately run charity hospitals for more serious conditions. These urban hospitals, which often served as important teaching centers, were frequently built near docks to minister to sailors and injured workers. Admission to the charity hospitals, like access to other forms of private benevolence, was strictly monitored. Patients with contagious or incurable diseases were routinely excluded. Some hospitals only opened their doors to the worthy poor bearing letters of entrance from a donor. Paupers who were ineligible for the charity hospitals generally ended up in an almshouse ward or in a nearby city hospital set aside for the poor. In many cases disease proved the great social equalizer, blurring the already tenuous lines between paupers and the working poor. Any urban worker was liable to fall into poverty if injury or illness even temporarily interrupted the flow of wages.[3]

Liverpool's Infirmary had stood as one of the city's leading charities since the mid-eighteenth century. Supported by popular subscription, the Infirmary admitted poor patients on the recommendation of a subscriber, as well as accident victims.[4] Many more poor Liverpudlians turned to the city's dispensaries—the oldest of which dated to the 1770s—for medical assistance. In the second quarter of the nineteenth century between 32,000 and 58,000 patients a year received medicine and minor medical treatment from the city's North and South Dispensaries. Like the Infirmary, the dispensaries relied on private subscriptions and (except in emergencies) only assisted those who had a note from a subscriber.[5]

In 1834 Liverpool responded to a rise in accidents in the northern part of the city by constructing the David Lewis Northern Hospital on Great Howard Street. The Northern Hospital was founded and supported through a combination of public funds—from both the parish and the Corporation—and private subscriptions. The hospital's "Rules of Management" excluded all persons of "notoriously bad character," patients "whose circumstances are such as to enable them to pay for their care," and those with certain infectious diseases. In 1845 the managers responded to increasing demand by opening a new 200-bed building on land provided by the Council.[6]

The Southern Hospital (initially the Southern and Toxteth Hospital) opened in early 1842, after four years of planning and fund-raising, to care for accident victims along the expanded docks at the southern end of the city. In their first report the hospital's managers proclaimed that "Its doors are about to be thrown open to the free entrance of the maimed poor of all classes, without reference to sect, creed, clime, or complexion—bodily suffering being the only test of their claim to become partakers of the benefits which with God's blessing, this charity is calculated to bestow." By 1845 the 62-bed hospital was treating over two thousand patients a year, three-fourths of whom were outpatients. Like the Northern Hospital, the Southern Hospital received property and small subsidies from the local government but relied chiefly on private subscriptions and donations from local churches.[7]

The Ladies' Charity sent midwives into the homes of poor women during childbirth. Established in the 1790s, the Ladies' Charity claimed to insist on the high moral character of its patients, restricting aid to married women with at least one living child or recently widowed expectant mothers. The organization joined many charities in weeding out aliens by instituting a twelve-month residency requirement. In 1841 the Liverpool Maternity Hospital opened on Scotland Road, providing institutional assistance to poor women in childbirth.[8]

Each of these benevolent bodies depended on a combination of subscriptions, periodic donations, and charity sermons for their operating expenses. But in an interesting blurring of private and public interests, the Council routinely voted contributions to Liverpool's leading medical institutions. Several councillors questioned the practice, suggesting that such efforts might discourage more appropriate charitable giving.[9]

Philadelphia's mix of medical institutions was generally similar to that in Liverpool, but with fewer separate institutions and a clearer distinction between private and public hospitals.[10] The Pennsylvania Hospital, nearly a century old when the famine migrants arrived, was the nation's oldest such institution, and until 1848 it was—apart from the almshouse hospital—the city's only general hospital. Like Liverpool's Infirmary and hospitals, this private hospital relied on charitable donations, with admission requiring letters of recommendation from subscribers. Patients with incurable diseases or doubtful morality were routinely denied admission. Unlike its English counterparts, the Pennsylvania Hospital—and other American private hospitals—accepted paying patients as well as charity patients, creating an economic hierarchy behind the hospital walls. In the hospital's first century of operation 24,659 of 58,508 patients paid some portion of their expenses. These patient fees also established the Pennsylvania Hospital as a distinctly private, self-sufficient institution in contrast to Liverpool's quasi-public charity hospitals.[11]

In the mid-nineteenth century the Pennsylvania Hospital had a shift in cases that mirrored the English experience. As Philadelphia grew, the expansion in building and industry resulted in a disturbing increase in accidents. In 1827 the hospital only admitted 140 accident victims; two decades later that figure had jumped to 400 accidents out of 1,277 total admissions.[12] But even this expansion did not match the dangerous Liverpool docks. In 1846 the Southern Hospital treated 470 accident victims as inpatients (out of 653 total inpatients) and another 1,126 as outpatients (out of 1,489).[13] In the same year the Northern Hospital's trustees reported relieving 1,300 accident victims—as inpatients and outpatients—out of 2,500 patients.[14]

As in Liverpool, members of Philadelphia's working poor who could avoid institutionalization turned to one of several charitable dispensaries for medicine and modest outpatient assistance for a small fee, which was waived on the recommendation of the Guardians of the Poor. The oldest city dispensary dated to the 1780s; two more were added in the north and the south during the 1810s. Although complete patient figures are not available, the fragmentary evidence suggests that Philadelphia's dispensaries treated far fewer patients than their Liverpool counterparts.[15]

Poor Philadelphians who lacked letters of introduction to the Pennsylvania Hospital, or who were excluded for moral or medical reasons, turned to the almshouse hospital which was administered by the Board of Health. Throughout the century, patients in this city-run hospital regularly outnumbered those treated in the more commodious Pennsylvania Hospital. With the construction of Blockley Almshouse in the mid-1830s, hospital physicians sought to remove the shame associated with admittance to the almshouse hospital by renaming it Philadelphia Hospital (later Philadelphia General Hospital). Still, the hospital's poor conditions and the stigma of pauperism kept all but the most desperate from its doors. In 1840–41, 46 percent of its patients were foreign-born. The Philadelphia Hospital also admitted small numbers of black patients, shunting them off to the least desirable corners.[16]

LIVERPOOL: THE UNHEALTHIEST CITY

By midcentury Liverpool had developed a disturbing, and richly deserved, reputation for unsanitary conditions and high mortality. In early 1843 Dr. William H. Duncan, then the physician to the South Dispensary, delivered a long lecture "On the Physical Causes of the High Rate of Mortality in Liverpool." After examining local mortality rates Duncan concluded that Liverpool, far from being a healthy environment, was in fact "the most unhealthy town in England." He continued with a strongly worded attack on Liverpool's poor housing—particularly in the Irish neighborhoods—and a detailed analysis of the various diseases that plagued the city.[17]

Through the 1840s various local and national studies, often thick with statistics, concluded that the nation's cities in general, and Liverpool in particular, were facing a serious health crisis.[18] In 1842 the Poor Law Commission, under the Benthamite Edwin Chadwick, issued a *Report on the Sanitary Condition of the Labouring Population*, which argued for environmental solutions to England's health ills. Two years later a Royal Commission study confirmed Chadwick's report and called for renewed attention to sanitation. Both of these documents, as well as a second Royal Commission report in 1845, included vivid testimony from Liverpool's famous Dr. Duncan. Meanwhile, the national Health of Towns' Association began staging lectures and circulating papers emphasizing the need for aggressive local action.[19]

The national discussion of health and sanitation, much like the debates over poor relief, stimulated parliamentary initiatives that expanded the government's role in local affairs. A decade earlier Parliament had responded to the 1832 cholera epidemic by creating a temporary Board of Health that called on city and town authorities to establish their own local boards of health. This crisis prompted a brief flurry of sanitary activity that did not last much longer than the epidemic itself, but it laid the groundwork for later national initiatives.[20] In 1848 rumors of cholera sweeping through Europe helped push Parliament to pass the Public Health Act, a bill first proposed the previous year by Lord Morpeth. Inspired by Chadwick's belief in the link between filth and disease and his strong faith in administrative solutions, the 1848 act established a General Board of Health while empowering local authorities to create their own boards of health to manage sewers, remove nuisances, and control local housing. Like the Poor Law Commission, the central Board of Health was designed to play a supervisory role, while having relatively little direct authority. Still, critics worried that this national legislation threatened local autonomy and private property. Even if the General Board had little overt power, the boards under its supervision represented an important step toward local centralization of traditionally disparate sanitary functions. "The great defect of English legislation in the matter of public health," the *Liverpool Mercury* insisted, "is the total absence of fixed principles." The appropriate solution was not merely central local boards but "general and uniform legislation" at the local level.[21]

Once again, Liverpool's case illustrates the diversity of local experience in England. Most communities had responded slowly or not at all to earlier calls for sanitary improvement, but Liverpool officials—conscious of the potentially devastating impact of the city's poor reputation—had already launched a series of ambitious health and sanitation reforms before the passage of Lord Morpeth's bill. Prior to the 1840s responsibility for sanitation and health rested with various Liverpool authorities, with none taking an aggressive lead. In 1842 the new Tory Council passed a modest Health of the Town Act, which had been proposed by the recently deposed Liberals. During the next several years Dr. Duncan's campaign for health and sanitation improvement yielded masses of documentation and widespread discussion. In 1845 concerned citizens founded a local branch of the national Health of Towns' Association, which met periodically to hear new evidence of Liverpool's disturbing morbidity. These discussions identified a tangled mass of sanitation and health problems (many of which are considered more fully in the next chapter), and an equally confusing array of public authorities with differing jurisdictions and overlapping responsibilities. Even if the circumstances demanded change, the appropriate focus for reform remained unclear. Insofar as destitution and disease moved hand in hand, the Select Vestry—charged with poor relief—claimed a voice in decision-making. The Council could rightly claim authority over issues ranging from housing to quarantines, but there was no broad consensus that it should tackle these problems, particularly where they went beyond the Corporation's boundaries. In 1846 the Council responded to the administrative muddle by sponsoring the revolutionary Liverpool Sanitary Act in Parliament. The Sanitary Act established a Health Committee of the Council with broad supervisory powers over health and sanitation. It created three new officers—a medical officer of health, an inspector of nuisances, and a borough engineer—who would oversee provisions of the legislation and report back to the Health Committee.

As a response to Liverpool's organizational ills, the Sanitary Act was a crucial chapter in the Corporation's administrative history, as well as an important step in the battle against filth and disease. Because it was the first local act of its kind, the bill served as a model for other English cities and towns as well as an important benchmark for generations of scholars. By consolidating sanitation and health efforts in a single committee of the Council, with crucial oversight and investigation bestowed upon a central trio of new bureaucrats, Liverpool followed a generally Chadwickian model that anticipated the goals of the national legislation of 1848.[22]

The Sanitary Act's most dramatic innovation was the creation of England's first medical officer of health (MOH), a position that went immediately to the energetic William Duncan, who served until his death in 1863. Despite the office's potential importance, the 1846 act had little to say about the medical officer's actual duties and powers. He primarily was charged with reporting on the sanitary and medical conditions of the town and advising city officials on the best means for improving sanitation and checking the spread of disease. Such a vague charge gave the MOH tremendous freedom to define the position as he wished.[23] Duncan came to his new position with a strong background as both a physician and an investigator. Born in 1805, he received his medical training at Edinburgh University before taking a position in Liverpool as a private doctor and physician to the dispensaries. During the 1832 cholera epidemic Duncan began drawing links between poor housing and disease, prompting him to become a leading advocate of public health reform and an important correspondent of Edwin Chadwick and the nation's leading sanitarians. Once in office he eventually elevated the position from a poorly paid part-time office to a full-time position with considerable influence over the Health Committee's actions. Meanwhile, in 1848, London named John Simon as its MOH. Simon, Duncan, and a handful of other local medical officers became central to England's sanitary movement. But despite the encouragement of Lord Morpeth's bill, most cities and towns failed to follow suit, and those officers who were named did not achieve the autonomy and authority enjoyed by Duncan and Simon.[24]

Almost as soon as Liverpool's Sanitary Act became law, the city was bludgeoned by a series of health crises arising out of the Irish famine migration and the concomitant spread of cholera across Europe. Although the newly established Health Committee was an important step toward organizing the city's health and sanitary activities, much remained to be determined. Apart from his duties as a gatherer of statistics, Dr. Duncan's role remained ill-defined. Duncan, the borough engineer, and the inspector of nuisances all reported to the Health Committee. Other than the members themselves—all town councillors—and these three agents, the Health Committee had no personnel to carry out its policies. Thus, it soon turned to the city police, under the authority of the Council's Watch Committee, for assistance. In the meantime, the Select Vestry maintained its own medical relief committee, which addressed the health needs of the parish's poor.

The next several years would forge important relationships among these and other local authorities.

The Public Health Act fits an interpretation of Victorian reform as defined by national legislation and driven by reformers bent on centralization and standardization. The Liverpool Sanitary Act demonstrates the limitations of this perspective. This parliamentary act—which predated Lord Morpeth's bill—reflected the continuing power of localism. Still, Liverpool's act was a centralizing measure, albeit at the local level, instigated by one of the new breed of scientific-minded reformers. The truly distinctive characteristics of Liverpool's evolving health establishment will be best understood by examining it in light of the famine migration crisis and then comparing it to the simultaneous experiences across the Atlantic in Philadelphia. Only through such a comparison can we fully grasp the advanced state of Liverpool's sanitary apparatus.

By the time the Council appointed a new Health Committee in January 1847, Liverpool was already feeling the effects of a typhus epidemic among newly arriving Irish famine migrants. Soon the papers were filled with inquests reporting deaths from "Irish fever" and letters and editorials blaming the blight on poor conditions in Irish neighborhoods.[25] Dr. Duncan had long reported that the city's highest mortality was concentrated in the overcrowded Irish cellars.[26] Now the problem became how to balance the demands posed by the emerging health emergency with the city's new long-term agenda for sanitation reform.[27]

In February the Select Vestry reported outbreaks of fever in the workhouse. Rather than turn the entire institution into a fever ward, parish officials opted to open temporary fever sheds in Brownlow Hill, adjoining the workhouse. This led to weeks of controversy as a neighborhood organization formed to protest the presence of sickly Irish in its midst.[28] By May a Council delegation to London had received permission from the Admiralty to use lazarettos on the river as floating fever hospitals, enabling the city to impose a temporary quarantine on ships from Ireland. The solution prompted some grumbling from shipowners but seemed to please local officials and concerned citizens.[29] Meanwhile, Duncan and the Health Committee recommended that the city open special fever hospitals for afflicted nonpaupers. These hospitals would charge modest fees and provide local workers with medical care without the ignominy of going on parish relief. Several months later the *Mercury* noted that the "influx of the thousands of wretches from Ireland" had overwhelmed the regular fever wards and called on the Select Vestry to "[establish] a place of refuge for those patients in the town who are not paupers, but whose position is such as to render recourse to a hospital highly desirable."[30] Thus, in the face of a medical emergency the *Mercury* perceived a public interest in providing citizens with medical care outside of the workhouse.

The fever wards and hospitals treated only a portion of the fever victims. Many sick Irish migrants preferred to remain in their cellar homes rather than risk death in the makeshift hospitals or forced removal back to Ireland. The Select Vestry responded to the first weeks of the crisis by hiring six new district medical officers to visit the poor. That spring several parish officers—both relieving officers and district medical officers—fell victim to typhus or smallpox while assisting the newcomers. Liverpool's Catholic clergy rose to the occasion, often at great cost. By summer ten local priests had died of disease after visiting the homes of Irish fever victims.[31]

The threat of disease, combined with the costs of poor relief, induced Liverpool officials to cast about for better solutions.[32] In July the Health Committee followed Duncan's advice and began accelerating the process of "clearing" and cleaning disease-ridden cellars. This measure tragically dramatized the poor communication among local officials, as police officers —acting as Health Committee agents—evicted Irish paupers from their homes without prior consultation with the Select Vestry. The city thus witnessed the horror of evicted Irish fever victims dying on the streets while awaiting assistance from parochial officials. This problem was soon addressed as the Vestry began coordinating its aggressive removal policy with the Health Committee's cellar clearance. In the meantime, the magistrates took an active hand in the process by imposing fines on people who returned to cleared cellars.[33]

By September 1847 the Irish fever had run its course and the Select Vestry had closed the lazarettos and ended its emergency measures. But Liverpudlians remained conscious of the damage to the city's already problematic reputation. When the government's Quarterly Tables of Mortality appeared for the quarter ending on September 30, the registrar-general's report included a scathing indictment of the Merseyside city:

Liverpool, created in haste by commerce—by men too intent on immediate gain; reared without any very tender regard for flesh or blood; and flourishing while her working population was rotting in cellars—has been severely taught the lesson, that a part of the population, whether in cellars or on a distant shore, cannot suffer without involving the whole community in calamity. In itself one of the unhealthiest towns of the kingdom, Liverpool has for a year been the hospital and cemetery of Ireland. The deaths registered in the four quarters of 1846 were 1934, 2098, 2946, and 2735; in the three quarters of 1847 ending September last, 3068, 4809, and 5669!

In his final report for 1847 Duncan estimated that 5,239 people in the parish of Liverpool had died from fever and another 2,236 from diarrhea. Smaller epidemics of smallpox and measles, which were also concentrated in the Irish districts, took roughly 380 lives apiece.[34]

❧

In March 1848 Duncan was pleased to announce to the Health Committee that mortality was the lowest in two years. He attributed this improvement to the policy of cellar clearing and hoped that this latest news would encourage people from the hinterlands who had worried about visiting Liverpool. But even as the MOH was declaring success, he was joining his colleagues in monitoring the ominous spread of cholera across Europe.[35] Before long this dreaded disease would eclipse the damage done by "Irish fever," forcing city health officials into another round of emergency measures.

The 1832 cholera epidemic had precipitated a wave of public health reforms that had, at least temporarily, expanded the powers of government. In the ensuing decade and a half medical research had failed to identify the living organism responsible for the disease. That discovery would be made by Dr. William Budd in 1849. Nonetheless, the state of medical knowledge had evolved. In 1832 many doctors and laypeople alike had viewed cholera as "God's will." By 1848 the miasmic theory was the most prominent of a myriad of explanatory models. Still, the medical terrain was crowded with contradictory opinions. As Anthony Wohl has pointed out, between 1845 and 1856 seven hundred different works on cholera were published in London alone.[36] In Liverpool, Duncan's policies met with continual attack from Dr. George Stuart Hawthorne—a favorite of the *Mercury*—who peppered the newspapers with letters claiming the success of his own mystery treatments while attacking Duncan's miasmic theories.[37]

Soon after the first rumors of cholera in Constantinople reached Liverpool, the Select Vestry—acting on the suggestion of the Health Committee—met to discuss arrangements. The chair read from a lengthy London report that described the disease as "a visitation of Providence, proceeding from the peculiar state of the air." It was, the report stressed, swift, deadly, and incurable. The best preparation was to emphasize cleanliness and ventilation. Rector Brooks concluded his presentation to a round of cheers when he insisted that "overcrowding is the thing of all others, gentlemen, to which we should direct our attention; and the inhabitants ought to cooperate with us in preventing this overcrowding, by discouraging, as far as they possibly can, the immigration of Irish poor into this town." He added that for the time being the principal duty lay with the Council's Health Committee. The Vestry's role would only begin when the city's poor began contracting the disease.[38]

For most of 1848 the Health Committee monitored cholera's approach while developing routine procedures for street cleaning and cellar clearing.[39] In August 1848 Duncan sent the committee a multitiered plan for attacking the disease. His proposals emphasized sanitation and water supplies as well as emergency hospitals for the destitute.[40] In October a joint committee of the Health Committee and the Select Vestry began meeting weekly to respond to complaints of unsanitary nuisances. Finally in December—after a year of editorials and worry—the MOH reported the city's first cases of cholera. For the next several months the Health Committee announced several new casualties each week, concentrated on Lace Street, a poor, predominantly Irish neighborhood known for its crowded cellars and lodging houses.[41] Meanwhile, the Vestry's decision to expand the Brownlow Hill fever sheds to accommodate cholera patients provoked another round of neighborhood complaints. By mid-June 1849 cholera deaths had climbed to 63 in a single week. A month later Duncan reported a staggering 375 deaths in one week, although he assured the Health Committee that "the ravages of the cholera were still chiefly confined to the destitute population in the lower districts of the town"—Vauxhall and Scotland Wards—where overcrowding and filth remained the rule. The weekly death totals reached 572 cholera victims in August, but then the crisis gradually subsided until October, when the *Mercury* announced that Liverpool was finally rid of the disease. In his final report Duncan calculated that in 1849 cholera had killed 4,189 people in the parish and another 1,058 in the surrounding wards.[42]

❧

Liverpool's battles against typhus and cholera tested the city and nation's newly restructured public health institutions. The policy of evicting paupers from unsanitary cellars called for the coordinated efforts of several government agencies. Initially, the parish authorities would contact Thomas Fresh, the Health Committee's inspector of nuisances, who would order the diseased cellars whitewashed. Later, Fresh arranged with the parish's emergency relieving officers to report nuisances and infected areas directly to the Health Committee.[43]

The relieving officers had particularly challenging roles: as policemen, they were technically employees of the Council's Watch Committee, but during the emergency they were on loan to the parish. Meanwhile, Inspector Fresh and the Health Committee also used men from the Watch Committee's force to inspect lodging houses and clean cellars. This shared use of manpower sparked repeated clashes between the two committees. Such jurisdictional disputes led a committee of the Watch Committee to recommend in late 1847 that the two committees be joined into a single entity. Two years later the Health Committee and the Watch Committee continued to coexist in a sometimes uneasy truce, with police officers distributing Health Committee notices on cholera, assisting Dr. Duncan in removing people from diseased dwellings, and serving as special lodging house inspectors.[44]

When the cholera death tolls mounted, Duncan and the Health Committee continually crossed swords with the Select Vestry's medical relief committee over appropriate responses. From the outset the MOH urged the Select Vestry to hire additional parochial medical officers for house-by-house visitations. In April 1849 the joint committee of the medical relief committee and the Health Committee asked the Vestry what was being done about treating the poor. Unsatisfied with the Vestry's responses, Duncan and the joint committee wrote to the new General Board of Health in London, which ordered the Vestry to hire a dozen new medical officers and establish two new cholera hospitals. The Vestry reluctantly complied, but only after expressing its outrage at the government's imposition on local autonomy, resources, and judgment, particularly when the same government had refused to offer Liverpool any material assistance. A few months later the General Board of Health, annoyed by the Vestry's insufficient actions, ordered the appointment of twenty additional medical officers and issued a report criticizing Liverpool's parochial officers.

The Board of Health's criticisms set off a flurry of special meetings of both the Vestry and the Health Committee. Some vestrymen admonished Duncan for embarrassing them sending unfavorable reports to London. The Vestry's medical relief committee defended its opening of emergency hospitals and dispensaries, insisting that it had always acted with Duncan's approval, and blamed the Health Committee for any deficiency in nuisance removal. The Health Committee, which had been spared official censure, enraged the Vestry by voicing satisfaction with the board's report. In late November, when the crisis had passed, the Select Vestry heard a report that placed cholera deaths at only 4,100. Several members argued against a vote of thanks to Duncan for his actions during the crisis, while criticizing the "'healthmongery' movement" that had cost the city so much money.[45]

The Vestry's occasional resistance to energetic health reform, even in times of epidemics, was typical of the English response to the public health movement. A factor that set Liverpool apart, other than its earlier legislation, was the presence of Duncan acting as an advocate for aggressive action, whereas other local boards of health resisted the use of their legislated power.[46] In July 1849, for instance, Duncan received permission from the General Board of Health to forcibly remove sick or healthy people from homes stricken with cholera. The medical officer of health lost no time in flexing his new muscle: the following day he ordered the police to remove a recalcitrant patient to the Fever Hospital. In the months to come, Duncan reported, he never had to resort to this compulsory power, "the knowledge that the power existed and might be resorted to being sufficient for the purpose."[47]

The typhus and cholera epidemics also underscored the centrality of commercial concerns in framing health and sanitation policy. From the outset the local branch of the Health of Towns' Association stressed the importance of battling Liverpool's stigma as the nation's unhealthiest city. Local editorials, exhibiting a similar booster spirit, worried that reports emphasizing local disease would discourage businessmen from traveling to Liverpool. In June 1847 the *Mercury*—following Duncan's line of analysis— called on other journals to tell their readers that the disease was concentrated in the city's poor Irish districts and did not pose a threat to commercial travelers. When cholera began spreading across the globe, local commercial interests recoiled from the threat of quarantine. In October 1848 the *Mercury* offered sarcastic praise when the Lords of the Council ordered the Customs Department to rescind the quarantine because cholera had already arrived in the country. "Had 'the Lords of the Council' been practical business men," the newspaper reported, "instead of mere sprigs of the aristocracy, appointed on considerations altogether apart from fitness for duty, no such ridiculous and mischievous order as that now rescinded would ever have been issued."[48] As local cholera deaths reached their peak, both the Health Committee and the Select Vestry discussed the dangers of "overreporting" local mortality to the international community.[49]

❧

Liverpool's public authorities responded to the typhus and cholera epidemics by establishing emergency hospitals and dispensaries in the affected districts, fever sheds adjoining the workhouse, and lazarettos floating in the Irish Sea. As Duncan reported, the victims of both epidemics—and the patients in the emergency hospitals—were predominantly Irish immigrants. The famine migration also placed some additional strains on the city's established public and private medical institutions. Dispensaries, which offered outpatient relief to the poor and working classes, reported unusual financial difficulties during the famine, but net declines in total patients. In 1846 the Northern and Southern Dispensaries treated nearly 47,000 patients, up almost 8,000 from the previous year. The next year the committee reported reduced donations "owing, no doubt, to the prevailing commercial pressure" and heavy demands accompanying "the influx of so large a number of Irish paupers." But despite caring for over 6,000 fever patients, the dispensaries treated only 37,256 total cases in 1847. In 1848 the dispensaries suffered through deep financial distress, leading to the closing of the Southern Dispensary and a reduction to about 32,000 patients. The records of the Liverpool Infirmary tell a similar story. The Infirmary received £4,800 in subscriptions and donations in 1840 and began the year with 219 patients. In 1848 the Infirmary's officers reported barely £3,000 in donations and a January 1 population of only 188. In 1846, 2,503 patients had entered the new Northern Hospital building; by 1850 that figure had climbed to 3,138. Most patients were accident victims, reflecting the heavy construction in the northern part of the city. The number of Irish-born patients rose during the famine years, but it represented a fairly stable proportion of the total (roughly 35 percent), suggesting that the Northern Hospital did not feel the severe effects of the famine migrants or the concomitant epidemic diseases.[50] The combined total of inpatients and outpatients at the Southern Hospital climbed from 2,009 in 1846 to 2,444 in 1847 and continued to rise steadily for the next several years. Although the hospital did not report places of birth, the chairman noted that three-fourths of the patients were Roman Catholic, reflecting the large Irish Catholic population in the vicinity. The Southern Hospital's reports attributed its fluctuating annual patient numbers to the amount of public works (and thus accidents) on the one hand, and the state of the economy (and thus available donations) on the other, rather than to the flow of Irish migrants.[51]

The combined pressures of increased demands and reduced donations led Liverpool's medical charities to employ extraordinary measures. In January 1849 the internationally renowned singer Jenny Lind ("the Swedish Nightingale") gave a charity concert for Liverpool's hospitals.[52] Later that year Mayor Bramley Moore and his wife—assisted by a committee of local women—staged a fund-raising fair in Prince's Park for the Infirmary and the Northern and Southern Hospitals. Although one volunteer (anticipating Yogi Berra) feared that the fair would not make much money, "the crowd being so great it was almost impossible to get near the sales," the Fancy Fair raised £11,000. This function, which was comparable to periodic charitable fairs in the antebellum United States, was an unfamiliar event in Liverpool, attracting tremendous popular attention. The Northern Hospital's trustees sent the mayor a letter thanking him for the fair, which they characterized as "totally unprecedented in any undertaking of a similar character." They included a special thanks to the "Mayoress" for helping the three institutions "[obtain] relief from accumulated debts arising from the Famine, commercial distress, and other difficulties of the last three years which caused a great falling off in their income."[53]

Despite this evidence of difficult circumstances during the famine years, the records of Liverpool's medical charities reflect their conviction that sick Irish paupers were properly the government's problem. Charitable medical institutions limited admission by requiring letters of introduction or—at the very least—established residency. As the dispensaries' managers explained, their role was to help keep the working poor off the parish rolls, not aid paupers and aliens. The responses to the occasional immigrant in charitable medical institutions underscore the expectation that they should have been public charges. In late 1848 the Lying-In Hospital became the center of controversy when rumors circulated that it had been improperly assisting Irish immigrants. This led to an investigation by the mayor, who, the *Mercury* reported, "was now fully satisfied that it was conducted with the greatest propriety, and confined to the relief of the inhabitants of the town." The Southern Hospital's 1851 report complained of excessive demand, arguing that roughly a third of its inpatients should "have come under the operation of the poor laws, and should be relieved out of parish funds." But the report acknowledged that although "the parish offices have made no provision" for these accident and surgical cases, "for *Medical* cases a laboratory and a suitable medical staff have been established at the workhouse."[54] With the 1851 opening of the new county asylum at Rainhill, Liverpool's Infirmary quickly stopped treating pauper patients in its own Lunatic Asylum, announcing that it would begin charging patients a small fee.[55]

✿

Coming on the heels of the dramatic changes in Liverpool's health apparatus, the famine migration had produced considerable strains between Duncan and the Vestry's medical relief committee. The MOH's localized vision of centralized, rational control quickly ran afoul of competing agendas and jurisdictional disputes, revealing the intransigence of the traditional local administrative structure. But his successful appeal to the Board of Health indicated an important new role for national authorities in shaping local policies and practices. In the meantime, the experiences of Liverpool's medical institutions demonstrated the enduring distinction between quasi-public charities—intended to address the needs of the city's own working poor—and public assistance for paupers under the Select Vestry. The fact that those members of the working poor who fell victim to typhus or cholera also fell under parish authority merely continued an established tradition: poor residents had long been one misfortune away from the workhouse. Finally, Liverpool's responses to the waves of medical crises must be understood in the context of powerful commercial considerations. Elected officials recognized the importance of addressing the port's reputation; thus they were driven by a desire both to reduce mortality and to reassure the world that the city's epidemic diseases were contained in the Irish neighborhoods and therefore posed no threat to travelers or merchants.

PHILADELPHIA'S HEALTH CRISES

In the second quarter of the nineteenth century Philadelphia enjoyed a reputation for cleanliness and good health, which contrasted sharply with Liverpool's image. The city had also become known as an important American center for medical research and education. At midcentury its various medical schools trained roughly 1,000 students a year and—according to the County Medical Society—Philadelphia County boasted nearly 400 "legitimate" physicians and nearly 200 other medical practitioners.[56] Perhaps such fame said less about Philadelphia's medical apparatus than about the state of urban health worldwide. Antebellum American policymakers typically responded to its epidemics—like its wars—*after* the first casualties had fallen. Philadelphia's medical responses to the Irish famine migrants, and to the accompanying diseases, partially reflect this tradition.

In 1832 U.S. cities faced cholera for the first time. As the disease moved from the Far East through Europe, Americans confidently assumed that rigorous quarantines and superior cleanliness would protect them from its worst effects. As Charles Rosenberg has demonstrated, Americans blamed cholera—when it finally struck—on various individual failings, ranging from immorality to intemperance. In New York, the disease eventually spurred the local Board of Health into a series of emergency measures to clean the streets and provide temporary hospitals. Municipal authorities in Philadelphia, Boston, and Baltimore made similar efforts, but Rosenberg argues that the 1832 epidemic left only a modest legacy for public health or sanitation.[57]

Less than twenty years later America's East Coast cities braced for the combined medical threats posed by Irish famine migrants and a second international cholera epidemic. Whereas Liverpool had already taken the first steps toward health and sanitation reform, under the direction of its new medical officer of health, most American cities had only rudimentary mechanisms for responding to medical emergencies. In Philadelphia, re-sponsibility for overseeing local sanitation and health measures fell to the Board of Health. The board was established in 1806, with members ap-pointed by the Council and the district commissioners. In 1849 the mem-bership included six city representatives and four members from each in-corporated district. Although named by local officeholders, the Board of Health was largely independent and technically under state authority. Its activities were funded by county taxes controlled by the state legislature. In addition to its own members—who served on various subcommittees—the board directed the actions of the port physician, the lazaretto physician, and the quarantine master, all appointed by the governor.[58] The board regularly communicated with the Guardians of the Poor, who were charged with running the almshouse and administering poor relief throughout the county. The late 1840s would prove an illuminating test for Philadelphia's public and private medical institutions.

The leading historian of U.S. hospitals has suggested that the famine "created something approaching a crisis in American hospitals." The arrival of sickly Irish paupers did not place equivalent strains on all medical institutions. As in England, many immigrants, especially those suffering with disease, quickly became public charges. Philadelphia's Guardians of the Poor reported steady increases in patients at the almshouse hospital throughout the late 1840s. In 1848 the hospital treated 3,548 patients, 1,605 of whom were Irish-born. Nearly half of its 5,000 patients in 1850–51 were Irish-born.[59] In addition to the Irish patients treated in the City Hospital, the city-run Wills Hospital for the Indigent Lame and Blind, established by a private bequest, in 1846 discharged 163 patients, of whom 56 were Irish. The following year the managers reported treating 148 residents, including 92 who were Irish-born.[60]

Among Philadelphia's established private medical institutions, the Pennsylvania Hospital played the largest role in caring for Irish migrants. From 1842 to 1845 the charity hospital treated between 886 and 1,044 patients annually, with roughly a third reporting Irish birthplaces. In the next five years (1846–50), in the midst of the famine migration, the total number of patients climbed dramatically, reaching 1,973 in 1849–50. Irish-born patients began outnumbering American natives by 1847. In 1847–48 the hospital treated 702 Irish immigrants out of 1,546 total patients, prompting the managers to append two small exclamation points beside the figure in their tabular summary. In 1850–51 the Pennsylvania Hospital treated 887 Irish natives out of a total of 1,935 patients. But even in its peak years the charity hospital did not approach the numbers (or proportion) of Irish patients treated annually at the city-run Philadelphia Hospital.[61]

Philadelphia's Catholic community, unlike its Liverpool counterpart, had the wherewithal to address the rising medical needs directly. In early 1848 the pastor of St. Joseph's Church called on his parishioners and other interested Catholics to assist the parish's distressed famine migrants. A February meeting resulted in the creation of the "St. Joseph's Society for the Relief of Distressed Immigrants from Ireland, and for the Establishment of a Hospital." In June 1849 St. Joseph's Hospital, to be run by the Sisters of St. Joseph, opened its doors for the care of patients "without distinction of creed, country or colour." In its first year the managers—who accepted both paying and charity cases—reported treating 185 patients, including 154 from Ireland and only 15 born in the United States. The following year the Sisters of St. Joseph treated 272 "in-door" patients, including 214 from Ireland, and 243 outpatients (177 from Ireland). Most (345) of these 515 cases were charity patients. In subsequent years the hospital continued to grow, with the vast majority of its patients coming from Ireland. Although annual reports stressed that patients from all religions were welcome, the hospital relied on local Catholic churches for donations.[62] St. Joseph's Hospital was one of the early examples of a mid-nineteenth–century boom in American hospital building in response to rising urban demands.[63]

Whereas financial strains forced Liverpool's dispensaries to cut back in the late 1840s, Philadelphia's more modest charitable dispensaries expanded their operations during the famine. The Northern Dispensary, for instance, treated only 619 patients in 1841 but 3,807 in 1850. In late 1848 a group of local citizens, led by philanthropist William J. Mullen, opened a new dispensary in Moyamensing explicitly so that the local poor would not be forced into the almshouse for medical aid. The Society for the Employment and Instruction of the Poor (PSEIP) added a dispensary in 1851 and the next year provided medicines to nearly 1,400 patients. The PSEIP dispensary's figures for 1854–55 indicate that nearly half (605 of 1,266) of its white patients with known nativity were Irish-born (it treated 131 black patients in the same year).[64]

As in Liverpool, most of Philadelphia's sickly famine migrants received public assistance in a city-run hospital. But the responses of charitable institutions in the two cities were distinctly different. Not only did the Pennsylvania Hospital and the charitable dispensaries expand their operations, taking in large numbers of Irish-born patients, but also philanthropic agents in Philadelphia responded to the new demands by founding St. Joseph's Hospital and at least two new dispensaries. During the same period Liverpool's charitable hospitals and dispensaries either cut back their patient totals—owing to financial strains—or experienced modest increases that their managers attributed to other variables. Thus, while Philadelphia's William Mullen was striving to protect the poor from resorting to the almshouse, Liverpool's charities appeared intent on maintaining a sharp distinction between paupers, who were the Vestry's concern, and the city's own working poor.

The increased demand on Philadelphia's medical institutions was only one of the medical challenges facing the city at midcentury. The periodic epidemics of diseases, sometimes associated with the Irish newcomers, presented Philadelphia's officials, like Liverpool's, with further dilemmas. The first line of defense was to keep diseases from entering the city. Between June 1 and October 1 of each year, arriving immigrant vessels were subject to quarantine under the supervision of the Board of Health. At all other times the port physician inspected incoming immigrant ships in search of contagious diseases. In April 1847, for instance, the physician discovered smallpox aboard the immigrant ship *Alabama* and ordered its two hundred Irish passengers to remain in quarantine at the lazaretto floating offshore.[65] And as we saw in the case of the *Provincialist* in 1848, local officials at all levels responded aggressively to efforts to circumvent the established health barriers.

Epidemic disease generally came under the purview of the Board of Health, but often the board's duties led it into contact—and sometimes conflict—with the Guardians of the Poor. In May 1847 the Guardians complained to the Board of Health that paupers suffering from typhus, or "ship fever," had been crowding the almshouse. The board responded that the diseased immigrants had arrived by land from New York City rather than slipping past the port physician. For the next several weeks the two bodies battled over which one should be responsible for the incoming typhus cases. The Guardians wanted to transfer the patients to the City Hospital, run by the Board of Health. The board resisted making any special arrangements for the fever victims until mid-June, when they named a committee of three doctors to investigate the problem. In the meantime, the Guardians had asked the city solicitor "to take such measures as he may deem best for the purpose of compelling the Board of Health to open a Hospital for the reception of Fever cases." Finally, the board agreed to accept typhus and smallpox victims in the City Hospital so long as the Guardians would cover their expenses. It also appointed a committee to visit Boston and New York to investigate how those cities dealt with diseased immigrants.[66]

In early November 1847 the Board of Health faced new rumors of a deadly disease—reported to be spotted fever—among African Americans living on Baker Street in Moyamensing. After sending a visitation committee into the neighborhood, the board promptly ordered much of the street vacated and the homes cleaned and boarded up. Although the board attempted to coordinate these evictions with the Guardians of the Poor, it appears that at least some people were left temporarily homeless. Meanwhile, the Guardians agreed to provide medicine to Moyamensing residents through private physicians working with the Society for the Employment and Relief of the Poor. By the eighteenth the Board of Health had begun allowing the survivors to return to their homes. The *Public Ledger* reported that the disease had taken 66 black victims. Two weeks later the visitation committee discovered a worse outbreak in nearby Bedford Street, prompting another round of emergency evictions and housecleaning. In a week's time 174 more Philadelphians—predominantly black residents of the Baker-Bedford neighborhood—had died. The *Ledger* praised the board for its prompt, aggressive action while blaming the outbreak on intemperance and the victims' "squalid mode of life." [67]

During the spring and summer of 1848 the Guardians of the Poor joined the Board of Health in another round of efforts to battle contagious diseases. In April the Guardians discussed plans to construct a hospital for the treatment of paupers with contagious diseases. The following month the arrival of the ship *Provincialist*—reputedly with smallpox victims aboard—provoked the complex series of responses discussed in Chapter 2. In the process, both the Guardians and the Board of Health acted to protect the city and their own budgets from financial impositions. That June, with the annual quarantine under way, the Guardians concluded extended negotiations with the Board of Health by agreeing to pay three dollars per week to place paupers with contagious diseases in the City Hospital.[68]

If fever and smallpox challenged Philadelphia's existing health apparatus, cholera threatened to overwhelm the city. By the end of 1848, reports of its progress across Europe had begun to filter into the United States. In August the *Ledger* summarized an English study linking cholera to atmospheric moisture and called on local officials to drain pools, ditches, and marshes.[69] Three months later the Board of Health's sanitary committee proposed a series of hygienic measures based on the English experience and closely paralleling the policies enacted by Liverpool's health officials. As the new year began, the frequency, and urgency, of published cholera stories mounted.[70] Philadelphia's initial response to the rising cholera panic—in editorials, letters, and official proclamations—emphasized the need for improved sanitation, an issue that is taken up in the next chapter. Before long city officials had to confront the disease as a distinct, and potentially devastating, medical problem.

Through the winter and spring the Board of Health turned to familiar devices to prepare for the medical emergency. Early in the year the board arranged to quarantine ships arriving from cities with known cholera outbreaks. In March 1849 it established special cholera hospitals and dispensaries, all the while taking pains to clean city streets. On May 11 the first American case of cholera was reported in New York City. A week later Philadelphian Arthur Ritchie wrote to a Georgian that "we fully expect the cholera . . . tho the people here do not seem to fear it much." On the twenty-fourth the *Ledger* announced that rumors of cholera in the city were so far unfounded and that the city should congratulate itself for avoiding the disease. A few days later the paper, echoing commercial concerns voiced in Liverpool, added that the false rumors threatened to harm the city's prosperous economy.[71]

Finally, on May 30, the Board of Health reported the city's first cholera fatalities: three Irish immigrants who had recently arrived from New York. For the next several months the city and the surrounding districts turned to emergency cleansing operations. The Board of Health issued a plan to establish ten emergency cholera hospitals: three in the city, two in Kensington, and one in each of the other outlying districts. Meanwhile, cholera patients would receive medical assistance from the city dispensaries.[72] Blockley Almshouse did not report its first case until June 27, but soon the disease swept through the facility, killing 85 of 1,546 inmates in a single week. Nonetheless, the Board of Guardians voted against hiring additional physicians, although it did eventually open two temporary cholera hospitals adjoining the almshouse.[73]

Although the emergency hospitals and the almshouse bore the brunt of the epidemic, Philadelphia's charitable institutions made substantial efforts to meet the crisis. On June 1 the managers of the new Moyamensing Dispensary issued an appeal for donations, pointing out that the neighborhood was among the city's filthiest and most susceptible to contagious disease. In July the affiliated Moyamensing House of Industry turned its building into a cholera hospital.[74] The Society for the Employment and Instruction of the Poor also transformed its building into a cholera hospital; the managers later claimed to have treated twice as many cholera patients as any other Philadelphia hospital.[75] Once again, Philadelphia's private benevolent bodies—unlike those in Liverpool—had responded to a crisis by expanding their existing activities and creating new emergency institutions.

The epidemic peaked in mid-July; by early August the worst was over and the Board of Health voted to close all but two of the emergency hospitals. Between May 30 and September 8, 1,012 county residents had succumbed to cholera. Roughly a third (358) of these cholera victims died in public institutions, including hospitals, the almshouse, and the county prison.[76]

❧

Although Philadelphians were generally concerned about the epidemic, members of the middle and upper classes clearly saw the disease as an affliction of the lower classes. As in 1832, many Americans viewed cholera as evidence of God's will, while others saw it as the product of intemperance and immoral behavior. Even those who adopted a more environmental interpretation blamed the disease on the personal circumstances and sanitary habits of its victims. Only a small minority of professionals on either side of the Atlantic had begun to recognize the medical importance of microscopic organisms. Philadelphians had every reason to view cholera as an Irish disease. The initial cases arrived on ships from Ireland, and although the *Ledger* accounts did not list the nativity of victims locally, the newspaper took pains to report the heavy concentration of Irish fatalities in New York, Boston, and other eastern cities.[77]

The Board of Health's official report presented tables locating the neighborhoods with the worst sanitary "nuisances" and the heaviest concentrations of cholera. The report consistently linked the most severe outbreaks with the personal depravity of the residents: Southwark's uncleanliness was owing to the "character of a portion of its inhabitants that reside in the more densely populated neighborhoods"; Moyamensing suffered from the "depraved conditions of hundreds of its inhabitants." The reader could easily recognize the city's Irish (and black) neighborhoods among those singled out for criticism, even though the report did not draw explicit links between behavior and ethnicity or race. Sidney George Fisher's private comments in his diary were typical. On July 7 he wrote: "The cholera still continues among us. . . . It is confined almost entirely so far to the lowest classes. Those who live cleanly & comfortably & avoid improper diet & excesses are in very little danger." Later, Fisher noted the even higher incidence of the disease in St. Louis and Cincinnati, where "the Germans & Irish, destitute, filthy, ill fed & wretched, arrive there in hordes, after crossing the Atlantic in crowded & dirty ships, & after a long journey from New York & other eastern ports in crowded steamboats & cars."[78]

As in Liverpool, some Philadelphians eyed the progress of cholera with a concern for commerce. But in the City of Brotherly Love the commercial classes had greater reason for optimism. In late June, as the local outbreak was nearing its peak, Arthur Ritchie informed his Georgian friend: "We have felt no alarm so far, nor should we leave the City on account of it, as we should probably be better off here, than any where else, our City is very clean, remarkably so . . . cleaner than it has been for years." New York, he reported, had been hit much harder, making business dull and keeping outsiders from visiting that city. Six weeks later the *Public Ledger* noted that Boston and New York continued to suffer, whereas travelers had already begun returning to Philadelphia. Consequently, the editorial noted, "Philadelphia will come in for a large share of the Western trade."[79]

CONCLUSION

Liverpool and Philadelphia faced the twin health challenges of immigration and epidemic disease with similar tools. In each case the first line of defense was to search incoming vessels and impose quarantines, a policy that routinely drew the ire of commercial interests. Both cities supported a variety of medical institutions, ranging from city hospitals and dispensaries to privately run charitable hospitals. Each local government had separate bodies charged with assisting the poor and protecting public health, although Philadelphia did not yet have a central figure comparable to Liverpool's Dr. Duncan. Moreover, the two cities were part of the same scientific world. Competing theories about epidemic disease and its causes traveled as rapidly as the diseases themselves. And the persistent links drawn between poverty, immorality, and disease only served to support such popular attitudes toward the poor in general and the Irish in particular.[80]

When hundreds of Irish immigrants in each port city began seeking medical assistance, they turned disproportionately to medical wards in the public almshouse (or workhouse) or to the outdoor medical relief provided by the city dispensaries. Epidemic diseases were also liable to drive other members of the working poor—including previous Irish immigrants —into public institutions. Liverpool's private hospitals followed the logic of the Poor Law, generally directing Irish paupers to the public authorities. Moreover, the city's charitable hospitals commonly refused patients with contagious diseases. Philadelphians left the chief responsibility for the sickly newcomers—and for the treatment of contagious diseases—in public hands. But the city's charitable hospitals pitched in to meet the crisis, and several new institutions—most notably, St. Joseph's Hospital—emerged in the midst of the famine migration.

If we consider the two cities in isolation, the similarity of their stories is clear and unremarkable. In each country the sickly poor—and particularly the alien poor—were presumed to be a public responsibility.[81] As the famine migration continued, the burden on taxpayers grew, prompting emergency efforts to minimize the public cost, either by regulating the flow of immigrants or by charging shipowners bonds for transporting people who were likely to become a public charge. But a comparison of the two cities suggests their distinctive characteristics beneath these shared assumptions. Although Philadelphians treated the migrants as a major health threat and the approach of cholera as a true crisis, the magnitude of those problems is put into perspective by comparing them to the far greater tragedy witnessed in Liverpool's Irish wards and fever sheds. Liverpool and the surrounding area lost nearly five times as many victims of cholera as Philadelphia County. This difference in degree, and the greater freedom of American ports to control the flow of migrants, provides further evidence of the importance of geography and distance in shaping national experiences. And despite Philadelphia's more modest health challenges, local charitable institutions took on a much more substantial role in caring for the famine migrants than did Liverpool's comparable private hospitals. Thus once again the two cities exhibited quite different levels of voluntarism, seemingly indicating differing presumptions about the respective roles of the individual and the state in society, particularly in moments of crisis.

When we turn our attention from the treatment of patients to more broad-based public health measures, further differences emerge. Government health officials in both cities followed conventional wisdom by undertaking vigorous efforts to clean the streets and remove unsanitary nuisances, thus dramatically elevating their public presence. The government agencies in both cities frequently battled over jurisdictions and responsibilities, but Philadelphia's health officers were never embroiled in the highly publicized controversies that characterized many of Liverpool's debates. Of course, this was partially because the epidemics hit Liverpool much harder. But Liverpool's battles also reflected a jockeying for position in the aftermath of the recent Sanitary Act. The city's new medical officer of health was a far more powerful public health official than Philadelphia, or any other American city, would see for some time. For the time being American urban conflicts were fought in a political atmosphere that did not yet offer much support for substantial health reform.[82] Under the new Sanitary Act, Dr. Duncan and his Health Committee were responsible for evicting hundreds of migrants from Liverpool's diseased cellars; such actions were much rarer in Philadelphia and were apparently reserved for the city's poor black population. This, too, may reflect Liverpool's greater sense of crisis, but it also supports the argument that Philadelphians—and perhaps Americans generally—clung more vigorously to a belief in the sanctity of private property than their English counterparts.

The two cities also differed significantly in the role played by the national government. Philadelphia's Board of Health reported to the state but was largely autonomous in its actions. The U.S. Congress played no role in the internal workings of the city's health establishment. In contrast, the British Parliament had devoted substantial energy to local health reform in the previous few years. During the cholera epidemic the General Board of Health saw fit to send emissaries to Liverpool to evaluate local health measures. And when the health crisis became overwhelming, the city sent a delegation to London in search of relief. The differences between the roles of the two national governments were indeed dramatic. Nonetheless, Liverpool's health efforts—like its poor relief—were actually much more independent than a cursory reading of national reforms might indicate.[83]

The famine migration and the cholera epidemic tested existing medical practices on both sides of the Atlantic. Liverpool's health authorities turned to aggressive tactics such as the widespread "clearing" of Irish immigrants from dirty cellars. America's health boards—where they existed— had fewer powers. In the short run, cities like Philadelphia opened temporary cholera hospitals. In the longer term, the migration persuaded private American philanthropists to construct new hospitals, such as Philadelphia's St. Joseph's Hospital.

The midcentury epidemics also helped produce an international cohort of sanitary specialists who meticulously recorded the carnage in their midst. Dr. Wilson Jewell began serving on the Philadelphia Board of Health in 1849. By the early 1850s, Jewell had begun delivering public papers based on his studies of local sanitation and disease. In 1853 he published a detailed analysis of the yellow fever epidemic that struck southern Philadelphia that August. Jewell's publications shared much in common with the work of Dr. Duncan in Liverpool, both in their meticulous statistical analyses and in their emphasis on environmental—rather than contagious— sources of disease. In 1857 Jewell hosted the first in a series of sanitation conventions, bringing together seventy-four of the nation's urban "sanitarians."[84] By the mid-nineteenth century sanitary reform was the central focus of public health officials in both English and American cities. The next chapter considers their efforts to control the evolving urban environment.

5. Environmental Reform

INTRODUCTION: SANITARIANS AND PUBLIC SPACE

By the middle of the nineteenth century, health professionals such as William Duncan and Wilson Jewell had convinced urban dwellers that poor sanitation and epidemic disease went hand in hand. Quarantines, hospitals, and dispensaries were only one part of the attack on urban disease. The public health movement was equally concerned with the environmental dilemmas posed by rising population density. Public officials in English and American cities took pains to map the worst neighborhoods, with their crowded housing, poorly ventilated buildings, and distressing assortment of foul-smelling "nuisances." These surveys commonly linked environmental discussions with broader analyses of poverty, health, and morality.

This chapter seeks to unpack these intertwined issues, focusing on the sanitary discussions while remaining cognizant of their links to related concerns. The first task will be to identify the environmental challenges in the two cities as they were viewed by contemporary observers. Professional "sanitarians" in both cities took pains to map the worst neighborhoods, suggesting a rising public concern for the urban environment. But in Liverpool the conditions were in fact much worse and the level of concern far greater. Then we will consider how health officials in each city tackled their perceived problems, with an emphasis on the responses to the 1849 cholera epidemic. The final task will be to step away from daily policy discussions to consider broader debates over utilities and housing. The Irish famine migrants were, once again, not so much the ultimate cause of the problems confronting Liverpool and Philadelphia as a crucial contributing factor that helped bring difficult issues to a head. In fact, environmental reformers on both sides of the Atlantic concluded that the Irish posed a specific sanitary threat, thus thrusting the newcomers into the center of ongoing debates.[1]

These environmental discussions also emerged out of an evolving sense of the nature of community, public space, and the role of public policy in controlling that community and shaping that space. Both societies approached these discussions with a clear sense that private property ought to be protected from unnecessary infringement by government authorities. But a comparison of the two cities suggests that Philadelphians—and Americans—were particularly concerned about the rights of the property owner as they came into contact with the state.[2] In the meantime, as Mary Poovey has pointed out, the image of the social body had taken hold in British public discourse, providing "a more dynamic picture of the relationship between organisms and their physical environment" than the competing image of the social machine. Poovey notes that this metaphoric image of the social body was sufficiently malleable to support a wide array of interpretive perspectives, but it was especially useful in supporting government-sponsored efforts to address—and cure—sanitary nuisances. Perhaps this metaphoric understanding of social ills, coupled with the distinctive magnitude of the environmental dilemma, supported Liverpool's early steps toward sanitary reforms even when they challenged the acknowledged sanctity of private property.[3]

MAPPING URBAN NUISANCES

Liverpool's Irish migrants packed into crowded neighborhoods near the docks, often taking up temporary residence in cellars, closed courts, or lodging houses.[4] Long before the famine began driving migrants across the Irish Sea, the borough's most crowded, unsanitary wards had already become the object of national and local concern. In 1840 the Select Committee on the Health of Towns' estimated that a fifth of Liverpool's working classes lived in cellars; Dr. Duncan testified that the city had 2,400 poorly ventilated courts where the residents overwhelmed the existing sanitary facilities.[5] Two years later local merchant John Finch published a detailed analysis of "more than five thousand families" of Vauxhall Ward—to the north of the city and stretching to the river—for the Liverpool Anti-Monopoly Association. Finch found that nearly a fifth (982) of the families lived in cellars and even more (1,082) resided in lodging houses and owned no furniture. Although Finch made his survey a half a decade before the famine, 45 percent (2,443) of Vauxhall's household heads were Irish-born.[6]

In 1843 Duncan delivered a lengthy paper to the Literary and Philosophical Society "On the Physical Causes of the High Rate of Mortality in Liverpool." Speaking to an audience that rarely ventured into Liverpool's poor districts, he provided a meticulous—and vivid—account of the city's courts, cellars, and lodging houses. The courts, he explained, "consist usually of two rows of houses placed opposite to each other, with an intervening space of from 9 to 15 feet, and having two to six or eight houses in each row. The court communicates with the street by a passage or archway about 3 feet wide—in the older courts, built up overhead; and the farther end being also in many instances closed. . . . the court forms in fact a *cul de sac* with a narrow opening. Such an arrangement almost bids defiance to the *entrance* of air." Duncan estimated that the city's 1,982 courts contained 10,692 houses and 55,534 inhabitants, or more than a third of the parish's working classes. Liverpool's inhabited cellars were even more disturbing. They were "10 or 12 feet square . . . frequently having only the bare earth for a floor,—and sometimes less than six feet in height. There is frequently no window, so that light and air can gain access to the cellar only by the door, the top of which is often not higher than the level of the street. . . . They are of course dark; and from the defective drainage, they are also very generally damp." Duncan reported that the parish's 6,294 cellars housed 20,168 people (with perhaps another 2,000 residents living in cellars within courts).[7]

For those who lived in buildings along the city streets, circumstances were not much better. Poor residents often slept in crowded lodging houses. "In every room of such houses, and with the exception of the kitchen or cooking-room, the floor is usually covered with bedsteads, each of which receives, at night, as many human beings as can be crowded into it; and this, too, often without distinction of sex, or regard to decency." The poorest lodgers slept in even more crowded cellars, which Duncan likened to "the Black Hole of Calcutta."

Across the parish, Duncan found disturbing evidence of insufficient—or nonexistent—privies, drainage, ventilation, and general cleanliness, all of which, he argued, contributed to the city's high mortality rate. He devoted much of his energy to mapping out Liverpool's most notorious districts, drawing special attention to the apparent link between Vauxhall Ward's poor housing and high fever rates. Sometimes Duncan added specific indictments of the local Irish population. The Irish, he claimed, ran (and occupied) the worst lodging houses and lived in the most foul cellars. "It may be said that this is merely the result of their greater poverty," he acknowledged,

> which deprives them of a proper supply of the necessaries of life, and compels them to select the most unhealthy (because the cheapest) localities as their places of residence. To a great extent this is true; but at the same time there appears to be, among the lowest classes of Irish, such an innate indifference to filth, such a low standard of comfort, and such a *gregariousness,* as lead them, even when not *driven* by necessity, into the unhealthy localities where they are found to congregate; and which they render still more unhealthy by their recklessness and their peculiar habits.

Thus, he concluded, "the districts of Liverpool, where we have seen fever to be most prevalent, are exactly those where the Irish are congregated in the greatest numbers."[8]

Such observations about Liverpool's housing and sanitation, often linked to discussions of health, morality, or ethnicity, became common currency in the 1840s. In 1842 the Domestic Mission Society passed a resolution decrying the physical and moral evils "arising from a miserably accommodated, dense, and destitute population." In his annual reports to the society, Rev. John Johns routinely remarked on the unsavory cellars, on one occasion suggesting that the Irish poor were unusually unclean (or at least unfamiliar with urban housekeeping). By the middle of the decade Johns had become fully vested in the notion that the moral elevation of the poor would only follow an improved environment.[9] On September 29, 1845, the new local branch of the Health of Towns' Association staged an enthusiastic public meeting at the Music Hall to promote improved health, sanitation, and ventilation. Samuel Holme rose to describe one especially unpleasant court in Vauxhall Ward, concluding that it would be impossible to teach morality to the poor living in such conditions. Thus, concerns about housing, sanitation, poverty, and morality blurred together in the years *before* the famine migration, and the Irish were already the subjects of special criticism.[10]

Liverpool's national reputation for filth and disease expanded at the same time that Edwin Chadwick was applying his estimable energies, and centralizing principles, to the problems of sanitation and public health. In 1842 Chadwick's *Report on the Sanitary Condition of the Labouring Popula-*

tion criticized conditions in Liverpool and other British cities. The following year the Buccleuch Commission issued its first report on the health of towns, making extensive use of Dr. Duncan's vivid testimony. As we have seen, this torrent of local and national attention led to the passage of Liverpool's Sanitary Act of 1846, giving the city England's first comprehensive local health legislation. The process that yielded Liverpool's Sanitary Act, and Lord Morpeth's Public Health Act two years later, represented a confluence of disparate—often seemingly contradictory—forces: evolving national ideology combined with persistent localism, national bureaucratic experts joined forces with local medical authorities, and innovative discussions of sanitary reform found receptive ears in a commercially conscious and disease-ridden port city. The results revealed the analytic power of the social body, in this case subject to ameliorative medical reforms. They also demonstrate the importance of historic contingency in shaping the effect of such metaphoric theory.[11]

America's midcentury urban reformers joined the British in finding environmental links to health, poverty, and morality. In New York City, John H. Griscom established himself as the nation's leading advocate for health reform with his 1842 report on *The Sanitary Condition of the Laboring Population of New York,* which he expanded and published in 1845.[12] But in the years before the Irish famine migration, American cities were generally "behind" their English counterparts—and Liverpool in particular—in addressing sanitation and public health. During the previous decades Philadelphia's public officials had made a few surveys of the condition of the poor, but it was not until the famine migration and the threat of cholera that the city undertook serious investigations along the lines of the earlier work by Duncan, Griscom, and a handful of other leading sanitarians.[13]

Philadelphia's relative inattention to environmental concerns, at least compared with Liverpool, can perhaps be explained by the city's reputation as an unusually clean, airy "city of homes."[14] In 1851 the *Philadelphia North American* published an editorial celebrating the county's low housing density of 6.68 people per house, a figure roughly half that of New York.[15] Philadelphia's housing stock was, indeed, dramatically different from—and generally not so bad as—that in Liverpool. Although the Pennsylvania city also had dark cellars and crowded courts, most of its worst housing was in a network of alley dwellings scattered over the city. Ironically, despite these differences in the nature of housing and in the quality of housing for their poorest citizens, at midcentury the two cities had nearly identical indices of household crowding.[16]

Philadelphia's typhus, cholera, and smallpox epidemics spawned periodic discussions of the city's worst neighborhoods, producing vivid descriptions comparable to Duncan's accounts of Liverpool's cellars and courts. The late 1847 fever outbreak in the Baker-Bedford section of Moyamensing prompted both a Board of Health investigation and a visit from the grand jury. Both bodies denounced living conditions in the neighborhood; as a result, many locals were evicted and their homes temporarily boarded up.[17] The managers of the Philadelphia Society for the Employment and Instruction of the Poor (PSEIP) chose to concentrate on the Moyamensing neighborhood "between St Mary's and Fitzwater streets on the north and south, and between Fifth and Eighth on the east and west" (which included the Baker-Bedford section) because it "had acquired for itself the name of *the infected District,* a name to which it was well entitled." Until the winter of 1847, the "unfortunate persons who lived in this district" had "remained unknown, save to the officers of the law and the unprincipled men who preyed upon their necessities." The PSEIP's visiting committees returned with horrific tales of "ill-built unventilated tenements, often no better in any respect than pens for cattle, [where] the discharged convict, the gatherer of bones and offal, the rag picker, dog catcher, and river thief found their wretched homes" and where "on the floor of a cellar trickling with unhealthy damps, they had found twenty-three ill-clad men and women."[18]

Several reports around midcentury presented a broader mapping of Philadelphia's housing and sanitary conditions. In December 1848 the Council named a special committee to respond to a circular letter from the American Medical Association (AMA). The special committee's 1849 report included detailed accounts of local housing and sanitation as submitted by the district collectors of vaccine cases and various other city officials. The authors noted specific streets and alleys with poor ventilation and cleanliness, occasionally blaming the inhabitants for their personal behavior, but only rarely noting their race or ethnicity. The special committee concluded that Philadelphia enjoyed good air flow, access to water, and street cleaning regulations, all of which contributed to making it a "comparatively healthy city." Nonetheless, they pointed out,

> there exists a limited district in one of our suburbs, a locality that is abundantly fruitful in originating and propagating disease. . . . In that almost isolated neighborhood, we find an excess of a vagrant popula-

tion, half fed and half clothed, crowded together in almost untenantable houses, and in open and humid cellars, located in narrow streets and narrower alleys, and pent up courts, badly ventilated and badly lighted. . . . many fruitful causes for disease, operating upon the half famished and bloated bodies of a depraved and mixed population, whose constitution have been undermined through the ravages of intemperance and exposure.

Interestingly, after detailed descriptions of specific alleys this passage failed to identify the offending neighborhood. One might reasonably surmise that the special committee was once again referring to the neighborhood around Baker and Bedford Streets, and that no specific address was necessary. Moreover, the committee's larger point was that the rest of the city had not fallen to that level.[19]

The same year Dr. Isaac Parrish officially answered the AMA's queries in his "Report on the Sanitary Condition of Philadelphia," which he submitted to the association along with the special committee's findings. Parrish, too, concluded that "the general character of Philadelphia for health, is perhaps equal to that of any large city in the world," suffering mainly from poorly planned expansion that had disrupted the natural air flow. According to Parrish, the greatest menaces to Philadelphia's health were the narrow alleys and closed courts that had cropped up across the city. "A lot," he explained,

of forty feet, by one hundred feet deep, encompassed by a high wall upon each side, and fronting upon a narrow street, would accommodate three small houses with large back yards; but the same premises, laid out as a court, would give place to seven or eight houses upon each side, with a common outlet of eight or ten feet wide, upon the alley. In such a court, the houses are, of course, built against a dead wall, and unprovided with any means for the access of air or light in the rear; they are without privies, or hydrants, and from the height of the surrounding walls, and the confined situation of the street on which the court has an outlet, it is often deprived of current air through it, and from the access of sun light, except during a small portion of the day.[20]

Parrish described the unsanitary characteristics of Philadelphia's alleys and courts much as Duncan had described Liverpool's a few years earlier. But there were profound differences in degree. Whereas Duncan's 1843 paper estimated that there were nearly two thousand such courts in Liverpool,

Parrish described only "upwards of fifty courts and alleys" in "the north-east district of the city" and at least forty more in the south-east district.[21]

Parrish also noted the connection between housing and "infectious disorders," drawing particular attention to the recent typhus fever epidemics that "have originated and been almost entirely limited to a crowded and filthy section of the district of Moyamensing, amongst a class of depraved inhabitants, who live in confined courts and cellars." His discussion acknowledged Griscom's New York City research as well as the findings from British cities, which, he suggested, experienced greater housing problems.[22]

In his annual report to the Committee on Public Hygiene in 1851, Wilson Jewell declared that "Philadelphia enjoys a high reputation, both at home and abroad, for its salubrity." He attributed much of that good health to a sound original city plan, but he warned that "there exist fruitful causes for the deterioration of public health," particularly "the rapid increase of our population and the continued influx of strangers from immigration." Jewell, like his predecessors, pointed to the dangers of "an over-crowded or excessive population in narrow or confined streets, or pent up courts and alleys, with small, contracted, and badly ventilated houses, with damp and foul cellars." Quoting from the 1849 report that he helped write, he noted that there were ninety-one " 'plague spots' " in the city and many more in the surrounding districts.[23] Two years later, his paper on the 1853 yellow fever epidemic along South Street Wharf included a comprehensive discussion of life in one such district. In his meticulous reconstruction of the fever victims' movements, Jewell exposed the overcrowded, unsanitary living arrangements of this largely Irish population.[24]

Perhaps the most dramatic published "map" of Philadelphia's poor neighborhoods appeared in 1853 under the title *The Mysteries and Miseries of Philadelphia*. This twenty-page pamphlet combined the latest grand jury findings with a vivid "Sketch of the Condition of the Most Degraded Classes in the City" written by Casper Souder Jr., a reporter for the *Evening Bulletin*. The grand jury inspected several key institutions and then visited "some of the houses in Baker and Strafford streets, Moyamensing, the resort of the most depraved," including one exceptionally crowded house owned by one Patrick Duffy. The jury members were shocked to find "a number of the depraved class alluded to, some half naked, huddled together, of all ages and sexes, without even a straw to lie upon, and no furniture of any kind," adding that "[t]he existence of such a scene of destitution in our midst had never entered the mind of any of our body." [25] In his more detailed description, Souder set out to demonstrate that Moyamensing contained scenes every bit as miserable as Dickens's London or Five Points in New York. Concentrating on the neighborhood between Fifth and Eighth Streets and between Lombard and Fitzwater, Souder took his readers on a guided tour as if to some foreign land. In scores of lodging houses he found "men and women—blacks and whites by dozens— . . . huddled together promiscuously" in filthy, dimly lit, and unfurnished rooms. Souder mentioned two Irish proprietors—including Patrick Duffy—by name, identifying Jemmy Quinn as "a hideous looking Irishman," but he made no effort to link the problems to either ethnicity or race.[26]

SANITARY REFORM IN LIVERPOOL

The approach of cholera gave sanitarians in both cities a new sense of urgency. Although theories on treatment differed, most agreed that the disease prospered in dirty, poorly ventilated, overcrowded urban areas. For Liverpool's Dr. Duncan and his colleagues, the looming disease forced a shift from ongoing reforms to emergency measures. Although cholera hit Philadelphia with less force, local public health officials saw the problem and its apparent solutions in a similar vein. For both cities, the threat of cholera tested, and illuminated, the existing sanitation systems.

Liverpool's sanitation apparatus had undergone substantial changes in the previous generation, reflecting the interplay of local and national initiatives. For years the borough and parish's various sanitary functions had been divided among different local boards and committees. In 1835 the newly established Corporation gave the Watch Committee authority over street cleaning, leaving other functions in the hands of the Highway Board. After 1842 the Health Committee had jurisdiction over court drains while the commissioners of paving and sewerage maintained their earlier functions. The Sanitary Act of 1846 gave the Council, and its Health Committee, control over street cleaning, sewerage, draining, and paving. The 1846 act also provided for the appointment of the borough engineer, the inspector of nuisances, and, of course, the nation's first medical officer of health (MOH). Two years later, with the Public Health Act, Parliament established a national General Board of Health and empowered local authorities to control of a wide range of sanitary functions.[27]

Liverpool's new public health officials served a city increasingly concerned with the problems of housing and sanitation.[28] The local Health of Towns' Association—which counted many of the town's leading physicians, politicians, clergymen, and (male) philanthropists among its members—became an important champion of sanitary reform, publishing its own journal, the *Health of Towns' Advocate,* and sponsoring regular lectures aimed at the working classes.[29] Among the familiar inventory of sanitary problems, the association stressed that the "first evil" was "too many people living in the same house," a dangerous circumstance that was notably present among "our Irish fellow townsmen." Often the association blamed those citizens who failed to keep their own homes and persons clean. The Irish immigrants were objects of public scorn in this regard. In November 1847 the *Mercury* called on local Catholic priests, "who have such extraordinary influence, [to] insist upon cleanliness among the wretched Irish population." On occasion, local priests took up the call, urging their flocks to pay closer attention to cleanliness. Even the Domestic Mission's John Johns, while deeply sympathetic to the immigrants' plight, called for the closing of cellars to combat both immorality and disease.[30]

The new Health Committee together with the new medical officer of health and the inspector of nuisances adopted a variety of strategies to combat Liverpool's environmental problems.[31] High on the agenda were the notorious cellars and their occupants. City officials, acting on provisions of the 1842 local act, had already cleared inhabitants from over a thousand cellars before 1846. The Sanitary Act established new maximum cellar dimensions, and so the Health Committee named four police officers to measure and inspect the borough's cellars as the first step in a gradual process of cellar clearance. By 1851 over 5,000 cellars had been closed and over 20,000 occupants evicted. The Sanitary Act also provided for the regulation of Liverpool's overcrowded lodging houses. Under the new rules, the medical officer of health inspected all lodging houses and determined their maximum occupancy. Once registered, lodging houses were subject to regular inspection by both borough police officers and the inspector of nuisance's special officers. Between 1848 and early 1851 Health Committee agents measured and inspected 1,165 lodging houses. As of March 1851 there were 659 registered lodging houses in Liverpool, including 286 classified as "emigrant lodging houses."[32]

Liverpool's new sanitary policies, like its poor relief reforms, were in place before the Irish famine migration began. Both Duncan and Inspector of Nuisances Thomas Fresh blamed the arriving Irish immigrants for increased overcrowding and the periodic waves of epidemic disease. In early 1847 Duncan estimated that "seven-eighths of all the patients in the Fever Hospital [were] *Irish*" and that "five-sevenths of them [were] from the crowded lodging-house district" between Scotland Road and Vauxhall Road.[33] Inspector Fresh added that "the worst [lodging houses] were those kept by low Irishmen, in courts and narrow streets, and they were chiefly frequented by migratory Irish people, vagrants and others."[34] Much of Duncan's campaign against the "Irish fever" involved clearing cellars and placing the afflicted in quarantine. In this fashion, the overwhelming numbers of newcomers proved a distraction from, rather than an impetus to, Duncan's long-term housing reform plans. As the MOH explained in his report to the Health Committee: "[A]ll these measures were but as a drop in the bucket so long as the Irish influx continued. No Sanatory or Poor-law engine could possibly extinguish the conflagration while such combustible fuel was so abundantly supplied."[35]

The policy of cellar removals and lodging house inspections represented the most aggressive piece in the Health Committee's attack. In addition to these incursions into the interiors of Liverpool's working-class housing, the committee and its agents adopted various measures to clean and drain the exterior environment. The Sanitary Act charged the inspector of nuisances with a variety of tasks including "the inspection and suppression of nuisances," the emptying of middens (refuse heaps), and the registration and inspection of various businesses (slaughterhouses, knackers' yards, cemeteries, and the like). The borough engineer was responsible for sewage and draining and street cleaning.[36]

The emptying of middens became a particular concern as the importation of guano (a fertilizer derived from seafowl excrement) meant that nightmen were no longer willing to empty middens for free. Under Fresh's system, individual property owners filled out written applications to have their middens emptied, whereas the police, the inspector of scavengers, and Fresh's own outdoor agents were all responsible for reporting overflowing middens outside crowded courts. In this fashion, the inspector of nuisances combined private responsibility with public inspection. Although local citizens occasionally complained about unsatisfactory contractors, Liverpool's system for emptying middens was ahead of much of the nation; health officials across the country reported persistent problems with cesspools for decades to come.[37]

Whereas the inspector of nuisances and the borough engineer were most responsible for Liverpool's day-to-day sanitary concerns, Dr. Duncan took on a broader, strategic role, collecting data on disease and mortality while working with local officials to battle disease. Duncan's understanding of the sources of disease helped frame his actions. Fever, he argued, was spread by contagion and "revel[ed] amidst filth and overcrowding." But he also blamed the spread of cholera on "atmospheric influences" that certainly prospered in unsanitary conditions but cropped up as well in places that had been resistant to fever. His chief answer to the fever epidemic was to attack Liverpool's most dirty and overcrowded housing by pushing for cellar removals. With the approach of cholera in late 1848, he oversaw a series of preventive sanitary measures stressing cleaning, drainage, and the removal of nuisances. Once the disease had been detected, Duncan—with the cooperation of the water committee—directed the repeated washing out of crowded courts in the most infected districts. In June 1849 he arranged for the Health Committee to supply parish authorities with "the materials for lime-washing." The parish hired paupers to clean out the interiors of nearly a thousand infected houses. Meanwhile, Duncan ordered property owners in the infected districts to lime-wash the exteriors of their own buildings.[38]

Both the emergency responses to epidemics and the ongoing efforts to address housing and sanitary needs tested Liverpool's newly established sanitation system. Thomas Fresh's 1851 report included a revealing sketch of day-to-day operations: "With the view of promoting unity of action in all the departments under the Health Committee, a daily communication and co-operation has been established between the town clerk, the medical officer of health, the borough engineer, the building surveyor, the water engineer, the head constable, and the inspector of nuisances." Inspector Fresh was pleased with the new structure, which placed the various offices of the Health Committee under one roof but each with "a separate suite of offices" as well as clearly delimited roles.[39]

The Health Committee's success depended on cooperation from other city officials. Both Dr. Duncan and Inspector Fresh relied on police officers on loan from the Watch Committee to serve as inspectors and to otherwise enforce the sanitary regulations.[40] Duncan also worked closely with parochial officials in clearing and lime-washing the cellars. The inspector of nuisance's office "report[ed] cases of peculiar distress, or destitution" to the Select Vestry while, in return, receiving periodic reports of unattended nuisances from the poor relief officers. Even local charities joined in the process, reporting unhealthy cellars to the borough inspectors and sometimes promising to assist the Health Committee in keeping the cellars vacant.[41]

The Health Committee's various officers also relied on the enthusiastic cooperation of the magistrate's office. Violators of the Sanitary Act were brought before magistrate Edward Rushton. In September 1847 Rushton heard the case of a Mr. Duckworth, a builder who had been charged with refusing to build proper privies outside houses he had put up along Scotland Road. The defiant builder questioned the Health Committee's authority to require such actions, but the magistrate would have none of it, imposing a fine of £5. In the same session Rushton fined several cellar owners "for permitting their cellars to be occupied as dwellings, after having been served with notices from the Health Committee as to their illegal construction." In both cases the magistrate refused to listen to appeals for leniency, declaring his intention of supporting the Health Committee with all of his authority.[42] In a typical magistrate's session the following April, Rushton fined thirty people for operating unregistered lodging houses, twenty for letting unhealthy cellars, and ten more for failing to clean cellars after receiving notices.[43]

Sometimes friction between competing civil authorities threatened this spirit of cooperation. The Health Committee, for instance, periodically complained to the Watch Committee that police officers were failing to report nuisances encountered on their beats. The Watch Committee claimed that it was not properly reimbursed for the services of its officers on loan to the Health Committee.[44] But these minor conflicts were less persistent or damaging than the jurisdictional battles between the Health Committee and the Board of Health during the cholera crisis.

The actions of Liverpool's Health Committee during the famine migration are open to interpretation. As Duncan and Fresh were quick to point out, it would have been nearly impossible to show absolute improvements in cleanliness or declines in mortality during the years when the city was absorbing thousands of famine migrants. Instead, both preferred to stress the incremental gains measured in cellars closed, lodging houses registered, middens emptied, and new regulations passed. In an organizational sense, the years from 1847 until 1851 also demonstrated the efficiency of Liverpool's new Sanitary Act. The popular concern for the state of local health and sanitation, which provided the impetus for the 1846 legislation, only grew during the famine years. Even if the most unsanitary streets were concentrated in heavily Irish neighborhoods along the docks, Liverpool's cleanliness remained a broad concern. In fact, the popular sense of crisis helped ensure the cooperation of public officials and private citizens who, following the metaphoric logic of the diseased social body, discussed sanitary reform much as they debated competing cholera treatments.

On the other hand, the human price of these reforms—particularly the wholesale cellar removals—was high, and the poor cellar occupants were not willing participants in the Health Committee's grand plan. Although filthy and disease-ridden, the cellars and lodging houses were often the migrants' only housing options. The inspector of nuisances regularly discovered that cleared cellars had been reoccupied, often by Irish immigrants. By the end of 1849 roughly three thousand cellars had been cleared for a second time. In many cases the occupants tried to circumvent the regulations, which outlawed *overnight* occupation, by removing their bedding during the day. Duncan's solution was to limit the rate of cellar clearings in hopes that other housing would keep pace. But by the mid-1840s Liverpool's builders had begun to shift their energies away from working-class housing, further limiting the options for even those new arrivals who could afford something beyond the unsanitary cellars.[45] The migrants' own interests were no better served by a collective understanding of the social body—which essentially cast them in the role of diseased parts—than they were by a rigid adherence to free market principles.

SANITARY REFORM IN PHILADELPHIA

In the years before the famine migration, concerns about public health and sanitation did not dominate debates in Philadelphia as they did in Liverpool. Residents routinely complained about certain homes or businesses, and calls for improved street cleaning were almost a summer ritual, but overall the citizenry celebrated its city as unusually clean and airy. Thus, Philadelphia's sanitary structure in the mid-1840s was designed to maintain a fundamental level of street cleaning while responding to complaints where needed.

At the center of that sanitary structure was the countywide Board of Health, which met weekly during most of the year and daily once the quarantine season began each June 1. In addition to inspecting incoming vessels and administering the quarantine, the board enforced Philadelphia's sanitary regulations.[46] Twelve subcommittees, including the sanitary and nuisances committees, attended to most of the day-to-day operations. Lacking Liverpool's network of nuisance inspectors and police officers, Philadelphia's Board of Health responded primarily to written complaints about unsanitary "nuisances" from individual citizens. Typically the board ordered an inspector to the scene and, if necessary, called for the removal of the offending nuisance, occasionally levying fines on individual property owners. The board also periodically responded to complaints about businesses or crowded housing by sending out investigatory committees. Thus, whereas representatives of Liverpool's officialdom regularly entered neighborhoods *in search of* dangerous nuisances, Philadelphia's authorities usually only responded to explicit complaints or petitions.[47]

Whereas the Board of Health had various regulatory and investigatory responsibilities, the city and district governments retained authority over sanitary functions requiring more substantial budgets. The Council's joint committee on highways attended to street paving, repairs, and nuisances in the street; the joint sanitary board controlled the street cleaning funds. The district commissioners directed similar activities beyond the city limits.[48] As in Liverpool, Philadelphia's Board of Health sometimes worked with other public agencies. For instance, in August 1848, as the heat of summer threatened public health, Board of Health president John Lindsay wrote to the Council "urging that the streets, lanes, and alleys of the city, be cleansed and scraped twice a week, and the gutters cleansed by running water on each day." The Council referred the request to its committee on cleansing, which negotiated a new agreement with its street cleaning contractors. A few weeks later the board sent a similar communication to the commissioners of Northern Liberties, who made a special appropriation to its highway committee.[49] On other occasions, violators of local sanitary ordinances appeared before the court of quarter sessions, much like Liverpool's magistrates' courts dealt with local transgressors.[50]

Although the 1848–49 cholera epidemic did not hit Philadelphia as hard as Liverpool, the approaching scourge provided the city with a significant test of its sanitary apparatus. The report from the English sanitary commissioners, blaming the disease's spread on atmospheric moisture, gave Philadelphians a focus for their preparations. In November the sanitary committee of the Board of Health published an eight-page pamphlet "embracing certain sanitary suggestions and recommendations." The report emphasized the need for improved public hygiene, street cleaning, and sewerage, with special attention directed to the "narrow courts and alleys, crowded densely with inhabitants." In addition to these immediate measures, the committee called for long-term legislation providing "for free ventilation in the construction of houses for the poorer classes, a better supply and use of water, and a restricted number of inhabitants to houses of limited dimensions."[51]

In the ensuing weeks the city rallied to the committee's call. The Council and the Kensington Board of Commissioners made express appropriations for street and gutter cleaning while calling on citizens to be vigilant in reporting nuisances. The *Ledger* promptly became an enthusiastic cleanliness advocate, stressing that the task demanded participation from citizens and officeholders alike. When Moyamensing's commissioners were slow to follow the Board of Health's advice, the newspaper took them to task, pointing out that the district's courts and alleys were overcrowded and in desperate need of cleaning.[52] In this fashion, the committee's report and the ensuing public discussion focused on Philadelphia's worst neighborhoods and housing.

For the next six months Philadelphians gradually grafted a set of emergency procedures onto their existing sanitary apparatus. The Board of Health appointed district sanitary agents to visit homes, factories, and vacant lots, reporting nuisances to the board's new district committees. In the meantime, commissioners in Kensington, Moyamensing, and Spring Garden hired special agents or assigned police officers and other public officials to make similar reports to the board. Moreover, newspapers and public officials continued to call on citizens to report nuisances.[53]

The following May the *Ledger* congratulated its readers for having successfully avoided cholera to that point. "This exemption," the paper suggested, "is no doubt the result of the pains taken to remove all the predisposing causes to disease which exist in *unclean streets* and impure corners, and it is only by a renewed effort and a more thorough and general cleansing of the city, with precaution on the part of our citizens and particular attention to diet, that we hope to keep off the evil altogether." Once the first cases of the disease were reported in Philadelphia, the Board of Health advocated an escalation of street cleaning and nuisance removal. The Council named a special sanitary committee that met daily to cooperate with the Board of Health and appropriated $10,000 for special street and gutter cleaning. The Council also divided Philadelphia into districts, with each councillor agreeing to visit his district three times a week to check for nuisances and provide cleaning materials. The commissioners of Northern Liberties, Spring Garden, and Kensington also each appointed a sanitary committee to inspect their streets and hired cartmen for additional refuse collection.[54] Meanwhile, Board of Health agents continued to patrol Philadelphia's streets, concentrating on the most infected districts. If, on later inspection, the nuisances had not been removed, the agents reported the infraction to the health officer for prosecution. (Supplementary legislation in April 1849 eased the board's task by empowering it "to remove the cause of nuisances" as well as the nuisances themselves.)[55]

Although it did not demand wholesale removals comparable to Dr. Duncan's campaign against cellars in Liverpool, Philadelphia's Board of Health did have the authority to evict people from housing that it deemed overcrowded, unsanitary, or diseased.[56] In June 1849 the board's agents reported on "the state of a number of adjoining dwelling houses in the city, occupied by *colored families*. Many of the rooms were not more than ten feet square, and the inmates of the same from three to eight, with accumulations of filth from cellar to garret." The board required the owners "to reduce the number of tenants one half, and cleanse the entire premises within 48 hours." Later that month health inspectors, responding to complaints, visited the Liverpool House—a waterfront boarding house on the corner of Ten Alley and Water Street that catered to "the lowest class of sailors and emigrants"—and found thirty-six beds crowded into the tiny, filthy building. The Board of Health promptly ordered the lodging house closed down until it was properly cleaned and threatened to take similar measures against neighboring establishments.[57]

After the epidemic had passed, the Board of Health issued an extensive report on its emergency activities. In the twelve months beginning in October 1848 the board had removed—or caused to be removed—6,573 nuisances in the city and surrounding districts. This figure included nearly 3,500 privies cleaned or purified, 918 "hog pens removed," and more than 100 stables and slaughterhouses removed. In recounting its emergency activities, the board expanded on familiar themes. "Whilst our City may enjoy, and well deserves the credit of being the cleanest in the Union," the board reported, "it must not be denied, that there do exist localities, and there may be found spots, hidden from the public eye, where nuisances of the worst kind abound, generating and entailing disease, and sowing the seeds of physical death upon all around." Once again, the board took notice of the primarily black and Irish Moyamensing neighborhoods around Baker and Bedford Streets, the scenes of "moral debasement and physical disorder . . . the very hot-beds of everything offensive and disgusting." But unlike the "mapping" of earlier years, the 1849 report painted with a broad brush, criticizing Southwark—a heavily Irish district—for the unclean "character of a portion of its inhabitants that reside in the more densely populated neighborhoods and to its numerous, confined, and illy ventilated courts and alleys" and assailing portions of Richmond—north of the city along the Delaware River—for the "character, habits, and occupations of a larger portion of its population." By October 1849 the board had ordered 561 cellars, 194 alleys, 340 houses, and 384 yards cleaned. Moreover, it reported that it had closed 63 houses, including 35 in the city proper and 15 in Moyamensing.[58]

Although Philadelphia's emergency responses to the cholera epidemic, in both the city and the surrounding districts, expanded on established sanitation practices, they did not break much new ground. The Board of Health adopted a more aggressive, proactive role, hiring agents to seek out nuisances rather than relying primarily on citizens' complaints. But these expanded efforts were of limited duration and paled in comparison with the emergency cleaning and cellar clearing in Liverpool supervised by Dr. Duncan and his colleagues (who, of course, faced far worse conditions). Meanwhile, despite the board's developing role, Philadelphia's various sanitary functions continued to be divided among a variety of local and countywide bodies.

The differences in their experiences reflect the extent of the challenge, the timing of events, and the theoretical understanding of the relationship between the individual and the larger society. Certainly Liverpool faced worse sanitary problems and a graver cholera threat. These differences were both a symptom and a cause of broader distinctiveness. Liverpool's more aggressive responses also reflected the contingency of events. The famine migration and the cholera epidemic became crucial tests for the city's newly established health bureaucracy. Although the crises slowed some of Duncan's larger plans, the prior existence of the MOH and the Health Committee gave Liverpool's operations a broader impact than that of Philadelphia's explicitly limited emergency measures. Finally, the image of the social body—more prominent in English discourse—helped mediate against the pull of individualism that remained the dominant American dogma. American individualism, and its corollary emphasis on the protection of private property, ensured that under normal circumstances individual citizens—not government agents—would be responsible for reporting unsanitary public nuisances,[59] and public officials would not have the same freedom to order wholesale evictions that Duncan exercised so freely. The periodic eviction of African Americans is the exception demonstrating the rule: In practice, this understanding of individual liberties, like many others, apparently varied along racial lines.

BROADER INITIATIVES

The popular interest in sanitation and public health, coupled with rising population densities, helped spur a variety of broader public and private initiatives in American and English cities. A brief survey of the debates surrounding three of these proposed reforms—expanded water supply, public baths, and model housing—will indicate further similarities between Liverpool and Philadelphia, as well as revealing differences in their responses to shared challenges.

Water and Sewers

During the second half of the 1840s—in the midst of concern for poor relief, epidemic disease, and sectarian conflict—much of Liverpool's most heated political rhetoric focused on water. For years city water had been supplied, however inadequately, by two private companies. In 1845 the Highway Board ordered an investigation into the complaints against the companies. The *Mercury* filled its pages with attacks on the greedy private suppliers, while Harmood Banner, representing the Liverpool and Harrington works, penned lengthy rebuttals. The Liverpool Corporation Waterworks Act of 1847 gave the Corporation the authority to purchase existing companies, which it did the following year. But the complaints about the water supply continued, leading to the controversial Rivington Pike scheme to pipe in water from distant rivers. The anti-Pikists attacked the expense of such an arrangement, preferring a more moderate solution involving local waterworks. After a lengthy round of debates the Pikists managed to secure parliamentary approval, despite opposition in the cost-conscious Council. By 1857 Liverpool was enjoying a steady supply of water piped from Rivington, at an ultimate cost of £1,345,969.[60] In the meantime, John Newlands, Liverpool's new borough engineer, was busy proposing extensive additions to the Corporation's sewage and drainage system. Under Newlands, Liverpool nearly doubled its street sewage system by adding forty-six miles of sewers and main drains by 1858.[61]

Travelers to Philadelphia routinely visited the famed Fairmount Waterworks on the Schuylkill River, where they marveled at the system of basins and waterwheels that pumped water throughout the city. The rapidly growing outlying districts followed various strategies for supplying water. Southwark and Moyamensing contracted to purchase water from Fairmount. Beginning in 1844, Spring Garden and Northern Liberties shared the costs of pumping their own water from the Schuylkill. Between 1845 and 1850 Kensington purchased water through the Spring Garden and Northern Liberties Joint Watering Committee, an arrangement that Kensington's commissioners eventually found too limiting. When Isaac Parrish surveyed Philadelphia's sanitary conditions in 1849, he emphasized the benefits of the city's "abundant supply of excellent water." [62] Parrish also praised the quality of the surface drainage of Philadelphia streets, as well as the system of twenty-seven and one-half miles of public sewers in the city and surrounding districts. But in the next few years both Wilson Jewell and Samuel Kneass, the city surveyor, criticized the quality and scale of Philadelphia's sewage system.[63]

By midcentury both Philadelphia and Liverpool had been recognized for their comparatively advanced water and sewage systems. And following Liverpool's purchase of its two private water providers, both cities had municipally owned utilities. How do these advances connect to our larger themes? In each city, proponents of improved water and sewage systems emphasized their potential benefits to public health, particularly for the poor. In Liverpool, where water supplies were often irregular, advocates of change drew direct links between cholera and inadequate water and sewer systems.[64] City councillor Samuel Holme declared in 1847 that he would rather spend public money on John Newlands's proposed sewer expansion than on relieving the incoming Irish poor. The former, he argued, would have a much more profound impact on public health.[65] Philadelphians expanded the city's water and sewage systems more gradually, largely because the period of sanitary introspection after the cholera epidemic found fewer problems requiring immediate attention.[66]

Public Baths

By the mid-nineteenth century medical experts had repeatedly drawn links between personal cleanliness and disease, often directing their attention to the urban poor. In the meantime, the middle classes celebrated cleanliness as evidence of moral virtue. It was only fitting that personal hygiene would become a focus for public policy. One response was the creation of public baths, offering the working poor—who often had only irregular access to running water—free or inexpensive bathing facilities.[67]

By the time of the famine migration, Liverpool already had an established history of public baths. In 1828 the Corporation opened St. George's Bath, constructed with public funds but charging modest fees to users. Four years later Kitty Wilkinson won national fame by inviting neighbors to use her kitchen to wash the clothing of cholera victims. In the years to come, Wilkinson, the wife of a Liverpool laborer, expanded her operations into a neighboring cellar with the assistance of the District Provident Society and leading Unitarian William Rathbone.[68]

With concern over disease and sanitation mounting, Parliament passed legislation in 1846 permitting local authorities to run bath and wash houses for the poor. In fact, Liverpool's Council acted long before this legislation, opening baths for the poor in 1841. But following the new legislation, and urged on by the enthusiastic support of the Health of Towns' Association, the Council voted to invest £9,000 in new baths and washhouses at Paul Street. The new baths experiment proved a tremendous success. Within ten months the Paul Street baths had received over 50,000 visitors, leading one councillor to call them "the greatest boon the people of Liverpool had ever received" and generating calls for new baths throughout the parish. The Council soon agreed to build new baths in Upper Frederick Street in the southern part of the city, under the supervision of none other than Kitty Wilkinson. In February the two locations served more than 2,400 men, 200 women, and 1,351 children, including 245 ragged school pupils. They also provided nearly 4,400 tubs for clothes washing. That spring the Health Committee sent a delegation to visit London's new baths; it returned home to Liverpool with ambitious plans for further construction. The expansion of public baths, and the cooperation of public authorities and private philanthropists, continued in 1849 when the Health Committee worked with the Rathbones to establish new baths on Cornwallis Street.[69]

The public baths were not established as pure charities. The organizers aimed their services at the city's working poor, who could afford small fees, as opposed to local paupers. The Paul Street baths were self-supporting almost from the outset. The Council did not object to providing free baths to children from St. Bartholomew's Ragged School, but they doubted that the busy baths could accommodate the added demand and they appeared unwilling to make any special arrangements. But with the rising concern over epidemic disease, the baths took to accepting penniless paupers as well as paying members of the working poor.[70] In less than a generation, an institution that had grown out of spontaneous private benevolence during the 1832 cholera epidemic had evolved into a citywide network of public bathhouses supported by national legislation.

In the United States, concerns for sanitation converged with the new water cure craze, which attracted support from the likes of health reformer Sylvester Graham. In the summer of 1848, as Philadelphia's Board of Health was gearing up for its intensive cleaning efforts, local charities took up the board's call for improved public hygiene. The Philadelphia Society for the Employment and Instruction of the Poor (PSEIP) offered washtubs and free public baths in its new House of Industry in Moyamensing. The following summer the American Medical Association's Committee on Public Hygiene responded to cholera fears by proposing cheap public baths for the nation's urban poor. Milwaukee established special baths for arriving immigrants, but most other cities failed to answer the call. In Philadelphia, the Northern Dispensary began offering free baths to poor women, and a new organization of "philanthropic ladies" opened an establishment on North Fourth Street promising "free baths for respectable females."[71]

The city's modest private efforts met with public approval but failed to gain official support. In 1848 the PSEIP petitioned the Council for free Schuylkill water for its baths. The *Ledger* thought this an excellent idea, as the cost of supplying the water was likely to be much cheaper than supporting diseased paupers at the almshouse. But the Council's watering committee refused the request, forcing the PSEIP to rely on its own resources. Three years later Wilson Jewell included a call for public baths in his list of suggested reforms, reasoning that they were one of the best vehicles for giving Philadelphia's poorest residents access to the city's ample water supply.[72] In 1853 Samuel Kneass, the city surveyor, told the Council that the availability of public baths "at little or no charge, cannot be too strongly insisted on, as connected with the hygiene of a city in such a latitude and climate as ours, as the free use of ablutions cannot be too largely encouraged, especially in a city so heavily devoted to manufactures as Philadelphia."[73] Despite such persistent opinions from local health and sanitation experts, Philadelphia's public officials continued to emphasize limited emergency responses to existing problems rather than aggressive, tax-funded preventive measures.

Elsewhere in the United States the experience was similar. Despite the widespread belief that baths helped fight disease and periodic calls for publicly financed baths, antebellum American cities failed to respond. In 1849 the New York legislature authorized the Association for Improving the Condition of the Poor (AICP) to offer public baths. The AICP's baths finally opened in the Lower East Side in 1852, providing nearly sixty thousand men and women a year with bathing and laundry facilities for a modest fee.[74] Nonetheless, America's public officials—local, state, and national—did not approach the government initiatives already under way across the Atlantic.

Model Housing

Urban reformers agreed that the problems of filth and disease required immediate sanitary measures, but many also concluded that the long-term solutions lay in rethinking housing for the working poor. Although it would be some time before either city constructed public housing, the midcentury housing discussions are an interesting reflection of contemporary assumptions, once again suggesting a greater English receptivity to publicly funded solutions.

Across the River Mersey, Liverpudlians gazed approvingly on the model worker housing constructed by the Birkenhead Dock Company. The *Mercury* noted that Liverpool's policy of taxing housing by the number of windows made it more difficult to imitate the Birkenhead example. The paper declared: "In vain shall we expect to find a healthy, happy, and moral people, until they are provided with comfortable dwellings, into which the air and light of heaven shall freely enter, and where they shall be removed from those scenes of filth and abomination by which many of them, from no fault of their own are now surrounded."[75]

In early 1848 a local architect, a Mr. Harris, presented the Liverpool Health of Towns' Committee with plans for local model housing. The *Mercury* threw its weight behind Harris's plan, insisting that the new housing would replace insalubrious cellars, thus improving Liverpool's poor reputation. Soon other locals entered the debate. Some argued for renovating vacant warehouses to house workers who had been displaced from cellars. One correspondent to the *Mercury* contended that more attention to worker housing, rather than religious instruction and the like, was the best solution to crime and other urban problems. Another writer called for the formation of a joint-stock company "whose object should be to throw down all courts or cottages condemned by the Health Committee, and to rebuild them on the most approved modern plan, thereby insuring a *through ventilation.* The fearful disorder now raging throughout Liverpool may be attributed, in a great measure, to the want of a purer atmosphere, and until this blessing is obtained, drainage, a supply of water, baths, washhouses, &c, are secondary considerations." Clearly some local citizens had come to see improved housing as the solution to various social ills.[76]

Some local businesses followed the Birkenhead Dock's example by experimenting with model worker housing; the most famous of such projects was the Prince Albert Cottages on Frederick Street. But costs limited the potential of private initiatives. In fact, one historian has argued that in the years immediately preceding the Irish famine migration, Liverpool builders shifted their investment from traditional worker housing to more expensive forms of housing.[77] Even the more innovative models for workers failed to address Liverpool's greater problem of housing for the poor.

In 1851 Parliament passed legislation permitting town councils and local boards of health to erect and maintain lodging houses for the laboring classes. Dr. Duncan urged the borough to take advantage of this option by building "a *model* lodging-house, — not designed to compete with already existing houses, but simply as a practical illustration to builders, of the possibility of erecting convenient and wholesome dwellings at no greater cost than inconvenient and unwholesome ones." Three years later Francis Bishop of the Domestic Mission Society called on the Liverpool Council to construct "a class of large and well-arranged houses, separated into apartments for the poorest class of the people, and to be let at the smallest possible rent. Such dwellings would not only tend to raise the morals of the community, but check the spread of fever, cholera, and other 'malignant diseases.'" It was well over a decade before the Council acted on such suggestions, finally opening St. Martin's Cottages — among England's first Council houses — in 1869.[78]

Philadelphians were well aware of the British discussion of model housing. But despite occasional approving comments, the city did not seriously contemplate publicly funded housing for the poor. In January 1847 a *Public Ledger* editorial connected poverty, immorality, and disorder with inadequate local housing and high rents, and noted recent housing experiments in Boston. The newspaper called on "some of our benevolent Quakers who 'invest in real estate'" to look into these ideas. Subsequent editorials and articles kept the discussion alive, proposing various plans to improve economic efficiency, sanitation, and morality. In one of its most radical statements, the *Ledger* declared that "it is high time for our laws to lend a helping hand to [reduce] poverty." "Human virtues cannot thrive in pig-pens," the editorial insisted. It urged the "most afflicted" districts to construct low-rent housing in the worst neighborhoods, thus providing public revenue while reducing crime, immorality, and disease. A few months later the newspaper once again took up the issue of "dwellings for the poor," praising Liverpool for closing poorly ventilated cellars and applauding housing efforts in New York and Boston.[79]

In his 1856 report to the Philadelphia County Medical Society, Wilson Jewell addressed the problem of "dwellings and social condition of the poor," concluding that the city's "overcrowded, filthy, damp, unventilated tenements" were "nurseries of beggary, depravity and sickness." The various "philanthropic efforts to remedy this eyesore," he argued, had "scarcely accomplished the first step, in a sanitary point of view, towards reforming their domestic habits, or removing them from their dark and dreary homes of physical obscurity and moral degradation." The solution was "the establishment of model dwelling and lodging-houses under proper management, in various parts of our city." To support his proposal, Jewell cited the work of British sanitarian Dr. Southwood Smith, who reported improved sanitation and health in London's model dwellings.[80]

Such proposals never won substantial support in Philadelphia. Despite encountering periodic descriptions of unsanitary dwellings, most policymakers remained satisfied that housing in the "city of homes" surpassed that of other American or European cities. Not until the Great Depression did Philadelphia, with the assistance of federal initiatives, turn to public housing. Even in New York City, where population density created a true housing crisis, talk of model housing initially fell on deaf ears. The city's Association for Improving the Condition of the Poor experimented, unsuccessfully, with a model tenement in 1854. In 1867, as Liverpool was planning its Council housing, New York passed the Tenement House Law. This legislation was an important milestone in American urban housing in that the state General Assembly gave the city's new Metropolitan Board of Health authority to regulate privately owned housing.[81] Still, New York's revolutionary law assumed that the state would only regulate private property for the public good, rather than proposing that the government should compete with private enterprise in providing public housing.

CONCLUSION

By the mid-nineteenth century the insalubrious environment had become a central trope for urban reformers. Disease, immorality, ignorance, and crime were not merely, or even principally, perceived as products of personal failings or divine wrath. Rather, such disamenities flourished in filthy streets and poorly ventilated cellars. Spurred on by mass migrations and epidemic disease, sanitarians on both sides of the Atlantic churned out reports advocating environmental reforms. Even where they faced differing physical environments and political climates, these reformers worked from a shared set of assumptions and routinely drew on each other's writings and experiences.

It comes as no surprise, then, that Philadelphia and Liverpool undertook many of the same environmental reforms at roughly the same time. Both cities responded to fears of epidemic disease by "mapping" their worst neighborhoods and enacting emergency measures to address the most pressing sanitary and housing dilemmas. Recognizing the need for more extensive environmental measures, public officials and private reformers in both cities advocated expanded public works—particularly water and sewage—as well as public baths and model housing. In most instances Liverpool and Philadelphia were among their nations' leaders in undertaking such reforms, often trailing only London and New York City.

Although from a distant perspective the similarities between Liverpool and Philadelphia, and between England and the United States, are indeed striking, the pace and magnitude of environmental reforms were actually quite distinct. By most measures Liverpool's reforms developed more rapidly than those in Philadelphia or any other North American city. The English city had its revolutionary health and sanitation apparatus, led by Dr. Duncan and Thomas Fresh, in place before the famine migration began. And whereas Philadelphia relied on a vigilant citizenry to report sanitary nuisances, Liverpool had an established network of public officers charged with seeking out sanitary violators. In response to the cholera crisis, Philadelphia and its neighboring districts named special sanitary committees, adopted emergency cleaning measures, and hired agents to report dangerous nuisances. During the same period Liverpool—which already had similar measures in place—undertook an aggressive policy of cellar inspections and forced removals, far exceeding Philadelphia's limited efforts to close the city's worst lodging houses. Liverpool's sewage, baths, and public housing reforms also proceeded further and faster than their American counterparts, with a far greater assumption of local government responsibility and national government input.

In both England and the United States these environmental reforms faced a mountain of structural and attitudinal resistance. A crucial triumvirate of values—tradition, localism, and the sanctity of private property—stood in the way of most of these initiatives. And if ideology alone was not a sufficient barrier, most environmental reforms came with a price that was more immediate and apparent than any potential benefit to the community. As Gerry Kearns has noted, the progress of England's public health reform owed much to Chadwick's successful integration of his own ideas about collectivism with the firmly held faith in private enterprise. The solution, Kearns argues, was not to cast public health reform and private property as antithetical, but rather to convince the electorate that the obstacles to "the sanitary idea" were in fact vested interests intrinsically at odds with private property.[82]

Such arguments make the important point that British health and sanitation reforms, even when prodded along by national investigations and advocates, never completely jettisoned the ideals of local control and private property.[83] Nonetheless, the contrast with the United States is telling. Dr. Duncan and his colleagues used the weight of national legislation to impose reform on private property owners, to say nothing of the immigrants themselves. Philadelphians, in comparison, adopted short-term emergency measures to clean the public streets but refused to support public baths, public housing, or large-scale eviction. Other prominent U.S. cities were similarly cautious in their approach to private property, opting for modest regulation rather than public ownership.[84] Even moderate American reforms came from local sources (sometimes with state legislative support) with no federal role whatsoever.

What explains the differences between the British and American cities? One explanation would emphasize differing ideologies: Philadelphians were simply more tenacious in their devotion to localism, voluntarism, and private property, resisting any talk of government encroachment in the name of sanitarianism. Another approach would stress the objective difference in the challenges faced by the two cities. Liverpool supported broader measures because the Irish immigrants created an environmental crisis far surpassing that experienced anywhere in North America. There is truth to both views. Certainly Liverpool had more migrants, particularly when one considers those who passed through the port on their way to other destinations. But on the other hand, Liverpool had a terrible health reputation and undertook revolutionary sanitary reforms *before* the famine. A full explanation must incorporate differences in the power of fundamental values and ideas as well as a recognition that the cities had measurable ecological and demographic differences, both before and during the famine. The English in general, and Liverpudlians in particular, were more receptive to challenges to localism, voluntarism, and private property, partially because new approaches to national reform and the centralization and expansion of local administration were wrapped in the rhetoric of protecting private enterprise (and in Liverpool's case, the protection of the port's commercial reputation) and in the metaphoric notion of ministering to the social body. American sanitarians, faced with more limited environmental problems and a political culture that was more vehemently resistant to government imposition, turned more slowly to a mosaic of regulations, often only enforced following private petitions.[85]

Analysis of these environmental reforms, coupled with the health reforms discussed in the previous chapter, must also address the distinctive characteristics attributed to the Irish poor. One might reasonably have supposed that the Liverpudlians would have viewed the Irish immigrants as their United Kingdom neighbors rather than as true foreigners. But, in fact, sanitarians in England and the United States appeared equally likely to link unclean personal habits to ethnic traits. And certainly Liverpool's ratepayers treated the Irish paupers as "others," rather than national brethren, when the migrants were forcibly evicted from cellars and sent home across the Irish Sea. The next two chapters examine the implications of the Irish immigrants' distinct religious and ethnic identities as those identities shaped local religious, benevolent, and educational institutions and as they created a complex interplay between the forces of disorder and order in each city.

6. Sectarian Conflicts: Churches and Schools

INTRODUCTION: IRISH IMMIGRANTS AND CATHOLIC COMMUNITIES

Our attention thus far has been directed at the real burdens and perceived threats posed by the sheer numbers of Irish famine migrants, compounded by their poverty, ill-health, and, in the eyes of many, uncleanliness. The famine migrants also presented intertwined sectarian and ethnic challenges to their host cities. Although earlier generations of Irish migrants were predominantly Protestant, the paupers who fled the famine were overwhelmingly—if sometimes only nominally—Roman Catholics.[1]

In both Liverpool and Philadelphia the immigrants found established Catholic communities. In addition to the parish churches, their new worlds included a wide array of Irish clubs, associations, and benevolent societies.[2] But neither established churches nor clubs guaranteed the immigrants an easy transition into societies dominated by Protestant majorities. Moreover, the huge influx of Irish Catholics in each city threatened to destabilize various institutional balances, thus creating the potential for serious sectarian and ethnic clashes.

This and the following chapter explore some of the repercussions of the Irish inflow. How did the native Catholic communities respond to the demands posed by these poor newcomers? How strong were the "anti-popery" forces in each city, and how did these hostilities evolve in the face of thousands of new Catholics? How, if at all, did public institutions—workhouses, schools, prisons—accommodate religious diversity? Both cities experienced extended sectarian conflicts over religious instruction in the local school systems. This chapter will close with a comparison of these educational battles and their aftermaths, providing a useful case study in institutional development. The subsequent chapter concentrates on cul-

tural and political conflicts and the development of police and penal institutions in each city. The concerns in these two chapters—the first emphasizing the sectarian and institutional, the second the social and cultural
—are intertwined. Although they may be pulled apart for examination, our
eventual conclusions must consider the combined effect of their evolving
religious and ethnic compositions on Liverpool and Philadelphia.

One key similarity provides an important context to this analysis: sectarian and ethnic tensions were deeply woven into the fabric of life in
both cities long before the famine migration. Each had high-profile Protestant ministers who routinely impugned Catholic teachings. Local Catholic priests, in turn, were skeptical about evangelical plots to convert their
flocks. Working-class Protestants and Catholics clashed over organizational
and geographic turf in ways that reflected each city's cultural traditions.
Often the most violent disputes were between Irish Protestants and Irish
Catholics. The famine migrants did not create any of these hostilities, although their numbers helped inflame long-standing conflicts, as did the
widely held prejudices about their cleanliness, personal habits, and perceived intemperance. But a full analysis of the issues will require a comparison of events and institutions beyond the chronological limits of the
famine itself and—where appropriate—consideration of the experiences
of other demographic groups in each city.

THE RELIGIOUS LANDSCAPE

England's 1851 census of religious worship, part of the national census
for that year, provides a useful if imprecise portrait of organized religion
in Liverpool at midcentury. Of 153 places of worship reported in the borough, 56 were Anglican, 62 were Nonconformist—representing a wide array of Protestant sects—and 13 were Roman Catholic. The official returns
recorded nearly 173,000 worshipers on census day, with 70,321 (40.7 percent) Anglican, 46,789 (27 percent) Nonconformist, and 52,005 (30.1 percent) Catholic. In contrast, the combined figures for England and Wales
were 48.6 percent Church of England, 47.4 percent Nonconformist, and
only 3.5 percent Roman Catholic. The census revealed a prospect of which
Liverpool's Catholic leaders were all too aware: that the famine migration
threatened to overwhelm local Catholic institutions. With nearly a third of
the census-day attendees, local Catholic priests reported a capacity of only
11,332 seats, roughly 10 percent of the borough churches' total capacity.[3]

The census estimated church attendance for a single day; it certainly was not an exact measure of religious affiliation or even of the relative weight of different religions in the population.[4] By some estimates, at least half of the Irish immigrants had not been regular churchgoers in their native land. Perhaps a third or less of the migrants who would have described themselves as Irish Catholics regularly attended church in England.[5] The fact that it was impossible to obtain a firm estimate of Liverpool Catholics at midcentury did not discourage contemporaries from taking on the task. The diocesan office estimated that there were 106,000 Liverpool Catholics in 1850;[6] in 1858 Abraham Hume guessed that there had been 81,000 Roman Catholics in 1851. W. J. Lowe has concluded that both figures are too low, but that the diocesan number was not far off the mark.[7]

In the half century preceding the 1851 census, Liverpool's Catholic community had experienced substantial demographic and political change. Between the 1801 Act of Union, which brought Ireland under parliamentary control as part of the United Kingdom, and the Catholic Emancipation Act of 1829, which finally allowed Catholics and Nonconformists to vote and hold office, Liverpool's Catholic population grew steadily. At the turn of the century there were only three Catholic chapels in Liverpool. By 1811 over 21,000 Catholics—largely Irish—lived in the parish. In 1830 a local Catholic leader estimated that between 50,000 and 60,000 Catholics lived in Liverpool. As the population expanded in the next decade, the local Roman Catholic church did its best to grow apace. Catholic committees raised funds and constructed churches in the north and the south of the city. Although these new churches were built to serve new Irish migrants, Catholic historian Thomas Burke argued that they were funded principally by wealthier English Catholics. In the 1840s five new Catholic churches opened in the borough, largely—but not exclusively—to address the needs of the poor Irish communities. By 1851 there were twelve Catholic churches in the borough, half in the densely Irish neighborhoods to the north. Still, in 1846 the *Catholic Directory* listed only twenty-one priests in the town of Liverpool.[8]

The Roman Catholic Church and particularly individual parish priests played a vital part in shaping the rural Irish community. In both England and the United States, parish priests assumed a similar, if less powerful, role in the cultural and spiritual lives of the Irish migrants, even when some members of their flock rarely saw the inside of a church. As we saw in the discussions of poverty and disease, Liverpool's clergymen had important personal contacts with the Irish paupers, many falling victim to typhus after ministering to diseased migrants. Although most of Liverpool's priests were themselves English, for the Irish immigrants—who were almost exclusively Catholic—identification with the church blended religious faith and nationalism. As we shall see, the priests made some attempts to control Irish processions and other potentially disruptive political events.[9]

The records suggest that even in the years *before* the famine migration it was all that Liverpool's Catholics could do to support local churches and schools, with only modest sums left over for the poor. From 1810 until the mid-1840s the Liverpool Catholic Benevolent Society raised small amounts through collections, which were distributed to the needy by parish priests. During the 1830s the society's subscriptions totaled between £222 and £423 a year. In 1839 the society received a huge £1,077 windfall from the proceeds of a charity bazaar, but by 1845 the society's funds had dwindled to almost nothing. It would not be until 1850 that Liverpool's Catholic Club acted to reinvigorate the moribund charity.[10] The Catholic Club, founded in 1844, brought together middle-class Liverpool Catholics for charitable, social, and political activities, but it is unclear what charitable efforts the club made during the famine years.[11] Meanwhile, the Society of Saint Vincent de Paul established a branch in Liverpool in 1845. By the end of the decade this Catholic charity had visited three hundred local families. Local Catholics also supported a small Catholic Orphan Asylum, which moved into new quarters in 1843; the Catholic Society of Mercy; and a Catholic Blind Asylum run by the Sisters of Charity.[12] Liverpool had no Catholic newspaper during the late 1840s; in the early 1850s three Catholic newspapers failed after brief appearances.[13]

Philadelphia's Catholic population, like Liverpool's, grew rapidly in the second quarter of the nineteenth century. In 1834 Bishop Francis Patrick Kenrick penned a lengthy portrait of the Philadelphia diocese, which at the time spanned Pennsylvania, Delaware, and western New Jersey and included roughly 100,000 Catholics. Kenrick, who had been bishop for only four years, noted that he was responsible for a diverse population consisting mostly of first- or second-generation migrants from Ireland, Germany, and—to a lesser degree—France. Kenrick reported that Philadelphia City's estimated 25,000 Catholics had only five churches, each served by two priests, with a sixth church under construction to the north of the city and a seventh desperately needed to the south.[14] Over the next two decades the energetic Kenrick oversaw the building of dozens of new churches in the city and across the diocese. In 1851 his diocese had grown to 92 churches, with 101 priests, serving a population of 170,000, and Kenrick had established himself as America's leading "building bishop." By the time of the 1854 consolidation, Philadelphia—which now encompassed the surrounding county—boasted 26 parish churches. Two of the churches founded during the 1840s had German congregations, but most of this building was in response to the heavy Irish migration into the city and surrounding districts.[15]

There is no good contemporary estimate of the number of Catholics in Philadelphia County at midcentury similar to the estimates for Liverpool. Following the riots of 1844 (discussed below) Catholic laity claimed that the city had "60,000 [Catholic] citizens"; the committee overseeing the construction of a new cathedral used the same figure in its January 1847 report.[16] But the origin of this estimate is unclear and not necessarily comparable to the Liverpool census. If we follow the logic of the Liverpool estimates, which were little more than guesses based on the number of Irish-born residents, we might reasonably conclude that Philadelphia's Catholic leaders—with 12,000 fewer Irish immigrants but nearly 23,000 German immigrants in 1850—drew from a slightly larger potential flock.

Whatever the number of actual churchgoing parishioners, Philadelphia Catholics supported more churches and more benevolent institutions than their Liverpool counterparts, both before and during the famine years. The Ladies' Catholic Benevolent Society, founded in the early 1830s, dispensed food, clothing, and funds to hundreds of Philadelphia families through a network of district managers. Several parishes had sewing societies that distributed clothing—sometimes through the Benevolent Society—to the poor. The Benevolent Society's activities, both in organizational complexity and in numbers assisted, went well beyond the organized charities run by Liverpool's Catholics. By midcentury there were seven Catholic benevolent institutions in Philadelphia, including two orphanages and the newly constructed St. Joseph's Hospital. The city's Catholics also enjoyed the benefits of their own newspaper, the *Catholic Herald*.[17] Perhaps the differences between the two cities were partially owing to the greater wealth of Philadelphia Catholics, but the degree and nature of the city's Catholic organizations also suggests a more substantial national commitment to private benevolence and institution building. Moreover, according to Dale B.

Light Jr., the American Catholic Church—and the Philadelphia diocese under Bishop Kenrick—underwent widespread reforms long before such impulses took hold in England and Europe. These "restoration reforms" included extensive institutional development both in response to Catholic immigration and in order to address larger doctrinal concerns.[18]

SECTARIAN POLITICS AND EDUCATIONAL CONFLICTS

In his analysis of "No Popery politics" in Liverpool, Frank Neal identifies a triumvirate of forces that promoted local anti-Catholicism in the decades before the famine: "an ultra-Protestant Conservative caucus on the town council," the "Irish evangelical clergy," and "the Orange Order."[19] Liverpool's first instance of Irish Catholic–Orange rioting occurred in July 1819, when a large group of Irish Catholics attacked an Orange procession that had marched down Dale Street, near Vauxhall Ward. In 1826 a group of local Catholics formed the Catholic Defence Society to answer what they saw as an "abusive torrent daily pouring out from that portion of the Press engaged in the services of the religious tract societies, and the weekly stream flowing from the pulpits of itinerant and illiberal preachers." The Defence Society held a series of public meetings and distributed its pro-Catholic literature.[20] So long as Liverpool's electoral system remained in the control of the freemen, the 1829 Emancipation Bill had little effect on the limited political voice of local Catholics. But with the passage of the Municipal Corporations Act of 1835, giving the municipal franchise to adult males with two years' residency, the role of sectarian issues in local politics changed dramatically.[21] In the 1835 elections Liverpool's reformers swept into power, winning 43 of 48 seats and ousting the conservative Tories. The new town Council contained only three Catholics; roughly half of the new members were Dissenters and fifteen were Unitarians. Neither political camp had a history of anti-Catholicism. But as Neal points out, in their battle to regain control of the Council, Liverpool Tories played the anti-Catholic card at every opportunity.[22]

On gaining power, the enthusiastic reformers inadvertently handed their adversaries an ideal rallying cry by tinkering with the Corporation's school system. Since 1827 the Council had run two small Corporation schools where pupils had daily prayers and catechisms from the Anglican "Authorized Version" and were required to attend Anglican services on Sunday. Although not officially excluded, only a handful of Catholic students took advantage of this tax-supported education. In their first year in office the Liberals revised the religious component in the Corporation schools to accommodate Catholic children. Following the example set by Ireland's educational reformers, the Liberals established a system whereby students would have daily nondenominational scriptural readings and one day a week clergymen from different denominations would instruct the children from either the Authorized Version or the Douay Bible.[23] The Council's efforts at reform were apparently an innocent response to the desperate educational needs of Catholic children in Liverpool as well as a means of bringing together the city's various religious groups. As of 1830 Liverpool's Catholic schools had only eight hundred spaces. According to one estimate, nine thousand Catholic children were not attending school, a number that was bound to rise in the decades to come.[24]

The school reforms met with enthusiastic support from local Catholics and Dissenters, but vehement resistance from Anglican clergymen. In 1835 Liverpool's Anglicans established a local branch of the powerful Protestant Association. Almost immediately flamboyant Ulster clergyman Hugh M'Neile emerged as the association's most celebrated antipopery spokesman, using the school issue to bludgeon the embattled Liberals. The Protestant Association found its constituency among middle-class Anglicans. Three years later the Operative Protestant Association established a local branch, delivering an anti-Catholic message to the Protestant working classes. These two associations, dominated by Rev. M'Neile and his Irish Protestant colleagues, played an instrumental role in keeping No Popery rhetoric at the center of political discourse. Between 1836 and 1840 Liverpool Tories—profiting from this intense anti-Catholicism—made steady political inroads until finally, in 1841, they regained control of the town Council, ending the Liberals' brief reign.[25]

The newly conservative Council did not wait long to reap the spoils of victory. In early 1842 its Education Committee issued new rules requiring Corporation school pupils to read the Authorized Version of the Bible. As expected, Liverpool Catholics responded by withdrawing their children and taking steps to expand the local Catholic school system. A few years later Rev. M'Neile did some reaping of his own as he oversaw the construction of a brand new church in Toxteth, funded by Tory donations. As Neal has noted, this ugly episode in sectarian politics probably reflected some combination of heartfelt concern for the Established Church and political opportunism from those who recognized the power wielded by M'Neile and his cohorts. Whatever the origins, Liverpool's No Popery politics left a multitiered legacy for the famine migrants. On the political level, Liberals recognized the potential liabilities in appearing to cater to Catholic concerns. Moreover, the flood of anti-Catholic rhetoric established a tradition of street violence that would continue into the next decade.[26]

Irish immigrants to the United States faced the intertwined hostilities of anti-Catholicism and nativism.[27] In Philadelphia the steady rise in the Irish Catholic population created tensions both within the Catholic community and with local Protestants. As in Liverpool, Philadelphia's sectarian tensions bubbled to the surface *before* the famine migration in a dramatic conflict over public schools in which the Irish Catholics' leading adversaries were Irish Protestants. And in both cities the hostilities combined concerns over religious practices with worries about party politics.[28]

American anti-Catholicism, which Ray Billington termed "the Protestant Crusade," found a receptive home in Philadelphia in the late 1830s and 1840s. In 1837 the Native American Party, committed to restricting suffrage to native-born Americans, staged its first local meeting in Germantown. During the next decade an assortment of anti-Catholic groups coalesced as the Union of Protestant Associations; by 1842 a new Protestant Institute was distributing anti-Catholic literature, and a newspaper—the *Protestant Banner*—had begun publication. Near the end of that year many prominent Protestant clergymen, concerned about Philadelphia's rising Catholic population, assembled to form the American Protestant Association. In each of these initiatives Philadelphia's anti-Catholics were in the forefront of national intolerance.[29]

The Philadelphia-based American Sunday School Union (ASSU), founded in the mid-1820s, was typical of the city's Protestant Crusade. In 1843 the ASSU annual report announced: "We feel bound to contend earnestly, though in the spirit of love and meekness, for the principles of the Reformation, in contradistinction to the mind-enslaving and soul-destroying errors and superstitions against which those principles were arrayed in the sixteenth century." Two years later ASSU officers published a pamphlet, *Addressed to Evangelical Churches and Other Benevolent Citizens of the United States,* warning of "the spread of popish errors and delusions; the influx of foreign ignorance, superstition and vice, and the consequent depravity of morals; the corruption of social virtue and the abuse of civil liberty."[30] Between these two publications, both typical of the time, Philadelphia erupted in some of the worst rioting that the city—and the nation —had ever known.

America's battles over religion in the public schools had their origins in New York City, where the Public School Society—a Protestant benevolent group—had long controlled the bulk of the city's educational budget, guaranteeing that young scholars read only the King James Version of the Scriptures. In 1840 the New York Council voted down a petition drafted by Catholics to receive public funding for their own parochial schools. New York's Bishop John Hughes responded with a vigorous, but initially unsuccessful, public campaign to convince the Council to protect Catholic children from the Public School Society's anti-Catholic Protestant teachings. The battle continued for over a year, until the state legislature finally placed city schools under the control of school commissioners elected by each ward, allowing for—but certainly not guaranteeing—the removal of sectarian influences. This acrimonious dispute heightened the city's religious tensions and fueled nativism, while elevating Bibles in the schools to a central symbolic position.[31]

Bishop Francis Kenrick of Philadelphia watched developments in New York with interest, because pupils in his city's local schools were also required to read from the King James Bible. School officials refused Kenrick's request that young Catholics be allowed to substitute the Douay Version in their readings, ruling instead that Catholic children would be allowed to leave the room when the Bible was studied. In early 1843 Louisa Bedford, a Protestant teacher in Kensington, complained that the new policy was disrupting her classroom, prompting an Irish-American school controller to suggest that Bedford end the Bible-reading sessions entirely. When word of this action spread, local Protestants, grasping the move's tremendous symbolic value, unleashed a torrent of protest.

Kensington proved particularly ripe for violence. Long a center of Irish Protestant weavers, the northern suburb had more recently become home to newly arrived unskilled Irish Catholics. In May 1844 the nativist American Republican Association, incensed over the school controversy, staged a rally in the heart of Kensington's Irish Catholic Third Ward. A mob of local Catholics attacked the meeting, forcing their adversaries to scatter. The American Republicans returned to the Third Ward a few days later, this time with a crowd of three thousand who had answered the call of placards placed throughout the city. Rain drove the Protestants to the Third Ward's Nanny Goat Market, where tensions soon erupted in gunfire. The local Irish Catholics, firing from neighboring homes and fire stations, had the better of the first day's fighting, but that night the nativists began their retaliation, burning homes and churches before the state militia finally stepped in. In three days of rioting fifty people were injured and $150,000 in property destroyed. Three months later a crowd of nativists attacked St. Philip de Neri's Catholic Church, in Southwark, where Catholics were rumored to be stockpiling arms. This time the local militia, chastened by its previous inactivity, waded into the fray with disastrous results. By the time the ashes had cooled several days later, fifteen people were dead and another fifty had been wounded.[32]

The school controversy and the subsequent riots had a tremendous polarizing effect on Philadelphia's religious world. In the aftermath of the first riot a grand jury met and placed the blame on the Kensington Catholics. The city's leading Catholics responded with a public meeting at the cathedral and a lengthy printed rebuttal, chastising the grand jury for its one-sided proceedings and insisting that Kenrick and Philadelphia Catholics had never intended "'to exclude the Bible from the Schools'" as charged. They also took pains to distance themselves from their disorderly brethren, insisting that "it would be unjust . . . to visit their offense on an entire community, from the mere accidental circumstance that most of them are said to hold the religious faith we profess."[33]

Meanwhile, Protestant observers joined the grand jury in targeting the Irish newcomers. Quaker merchant Thomas P. Cope's diary entries following the first riots were typical: "The disturbances of the public peace are greatly to be deplored. The Catholics have become numerous among us & seem disposed for mischief. Several new chapels have lately been erected in the City & districts & in fact generally over the U. States. The indigent poor & discontented of Europe are constantly arriving among us & exercise no small influence at our ballot boxes. . . . No considerable part of our poor rates are expended by these people." Cope not only blamed the immigrants for the disturbances, but also took the opportunity to question their impact on the city's political and welfare systems: "Catholicism, as practised under the discipline of the Church of Rome, is not consistent with our free Institutions. With the pope at its head, issuing his mandates to all his various subordinates . . . the rank & file can scarcely be said to have a will of their own."[34]

The second round of rioting in July heightened sectarian tensions while prompting a public outcry against escalating street violence. Twenty-one-year-old Isaac Mickle, a strong opponent of the nativist movement, ventured into the streets during the July 7 rioting and discovered that "it was extremely dangerous to make a remark not fully approving of cutting Catholic throats, and burning all Catholic churches. I nearly got into a scrape for daring to express the abhorrence I have for mobocracy."[35]

Prior to the riots, Bishop Kenrick and the Catholic clergy had adopted an aggressive proselytizing strategy, battling Protestant ministers for the souls of the immigrant working classes. Newly constructed churches in Irish neighborhoods dispensed with pew rents and enticed converts and lapsed Catholics with temperance societies, reading rooms, and a broader associational world. With the 1844 violence, Kenrick backed off from his more assertive mission activity for fear that it might provoke further attacks. The riots thus left a legacy of conservativism that lasted to the eve of the famine migration.[36]

The sectarian conflicts in Liverpool and Philadelphia had striking similarities. At almost precisely the same moment, anti-Catholicism coalesced into a powerful movement, with important organizations and leaders based in Liverpool and Philadelphia. The rhetoric of Liverpool's Protestant Association, established in 1835, shared much in common with that of the Native American Party and Philadelphia's various Protestant organizations. In Liverpool, the Liberals' efforts to accommodate Catholic children in the schools was the catalyst for injecting sectarian differences into the town's political discourse. In the United States the intertwined hostility to immigrants and to Catholics launched the Native American Party; the battles over public schools in New York and Philadelphia helped bring the nativists' agenda to the forefront. The added intra-ethnic dimension of England's Orange Lodges was matched by Philadelphia's Irish Protestant weavers, who proved instrumental in turning Philadelphia's school controversy into violence.[37]

It is telling that the conflict in both cities turned on Bibles in the schools. At one level these conflicts reflected a concern for youthful souls. Evangelicals were anxious to protect children from the evils of popery; Catholics were equally worried that their youth would be indoctrinated with Protestant teachings. A similar concern for future generations shaped discussions of crime and juvenile delinquency as well as educational reform and poor relief. On a broader level, the school controversies turned on the role of government institutions in religious affairs. In essence, the participants were really debating the position that the government should take on religious diversity. Should the state use its power to impose a particular religious perspective? Conversely, should government institutions accommodate differing beliefs? Or should they—as Louisa Bedford would have preferred—dodge the issue altogether by removing religion from public institutions? One might reasonably assume that England, with its Established Church, and the United States, dedicated to the separation of church and state, would fall on opposite sides of this question. But in practice the terms of debate were nearly identical in the two cities. Some voices insisted on purely Protestant classroom teachings, whereas others sought some compromise that could accommodate Catholic children. The results owed more to the power of Protestant political muscle at the local level than to the weight of any grander ideological conviction.

All of this heat and passion predated the famine migration. The rest of this chapter will examine how the two cities, both barely healed from intense sectarian strife, dealt with the religious challenges posed by the famine migrants themselves. How did Catholics in Liverpool and Philadelphia respond? What, if anything, did private and public institutions do to accommodate the new Catholic inmates? Finally, how did each city answer the immigrant children's educational needs?

LIVERPOOL AND THE CATHOLIC MIGRANTS

According to Thomas Burke, "distinctions of race, religion, and party were obliterated in [the] presence" of the Irish potato famine. Liverpool's religious leaders of all persuasions called on their flocks to send assistance across the Irish Sea. There were, as Burke notes, some exceptions. Hugh M'Neile continued to attack Irish priests and publish sermons attributing the famine to God's wrath.[38] In the meantime, Catholics remained at the center of Liverpool politics. During the general election of 1847 local Catholics staged a special meeting where they devised a strategy that helped defeat the hated ultra-Protestant Sir Digby Mackworth.[39] Three years later antipapists raised a hue and cry when the pope divided England and Wales into dioceses. In Liverpool, home of a new bishop, citizens signed a petition protesting "Papal aggression" and cheered when Parliament passed the controversial Ecclesiastical Titles Act. Catholics responded with a huge public meeting to defend themselves. Unitarian George Holt Sr., a town councillor of long standing, observed the controversy with chagrin. "When shall we get strength to treat all Priestcraft with the quiet firm contempt it deserves?" the diarist asked. The answer to papal aggression, Holt insisted, lay not in public protests but in "personal attention to duties, education & enlightenment against the bigoted & arrogant pretensions of Romanist superstitions & principles." The following year Rev. Verner M. White published a sixty-page sermon on "Popish Intolerance." The Catholic voters got a measure of revenge during the election of 1852, when they helped remove one Liberal member who had voted for the anti-Catholic bill.[40] But despite the occasional controversial issue or inflammatory sermon, the famine migration does not appear to have heightened the level of sectarian political debate in Liverpool. The more immediate challenge was what to do with the flood of new Catholics.

In January 1847 Liverpool Catholics held a public meeting at the Concert Hall to collect subscriptions and discuss strategies for assisting the starving Irish while each congregation contributed the returns from a special collection.[41] Before long those energies and resources would be diverted to challenges closer to home. When typhus struck the Irish immigrants a few months later, local priests earned international praise for their self-sacrificing work with the sick. By the end of the year ten priests had fallen victim to the disease. (John Johns, of the Domestic Mission Society [DMS], was the only Protestant minister to die of typhus).[42] Catholics in the city resolved to honor the memory of the fallen priests by building a new church and school near Great Howard "to supply the crowded and daily increasing population of St. Mary's district." The *Mercury* called on Catholics from wealthier neighborhoods as well as members of the larger community to support the project in the interest of "general morality and welfare." In September 1849 the new Church of St. Augustine opened with a capacity of 1,200.[43] St. Augustine's was only the most noteworthy of the Catholic Church's institutional responses to the famine migration. According to the *Mercury,* Irish Catholics in Liverpool's poorest neighborhoods had recently been "aided by their brethren of the town generally, and by the munificence of the public at large" in financing St. Mary's Church in the same district. In March 1849 the newspaper reported that Samuel Holland Merton, Esq., had funded the new Church and School of the Holy Cross on Great Crosshall Street "solely with the view of providing, almost at the very doors of the poorest Catholics of Liverpool, a place of worship for themselves, and a school for their children." But although Liverpool's Catholics built five new churches in the 1840s, and the clergy supplemented these houses of worship with makeshift arrangements in empty buildings and warehouses, the religious census of 1851 still found local church seating woefully inadequate.[44]

Even while they struggled to meet the spiritual needs of their ever-increasing flock, local Catholic leaders battled the array of social challenges that accompanied the Irish migration. In May 1847, as the Health of the Town movement gathered momentum, St. Joseph's Rev. Walmsley delivered an impassioned sermon calling on his flock to attend to its own hygiene. The following month another clergyman warned his parishioners that if they did not improve their sanitary habits they would end up killing off all the local priests. A week later that priest was stricken with typhus. In February a self-styled "Protestant, but no bigot," praised St. Mary's Rev. Lane for "exhort[ing] his congregation . . . to a strict observance of the rules and practice of cleanliness and sobriety, not only with a view of avoiding disease themselves, but as a highly religious, moral, and social duty."[45]

Concern about health and sanitation notwithstanding, the overwhelming poverty of the migrants presented the most pressing, and intractable, dilemma. Each Sunday Liverpool's Catholic churches attracted hundreds of impoverished Irish beggars, prompting complaints from parishioners fearing for their health and safety and official charges that "indiscriminate" giving by Catholics was exacerbating the citywide problem. With the Catholic Benevolent Society lying inactive for most of the famine, clergymen had to rely on charity sermons and collections to fund their own good works. In early 1848 St. Patrick's Rev. Crook canceled the annual collection for the Southern and Toxteth Hospital (which treated many of his flock), because the parish was overwhelmed by its own financial needs. Every winter the annual Catholic Charity Ball raised modest funds for "the Female Orphan House and other Catholic charities of Liverpool."[46] In 1847 the orphan asylum's managers were already facing financial difficulties, reporting that the asylum had aided only forty to fifty girls in the last year despite a capacity twice that number.[47] Meanwhile, the new local branch of the Society of St. Vincent de Paul struggled through tough times with limited funds. In 1849 the society reported that "the present amount of poverty and distress is enormous, and that their funds are nearly exhausted."[48]

With the rebirth of the Catholic Benevolent Society in 1851, Liverpool's Catholics once again had an institutional focus for their compassion. In that first year the society collected £244 from subscriptions, donations, sermons, and the modest proceeds of the Charity Ball, nearly all of which it distributed to the "sick and destitute poor" through parish priests. For the next several years the society annually distributed about £240–270, which jumped to £382 in 1855 and 1856. The society had distributed an average of £332 annually between 1841 and 1843.[49]

The efforts of individual Catholic almsgivers and a handful of Catholic charities could barely scratch the surface of the rising demand for relief. Immigrants who turned to other private benevolent bodies often faced disappointment. Many charities explicitly excluded outsiders, while others tied assistance to training in the Established Church.[50] But there were exceptions to these rules. When the Southern and Toxteth Hospital named an Anglican chaplain, the hospital's managers insisted: "It is very important to add, that, although for the purpose of insuring regular worship in the building, it has been now necessary to appoint a chaplain, every patient is at perfect liberty to call in a minister of his own persuasion, and the committee takes this occasion of respectfully inviting clergymen of every denomination to visit, in such manner as they may think best calculated to promote Christian feeling, piety and resignation." Soon after taking office, the new chaplain announced that "though he was chaplain and held services in the hospital on Sunday afternoons, still he always was wishful for every patient who preferred his own pastor to see him," particularly because three-quarters of the patients were Roman Catholic. The regulations of the Liverpool Female Penitentiary (for reforming prostitutes) also provided for religious services "conducted by the Ministers of any denomination of Christians."[51]

Even where Protestant philanthropies opened their doors to other religions, Irish Catholics remained suspicious. In 1841 a local Catholic charged the Liverpool School for the Blind with pressuring Catholic pupils into converting in order to receive musical training. The committee that investigated the claims acquitted the school of any wrongdoing, but not before charges and countercharges had been aired in the press. The Catholic migrants were especially skeptical—often with good reason—when benevolent visitors entered their neighborhoods. The agents of the Liverpool City Mission, who went into the field to bring religion to the working classes, were instructed not to attack Catholics but to "explain" to them that "no man living can be justified by his own works." On several occasions agents reported encountering hostile Catholics who objected to Protestant proselytizing. In 1851 the City Mission targeted Irish immigrants by hiring an Irish-speaking agent. Before long the mission was reporting less hostility from Catholics and a steady flow of conversions. Robert Day, an agent for the Mersey Mission to Seamen, visited arriving vessels with evangelical tracts. After one visit to the docks, Day wrote in his journal: "I was pleased to see some Irish Roman Catholic sailors receive them, one who was at work up aloft seeing me going away sang out leave me one of them tracts before you go, indeed they receive them on Board of all the Irish vessels that I visited, only one sailor refused and he was as full of Bigotry as an Egg—and said it was impossible for any one to be saved who did not belong to the Church."[52] Such strategies and attitudes made the work of John Johns and the Domestic Mission Society that much more challenging. The DMS truly was committed to nonsectarian Christian benevolence, but its ministers to the poor often had a difficult time convincing the Irish Catholics. Johns and his successor found that some Catholics were—at least at first—openly hostile, expecting the worst from these Protestant intruders. And, to his dismay, Johns reported that other poor immigrants offered to convert (presumably to the religion of Johns's choosing) in exchange for assistance. Francis Bishop, who replaced Johns when the former minister died of typhus, heard a few such offers but added that most poor Catholics "would rather die than barter their consciences." Generally DMS ministers were pleased to report that they built excellent working relations with Irish Catholics and their clergymen, but the initial reactions suggest an atmosphere in which religious conversion was often the assumed price for material assistance.[53]

Some of the most dramatic debates concerned religious practices within the hated workhouse. In 1839 a Catholic clergyman charged that the master of the workhouse school had declared to his pupils that "every Catholic would go to Hell with a Testament in his hand," adding—for the special benefit of the Catholic children in his audience—that the wafer he held in his hand was "the God of the Papists."[54] Under the Old Poor Law only Established Church services were permitted in the workhouse; every Sunday Catholic and Dissenting inmates were permitted to leave the grounds to attend their own services. In the first half of the 1840s Liberal members of the new Select Vestry periodically called for Roman Catholic masses in the workhouse. But these arguments, offered on the grounds of both equity and discipline, repeatedly met with stern resistance from the Tory majority. Finally, a coalition of Liberals and Catholics won a majority of the Vestry seats in 1846 and immediately moved to set aside a room in the workhouse for Catholic masses.[55]

This solution lasted only as long as the Liberals controlled the Select Vestry. In January 1847 an Irish Catholic workhouse inmate wrote to Mr. Rushton, complaining that he had not been allowed to leave the grounds to attend Sunday services for four months. Rushton explained to the Vestry that the man, a Mr. M'Loughlin, had gotten drunk the last time he had left the workhouse for church; nonetheless, the magistrate ordered that in future M'Loughlin be allowed to go "along with the other Catholic inmates." The tensions in the workhouse apparently did not subside. When the Select Vestry elected a new workhouse chaplain at the end of 1847, one Protestant member declared that he had only voted for the new chaplain in hopes that he "would let the poor Catholics alone." The following June the Vestry had still another heated debate about Catholic services. Mr. Cafferata moved that Liverpool follow Manchester's example and set aside a room for Roman Catholic masses. Others objected to changing the status quo by bringing sectarian differences—and perhaps conflicts—within the workhouse walls. The Vestry voted the measure down 17 to 6, but not before charges of "bigotry" had filled the room. Two weeks later the vestrymen approved a motion from the workhouse committee ordering an officer to accompany the Roman Catholic inmates who left to attend Sunday masses, thus answering the earlier concerns about discipline. In 1855 the Select Vestry revisited the debate yet again, with the Catholic-Liberal coalition losing 13 to 11. Finally, in 1857, the Vestry agreed to set aside a room for Catholic services with the expressed provision that not more than one Catholic priest be allowed in the workhouse at a time. The vote turned less on a commitment to equity than on a long-held suspicion that poor Catholics had been abusing their Sunday excursions with theft, drink, and other rowdiness.[56]

The seemingly endless debate over religion in the workhouse, coupled with Irish Catholics' suspicions of private philanthropists, suggests the character of Liverpool's sectarian tensions. Although—or perhaps because —roughly half of the workhouse inmates were Catholics, the Vestry persisted in protecting the prerogatives of the Established Church.[57] To some these battles may have been largely political or symbolic, but for many voters the theological differences were deeply held. Both the theological and political battles were firmly in place before the famine.

Philadelphia remained a well-known center for nativism and anti-Catholicism throughout the famine years. But, as in Liverpool, it is not clear that the flood of immigrants in fact increased the venom aimed at foreign Catholics.[58] A resolution passed by the General Assembly of the Presbyterian Church, which met in Philadelphia in May 1849, was typical of much American evangelical thinking: "Resolved: That we should make efforts to induce children of *emigrants* to attend our Sabbath Schools, and the adults our congregations; and when they are converted, to join our churches, or to organize churches of their own, in connection with us, that as soon as possible they may be Americanized in the language and feelings, and become evangelical in their religion." The assumption—phrased with affection rather than hostility—was that the process of religious conversion and "Americanization" would go hand in hand.[59] In the meantime, nativist politicians continued to be powerful in Philadelphia in the decade after the 1844 riots, particularly when they joined forces with local Whigs.[60] In 1854 Robert Taylor Conrad, the Whig–Know-Nothing candidate, defeated well-known Democrat Richard Vaux, who had close ties with the immigrant and Catholic communities, in the first postconsolidation mayoral election. Conrad's success was especially disturbing to local Democrats: not only did he capture the traditionally Whig center city, but also his nativist rhetoric appeared to have made substantial inroads in traditional Democrat strongholds in Philadelphia County. Both the evangelicals' "Americanizing" rhetoric and the Know-Nothings' attacks on immigrants point to the distinctive national character of nativism. In addition to representing a threat to Protestant hegemony, the Irish immigrants were *outsiders* to be either schooled in the ways of U.S. citizenship or embroiled in partisan political conflicts. In fact, Dale B. Light Jr. has even argued that the Catholic Church was so distinct that "mid-century immigrants had to be assimilated not only to American culture but also to American Catholic culture." [61]

How did Catholic immigrants fare in this atmosphere of evangelical fervor and political hostility? As we have seen, the famine migration found Philadelphia and Bishop Kenrick in a period of prosperity and energetic growth. Construction on fourteen new churches was started in the decade beginning in 1845, largely in areas with rising Irish Catholic populations. Others, including the Kensington churches burned in the 1844 riots, underwent major renovation or expansion. Each of these projects prompted a new round of fund-raising meetings and charity sermons.[62] Meanwhile, Kenrick combed the nation for religious orders that would help administer the city's burgeoning charitable institutions. Four sisters of St. Joseph arrived from St. Louis in 1847 to direct St. John's Orphan Asylum for boys. In the next two years members of the School Sisters of Notre Dame, the Sisters of the Good Shepherd, and the Visitation nuns all descended on Philadelphia to take charge of schools, orphanages, and other benevolent activities.[63] In September 1846 Kenrick oversaw the laying of a cornerstone for the new cathedral. But this pet project stalled for years, losing out to other demands, not the least of which were the famine migrants.[64]

As Kenrick artfully orchestrated the growth of the diocese's infrastructure, the Catholic rank and file faced various financial requests.[65] Before long, news of the Irish famine began to absorb much of Philadelphia's benevolent attention. Local Quakers orchestrated a citywide collection and sent large sums to Ireland. The *Catholic Herald* collected money for the fund, as did each of the city's Catholic churches. Tales of the famine victims sparked similar emergency fund-raising efforts up and down the East Coast and across the country. In the meantime, Irish immigrants—in Philadelphia and other immigrant centers—acted independently, mailing small sums to loved ones left behind.[66]

Closer to home, the arriving famine migrants presented Philadelphia's Catholic charities with new challenges.[67] The manager of the first district of the Ladies' Catholic Benevolent Society reported a surge in clients, "nearly all of whom were newly arrived emigrants in the most abject state of destitution." As it had for years, the Catholic Benevolent Society depended on charity sermons for cash donations while sewing groups and Dorcas Societies connected with the churches provided clothing and other donations.[68] In addition to expanding existing charitable organizations, the famine migration spurred local Catholics to energetic new institution building. In 1849 St. Anne's Widows Asylum opened. Two years later St. John's Orphans' Asylum constructed a new building in West Philadelphia, the Society of St. Vincent de Paul launched a local branch, and fund-raising began for the new House of the Good Shepherd for unwed mothers.[69]

This spate of Catholic institution building had its parallels across the United States, reflecting the intertwined concerns for the Irish migrants' physical well-being and their spiritual health in the hands of proselytizing

Protestants.[70] In 1847 Bishop Hughes of New York responded to claims that the Catholic clergy had been denied access to patients in the almshouse and public hospital by calling for the construction of a separate Catholic hospital. The following February "the St Joseph's Society for the relief of the distressed emigrants from Ireland" began raising money for a hospital in Philadelphia. In 1849 New York's St. Vincent's Hospital and Philadelphia's St. Joseph's opened their doors, each under the administration of the Sisters of St. Joseph. Although the hospital's clientele was predominantly Irish Catholic, St. Joseph's managers assured the city that cases were accepted "without distinction of creed, country or colour." Moreover, the charter stipulated that patients were free to "obtain the spiritual aid of a Clergyman of his or her persuasion."[71]

Some of the city's Protestant philanthropies welcomed Catholic immigrants, with no apparent conflicts over conversion. The visitors for the Quaker-run Union Benevolent Association were quick to discuss the moral shortcomings of the poor—and to distinguish between the deserving and undeserving—and they were clearly concerned about the increasing demands of immigrants. But their annual reports rarely mentioned religious affiliation and never religious tensions. The Philadelphia Society for the Employment and Instruction of the Poor (PSEIP) reportedly held religious services of "several denominations" in the house of industry, although they appear to have been exclusively Protestant services. Patricia Clement notes that the Christian Home Missionary Society, which became the PSEIP, had as its "chief object . . . to preach temperance and religious conversion." Still, its annual reports do not refer to sectarian tensions of the sort that appeared regularly in the reports of some Liverpool societies.[72]

Other new Protestant charities, often acting in the tradition of the American Sunday School Union, were clearly interested in proselytizing, sometimes echoing comments made by the Liverpool visitors. The Evangelical Home Missionary Society of Kensington was established in the early 1850s "to supply as far as possible the spiritual and temporal need of the destitute population of this District." Its missionaries were directed to "avoid all interference with the distinctive tenets and forms of the churches *co-operating with this Association*" (emphasis added), implicitly leaving the way clear for "interference" with Roman Catholicism.[73] The Young Christians' Missionary Association (YCMA) was founded in 1852 to "ameliorate the temporal and improve the spiritual condition of the inhabitants of those wretched courts and alleys in the lower part of the city; the dwellers in cellars and holes, into whose cavities the sun of Heaven shines as seldom as does the light of the Gospel into the gloomy recesses of the souls of their occupants." YCMA missionaries, who took their evangelical message into the notoriously impoverished, and heavily Irish, Bedford, Baker, and Spafford Street area, reported strong resistance from local Catholics, particularly when they tried to found a Sabbath School for children who were "all under the jurisdiction of the Church of Rome."[74] This integration of material assistance with moral exhortation and evangelical conversion marked much of midcentury philanthropy, particularly where Protestant reformers perceived the Irish immigrants as equally lacking in both body and soul. Such efforts, in turn, helped stir American Catholics to more energetic institutional development.[75]

Most of the institutions housing orphans, delinquents, and other children deemed at risk stressed moral training while insisting that they were nonsectarian. The Quaker-run house of refuge welcomed clergy from various denominations, but its annual reports never mention visits from Roman Catholic priests. The Northern Home for Friendless Children, founded in 1854, gave its children Christian training while stressing that "sectarianism is, of course, excluded." Stephen Girard took his own stand on the city's sectarian conflicts by insisting in his will that Girard College for Orphans should offer a distinctly nonsectarian education to those local (white) boys who were "taken from a class not likely to have received that very early discipline, so necessary for the success of efforts directed towards their moral culture." But in the months before the orphanage opened in January 1848, the *Catholic Herald* reported a brewing controversy over talk that it would exclude the Catholic Bible and thus—the paper suggested— effectively exclude Catholic children. Skeptical about the religious training available in these institutions, Philadelphia Catholics responded to the famine migration by expanding their two orphanages to accommodate 350 children by 1850.[76]

Although Catholic Philadelphians, unlike their Liverpool brethren, did not have to contend with an antagonistic Established Church, Catholics in public institutions still faced obstacles to religious observance. The minutes of the Board of Guardians are largely silent on religious matters, but two entries on May 29, 1848, suggest unrecorded storms. On that day Rev. Devitt, a Catholic priest, petitioned the board for the use of a room where Catholic inmates "may assemble for religious exercises & instruction as heretofore." In the same session one of the Guardians resolved "that the Catholic Female population of this house be permitted to continue their devotional exercises in the room lately occupied by them for that purpose until otherwise ordered by the Board." The board voted to "postpone" both resolutions.[77] These entries indicate that for at least a time Catholics in Blockley Almshouse were allowed to celebrate their own mass. One is left to wonder whether the board had changed a formal policy or simply ordered an informal practice stopped. The matter does not reappear in the minutes.

Other evidence suggests that some forms of religious worship continued at the almshouse. In December 1848 the Guardians' Committee on the Almshouse heard a report concerning "improper conduct"—apparently between the sexes—among inmates who had assembled for worship.[78] The following February a John Simpson petitioned the Board of Guardians for "a suitable apartment in the House in which to hold public worship." The Almshouse committee ordered the steward to prepare a vacant room as "a place of worship" and "allow such old men as he may deem proper persons to attend divine services there." Perhaps this decision to accommodate elderly men was comparable to efforts in Liverpool to make special arrangements for inmates who were too sick to travel into town for services. But the brief notes concerning these two episodes make no reference to particular religions, a silence implying that the arrangements were for Protestants. Beginning in 1843 the prisoners at the Philadelphia County Prison received weekly religious instruction from Rev. John Woolson, a Methodist minister. Until 1849, when the prison inspectors voted him a government salary, Woolson had received a small stipend from voluntary contributions. In paying him the government officials were effectively supporting a private Protestant initiative, but the decision seemed more to support Rev. Woolson's ongoing philanthropic efforts rather than any particular sectarian agenda.[79]

An episode before the Orphans' Court does suggest the state's willingness to protect Catholic interests. In June 1848 the court heard the case of the orphaned children of Patrick Quigley, a Catholic. Some witnesses claimed that Mrs. Quigley had also been a Catholic, whereas others insisted that she had been a Methodist. The case, still unresolved when the *Public Ledger* reported it, attracted attention because a Protestant uncle had petitioned for custody of the children, who had been living with a Catholic aunt. According to state law, the court could not grant custody to non-Catholic guardians if both parents had been Roman Catholic.[80] This case, and the state law, was an acknowledgement of sectarian differences as well as a willingness to protect Catholic autonomy. It also reflected concern for the spiritual well-being of Philadelphia's children. This concern, which was at the heart of the earlier school conflicts in both Liverpool and Philadelphia, continued to be the most important point of sectarian controversy in both cities.

RELIGION AND EDUCATION

Catholics in Liverpool and Philadelphia shared a commitment to support separate parochial schools. In the years before the famine, sectarian school conflicts in each city had stiffened that resolve. Thus, the Irish Catholic newcomers were largely a cause for expansion rather that a catalyst for new educational programs. Despite these similarities, educational developments in the two cities reflected distinctive national and local patterns.

In 1847 the Roman Catholic schools in Birkenhead, across the River Mersey from Liverpool, were shut down until the old master could be replaced. When the new master took office, he chastised those parents who had temporarily placed their children in other schools, declaring — according to one disgruntled parishioner — that their children's "religion and morals would be tampered with" in Protestant schools. A year and a half later the *Mercury* lamented the "great want of school accommodation in this large and populous town for the children of the poor and working classes."[81] These two concerns — the Roman Catholic apprehension about Protestant education and the broader public outcry about inadequate schooling for the poor — framed public discussions throughout the 1840s and 1850s.

In the absence of a comprehensive public school system,[82] Liverpool's poor children received a rudimentary education, if any, from a patchwork of government and private schools, none of which were free of sectarian concerns. The Tory-dominated Town Council continued to administer two Corporation schools, for roughly 1,400 to 1,800 pupils, under the auspices of the Established Church.[83] Beginning in 1847 Liverpool's network of ragged schools offered basic education and moral training to thousands of poor children. When the ragged schools first opened, the *Mercury* celebrated this ostensibly nonsectarian effort to reach the city's most needy children, suggesting that the Town Council could follow the same path were it not for the fact that "the predominant party in the Council, owing to zeal for exclusive doctrines, seems 'with one consent,' to have abandoned the great mass of the poor and the needy." In fact, students who attended schools directed by the Ragged School Union read from the Authorized Version of the Bible, thus effectively excluding Roman Catholics as much as the Corporation schools.[84] The Industrial Ragged Schools, aimed at a still lower strata of Liverpool's poor children, opened in 1849 to provide food, trades instruction, and religious instruction "from the authorized version of the Bible imparted to them." The Domestic Mission Society's small ragged school was the exception in their adherence to true nonsectarian goals. In early 1848 the school's committee resolved "to introduce a regulated [and noncompulsory] use of the sacred scriptures in the schools, with the express understanding that they are to be put to no sectarian use."[85]

The Kirkdale Industrial Schools, established by the Vestry to separate pauper children from the adult population, became the center for vigorous debates that ran parallel to those concerning religion in the workhouse. In 1845 the Board of Guardians' Industrial Schools Committee voted to follow the practice of the workhouse and allow Roman Catholic children to leave the premises on Sundays "for the purpose of attending their Chapel." A few years later it resolved to set aside a portion of each day for the "religious instruction of the children in the Holy Scriptures and the Catechism." Perhaps it was this expansion in Protestant religious training that prompted a letter from Rev. George Fisher, a Catholic priest, who posed "a number of queries in reference to new arrangements for the religious instruction of the Roman Catholic children in the schools." The Vestry offered to give Rev. Fisher access to the entry books on Catholic children but said that "they cannot agree to the other arrangements suggested in his letter."[86] Whatever Fisher's suggestions may have been, the question of religious education continued to crop up in the Industrial Schools Committee minutes. Finally, in September 1851 the Vestry hired a man to escort Catholic children to Sunday mass, but it twice deferred a proposal to allow a "Roman Catholic lay brother" to go to the school to instruct Catholic children while "Protestant children are at service."[87] In the following year a subcommittee rejected a charge that the religious education of five Catholic children had been interfered with in the industrial schools.[88]

In 1854 the two Catholic members on the Select Vestry expressed their shock at the religious ignorance of the workhouse's Catholic children and asked permission to hire their own lay teacher. When the Vestry voted down the proposal, one of the members claimed that whereas Catholic teachers had been blocked, non-Catholics had been proselytizing Catholic Kirkdale children at will. A few months later the Schools Committee rejected a motion to ask "the Select Vestry to apply to the Poor Law Board for permission to allocate such a sum from the Parochial Funds for providing proper means for the religious instruction of the Roman Catholic pauper children in the schools as may be deemed just." But in November the committee did agree to recommend the purchase of Douay Bibles for the Catholic children and to allow priests to enter the schools for limited hours. These recommendations lost by a close vote, but in 1856 a slightly changed Vestry finally agreed to arrange for Catholic instruction in the Kirkdale schools.[89]

In the face of evangelical enthusiasts and hostile government officials, it is little wonder that Catholics in Liverpool did their best to educate their own children. Before 1840 they supported four parochial schools. During the next thirteen years, with the Irish Catholic population rising and the Corporation schools proving unacceptable, the church added nine new schools. By 1853 Abraham Hume estimated that the city's Roman Catholic schools, including those still under construction, could accommodate over 10,000 students (which was still only a fraction of Liverpool's Catholic children). Like the church buildings that often accompanied them, these new schools were almost exclusively in areas with heavy Irish Catholic concentrations, often relying on citywide fund-raising or large philanthropic gifts to supplement the meager local resources. And much like Kenrick's recruiting efforts in the Philadelphia diocese, Liverpool's Father James Nugent invited members of the Sisters of Notre Dame to help run schools for the poor.[90]

The development of Liverpool's Catholic school system proceeded amid local and national discussions of educational reform. At midcentury the national government's position on education was neither deeply rooted nor clearly defined. The emerging parliamentary role followed incremental efforts to address small gaps in the existing educational system—usually with modest grants or other supplemental assistance—rather than pursuing a broader theory of state involvement in schooling. In 1833 the government passed a small grant to support school building, followed shortly by national involvement in teacher training. Six years later, as Liverpudlians were engaged in sectarian conflicts over their Corporation schools, national defenders of Church of England prerogatives successfully resisted a move to establish nondenominational teacher training colleges under the newly organized Committee of the Privy Council. For the next several years the competing interests of Dissenters, sometimes allied with Roman Catholics, and Anglicans blocked any substantial progress toward a nationally funded school system. In 1846 the committee's first secretary, Sir James Kay-Shuttleworth, orchestrated a new program for state supervision of teacher training that met with Anglican and Wesleyan support but strong Dissenter resistance. This program, which provided government grants to schools and introduced an important role for inspectors, became a central component in the government's growing role in education.[91]

Roman Catholics across the nation initially believed that the educational plan excluded their schools. Liverpool Catholics met at the Music Hall "to express their sense of the injury and insult inflicted upon them, by the practical exclusion of their body from all participation in the grant for education from the national funds." But Kay-Shuttleworth managed to answer these concerns by adding new language explicitly including Catholic schools and ensuring that they could receive state aid without jeopardizing their religious beliefs. In February 1848 the nation's bishops called for donations to the new national Catholic Poor School Committee, which would work with the Privy Council committee to protect Catholic interests.[92]

S. Nasmyth Stokes, one of the Lancashire representatives on the Catholic Poor School Committee, immediately set about lobbying for government funds, insisting that Manchester and Liverpool were in particular need because of the influx of Irish immigrants. "From Liverpool I have been requested to ask your favourable consideration for St. Mary's Schools," Stokes wrote to the secretary of the Committee of Council on Education. "The congregation of St. Mary's is represented to be *the* poor Irish congregation of the town, containing thousands of poor children. The managers are anxious to place the girls' school under inspection, and to obtain pupil-teachers, and augmentation of the mistress's salary." Stokes pointed out that the congregation was simply too poor to collect substantial contributions; he urged the committee to set aside the government's regulation requiring that assistance go only to those who had already raised their own funds. The acting assistant secretary replied that, given limited funds and "the state of public opinion," the government could do no more than supplement existing resources rather than directly answer the needs of the nation's poorer districts. The following year both the Catholic Poor School Committee and the Committee of the Privy Council rejected requests to aid the existing Holy Cross parish schools, but each body promised that it would provide grants to assist *new* school construction if such projects were undertaken.[93]

The impact of local and national educational policies is perhaps best seen in the evolving character of Liverpool's Hibernia schools. Founded in 1807 by the Benevolent Society of St. Patrick, the Hibernia schools provided education for the "offspring of indigent Irish." Although most of the pupils were Roman Catholic, the schools stressed nondenominational education and received donations from across the religious spectrum. Near the end of the 1830s they fell on hard financial times and reported that "the corporation have refused us any assistance." In 1842 the embattled schools—now under the stewardship of William Rathbone—began charging small fees and accepting students of all nationalities, but still giving preference to Irish children. As the year came to a close, the schools' committee published a special notice in six local newspapers:

> The committee of these schools have [*sic*] found it necessary greatly to enlarge their means of instruction in consequence of a large majority of that portion of our population confessedly standing most in need of education and least able to procure it—The Irish Poor being deprived of all use of the Corporation Schools, without a compliance with regulations forbidden by the rules of their church. Under these circumstances the Committee have made great efforts to secure able teaching, and to adopt such a system of instruction as may best prepare the children to fulfill their duties in after life, without interfering with the religious liberty, which it was the object of the founders to secure to *all*.

The notice went on to call for donations to support this enlarged venture, particularly from those "who are alive to the *extent and degree of juvenile depravity in Liverpool*."[94]

When the Privy Council passed its new provisions, Rathbone and the Hibernia schools were quick to act. In early 1848 the schools followed the government plan by elevating four girls to pupil-teacher status, leading the Committee of the Council on Education to approve a request for assistance "for Govt Aid & Inspection." For the next several years the Hibernia schools reported regular grants from the Committee of the Council on Education, while celebrating the fact that "in a town where party and polemical bitterness is often carried to such a violent and dangerous excess amongst the working classes, the Hibernia school, by opening its doors to all parties, without requiring a compromise of principle on the part of any, should inculcate daily a lesson of forbearance and love." Thus by opening its doors to all ethnic groups and by stressing its role in promoting an orderly society, the Hibernia schools managed to earn public support and government assistance in the midst of sectarian conflict.[95]

In the meantime, Liverpudlians continued to discuss the nation's broader educational shortcomings. The Lancashire Public School Association, founded in 1848, called for the establishment of new schools—funded by local taxes and run by elected officials—that would exclude "all theological tenets from the instruction." The arguments for such schools stressed the need to set aside sectarian differences in order to address larger social ills. Some Liverpool Protestants rallied around proposals to establish national schools under the Church of England.[96] But despite years of discussion, not until the Education Act of 1870 did the state go beyond merely subsidizing existing voluntary school systems.

The Lancashire Public School Association's publications routinely called attention to the American example of nondenominational public schooling, insisting that England could learn from it. But at least one resident, Anne Holt, was not so sanguine about the concept. In 1851 the thirty-year-old Unitarian teacher traveled to Philadelphia, where she recorded her thoughts on developments in America:

> I doubt whether the American system of public instruction has not reached what I should consider its best point & is not already on the decline. Sectarianism is displaying itself strongly. The Catholics have already almost entirely seceded from the public schools & established others where their mode of faith is exclusively taught. Such is also the strong tendency of the Episcopal Church . . . is it to be expected that these bodies will long continue to pay the state tax for benefits they will not share?[97]

The American schools did, in fact, provide an interesting contrast with the English model, even though the Philadelphia example was hardly free of sectarian divisions.

From the outset William Penn envisioned that his City of Brotherly Love would support education. Initially Philadelphia's schoolhouse was under the auspices of local Quakers, but by the early 1800s the city had at least a dozen church-sponsored charity schools, in addition to a wide array of other educational institutions. In 1818 the state legislature took an important step in consolidating Philadelphia's charity schools when it created Pennsylvania's "First School District," encompassing the city and county of Philadelphia. The 1818 act placed the charity schools under a board of controllers; provided for public monies for school construction, teacher training, and books; and standardized the implementation of the Lancastrian system of teaching, which had recently been imported from England. Eighteen years later the legislature opened the schools to all students rather than only the poor—thus somewhat easing the stigma of attendance—and expanded public schooling to the entire state. By 1840 the city and county schools had over 23,000 pupils; at midcentury that figure had more than doubled, to 48,056 pupils, a figure that dwarfed the population of Liverpool's two Corporation schools.[98]

Catholic schooling in Philadelphia dated back to the 1780s. But for the first third of the nineteenth century parochial education remained limited and therefore many Catholics relied on the city schools. In 1834 the state's public school controllers resolved that "the introduction of any religious or sectarian forms" into the schools would be an infringement of religious freedom, but according to one scholar this declaration of tolerance was already flying in the face of rising anti-Catholicism. As we have seen, ten years later the issue of religious training in the public schools came to a head, triggering some of the nation's worst urban rioting.[99] One of the many repercussions of the 1844 rioting was a new Catholic commitment to separate schooling. In the next seven years Bishop Kenrick, who had already made some progress in that direction, placed increased emphasis on what would become one of the nation's most extensive systems of free parochial schools. When Kenrick moved on to the Baltimore diocese in 1851, his successor, Bishop John Neumann, maintained the same emphasis. In 1850 the city had five parish schools; ten years later that number had jumped to fourteen.[100]

The Irish famine migrants entered a city that already had a large and growing public school system and a strong Catholic commitment to parochial schools. During the famine years the city and county schools continued to expand, and the Catholic Church continued to build new schools.[101] Although the immigrants increased the demand for parochial schools, it does not appear that the Irish newcomers changed the direction of Philadelphia's school development. Rather, the legacy of earlier conflicts in New York City and Philadelphia was a strong commitment to separate Catholic schooling in cities across the United States. Of course, this commitment did not always translate into widespread Catholic abandonment of public schools. Boston presents an interesting counterexample. Although the Massachusetts city had its own prefamine history of nativist violence and battles over school texts, efforts to produce a strong parochial school system never really took hold. James W. Sanders attributes Boston's relatively weak system to several forces: a poor local Catholic population, a preference for "monumental churches" over school building, generally strong public schools, a Protestant School Committee willing to make some compromises, and a rather passive Catholic leadership. Thus a comparison of the results of Boston's school battles with those in Philadelphia and New York City points less to clear demographic and economic differences than to the importance of historic contingency as played out in particular divisive events and leadership decisions.[102]

Philadelphia was also similar to Liverpool in its contributions to ongoing discussions of national educational reform. In October 1849 Philadelphians hosted a National School Convention, prompting one correspondent to suggest that the convention should ask why the city and county paid tremendous sums for education and "still crime, fraud, violence, riot and murder increase." Such concerns were among the catalysts for the Industrial Ragged Schools, houses of industry, and evening schools that opened in Philadelphia during the late 1840s. These charitable schools typically stressed cleanliness, industriousness, moral training, and law and order over sectarian agendas. Nevertheless, local Roman Catholics were sometimes wary of Protestant proselytizers disguised as philanthropists.[103]

CONCLUSION

The histories of civil and sectarian schooling highlight the broad similarities between religious experiences in Philadelphia and Liverpool, while also pointing to several illuminating differences. As we have seen in earlier chapters, the timing of the migration was crucial in determining its effect on urban development. In both of these narratives of sectarian conflict, the crucial chapters had already been written in the decade before the Irish famine migration. Each city also had its own history of local battles over schooling, while playing an important role in ongoing national debates on education. The impassioned conflicts over Bibles in government-funded schools developed in an atmosphere already tense with sectarian hatred and distrust; the school debates in both cities further inflamed those tensions. In both Liverpool and Philadelphia, Catholic churches, schools, and institutions provided a refuge from antipopery or nativism.[104] And where circumstances placed Roman Catholics in other government institutions such as workhouses or penitentiaries, they used arguments for separate religious observance that had become more finely honed by the battles over school Bibles.

How do the famine migrants fit into this comparison? Even the conflicts that predate the migration were largely about the spiritual fates of Irish Catholic newcomers. The flood of famine immigrants forced the Roman Catholic hierarchies into a range of emergency responses as well as long-term institutional expansion. Catholics in both cities had already made plans for expansion before the migration, but certainly the enormous numbers pushed them to more energetic levels, while forcing some projects, like Philadelphia's cathedral, onto the back burner. However, the crucial commitment to separate parochial schools had already been made before the famine.

Another way in which the famine migrants shaped this story is in their wariness toward strangers, most notably toward Protestants bearing gifts and Bibles. In many day-to-day situations the migrants must have felt that their fates were in the hands of quarantine officers, relief officials, policemen, or Guardians of the Poor. But when it came to the marketplace of religious ideas, the immigrants could exercise more autonomy, rejecting the message and sometimes the messenger. Parents accustomed to fairly secular local schools and an Irish national school system that guaranteed all clergy access to the pupils, routinely refused to send their children to schools providing only the King James Bible. And philanthropists bent on social control would have to moderate their approach to reach these Irish Catholic newcomers.[105]

Clearly the Roman Catholic experiences in Liverpool and Philadelphia shared much in common in the decades surrounding the famine migration, underscoring the ubiquity of sectarian conflicts. Nonetheless there were telling differences. Although the numbers of potentially practicing Catholics in the two cities were fairly comparable, by most measures Philadelphia's Catholics seem to have out-built and out-organized their Liverpool counterparts. The 1851 census showed thirteen Catholic churches in Liverpool; three years later consolidated Philadelphia had twenty-four parish churches. And whereas Liverpool's Catholic charities struggled during the famine years, Philadelphia's more substantial network of charities expanded and the city added a new orphanage and St. Joseph's Hospital. Interestingly, the two cities were closest in their early development of a parochial school system. By 1853 Liverpool's Catholics had opened thirteen such schools; seven years later Philadelphia had fourteen.[106] This may be partly owing to the fact that some of Philadelphia's Catholics continued to rely on the extensive city school system, whereas few Liverpool Catholics took advantage of the Corporation schools run under the auspices of the Established Church. In 1858 Hume estimated that Liverpool had places for only 44,767 children in all schools; 10,663 of them were in Catholic Schools. In 1860 Philadelphia's *public* schools had 63,530 students. In the next decade Kenrick's vision of a separate parochial school system really took shape, growing to twenty-six schools by 1870.[107]

This contrast in institution building indicates some combination of various factors: differing national traditions of voluntarism, differing levels of Roman Catholic wealth, and the different timing of Catholic reform movements on either side of the Atlantic. Meanwhile, a comparison of the two cities' sectarian conflicts suggests local—and perhaps national—differences in political processes and decision-making. In Liverpool, conflicts over religious beliefs folded into the existing party structure, enabling the Tories to regain control of the Council and thus the Corporation schools. In Philadelphia, and the United States as a whole, religious antagonisms combined with hostility to immigrants—a factor that was not present in the Liverpool debates—to contribute to a dramatic reshaping of the party structure. Certainly the presence of the Established Church had everything to do with England's distinctive school debates. Whereas the impetus for parliamentary oversight produced major inroads in other areas of social reform, parallel talk of national schools foundered on the rocks of sectarianism, leaving the government with a modest role in supplementing a variety of schools rather than successfully establishing its own system. Anne Holt was correct in noting the sectarian forces at work in Philadelphia's mixed educational system, but the ostensible separation of church and state enabled Pennsylvania to push well beyond the English example in building a public school system, even while many local Catholics were abandoning that system.

The final difference may be the most telling. When the school issue came to a head in Liverpool, the disputants battled it out, over a number of years, in voting booths. Philadelphia had its share of political battles over nativism, but the central moment in the city's sectarian drama occurred in

May 1844 at Kensington's Nanny Goat Market, when enraged Irish Catholics fired on a gathering of American Republicans. The riots that followed, and the return engagement in Southwark several months later, were a stark reflection of Philadelphia's disorderly world. And those events would, in turn, play a crucial role in shaping the years to come. The nature of disorder and the pursuit of order in each city are the focus of the next chapter.

7. Street Violence and the Pursuit of Public Order

INTRODUCTION: POLICING AND PUBLIC ORDER

In 1829 Robert Peel, England's home secretary, engineered the creation of London's Metropolitan Police, a benchmark in the history of professional policing. The history of urban policing can be analyzed in various ways. On the one hand, it can be seen as a series of incremental—widely agreed on—responses to the problems arising out of growing city size, population density, and urban anonymity: uniformed police departments developed and grew as cities became more dangerous and individuals could no longer police themselves. On the other hand, the story can be told as a conflict between competing agendas: social and economic elites supported the development of professional police forces to protect property and commerce, suppress unruly elements, and maintain political control.[1] Either interpretation could portray the development of professional policing as an inexorable consequence of larger nineteenth-century forces—urbanization, industrialization, the continuing rise of capitalism—as experienced first in London and New York and later in other cities and their hinterlands. A different, potentially complementary, approach shifts the focus away from national and international patterns toward the defining role of local circumstances: communities adopted organized policing through a process of highly individualized decision-making in response to specific events and local challenges.[2] Whatever the explanatory model, the Irish famine migrants found themselves in the thick of debates over crime, public disorder, and policing in both England and the United States, particularly in Liverpool and Philadelphia.[3]

The famine years are an unusually interesting period in each city's police history. In Liverpool, the Watch Committee was asked to take on expanded bureaucratic tasks, sectarian tensions periodically spilled out into violence, and the city braced for anticipated Chartist rioting in 1848. Meanwhile, Philadelphians grew so incensed over street violence and fire company rioting that they embarked on major administrative reforms. The police reforms in both cities fit into the pattern of developments in London, New York, and elsewhere, but each city also responded to its own unique characteristics and concerns.

This chapter returns to many of the themes that have recurred throughout this book. The comparison of responses to crime and disorder in Liverpool and Philadelphia offers some opportunities to sift through the explanatory power of these various interpretive models. Rising population densities and economic elites committed to social order indeed shaped the discussions about policing in both cities, prompting important reforms. But whereas these larger problems and concerns were shared, the responses in the two cities diverged. Thus, we will return to the importance of historic contingency—the timing of crucial events and circumstances—and the power of distinctive national characteristics for explanations. Differences in governmental structure, political ideology, and demographic diversity all played a role in directing the trajectory of essentially similar local histories. The arrival of the famine migrants, stirring up existing ethnic, sectarian, class, and racial hostilities, was not so much a direct catalyst for enduring change as an important factor shaping ongoing debates. And, as in the comparative history of sanitary reforms, the migrants' impact on the discourse on public order was directly related to the state of local affairs at the moment of their arrival.

LIVERPOOL: SECTARIAN VIOLENCE AND FISCAL FRUGALITY

The Police Establishment

Prior to Peel's ambitious reforms in London, English and American communities typically had some patchwork arrangement of public officers and private police forces to protect people and property and enforce the law. Small parishes followed tradition by relying on elected constables during the day and night watchmen after dark. Some larger towns had a paid police force, but these daytime officers still typically shared responsibilities with a night watch and perhaps with private forces patrolling docks or other private property. Such patrols might stumble on a crime in progress or be available to break up a melee, but they were too small and too poorly organized to play an important preventive role. Cooperation between adjoining jurisdictions was generally weak, detection and criminal investigation were barely existent. The creation of the Metropolitan Police in 1829 offered a new template. London's three thousand uniformed constables were more numerous, more visible, and better organized than any earlier police force. Of course, this is not to say that Peel's reforms were universally praised or that other cities were anxious to adopt a police model that raised the twin specters of standing armies and high costs.

A principal aim of the Municipal Corporations Act of 1835 was to create uniformity in the administration of the 178 boroughs in England and Wales. The new Councils were to appoint Watch Committees that would name and supervise reformed police forces. The following year Lord John Russell acceded to Edwin Chadwick's call for a Royal Commission on rural policing. The commission's findings, published in the *Constabulary Report of 1839,* reflected Chadwick's firm hand. Building on early findings on poor relief and public health, Chadwick hoped to make a case that local policing establishments were in complete disarray, requiring the creation of a national policing agency with the Metropolitan Police at its core. His colleagues on the commission rejected his more radical centralizing impulses, but the printed report did support Chadwick's views by emphasizing "colourful thieves tales" while ignoring ongoing local reforms. The Rural Constabulary Act that finally was passed in 1839 left crucial authority in the hands of the county magistrates, but legislation in the same year— motivated by fears of urban disorder—placed the police of Birmingham, Bolton, and Manchester under central control.[4]

Under the old Council, Liverpool's modest police force was divided between a small day police of 44 constables, a night watch of 166 men, and an energetic dock police with 154 officers; each force reported to a different government body. The new, reformed Council wasted no time in establishing a 24-man Watch Committee, which soon created a full-time force of 350 men under Head Constable Michael James Whitty, an Irish Catholic. The new force quickly absorbed the separate dock police; by 1838 the Corporation's combined police force numbered 574 men.[5]

In many ways the new police force followed the London model, with military-style uniforms and an emphasis on crime prevention. On the other hand, many of the new officers had served the old Corporation as constables or watchmen, and the Watch Committee retained a strong commitment to frugality, suggesting important continuities with past practices. And the timing of the reforms owed less to external political stimuli than one might suppose. When the 1835 legislation passed, the Corporation was already in the midst of plans for a private parliamentary bill to establish a unified police force.[6] Rather like the Sanitary Act of the next decade, Liverpool's local bureaucratic reforms moved almost in tandem with Chadwick's national reform agendas.

Although an improvement on what had come before, the new police force still was enmeshed in a complex tangle of responsibilities and authorities. The head constable reported to the Watch Committee, which was under the Liverpool Council (although largely independent), but the officers often reported directly to the stipendiary magistrate. Moreover, police officers cooperated with the Health Committee in inspecting and clearing cellars, and with the Select Vestry in acting as emergency relieving officers, creating ample opportunity for muddled responsibilities and frayed tempers.[7] These organizational complexities took on a sectarian quality in 1844, when the mayor learned that as many as sixty police officers were reputed members of the controversial Ulster Protestant Orange Lodges. Magistrate Edward Rushton addressed the issue in consultation with the mayor and head constable but did not notify the Watch Committee, which included a few leading Orangemen. When it became known that the magistrate had ordered several officers to renounce their lodge membership or lose their job, Rushton and members of the Watch Committee exchanged angry words about abuses of power.[8]

The internal conflicts persisted. Whitty resigned in 1844 and his successor failed to last out the year before the Watch Committee dismissed him for insubordination. M. G. Dowling—who had been a London police officer, superintendent of Liverpool's dock police, and, most recently, Whitty's deputy—took over at the end of the year and soon found himself overseeing a sometimes unruly and not always popular force. Between 1844 and 1846 the committee received roughly 2,000 reports per year of constables committing various infractions; 327 men were dismissed during that three-year period. Nevertheless, on the eve of the famine migration the borough boasted one of England's most substantial and best-organized police forces.[9]

Public Processions and Collective Violence

Long before the famine migration Liverpool had been plagued by collective violence—ranging from election day conflicts and labor disputes to sectarian rioting. In the two decades prior to the 1835 Municipal Corporations Act, Anne Bryson has identified seventy-four violent episodes involving ten or more persons and several other cases where authorities took preventive measures in anticipation of political clashes. Two of these incidents, in 1819 and 1835, were conflicts involving Irish Catholics and Protestants following July 12 processions when Orangemen celebrated William III's 1690 defeat of the Irish Catholics at the Boyne. Bryson's research shows increases in most types of disorder between 1836 and 1860 (which may reflect differing levels of reporting over time), with a marked jump in attacks on the controversial police officers.[10]

During the brief period of Liberal political control, sectarian tensions ran high, due in part to the efforts of Hugh M'Neile, but only rarely erupted into serious street violence. The worst episodes occurred in 1841–42. In June 1841 a mob of shipwrights' apprentices attacked Irish Catholics at an Anti-Corn Law Association meeting, which led to several days of clashes. More than 175 people were arrested in election day rioting the next month. The following July several small Orangemen's processions were disrupted by minor conflicts with Irish Catholics. Throughout the 1840s the Orange Lodges grew increasingly numerous and active, but local authorities—often employing heavy preemptive measures—prevented further July 12 violence until 1850.[11]

St. Patrick's Day was not as inherently divisive as the Twelfth of July, but by the 1840s the March holiday had become identified with Irish Catholics. In 1846 and 1847 the Catholic clergy did their best to discourage organized celebrations, which typically resulted in disruptive drunken revelry. In 1847 Bishop Brown issued the following letter to be read from Lancashire pulpits:

> I have been credibly informed that a numerous party in Liverpool, having the name of Catholic, have begun to make preparations for a public display and procession through the streets of the town on the festival of St. Patrick. As such demonstrations as these are incompatible with that spirit of charity and brotherly love which our holy religion inculcates, and as they have been found by experience to lead to disgraceful breaches of the peace and many other evils, I earnestly request you to dissuade from the pulpit to-morrow and the following Sunday. . . . I also desire you to use all your influence in trying to stop the processions entirely. They are bad at all times, but at present when our fellow subjects are actually dying of hunger it would be inhuman, disgraceful, and

wicked in the highest degree for their countrymen to spend in such fool-ish and uncalled for exhibitions, that money which, if better employed, may preserve the lives of many fellow creatures who are pining in the agonies of death from starvation.

The bishop thus attempted to use the image of starving Ireland to help maintain order among the Irish in Liverpool. On this occasion the clergy's efforts were fairly successful: the day's procession was small, largely peace-ful, and culminated in a sermon stressing education, temperance, and cleanliness.[12]

Liverpool's Irish famine migrants, then, entered a town that had a re-cent history of sectarian and economic conflicts but that also boasted a reorganized police force and recent success in anticipating and stopping street violence. Moreover, the arrest data indicate that the police were be-coming increasingly energetic in their day-to-day activities: between 1844 and 1846 the number of prisoners arrested and brought before the magis-trates had risen steadily from 15,286 in 1844 to 18,171 in 1846.[13] The com-bined impact of heavy Irish immigration, an expanding Orange Lodge membership, and fears surrounding the national Chartist movement would make the next several years especially challenging for Liverpool's police and judicial establishment.

Throughout 1848 nearby and distant events gave Liverpudlians every reason to believe that their city could erupt into violence at any time. In February, they read news of revolution in France, soon followed by a string of revolts across Europe. Closer to home, England's Chartists embarked on another round of mass demonstrations in pursuit of political reform, while various working-class groups seemed to be threatening class warfare. In both Ireland and England Repealers mobilized to call for the end of the Act of Union while Irish Confederates pursued their own national-ist agenda. In fact, Liverpool survived the "year of revolution" with more smoke than fire, thanks in part to aggressive preemptive measures.[14]

At the year's first Council meeting, Samuel Holme complained of re-ported robberies on the outskirts of town. Mayor Horsfall responded that he had already ordered a hundred armed constables to be stationed in the vicinity and declared that the city had never been safer.[15] Two months later, with stories of violence in other cities arriving almost daily, Liverpool's un-employed porters, including many Irishmen, began gathering at Exchange

Square to protest changes in the system of porterage, raising concern that class conflict was coming to Merseyside. On March 11 anonymous placards signed by "A British Artizan" called for a public meeting at Exchange Square "to take into consideration why British artizans should have to pay dearer for every thing they consume than any other people under heaven." The mayor and magistrates called on the "loyal population" to ignore these notices posted by unknown "strangers." The few hundred curiosity seekers who gathered at Exchange Square on the appointed day found no meeting but a large force of armed police on hand and reserves stationed nearby. Constable Dowling observed a few tense moments with some "blackguards from Vauxhall Road and Toxteth Park," but before long the constables had cleared the area.[16]

Although the *Mercury* termed the March 11 placards "a fraud," the popular fears and official preparations were real, fueled by reports from Dublin and Glasgow that the Repealers and Chartists had joined forces to burn Manchester and Liverpool. One letter from Glasgow to Liverpool's mayor blamed the plans on "the Irish and low-English and Scotch." The magistrates swore in a thousand "merchants, brokers, and others" as special constables and made emergency plans to protect the commercially vital Albert Docks and warehouses.[17]

If the tension-filled city was going to explode, St. Patrick's Day seemed likely to produce the spark. Wealthy banker and merchant George Holt was sworn in as a justice of the peace just in time to deliberate on "the necessity of being prepared for St. Patrick's Day, it being intended by the Repealers & Chartists conjointly to kick up a row." The Catholic clergy and Mayor Horsfall called for the cancellation of the planned processions; the Hibernia societies distributed placards urging that this advice be heeded. The *Mercury* suggested that the working classes should assist the needy rather than wasting their money on inflammatory displays. Horsfall reported to a concerned Home Office that Liverpool was still swearing in special constables, "chiefly consisting of the upper classes," with hopes of soon having five thousand armed men. The magistrates banned gatherings at the Exchange and ordered firearms and powder removed from gun shops.[18]

St. Patrick's Day passed peacefully, although the city took on an unaccustomed martial air. The constables assembled in the morning and then dispersed to await further calls, the police were ready at the station house, the county police were at the Old Swan, and several military forces—including the 11th Hussars, the 52d Regiment, and the 60th Rifles—were scattered throughout the city. The *Mercury* reported that there was scarcely a "drunk Irishmen" to be found. Horsfall received a warm letter from Liverpool's merchants, bankers, and clergymen applauding his efforts.[19] Other parties were less enthusiastic. Local Repealers held a large gathering a few days later and criticized the mayor and magistrates for raising anti-Irish feelings and taking steps calculated to "goad their countrymen into acts of outrage and violence." Why, they asked, was such an armed force necessary when the Irish clubs had promised not to parade and when there was no great history of St. Patrick's Day disturbances? The Repealers also attacked the magistrates for swearing in only Englishmen as special constables, and they claimed that Irish clubs—not English Catholic priests—deserved credit for maintaining the peace.[20]

For the next several months the local authorities remained vigilant and the Repealers and Irish Confederates continued to meet, making for persistent controversy and rumor but not the same level of public tension.[21] The Chartists were another matter. In April twenty thousand Chartists, and a now familiar array of police and military forces, attended a peaceful open air gathering. In the days before this meeting, police officers blocked Lawrence Reynolds, a leading Confederate allied with the Chartists, from selling swords out of his shop, which caused a scuffle with a crowd of workers. Reynolds charged the officers with unlawful obstruction. Magistrate Rushton reprimanded the officers but took no further action because of the recent "threats of arming and of open insurrection."[22]

Soon the policing emphasis shifted from dealing with public gatherings to handling rumors of dozens of subterranean Irish Confederate clubs, whose local sectarian battles were intertwined with conflicts in Ireland. In May Rushton heard a case involving a gang of Irishmen who had beaten a publican at his home on Mill-Lane, a reputed Orangemen's meeting place.[23] Two months later the *Mercury* complained that despite enormous expenditures on relief for the famine immigrants, "Irish clubs are forming here to threaten Liverpool!" In fact, the paper reported, there were already as many as fifty Irish clubs in Liverpool of a hundred men each.[24] The magistrates swore in twenty thousand special constables, largely from the propertied classes, and the government deployed several military regiments near Liverpool. On July 20—as rumors of Irish clubs circulated through the city—George Melly, the son of a prosperous Unitarian merchant, received this news from his father: "The town is quiet so far, but the magistrates & the privileged persons . . . are uneasy & wear a very gloomy appearance, every steamer from Ireland is waited for with fears by those who are to keep the peace, hope by those who intend to break it on the first favorable opportunity, preparations are however so complete that if there be any stir I fully expect that the friends of order will succeed." Meanwhile, the police staged several raids, seizing pikes and bullets from known Confederates, and four hundred leading citizens, including the mayor and magistrates, petitioned Parliament for permission to suspend the writ of habeas corpus, allowing for arrests without formal charges. In early August the police struck pay dirt, discovering a cache of five hundred cutlasses and canisters of gunpowder hidden in a cellar.[25]

The *Mercury*'s editors described the disturbing events with caution, fearing that local merchants would suffer lost business as they had during the 1847 fever. They assured their readers that the police, special constables, and military were well armed and quite prepared to maintain the peace. The newspaper was particularly pleased with a letter from "A Working Irishman in Liverpool" who acknowledged that "there are many Irishmen in Liverpool ready at a moment's notice to 'rise' and create a 'diversion' here, in the event of a revolt in Ireland" but that there were many more loyal Irishmen ready to be sworn in to preserve the peace. The newspaper concluded a lengthy July 25 editorial on "The state of the Town" by declaring that "we see no occasion for exciting great alarm in the public mind." In fact, "All our readers in the surrounding towns, and, indeed, throughout the kingdom, may be assured that they and their families may visit Liverpool at this season, for excursions, in perfect safety and peace. The streets are orderly and lively as ever; and the precautions to preserve the peace are satisfactory indications of a manly forethought to guard that blessing."[26]

A week later the threat of Confederate conspiracy had once again passed without serious incident, collapsing—according to John Belchem—"in the face of rigorous police action and in the absence of effective leadership." Sixteen of the leaders were indicted for seditious conspiracy, although several managed to elude arrest. The *Mercury* once again adopted a booster role, declaring:

> To our distant readers we can give the assurance of Liverpool being in a condition of perfect security and good order. Yesterday our streets were as gay as we ever remember them to have been, in an ordinary state of affairs. The utmost confidence prevails. The presence of the military, though only perceptible at intervals, rather adds to the animation of our public places; and the unmistakable loyalty and union of heart among all classes of English society, and a large portion of the Irish, too, requires not to be looked for—it presents itself on all hands, and gives a

tone to the public feeling unknown where either despotism or anarchy prevail.

But all of this good cheer was not without a cost. The weeks of tensions had pitted the Irish against the English; workers against capital. Five hundred dockworkers who refused to sign on as special constables had lost their jobs. Some locals called on their fellow citizens to hire only English workers. One open letter from "True Orange Men" to Liverpool's master tradesmen tried to remind local employers that the troublemakers were Irish Catholics: "We as a boddy of Church Men wish to inform you that we hair fully determined to doo away with all Roman Cathalicks from all Employes in this Town. We now give you Notice to turn from your Employ thoes too Romans, on or before Satherday Next, or Certainly we shal doo Either you or yours a Private Injury." Meanwhile talk of suspending habeas corpus—which had never proved necessary—had created rifts over civil liberties.[27]

The year 1848 left Liverpool untouched by its revolutionary flames. Even the widespread fears and intensive preparations left some members of the propertied classes unimpressed. In March, only a week after the St. Patrick's Day scare had sent the city into a panic, diarist George Holt Sr. summarized events in Europe and added, "In this country happily we keep at peace & have no fears of disturbance, except from the want of Employment and Food." On July 25, with thousands of special constables drilling in Liverpool, Louisa Melly wrote to her brother that "the talk here is rather dull to me—'Irish disturbances' etc. The world seems to going to rack & ruin all but dear little England & Switzerland who is quiet I believe—I went round the district with Mamma yesterday one woman had heard a report of the Irish coming to burn the town which she wanted to know the truth of they had better wait to burn it till the cholera comes, they may then do some good."[28]

Historians have been no more unanimous about the true character of Liverpool's 1848 civil disturbances. Louis R. Bisceglia argues that there was a strong, albeit informal, Confederate-Chartist alliance in Liverpool, although he acknowledges that the Confederates' interests really dictated local activity. Kevin Moore agrees with those Chartist historians who note Liverpool's relatively weak Chartist movement, even during the 1848 resurgence. Rather than attributing this solely to sectarian tensions undermining working-class solidarity, Moore contends that Chartism foundered in Liverpool by failing to mesh well with distinctive local party conflicts over free trade and protectionism. According to John Belchem, although Liverpool had had a strong Irish Repealer movement, by late 1847 the energies of the Irish middle class had shifted to the Confederates. In his discussion of 1848, Belchem emphasizes the widening role of the Irish Confederates—whose secret clubs soon attracted the famine migrants and members of Liverpool's Irish Catholic working class—while minimizing the importance of true Chartism and of the attempted Irish-Chartist alliance in Liverpool.[29] W. J. Lowe joins Belchem in focusing on Liverpool's Irish Confederates. But whereas Belchem found the secret clubs numerous and, at least for a short time, having the potential for armed insurrection, Lowe concludes that "as sinister as the Confederate clubs most assuredly were, it appears that there simply was not much going on."[30] In his study of Liverpool's sectarian violence, Frank Neal stressed the highly organized Orange Lodges while downplaying the level of Irish Catholic political organizing, especially in the 1840s. Neal thus found the Confederates' "boasts" in 1848 of their strength "ludicrous" and the official responses excessive.[31]

Whether or not they were excessive, these official responses—notably the deployment of large military forces and the deputizing of a small army of special constables—revealed a local government, supported by national resources, prepared to go to extreme lengths to preserve public order. These emergency measures showed a recognition that the established police force would be no match for a major armed insurrection. Such powerful responses to shadowy rumors reflected the larger international political context, a clear concern about the city's dangerous ethnic and class tensions, and a commercial interest in maintaining the appearance of calm and order. This last emphasis on Liverpool's reputation was comparable to the common concern for lost commerce if the port were to become known for epidemic diseases.

The 1848 disturbances—both real and imagined—drifted from the public consciousness almost as quickly as they appeared. For several years the traditional procession days passed without much commotion. In March 1849 the local Hibernia societies distributed placards announcing plans for a return to the traditional St. Patrick's Day procession. The following year the placards were countered by anonymous notices threatening to dis-

rupt the proceedings. In both years the head constable took special precautions, and St. Patrick's Day came and went without serious incident.[32]
July the Twelfth also passed peacefully for several years during the height
of the famine migration, with Orangemen staging their annual dinners but
agreeing to eschew parades. This uneasy peace threatened to fall apart in
July 1850, when some Orangemen insisted on holding a procession because their Catholic adversaries had marched on St. Patrick's Day. At the
end of the day the police dispersed a crowd of Irish Catholics gathered at
a public house where Orangemen were dining. The next day the Catholic protesters returned and shots rang out from the pub, wounding several
people—one fatally.[33]

Over the next twelve months sectarian tensions recurred. In September 1850 the pope restored the Catholic hierarchy in England and Wales
and named a Roman Catholic bishop of Liverpool, exacerbating the city's
already powerful anti-Catholic impulses.[34] That November, Protestants in
Birkenhead, across the River Mersey from Liverpool, called for a meeting of ratepayers to protest the recent developments. The situation was
ripe for conflict. A large number of Birkenhead's Irish Catholics, instigated by parish priest Father Browne, descended on the small town hall
to protest the gathering. Birkenhead police officials, anticipating trouble,
had arranged with Liverpool's Watch Committee for thirty men on standby.
When the crowd outside the town hall overwhelmed twenty policemen,
they called in the Liverpool reinforcements, who waded into the Irish
crowd with brutal enthusiasm. The crowd soon gathered reinforcements
of its own, as more Irishmen arrived armed with rocks and iron rails, and
the melee became a full-fledged riot. Father Browne managed to calm the
mob, but not before several officers had been severely beaten. That afternoon Constable Dowling arrived with fifty more Liverpool constables, followed shortly by an armed detachment from the 52d Regiment.[35]

The Birkenhead Riot fed Catholic suspicions that the public authorities were sympathetic to the hated Orangemen. The celebrated trial of
six of the alleged rioters became an occasion for airing these grievances.
Mr. Roebuck, the lead defense counsel, attacked the Birkenhead magistrates "who stirred up this riot, and who lighted the fire of religious ani-
mosity." He then offered testimony characterizing the episode as a police
riot against a hostile—but peaceful—crowd of Irish Catholics. The jury
found five of the six men guilty of riot, but Justice Williams was at least partially persuaded by Roebuck's argument, declaring that the initial police

action had been "illegal and unjustifiable," before sentencing the men to a year in jail.[36]

Despite the disturbances of the previous year and new rumors of the impending arrival of armed marchers from Ireland and elsewhere in England, Liverpool magistrates—acting on Constable Dowling's assurances—did not ban the Orange Lodges' July 1851 procession. When the first marchers assembled on London Road, they were attacked by Irish Catholics from the nearby docks, who were in turn driven off by more saber-wielding Orangemen. The eventual parade was unusually large, with two to three thousand official marchers and numerous other young enthusiasts. The police, absent during the first clash, helped maintain order along the route, but there still were many minor incidents and arrests. Afterward the crowds—and the disorder—dispersed throughout the city; two Irish Catholics were killed in separate incidents. The day's events reconfirmed many lessons learned over the last decade. First, whatever one's personal loyalties, Liverpool's sectarian tensions, which had become central to political discourse in the midst of the debates over the Corporation schools, were an ongoing threat to civil order. Second, the police had once again left themselves open to criticism as either inept or partisan. Some critics claimed that the officers were on hand to protect and support the procession, while allowing Irish Catholic protesters to be beaten mercilessly. Cynics pointed out that all seventy people arrested were Irish Catholics. And third, a consensus was emerging that the city could no longer afford to continue its tradition of sectarian parades.[37]

The 1851 violence helped engender a new round of investigations into the alleged anti-Catholic biases of the police force. This reform spirit gathered momentum the next February, when local police, acting on incorrect information, viciously attacked a group of Catholic worshipers. The ailing Constable Dowling left office in disgrace when it was discovered that he had altered a report implicating his officers in the incident. Following Dowling's departure, the magistrates renewed their efforts to identify and remove Orangemen from the police force, while the new head constable, J. J. Greig, began tightening discipline on the men who remained. In August 1852 Greig's force broke up an Orange procession, taking fifteen prisoners and effectively pushing all future demonstrations beyond the borough limits. That November Liverpool banned potentially divisive parades and other exhibitions, ending the more public aspects of both the St. Patrick's Day and Orangemen's Day ceremonies.[38]

The Famine Migrants and Public Disorder

The famine migrants did not create all of the tensions that bubbled to the surface in Liverpool between 1847 and 1851, but their presence certainly helped shape grassroots political organization and public celebrations, much as they framed contemporary partisan political and religious debates. In his examination of Irish immigrant culture, John Belchem stresses the importance of "Ribbonism"—the network of secret clubs that had a long history in Ireland—during the famine years and beyond. According to Belchem, Liverpool's ribbon societies, developed in the male world of Irish pubs, promoted an associational culture emphasizing mutual aid, nationalism, and sectarian identity that was quite apart from the sanction or control of the Catholic hierarchy. Although the ribbon societies had fallen from prominence by the late 1840s, the Irish Confederate organizers were able to mine the same veins in building their secret societies. Meanwhile, Belchem sees the linking of nationalism and religious identity—legacies of the ribbonmen—as crucial to the subsequent development of the Catholic Church's position in Irish Liverpool.[39] And, of course, the pub-based world of political and cultural mobilization and the parish-based network of religious institutions and associations developed partially in response to the threats posed by Liverpool's Orange Lodges, which owed their existence to transplanted Ulster Protestants.

Beyond their roles—as participants and targets—in Liverpool's collective violence, the famine migrants were reputed to have raised the city's general level of crime and disorder. Assumptions about the disorderly and criminal Irish long predated the famine, supported by periodic reports from constables in Liverpool and across the nation. The accuracy of such charges, and their true meaning, is not entirely clear. Arrest data reflect the interplay of various forces: police numbers and procedures, local statutes, the nature and location of illegal behavior, and the accuracy of reported information on nativity. In his survey of the available nineteenth-century criminal statistics, Roger Swift found that the Irish were indeed "more likely to be prosecuted and convicted for law-breaking than their English, Scottish or Welsh neighbours." But Swift pointed out that the Irish were often disproportionately involved in petty crimes or alcohol-related disorders rather than more serious infractions. Moreover, he noted, many of the characteristically Irish infractions, including vagrancy, reflected the disproportionate poverty of the Irish in England. Other arrest patterns can be linked to anti-Irish prejudices, which helped provoke violence and ongoing tensions between the immigrants and the police.[40]

Liverpool police and judicial authorities, perhaps reflecting this long-held hostility to the Irish, periodically pointed their fingers directly at the famine migrants. In April 1847 the chair of the Watch Committee reported that the recent "augmentation in crime must in a great measure be attributed to an increased population, particularly of the lower order resulting from a large influx of Irish emigrants and of navigators and labourers employed by the Railways, New Docks etc."[41] Head Constable Dowling, noting increases in total offenses and total arrests in 1847, concluded that "the increase of crime is not merely attributable to the natural increase of population, but when it is considered that the immigration of Irish which inundated the town of Liverpool with Paupers . . . it will appear extraordinary that the result was so small an increase in crime."[42] In November 1847 Magistrate Rushton told the Select Vestry that the new removal rules had led many migrants to turn to crime in hopes of finding sanctuary in jail. "During the whole pressure of last winter," he reported, there was scarcely a case of crime amongst these poor people, but since the passing of the act, rather than become chargeable to the parish, they become thieves. Within a given space last year, the summary committals of Irish for petty thefts amounts to 350 or 360. For the same period this year, and since the passing of the act for sending them back to Ireland the number had increased to 838."[43]

These reports suggest that if the famine migrants increased Liverpool's crime (or at least arrest) rate, it was largely by committing the crimes of pauperism as opposed to creating serious disorders or violence. In her study of rioting, Bryson found that the Irish were involved in more than their share of "private battles" and she reasonably suggests that many more went unrecorded in isolated courts and alleys.[44] Few such episodes found their way into the *Mercury*'s pages. In fact, during the famine years published reports charging police brutality *against* the migrants appeared more frequently. The most damning description of Irish disorder came from Constable Dowling, who, in July 1849, reported that "several men of the force have been seriously wounded and others severely bruised and beaten by the Irish Population of the North Division of the Town, where almost daily fights and broils occur, which but for the presence of the police would be a scene of constant uproar and bloodshed."[45]

New data published in 1849 gave Liverpool officials the hard evidence to make the case against the Irish: in 1848, 8,794 (39.9 percent) of the borough's 22,036 prisoners brought before the magistrates were Irish.[46] In his open letter on "Irish Immigration" to the secretary of state, Edward Rushton used these new data to suggest the disproportionate Irish share in Liverpool's rising arrests, which had jumped from 19,719 in 1847. The new evidence, he insisted, confirmed what he had been declaring for years: within twelve hours after landing, the migrants could "be found among one of three classes; viz., paupers, vagrants or thieves":

> The number of Irish brought into the Police court as prisoners during the year 1848 was 8,794; the number of Irish sent to trial or summarily convicted of felony during the same period 4,661; the English during the same period were 5,104. Now the Irish form but about one-fourth of the population, and yet they give very nearly half the criminals. The truth is, that gaols, such as the gaols of the borough of Liverpool, afford the wretched and unfortunate Irish better food, shelter, and raiment, and more cleanliness, than, it is to be feared, many of them ever experienced elsewhere.

Such evidence became a crucial piece in Liverpool's argument for expanded government assistance and removals.[47]

In 1849 there were 19,485 total arrests in Liverpool, more than 2,500 fewer than the previous year and roughly the same number as in 1847. For the next three years that figure remained below 20,000. Some of this decline may have been due to the aggressive policy of removals. But the parochial authorities were already removing large numbers in 1847 and 1848 and, despite Rushton's pleas, received no more assistance from the government after that date. The source of the 1848 bulge in arrests may lie more in the behavior of the police. David Jones has demonstrated that arrests for vagrancy, including a disproportionate number of Irish immigrants, peaked in 1848 before settling down to previous levels. An emphasis on vagrancy and other minor offenses would also help explain the relatively large share of Irish women among 1848 arrests. Women comprised 3,514 of the 8,794 (40 percent) Irish prisoners in 1848, compared to less than 32 percent among non-Irish prisoners.[48] In comparing the year's statistics with those for 1847, the head constable reported that roughly half of the increase—1,494 cases—involved arrests for some form of disorderly conduct. This increase may have reflected a more aggressive crackdown on public behavior during the tense months of 1848. Moreover, the rise in arrests almost certainly reflects the mid-1848 emergency expansion in the police force, which jumped from 830 total employees (including clerks) in late July to 1,090 men in mid-September.[49]

Liverpool's officials and citizenry rarely seemed as concerned with day-to-day disorder as they were with having an efficient, cost-effective police force. The *Mercury* routinely printed letters criticizing the organization and costs of the local police force. Some of the most heated discussions related to the composition of the police force, particularly what Samuel Holme called "the vexatious questions of Orangemen and Ribbonmen." In May 1848, in the midst of Liverpool's sectarian conflicts, one "Old Police-Officer" charged that since 1844 (the year Constable Dowling took office) influential members of the "Orange Society" had been dictating police appointments. Two weeks later Dowling, perhaps sensitive to such criticism, took pains to report that "during the late excitement the whole force of necessity underwent considerable extra exertions and fatigue . . . without a murmur, leaving no doubt upon his mind as to their loyalty and determination to do their duty to the utmost."[50]

Other discussions centered on the size and structure of the police force. In late 1847 a committee of the Liverpool Council visited Birmingham and Manchester and returned with recommendations to streamline the bureaucracy by combining the Watch Committee and the Health Committee and giving more authority to the head constable than the Watch Committee.[51] By early 1849 the return to calm led some councillors to question the size of Liverpool's police force, which—they pointed out—had far more members per capita than Manchester's. Head Constable Dowling reluctantly presented the Watch Committee with a plan that could reduce the force by fifty men, for a savings of "upwards of £6,000 per annum." It was in the midst of these discussions that Dowling offered his dramatic portrait of Irish violence while also pointing out that in the previous several years his officers had been "almost constantly employed in passing medical reports to the health and sanatory officers for district and other surgeons." Nonetheless, in 1850 Liverpool's police force dropped to 806 men, down from 892 the previous year. The force stayed at that size for several years and did not rise above 900 men until 1856. In 1849, the peak year, the regular police force numbered one officer for every four hundred people.[52]

These reductions in the size of the police force fit with the larger sense of Liverpool's midcentury priorities. The local reforms of the late 1830s had expanded the police force while also stressing centralization and improved organization. Throughout the 1840s day-to-day crime was less of a public concern than explosive public riots and rumored secret societies.

Large public disturbances remained under the jurisdiction of the mayor and magistrates, who repeatedly used their authority to enlist large forces of special constables, rather than the Watch Committee and the regular police. So long as the city's mercantile interests were protected, by banning ethnic processions and patrolling the docks, and so long as the Irish contained their worst violence within their own courts and alleys, officials seemed more interested in frugality than expanded routine policing. This emphasis on controlling certain kinds of civic disorders also placed Irish *men,* much more so than women, at the center of public concerns. Although Irish women were well represented in the city's arrest tallies, the policing focus on secret societies and ethnic processions directed public attention to masculine forms of collective action.

PHILADELPHIA: DISORDERLY CITY

Policing in Prefamine Philadelphia

Colonial America's police forces evolved much like those in England and across Europe. By the early 1800s the typical American city had some patchwork system of constables who patrolled the streets during the day and a night watchman who lit lamps, watched for fires, and otherwise kept the peace until dawn. Over the next several decades the pressures of increased population density, a popular perception that crime was growing worse, and growing demands for urban services strained this traditional system. Meanwhile, the developments in London prompted calls for similar reforms in American cities.[53]

By the end of the eighteenth century Philadelphians had taken steps to replace the old system of citizen-officers with a paid, somewhat regulated, force of night watchmen and day constables. In 1811 the city had fourteen constables and thirty-eight night watchmen. Two decades later the size of the watch had grown and the surrounding districts had their own small forces, but the essential structure was unchanged, with the watch reporting to city commissioners and the small constabulary appointed by the mayor. In 1833 financier and philanthropist Stephen Girard expressed both his admiration for Peel's London reforms and his concern for Philadelphia's disorder by providing funds in his will to improve the efficiency of the local police force.[54]

Over the next several years the Philadelphia police underwent a series of reforms, culminating in a new structure that divided the city into four watch districts, with all forces reporting to the mayor. The new system was more efficient than the one it replaced, but the division between daytime policemen and night watchmen remained. Moreover, despite talk of establishing a truly "preventive" police force, and despite the financial assistance from Girard's bequest, the city Council opted for a relatively small force of 120 watchmen, 24 policemen, 12 inspectors, 4 lieutenants, and a captain.[55]

David R. Johnson has argued that American reformers had to contend with distinctive cultural resistance to police expansion. Viewed through the lens of the dominant republican ideology, the English reforms smacked of dangerous centralization and militarism, threatening individual liberties. Moreover, the case for reform had to be made in the face of concerns over excessive costs. Despite much talk of reform, in 1836 New York City Council voted down a proposed police reorganization, and seven years later it rejected a measure to expand the force to six hundred men. Chicago's 1837 charter provided for seven constables, but city authorities chose to leave most of those positions unfilled. Even the modest expansion of Philadelphia's police force was deemed excessive: in 1835 the frugal Council trimmed the number of day police and the number of watch houses.[56]

The barriers to change notwithstanding, Philadelphians undertook substantial policing reform during the 1840s. By the start of the decade, Philadelphia had already developed a disturbing reputation as a disorderly city. Small street fights and larger riots routinely disrupted life in the City of Brotherly Love. Handloom weavers battled employers, southern sympathizers attacked abolitionists, political partisans turned election days into public melees. Between 1829 and 1849 African Americans were the victims of five major riots, and the city's racial tensions erupted in innumerable smaller clashes.[57] Many of the most notorious episodes involved volunteer fire companies, which regularly fought over terrain, reputation, and for pure recreation.[58] Often fire companies had affiliated youth gangs, who joined in their elders' affrays or staged their own street battles. In the 1840s alone, Johnson found eighty-three stories about gang activity in the *Public Ledger,* with twenty-six different gangs identified by name.[59] The problems with managing these disorderly episodes were exacerbated when the conflicts strayed beyond the city boundaries into Philadelphia County, where each district had its own small police force. Disruptive gangs could elude arrest simply by fleeing their pursuers' jurisdiction into a neighboring district.

The nativist riots of 1844 were a particularly dramatic catalyst for change. The riots' two stages, separated by several months and occurring in different neighborhoods, underscored Philadelphia's explosive sectarian tensions, notably between Irish Catholics and Protestants; they also called into question the effectiveness of the city's police and militia establishment. Earlier that year the state legislature had taken a stab at reforming Philadelphia's still unwieldy police apparatus, considering—but not passing—a bill that would have attempted to "condense the police business into an efficient system" while also increasing the number of police judges. The bloody and humiliating 1844 disturbances shifted the weight of popular opinion toward more meaningful local reforms. Following the first round of rioting, many residents faulted public officials for doing too little. Acutely aware of such criticism, the militia's General George Cadwalader employed his troops aggressively—and disastrously—when the tensions returned the following July, leaving four nativists dead. Before long, prominent Philadelphians were calling for new solutions to bolster the police force and remove the need for cumbersome military intervention. In this fashion, Philadelphia's police reforms reflected the same sort of booster spirit that drove Liverpool's sanitary reforms. And, again like Liverpool's Sanitary Act, the crucial impetus behind Philadelphia's police reforms predated the famine.[60]

In July the grand jury proposed that the city and surrounding districts appoint a new force of 450 men, combining day and night police under the mayor's direction. This plan confronted Philadelphia's central conundrum: the multiplicity of independent districts had become a bureaucratic and policing nightmare. Soon more ambitious proposals emerged, calling for the full political consolidation of metropolitan Philadelphia. For the time being such measures proved too ambitious for the city. Instead, the state legislature approved a far more conservative plan to enhance cooperation between municipal and district police forces while establishing minimum police forces for the adjoining districts. In the meantime, New York, with roughly contiguous city and county boundaries, had managed to pass major police reforms aimed at enhancing centralized efficiency while maintaining local democratic controls.[61]

Disorder and Reform during the Famine Years

The year 1847 began with no clear consensus about the state of crime in Philadelphia. When the court of quarter sessions convened in January, Judge Parsons reviewed the past several years and concluded that the 1844 riots had awakened the citizenry from its apathetic stupor, leading to improved policing and public vigilance, which had produced a gratifying reduction in crime.[62] But even as the judge was addressing the grand jury, Moyamensing's commissioners faced hostile calls for a public meeting to address the district's latest violent "outrages." The *Public Ledger*—clearly conscious of the importance of the city's good name—celebrated Parsons's optimistic assessment and sided with the Moyamensing commissioners, insisting that "[t]here seems to be a studied effort on the part of the journals of other cities to defame Philadelphia, and to denounce it as an immoral and disorderly city" even in the face of such positive reports. Other evidence leaves one wondering if the paper did protest too much. While the *Ledger*'s editorial page protected Philadelphia's reputation, the newspaper's chronicle of events routinely noted street disturbances, often directing the attention of the police or public officials to a particular street corner or neighborhood where the locals, typically gangs of boys, had gotten out of hand.[63] Near the end of the year the newspaper finally unleashed an angry editorial attacking "The Spirit of Rowdyism" on city streets and calling for increased police vigilance.[64]

In 1847 and 1848 local disturbances continued to weigh heavily on the public mind, prompting repeated calls for further expansion and reorganization of the various police forces.[65] Once again, the worst offenders were the volunteer fire companies. In November 1847 the *Public Ledger* applauded the ongoing initiatives to expand both the day police and the night watch, but clearly further steps were needed. Another spate of fire company riots that winter—largely in the adjoining districts—led to renewed calls for a consolidated police force and talk of replacing the volunteer fire companies altogether.[66] In early 1848 a new Police Bill expanded day and night police and reorganized the city's force into four districts. In the meantime, the commissioners of Northern Liberties and Kensington enhanced and reorganized their own small forces,[67] and the legislature mandated severe punishment for city and county fire companies that engaged in rioting.[68] But these reforms proved too modest to stop the unruly firemen. In July and August the surrounding districts reported unusually heavy disturbances involving hose companies, leading the Northern Liberties constable to invoke new regulations permitting him to call for assistance from special constables appointed by the court of quarter sessions. A few months later public attention turned to Moyamensing, where rival hose companies and gangs battled in a series of highly publicized affrays.[69]

When the court of quarter sessions opened the following February, an angry Judge Parsons prepared the jury for a range of cases of public disorder, including "rowdyism practiced by half-grown boys . . . sometimes upon the blacks in the southern part of the city" and annoying riots by volunteer fire companies.[70] But even as these disturbances grew increasingly irksome, that April the court, after making a detailed analysis of data on recent crime and poverty, concluded: "From all these statements, it is apparent that the last five years have not increased the pauperism and crime of Philadelphia. Let the increase of population be what it may, the number of criminals and paupers, taken as a whole, has diminished." The problem was not the city's overall criminal and economic health, but rather the specific threat posed by the "increase of juvenile offenders, resulting from the various associations of young men that throng the street corners, and find shelter in engine and hose houses, and who are banded together to commit crime, under the names of Rats, Bouncers, Killers, &c." In a moving final statement, the judge called on the grand jury to focus on "the suppression of this evil . . . so that they may suggest to the community some feasible check to what appears to be the only threatened source of demoralization."[71]

The evil would grow worse before it got better. In May and June 1849 there were almost daily reports of fire company and gang violence, generally in Moyamensing just south of the city. Although the sheriff of Moyamensing called out a special posse and the local commissioners urged extra vigilance, the violence continued unabated.[72] The image-conscious *Public Ledger,* sounding much like Liverpool's *Mercury,* expressed concern that such reports would "go forth through all the newspapers of the country . . . though it is probable that ninety-nine hundredths of the inhabitants of Philadelphia were entirely ignorant that such a dreadful condition of affairs existed throughout the day."[73] But even the most unreconstructed urban booster could not turn a blind eye after Moyamensing's full-scale riots in mid-June that left one fireman dead and several others wounded by gunfire.[74]

The investigation of Moyamensing's 1849 riots seemed to indicate that new regulations to deal with public disorder had not been properly heeded. Moyamensing's sheriff insisted that he had called on the Philadelphia mayor and the Southwark police magistrate to use their emergency powers to send him reinforcements, only to have both claim they had no jurisdiction. An irate Judge Parsons found many targets for his wrath. He was furious with the fire companies for their continuing violence, astonished by the recalcitrant conduct of the mayor and police magistrate, and skeptical about whether Moyamensing had followed the 1845 law in maintaining 1 officer for every 150 ratepayers. A month later the Moyamensing rioters were sentenced to jail under a new law that made rioting a felony.[75]

Within days of the worst Moyamensing riot, citizens of that district gathered at a mass meeting to discuss "Law and Order in Moyamensing" and determined to form voluntary bodies in each ward "to quell riot and suppress disorder." They further resolved "[t]hat this meeting approve and commend all individual and associate efforts for the moral, religious and physical improvement of the masses and deprecate and condemn all abuses of such efforts." In short, the men of Moyamensing created *voluntary, local* bodies to answer emergency calls, while declaring that voluntary moral and material assistance for the poor was a key component of social control.[76]

The attacks on African Americans, which Judge Parsons noted in February, remained another source of concern. In late August a large melee at 6th and St. Mary's Streets between Moyamensing rowdies and "some colored fellows" attracted police from Southwark and Moyamensing.[77] Six weeks later—on election night—a Moyamensing gang paraded down St. Mary's Street and passed the California House, a tavern owned by a mulatto man married to a white woman. Anticipating another attack, local African Americans assaulted the revelers; the consequence was a pitched battle in the southern Moyamensing neighborhood. The unarmed policemen who arrived on the scene were quickly driven off by the white mob, which then overran the California House, setting it ablaze. When several hose companies arrived, the rioters opened fire, forcing the firemen to flee. The rioters dispersed temporarily when they learned that the militia was on its way, but they returned a few hours later and continued to fight it out with local blacks until the next morning, when the militia returned with two cannons. Four people—two firemen, an Irish onlooker, and a black youth—were killed, and two dozen others were wounded and taken to the hospital.[78]

This terrible race riot occurred in the midst of accelerating calls for true police reform. A few weeks earlier the grand jury for the August term had celebrated a wide range of improvements but concluded that something must be done to address the "alarming increase of riots," particularly among fire companies. The answer, the jury declared, was to consolidate the city under one municipal government. The day after the California House riot, Joel Jones and the Independent People's Ticket defeated the incumbent Democrat in a mayoral campaign that emphasized the battle against crime and political corruption. The forces for consolidation rapidly gathered strength but required cooperation between the Democratic city Council and the Whig-dominated county governments.[79]

Full municipal consolidation would have to wait until 1854, but the 1849 riots helped convince Philadelphians that policing could no longer rely on decentralized administration. Some participants in the debate noted London's success in consolidating its police forces, suggesting that Philadelphia could profit from the English example. Others joined the chorus for consolidation with fiscal considerations in mind, pointing out the accumulating damage to the city's commercial reputation or noting that disorder in the districts was hindering potentially profitable development.[80]

In May 1850 the state legislature finally acted, but with characteristic caution. Rather than passing a full consolidation plan, it established a "Marshall's Police" under the direction of a Police Board with representatives from each district. The Marshall's Police had authority to roam across the entire metropolitan area, working with the local forces to put down disorders. The solution met with opposition from both sides: advocates of local autonomy feared the imposition of armed outsiders; proponents of full consolidation found the new force too limited. The board had the authority to name 1 officer for every 150 taxable residents, but in practice it assembled a much smaller force of 167 officers and 1 lieutenant for each of the twelve divisions, or roughly 1 man for every 400 taxables. By July 1851 the Marshall's Police had made over 7,000 arrests, more than half for breaches of the peace. Many observers were pleased with these results. An enthusiastic *Pennsylvania Journal of Prison Discipline and Philanthropy* celebrated the new armed body, declaring: "There are not a few persons in such a community as ours, who are restrained much more by fear than by any other motive." In his 1887 history of the Philadelphia police, Howard Sprogle concluded that the 1850 reforms had a "wonderful" effect in subduing "the lawless clubs and associations which had for years committed disorder and crime." But as anticipated, the new system did not satisfy everyone. Moyamensing continued to be plagued by disorder, leading disgusted locals to establish their own citizens' patrols. Even Sprogle acknowledged that the worst "ruffians in the districts . . . were not much interfered with." Meanwhile, the Marshall's Police periodically clashed with local police, underscoring the difficulties created by the new overlapping jurisdictions.[81]

From a distance, Philadelphia's 1850 police reforms conformed to several models of police development. They were certainly the logical next step for a large city that had outgrown its earlier police establishment and limited jurisdiction. They were also a clear attempt to ensure "social control" in the name of social order and economic prosperity: the driving force for reform was not a widespread increase in crime, but rather the disorderly behavior of gangs of young men and boys. The chain of events from the 1844 nativist riots through the 1849 Moyamensing riots can be used to support a thesis that police departments emerged and expanded in response to specific events, but the real catalyst for reform was less a single dramatic moment than the building public perception that city streets were becoming an ongoing battle zone. Here Philadelphia's story is very different from Liverpool's, undermining an analysis that depends on the universality of urban experiences. Liverpool answered its major threats to public order by naming special constables and ordering out the military rather than reforming the established police. These emergency measures (which were not even directed by the Watch Committee) suggest a different way of doing things, but they also point to a different set of challenges. Liverpool's most worrisome public disorders often occurred during celebration days or at announced assemblies or events, allowing for the use of short-term armies of soldiers and special constables. Philadelphia's disruptive fire companies and gangs followed no such predictable agenda and were generally smaller in scale, thus calling for a jurisdictional solution while not allowing for emergency militia responses. Whatever their differences, both cities' challenges to public order found the Irish at center stage.

The Disorderly Irish?

Philadelphians who scrutinized published arrest and prison statistics would have had little reason to point an accusing finger at the Irish, at least not until the mid-1850s. Between 1827 and 1847 only about 8 percent of the prisoners incarcerated in the Eastern State Penitentiary were Irish; in 1849 the penitentiary committed 128 prisoners, including 22 Irish natives (16 percent).[82] The inspectors of the Philadelphia County Prison began publishing their annual reports in 1848, including brief tables listing the nativity of prisoners sentenced to hard labor. In 1847 only 21 of 175 (12 percent) of these prisoners were Irish-born. During the next three years, as Irish migrants flooded into the city, the share of Irish-born among prisoners sentenced to hard labor climbed slowly; but in 1850—the year that the legislature established the Marshall's Police—the Irish-born were still only 21 percent of the total. (In 1850 roughly 17 percent of Philadelphians were Irish-born.) The largest increases occurred in the next several years: in 1852, 86 of the county's 317 (27 percent) prisoners sentenced to hard labor were Irish natives. A closer look at the data reveals that African Americans, who made up less than 5 percent of the county population, comprised over two-fifths of the hard laborers during the peak famine years. Thus, the Irish were substantially overrepresented among white convicts, with between 26 and 37 percent of the annual figures; often half or more of the handful of women sentenced to hard labor were Irish.[83]

These county prison data obviously reflect the effects of some combination of criminal behavior, legal statutes, and police and judicial enforcement. The relative poverty of Irish immigrants could easily explain their disproportionate appearance among white convicts. The fact that both African Americans and Irish natives appeared disproportionately among the county's hard laborers illustrates Noel Ignatiev's point that at midcentury the Irish were engaged in a struggle to define themselves as truly "white" and thus distinctive from American blacks. This tension over status and community perceptions helps explain the long-standing racial antagonism that Philadelphia's Irish population felt toward the African American community.[84]

But if we are most concerned with how and why the city's police institutions evolved, the overall criminal behavior of the famine migrants might be largely irrelevant. After all, in 1849 Philadelphia was celebrating an overall *decline* in many indices of criminality, including inmates of the state penitentiary, convicts in the county prison, and persons held before the magistrates for misdemeanors and other minor offenses. As the court of quarter sessions concluded in April 1849: "Let the increase of population be what it may, the number of criminals and paupers, taken as a whole, has diminished." In fact, in July 1849—as Philadelphians were crying out for an improved police establishment—the *Pennsylvania Journal of Prison Discipline and Philanthropy* ran a brief story on "Crime in Liverpool", declaring that Philadelphia, with a very similar population, had far lower arrest rates and fewer Irish convicts. The article quoted the latest annual data from Liverpool listing 4,661 Irish natives among 10,706 jail commitments, comparing them with the recent Philadelphia County Prison report listing a mere 128 commitments including 22 who were Irish.[85] The inspectors of the county prison were unusual in reporting the nativity of their inmates during the famine years. Even the statistically minded *Pennsylvania Journal* only occasionally indicated the ethnicity of criminals. A noteworthy exception (several years after the famine) was in 1856, when it reported that of 36,657 arrests in Philadelphia in 1855, "TWENTY SIX THOUSAND of these offenders were of foreign birth—nearly 22,000 being from Ireland alone." Later published data confirmed this conclusion: throughout the late 1850s Irish immigrants were arrested for minor offenses at a rate far beyond their share of the population. But whether or not such evidence provided an accurate portrait of Irish criminal behavior, and even if the (unpublished) data from the years before 1855 showed similar rates of Irish arrests, the overall arrest rates were not the main catalyst behind the push for police reforms.[86]

The persistent calls for police reform during the late 1840s focused on street disorder, especially those episodes that were either too large for the existing police forces to handle or that confounded the limited local jurisdictions (that is, when savvy gang members escaped arrest by fleeing to neighboring jurisdictions). During 1848 and 1849 newspaper stories, editorials, letters to the editor, and official reports routinely mentioned the youth gangs, unruly fire companies, and disreputable types hanging out at street corners. In short, middle-class Philadelphians were upset that the "disorderly sort" was taking control of the city's public space, particularly in working-class neighborhoods in Moyamensing and Southwark.

Were Irish immigrants joining these disruptive groups and exacerbating the problems? Many youth gangs and fire companies organized along ethnic lines, often with a distinctly Irish character. Moreover, whereas many battles were strictly "recreational," with little more than turf or ethnic pride at stake, the patterns of conflict did reflect larger political and ideological conflicts—often grounded in nativism, anti-Catholicism, or racism—in which the Irish were central participants.[87] The antiblack attack on the California House, for instance, was led by the notorious "Killers," a gang with a distinctive Irish Catholic character. Southwark's nativist Schiffler Hose Company and the affiliated Schiffler Association youth club took their names from a Protestant who fell during the 1844 riots.[88]

The timing of the heightened public outcry over street violence matches the famine migration, supporting a hypothesis that arriving Irish boys and young men turned to gangs and hose companies for companionship and cultural identity in their new environment, thus embracing a distinctive form of American associational voluntarism. In the early 1850s several published reports on Philadelphia's volunteer fire companies lamented recent changes in their composition. A committee appointed in 1852 to study the problem reported that for many years the city's volunteer fire companies had been a source of pride, but sadly they had "passed from the hands of the men of the town into those of minors" who preferred violence to order. Other reports listed fire companies that had been ordered out of service or appeared on court dockets for disorder. But none of the published reports or the many newspaper stories on street disorder directly blamed the Irish newcomers. In fact, the accounts rarely mentioned that Irishmen were involved (perhaps assuming that their last names identified their ethnicity).[89] It would appear that the young male Irish newcomers who swelled the ranks of Philadelphia's disorderly gangs and hose companies were so well assimilated into this distinctly local, ethnically divided, associational world that their immigrant status—as opposed to their class, age, and gender—did not merit comment.

Whereas the famine migrants—or at least the young men—almost certainly contributed to the escalating street violence by joining gangs and hose companies, the Irish immigrants who entered the city's broader associational world played no such disruptive role. Like Liverpool, Philadelphia's Irish cultural world stretched well beyond the bounds of the Catholic Church, encompassing a wide array of social and fraternal societies. However, as Dale Light has demonstrated, much of this Irish associational world took shape *after* the famine years. The clubs and societies already established before the mid-nineteenth century were largely, like the elite Hibernia Society for the Relief of Emigrant Irish, nonpolitical, although Light does note periodic spates of nationalist organizing among prominent Philadelphia Irish. During the famine years, Philadelphians followed the Chartist movement with interest, but the City of Brotherly Love had nothing akin to the ribbon societies or the other secret nationalist organizations that preoccupied Liverpool's Watch Committee.[90] Philadelphia's Irish civic rituals were also a pale imitation of their Liverpool counterparts. The Hibernia Society celebrated St. Patrick's Day each year quietly, with a dinner and a series of patriotic toasts (a tradition they set aside in 1847 to send the savings to the starving peasantry in Ireland). Both St. Patrick's Day and the Twelfth of July were occasionally marked by parades, but there appears to be no evidence of violence or unusual public precautions during the famine years.[91] In short, the associational world of the Philadelphia Irish played a vital role in building community at various socioeconomic levels, but during the famine migration there was no subterranean political world comparable to the societies that so vexed Liverpool officialdom.

Consolidation

In 1854 the state legislature finally passed the Act of Consolidation, placing Philadelphia and its surrounding districts under a new reformed government with a Council and a single mayor. This dramatic step addressed many of the logistical problems that had been accumulating over the previous decades, as growing populations and a multiplicity of political jurisdictions had made the delivery of services increasingly complex. Many factors contributed to the mix, but the driving force for change came from the city's police and fire company controversies. The new law dissolved Philadelphia's various district and township police forces, replacing them with a consolidated force organized in sixteen districts and controlled by the mayor. Making policing the first order of business, Mayor Robert T. Conrad and the reformed Council hired 100 new policemen, bringing the total to 820 men excluding officers.[92]

From an American perspective, these developments were substantial, placing Philadelphia on a tier with New York City as possessing the nation's most organized professional police forces. On the other hand, Liverpool's police force had been consolidated and reorganized for almost two decades and had numbered nearly nine hundred men at midcentury before undergoing *cuts* in the early 1850s. Even after consolidation, Philadelphia's police, like their compatriots across the United States, resisted donning official uniforms, a response in keeping with the long-standing American hostility to standing armies. Mayor Conrad did not get his officers into full uniforms until the end of the decade. In contrast, Liverpool's Watch Committee adopted a military-style uniform—following the Metropolitan Police model—as part of the borough's 1836 reforms. Thus, although it is important to consider the ebbs and flows in police reform in both cities, we must keep in mind that Liverpool's police establishment was well "ahead" of Philadelphia's during the entire period.[93]

Despite these differences, the police in the two cities shared much in common. Both forces faced periodic internal conflicts, often with ethnic differences at their root. In the early 1850s Liverpool's Watch Committee removed suspected Orangemen from the force. On taking office in Philadelphia, Mayor Conrad, a Whig who owed his success to Know-Nothing support, insisted that all police officers be of "American birth." When the Democrats temporarily reclaimed office in the following election, nativists underwent a similar purge.[94] Both cities also had problems with police brutality and discipline. In many cases the policemen charged with battling

Philadelphia's rioters were former gang members and firemen, suggesting that the police establishment did not so much reform as co-opt a portion of the city's violent street culture. David R. Johnson has argued that American policemen exercised more personal autonomy and were much freer with the use of violence than were their British counterparts. Certainly Liverpool's officers were the subject of frequent complaints about excessive violence, but it is impossible to judge whether "excessive" had a significantly different meaning on each side of the Atlantic.[95]

In his examination of the history of American policing, Eric Monkkonen placed policing within the context of emerging urban services and stressed the importance of urban "size hierarchy" in determining when each city adopted a uniformed force. As Monkkonen sees it, information and innovations trickled down from the larger cities, which had first encountered the problems of population density.[96] Clearly information passed freely back and forth across the Atlantic, with American cities paying particular attention to developments in London. But the differences in timing suggest that—in this instance—although Philadelphia and Liverpool were part of the same intellectual world, they did not share the same ideological system. Beyond their distrust of uniformed standing armies, the U.S. resistance to expanded and centralized police forces—in the face of disturbing waves of disorder—indicates the prominence of republican ideology in shaping American politics. In its mid-nineteenth–century form, republican ideology was not the stuff of partisan politics, but rather it encompassed a set of fairly vague, but widely shared, political values that were especially at odds with an expanding police presence. Philadelphians clung to a faith in individual liberties, democracy, and local autonomy while maintaining a healthy skepticism about any encroachment from centralized authorities, particularly where they might intrude on private property. It was one thing to call out a volunteer militia when riot threatened the city and quite another thing to support an armed force of outside interlopers. Thus, Moyamensing's voters initially called for volunteer citizen patrols when gang violence got out of hand and only grudgingly accepted outside assistance. Of course, ideological differences should not be overstated in this case. After all, Philadelphia and Liverpool eventually came to similar policing solutions, even if the Pennsylvania city—with greater urban violence—took longer to adopt major reforms.

Police reform was only the most direct response to the growing concern about urban disorder across England and the United States. The campaign to control public behavior, notably among the poor and working classes, was waged on many fronts.[97] Often the case for reform emphasized the moral shortcomings of the poor that led them into lives of crime. For instance, advocates of poor relief reform routinely saw intemperance as both a cause of poverty—and criminal behavior—and the product of indiscriminate giving. Temperance was not a purely Protestant issue on either side of the Atlantic; Roman Catholics of all classes embraced the total abstinence movement of the 1840s as both a source of personal virtue and a route to social respectability. In fact, the histories of the temperance movement in Liverpool and Philadelphia are directly linked in the person of Irish Catholic temperance crusader Father Theobald Mathew. In 1849 Mathew visited both cities and persuaded thousands of Catholics and Protestants to "take the pledge." Conflicts over alcohol did have an inherent class and ethnic dimension insofar as working class and immigrant drinking—and drunkenness—was most likely to occur in public places. This emphasis on controlling behavior in public places is reflected in the large number of midcentury arrests for drunkenness, disorderly conduct, and related misdemeanors. We thus come full circle: concerns about poverty and civic disorder promoted attacks on alcoholic beverages, which helped turn public drinking into a crime, which was committed most frequently by the poor, who were often Irish immigrants.[98]

Civic disquiet over personal conduct was also behind the upsurge in institution building in the second quarter of the century. Some of the most innovative discussions in the decades before the famine migration centered on the development of new forms of penitentiaries, designed to reform as well as imprison.[99] In 1829 Pennsylvania's Eastern Penitentiary opened its doors in Philadelphia, patterned after the Western Penitentiary in Pittsburgh. Two years later the state legislature authorized the construction of a new county prison in Moyamensing, which replaced the notorious old Walnut Street Prison in 1835. Built following the revolutionary principle of isolated confinement, both prisons were designed for the extended incarceration of a fairly limited number of prisoners; each had roughly four hundred separate cells. In 1836 the prison commissioners approved the construction of a new building adjoining the county prison for short-term prisoners. In 1848 the county prison held a total of 4,423 such prisoners, mostly for very short periods. This local and statewide prison system served Philadelphia for several decades, while attracting extensive scrutiny from prison reformers worldwide.[100]

Liverpool's prisoners were also confined in several facilities, depending on the gravity of the crime. Minor offenders went to the old borough jail on Great Howard Street, controlled by municipal authorities. More serious offenders were incarcerated in the Kirkdale Gaol to the north of the borough, one of four jails in Lancashire County. Rev. John Clay, the influential chaplain of the county's Preston Gaol, followed the American prison debate with interest. Clay concluded that the Philadelphia system of separate cells was superior to the less expensive "silent system" that had been developed at Albany, New York. In 1846 a committee of Lancashire justices, following Clay's recommendations, voted to adopt the separate system in Kirkdale and other county jails. In practice, this decision was not so sweeping; seventeen years later Kirkdale still had only 162 separate cells. By the late 1840s the press of numbers and the push for prison reform were putting serious pressure on the local and county prison facilities. In 1848 the Council and magistrates finally approved plans for the construction of a large new borough jail. Although "increasing prosperity and . . . fuller general employment" actually reduced committals in the early 1850s, the grand new Walton's Prison opened its doors in 1855.[101]

The most confident reformers believed that well-run prisons would reduce crime by reforming criminals, but even these optimists conceded that it would be far better—and less expensive—to keep impressionable youths from turning to crime. The widespread concern about juvenile delinquency was at least partly behind the midcentury establishment of charitable schools, orphanages, and ragged schools in every British city. In 1842 Liverpool's Hibernia Schools issued an impassioned appeal for assistance aimed at "all who are alive to the *extent and degree of Juvenile depravity in Liverpool.*" A few years later Liverpool diarist Anne Holt described a dinner conversation in which she advocated free schools for the poor as "the best 'prevention of crime society' that could be instituted." By the 1840s several American cities had already built separate reformatories for troublesome youths. The managers of Philadelphia's house of refuge—established in 1828—routinely stressed the importance of providing its inmates with discipline to spare them from a life of crime.[102]

With the famine migration, anxieties about unruly youths in both cities heightened, promoting new and expanded institutional responses.[103] The number of youths admitted to Philadelphia's house of refuge climbed steadily in the late 1840s and early 1850s, with first- and second-generation Irish comprising a disproportionate share of their numbers. The institution's midcentury reports paid special attention to the growing problem of juvenile delinquency, noting that it shared this concern with English reformers. Philadelphia's grand juries and courts of quarter sessions followed the house of refuge evidence carefully, issuing regular warnings about the rising problem of delinquency. Girard College opened in 1848 to provide a home for orphaned boys "taken from a class not likely to have received that very early discipline, so necessary for the success of efforts directed towards their moral culture." With reports of youth gangs becoming commonplace in Philadelphia in 1849, discouraged citizens proposed all manner of answers, ranging from evening concerts and lectures to a special "correctional police" charged with arresting rebellious youths "who defy the authority of natural guardians."[104] In England and the United States, schools for poor children were celebrated as inexpensive crime deterrents. The supporters of Liverpool's Industrial Ragged Schools—established in 1848—routinely praised them as a possible solution to the recent "fearful increase of crime," sometimes making the explicit case that such schools were a good investment if they reduced future prison costs. A handful of benevolent Philadelphians acted on the English example by opening the Logan Evening School on Callowhill Street. Judge Kelley applauded the school as "an auxiliary to the police" in the neighborhood and called on public school controllers to open night schools similar to those already established in New York and Providence, Rhode Island.[105]

Since 1845, Liverpool's poor children had been sent to the Kirkdale Industrial Schools rather than the workhouse, but unlike the major American cities Liverpool had no special public institution for delinquents. As early as 1846, Magistrate Edward Rushton began collecting data on juvenile delinquency and petitioning Parliament for a government solution, but it was not until 1850 that the Council named a Juvenile Offenders Committee to confer with the magistrates and vestrymen about a possible new asylum. Even this modest effort stalled over finances and the asylum's proposed location until 1854, when Parliament passed the Youthful Offenders Act. With this new legislation, existing local reformatories funded by private donations would receive government grants in exchange for Home Office inspection. Under the reformed system, local courts could sentence juveniles to the reformatories rather than local prisons. Spurred on by the promise of national assistance and the expectation that "several influential Gentlemen" would make donations, the Council approved a £2,000 contribution to purchase land and build the new reformatory.[106]

Liverpool Catholics watched these developments with mounting concern. In August 1856 Bishop Goss presided over a public meeting "for the purpose of making provisions for the Catholic children of the diocese who may become subject to the operation of the act for the reformation of Juvenile offenders." The meeting named a Catholic Reformatory Association, which arranged with the abbot of Mt. St. Bernard in Leicester to take charge of Catholic children who would otherwise have been sentenced to the new reformatory. By February the committee announced that a hundred boys and forty girls, "taken from the most part from the most destitute and abandoned class, for the most part criminal from no fault of their own, have been provided for & are receiving a thoroughly Catholic & Industrial Education" with the abbot. In the meantime, the committee began raising funds to build a local Catholic reformatory.[107]

The histories of juvenile reformatories in Philadelphia and Liverpool suggest fundamental similarities and larger differences between the two societies. Boston, New York, and Philadelphia all had reformatories by 1828. The major push for reformatories in England did not come until the 1850s. In Liverpool's case, Rushton's much-publicized comments about delinquency—which were comparable to Judge Kelley's in Philadelphia— failed to achieve local reforms until Parliament provided the added financial and administrative impetus in 1854. But although established more than a generation apart, the two cities' reformatories functioned in similar ways. Founded, financed, and run by private citizens, Philadelphia's house of refuge was incorporated by the state and enjoyed an official relationship with the local courts and the Guardians of the Poor. Liverpool's reformatory depended on a parallel mix of private contributions and public authority, but with the tremendous difference that the English model relied on Home Office supervision and subsidies. As the timing of these reforms indicates, the famine migrants did not *create* a public understanding that juvenile delinquency was an important concern, but their numbers promoted greater debate on the subject. And once again, the development of a national government solution in England encouraged Liverpool Catholics to develop their own institutional response to the problem.

CONCLUSION

The shared responses to disorder in Liverpool and Philadelphia illustrate many of the broader aspects of midcentury bureaucratic development.[108] Between 1840 and 1860 police departments, prisons, and reformatories in both cities evolved at a different pace but along parallel lines. The gradual process of police expansion and organizational consolidation was a natural response to the challenges of population growth and the lessons from other cities. The emphasis on preventing riots and suppressing disorderly conduct demonstrates the shared understanding that policing should be primarily concerned with maintaining order in the streets, especially where "respectable" citizens would be doing business. The discussions of prison reform and Lancashire's adoption of a modified version of the Philadelphia system offer further evidence that the two cities operated within the same intellectual and ideological universe.[109] The push for juvenile reformatories and night schools followed jointly held convictions that youths were learning the lessons of crime on the streets and that it was in the public interest to provide alternative lessons. Finally, in all of these public discussions politicians, reformers, and editors were liable to stress the importance of order in shaping the city's reputation and thus its commercial prospects.

The differences between the two cities' experiences reinforce the conclusion that urban centers did not develop in lockstep fashion. They also suggest that national characteristics—both structural and ideological—and not merely local idiosyncrasies, played an important role in shaping these institutional histories. Most important are the differences in the timing of reforms and the role of the central government. Liverpool's police reforms were local initiatives, but they still bore the mark of Chadwick's theories and Home Office input. The city's slow commitment to juvenile reformatories provides more dramatic evidence of the importance of a national impetus in the form of both financial incentives and governmental inspection. Philadelphia's—and America's—much slower acceptance of a uniformed, consolidated police force, even in the face of rising population and ongoing gang violence, supports a hypothesis of distinctive national characteristics. Although our two national observations are insufficient to determine which stance was truly "distinctive," the events in Philadelphia suggest an enduring republican resistance to standing armies. The much earlier establishment of the house of refuge and the tradition of independent-minded volunteer fire companies are two different manifestations of the American voluntarism that Tocqueville celebrated. Meanwhile, the resistance to centralized citywide policing fits with the militant localism that characterized so much of Philadelphia life.

Despite the generally similar responses, Liverpool and Philadelphia did not face identical challenges to civic order. Both had sectarian and ethnic conflicts, often with a distinctly Irish and masculine flavor, but those battles played themselves out in different ways. Liverpool's worst troubles had a political character: Chartists, Irish Confederates, and violent Orangemen were the sources of the greatest concern; the infiltration of secret societies and preemptive attacks on disruptive processions were the most important policing responses. When fear grew most intense, the mayor and magistrates—not the Watch Committee—called out special constables and armed troops. Philadelphia's most disturbing public disorders were more persistent and less easily anticipated. When volunteer fire companies or street gangs did battle on the streets, they did not distribute placards announcing their intentions. These dissimilar threats to public order, which became most pronounced in each city during the peak famine years, yielded distinct organizational responses. Liverpool turned to emergency measures that had little to do with the established (and already reformed) police force, whereas in Philadelphia the gangs' habit of fleeing from one jurisdiction to another provided a major impetus for police consolidation.

Although it would be almost impossible to measure, it does appear—judging from police records, grand jury reports, and newspaper accounts—that the City of Brotherly Love was a more violent place than Liverpool, supporting another aspect of supposed American distinctiveness. It was certainly the case that street violence between quasi-organized groups of boys and young men was of greater concern in Philadelphia's public discourse and thus played a more important role in influencing reforms. What might explain this difference? Philadelphia's greater demographic diversity, with its accompanying social hierarchies and tensions, encouraged collective violence. This is most obvious in the city's history of racial rioting, but it also promoted ethnic and occupational conflicts between groups competing for social, political, and economic status. In fact, Ignatiev has suggested that the Irish were also perceived as racially distinct in the United States. Unquestionably, their perceived distinctiveness contributed to street violence. The violence also reflected the associational—and recreational—patterns of many young people in Philadelphia and therefore should be seen in the context of a different cultural pattern of voluntary associations, an associational world that immigrant youths appear to have embraced with enthusiasm.[110] The street fighting also indicates a distinctive use of urban space. These gangs and volunteer fire companies battled in a world of contested public space, where their conflicts encroached on the lives of other Philadelphians, who, in turn, called for public solutions. True, Liverpool's public streets and thoroughfares were also potential battlegrounds. The city's most effective preventive measures were in curtailing parades on St. Patrick's Day and the Twelfth of July. But Liverpool officials managed to receive cooperation from the local clergy and Hibernian leadership, whereas Philadelphia's gangs answered to no such leadership and the city's ethnic conflicts knew no formal calendar. Perhaps the public nature of Philadelphia's disorders magnified their importance. It may have been that Liverpool's worst violence, especially that involving Irish immigrants, was hidden away in courts and alleys, as Head Constable Dowling indicated in his 1849 report. But even if that were the case (and one might reasonably suppose that Philadelphia had comparable amounts of unreported "private" violence), the fact remains that it was the very public nature of Philadelphia's conflicts that contributed to a distinctive culture of violence that, in turn, eventually produced widespread calls for reform.[111]

How much were the Irish famine migrants responsible for these developments in each city? On the one hand, Irish-born residents were at the heart of much disorder in both Liverpool and Philadelphia. But on the other hand, their differing experiences in the two cities suggests that the immigrants were adjusting to, rather than recasting, the established patterns of the host culture. In Liverpool, they entered a world of divisive sectarianism and subterranean Irish nationalist politics. Philadelphia's religious, associational, and political patterns were quite different, and thus the newcomers found themselves cast in different roles—both as participants and as victims.[112] The patterns of conflict and the essential policing apparatus were already in place before the famine. The Irish did not create the problems, but their sudden arrival certainly contributed to the timing of reforms.

Conclusion

COMPARATIVE EXPERIENCES

By 1846 Liverpool and Philadelphia had taken different routes to similar positions. While the potato blight was crippling the Irish food supply, both of these booming cities were enjoying national and international prominence. Steady demographic growth had also produced a host of new tests. The next few decades would prove crucial in determining how the two cities would meet these challenges. And whatever solutions Philadelphia and Liverpool chose would eventually help shape experiences in dozens of smaller cities. Into these evolving worlds came boatloads of starving Irish Catholic immigrants.

This study began with the journeys of a few famine migrants and with the observation that several forces had joined to force their tragic exodus: material preconditions, ruling ideologies, and a huge ecological disaster came together at that particular moment in time. The effects of the famine migration on Liverpool and Philadelphia were part of the next falling domino in the series of events unleashed by the potato blight. The comparison of the two cities' experiences—especially their responses to shared emerging urban problems—helps reveal the relative importance of material conditions, dominant ideologies, and the magnitude of the migration in each port. It also underscores the significance of timing and chronology in explaining events.

The material conditions in each city in 1846 were certainly not identical, but in terms of new urban challenges they were in fact similar. Each of the major themes addressed in the preceding chapters—poverty, sanitation, housing, disease, sectarian and ethnic conflict, crime and policing, education and delinquency—had been ongoing subjects of public debate in both cities. Local circumstances might dictate differing priorities, but these were central among the commonly acknowledged social challenges that accompanied urbanization at midcentury.

The two cities, and their nations, also shared many of the same core values insofar as they affected these urban policy discussions. Both political cultures had a declared faith in localism, voluntarism, and representative government and a skepticism about corruption and taxation. More broadly, they shared certain ideas—and debates—about individual and collective behavior. Contemporary discussions on the spread of disease, the proper design of penitentiaries, and the appropriate form of poor relief all reflect a larger struggle to find an orderly path in a world that— especially in an urban context—seemed increasingly complicated. Each of these debates, and many more, had a distinctly scientific bent, with published treatises thick with charts and graphs. In a more abstract sense, these discussions implied competing models of human interaction. A faith in the market and Adam Smith's laissez-faire principles could easily translate into arenas beyond commerce. Conversely, one might apply an anatomical model and see the city as a living, interdependent organism where one part's fate would have an important effect on the larger "social body."

The point here is not to suggest that Liverpool and Philadelphia were at identical points when the famine migration began, but to argue that they shared a fundamental set of pressing urban challenges and common intellectual assumptions. As we have seen, their responses to these problems during the famine years were also often comparable. But in other instances they differed. The seven interpretive models introduced by Derek Fraser in his history of the British welfare state (summarized in Chapter 1) are equally applicable to Philadelphia and Liverpool. Those seven perspectives, once again, are *Whig, pragmatic, bureaucratic, conspiratorial, capitalist, democratic,* and *ideological.*[1] All have some utility in explaining each city's history, but most are less fruitful as avenues for comparative analysis.

The *Whig model,* which understands the past largely as a linear progression to the (generally happier) present, is most useful in laying out a comparative path that we should avoid: we should not "rank" reforms according to their proximity to the present. The *pragmatic model,* which sees reforms as small, incremental responses to the specific problems posed by industrialization, avoids the Whigs' presentist pitfalls, but still has only limited explanatory or comparative value. At one level it explains—if any explanation is necessary—why Philadelphia and Liverpool addressed certain urban problems before those smaller towns that had yet to feel the press of population density. In a more subtle sense, the pragmatic model understands the importance of contemporary perceptions of need. Thus, perhaps reformers in Liverpool and Philadelphia might have understood problems differently and therefore moved in different directions.

This leads to the *bureaucratic model*, which stresses the role of anonymous officials and administrators. In both Liverpool and Philadelphia there were crucial officeholders, not always anonymous within their own communities, who played important roles in dictating how policies developed. For instance, things would have been very different in Liverpool if Dr. Duncan had not been present (although one might better classify Duncan as a reforming ideologue rather than as a mere bureaucrat). Moreover, clashes between local officeholders and committees repeatedly played a role in determining the next stage of administrative development. But even if we allow for the importance of the "statesmen in disguise" who implemented local policies, our comparative analysis would soon return to the larger world that created those policies, shaped their implementation, and selected the local bureaucrats.

Whereas the pragmatic and bureaucratic models are nearly value-neutral, and in fact describe policies evolving almost in an ideological vacuum, the *conspiratorial* and *capitalistic models* understand the emergence of the welfare state as part of larger—often hidden—agendas. Advocates of the conspiratorial perspective, most prominently Michel Foucault, have argued that the rise of the welfare state and the concomitant development of various institutions and asylums were all part of the pursuit of social control. Those in power created institutions and policies specifically to control the disorderly poor and "dangerous classes." The *capitalistic model* sees society's economic goals as driving the emergence of welfare policies. Like the conspiratorial model, the assumption underlying this perspective is that policies that on the surface appear to be aiding those in need are actually supporting the interests of the ruling classes, or at least those with ties to business and industry. The subterranean motives implied in these two perspectives do not lend themselves to systematic proof, nor would either necessarily be the only factor behind policy decisions. Both models contribute to our understanding of aspects of development in Philadelphia and Liverpool, but neither appears particularly useful in explaining differences between the two cities. For instance, discussions of both poor relief and educational reform in each city routinely turned on some combination of social justice, Christian charity, and a desire to control disruptive behavior. This last motive could fit the conspiratorial perspective, but it does not help us distinguish between the two cities: public discourse in both Philadelphia and Liverpool seemed equally concerned with the problem of social control. Public policies in these cities were also routinely influenced by economic concerns, which could support the capitalist perspective. But once again there is little evidence to argue that the two cities had differing commitments to capitalism.

Each of the last two perspectives bears an inverse relationship to what Fraser termed the *democratic model*. In this perspective, the expanding forces of democracy shifted the emphasis of public policy to working-class concerns. By midcentury England had undergone substantial electoral reform, expanding the local franchise to male ratepayers. In the meantime, universal white male suffrage was already the norm in the United States. Local political developments in each city reflected these democratizing forces. Immediately following the 1835 Municipal Reform Act, Liverpool elected its first Liberal Council; Philadelphia's complex party dynamics—with the demise of the Whigs and the temporary rise of local nativists—bore the imprint of Jacksonian political rhetoric and practice.[2] Although both political systems had become more open in recent decades, this perspective would presumably predict that Philadelphia's government—with its higher degree of electoral participation—would have been more sensitive to the demands of the masses. To some extent this was indeed the case. Even Liverpool's reformed Council maintained the traditional emphasis on commercial concerns, paying special attention, for instance, to the health of the dock estate. In Philadelphia, "Good Municipal Government" may have been more broadly understood in theory, even where common practice did not differ dramatically. But if Philadelphia did not have Liverpool's tradition of a local government run for and by the economic elites, neither did the American working classes have the unanimity or traditions required to promote a class-based political agenda. In short, this perspective has greater explanatory power in describing events many decades after the famine.

Fraser's final perspective is the *ideological model*.[3] Pragmatic concerns and faceless bureaucrats may have bent policy goals in idiosyncratic directions, and members of the elite may have used government to pursue their own social and economic agendas, but—as Fraser notes—"the ideological perspective makes it possible to relate social policy to the prevailing cultural climate."[4] In terms of the history of the welfare state, this perspective posits important transformations in those central ideas and values that shaped public policy. Thus it is useful for the historian seeking to explain changes over time. In our comparative project the ideological perspective offers somewhat different benefits. Rather than seeing Liverpool and Philadelphia at different stages of ideological development, we may see the two cities—or policymakers in each city—as selecting from among a shared array of ideas and values. As we have seen, the core values in one nation would certainly have been recognized, if not equally embraced, in the other nation. And beyond those core values there was an important constellation of shared theories and interpretations that had developed to address recent social challenges. The ideological perspective asserts that ideas really do matter in shaping events. But if the central ideas were available in both cultural universes, the perspective begs the larger question: Where their paths diverged, what forces led the two cities in different directions?

NATIONAL DISTINCTIVENESS?

Fraser's seven perspectives all provide important, often complementary, insights into the origins of the welfare state and the roots of a broader range of nineteenth-century urban social policies. They are not as useful in comparing concurrent processes in different settings. The ideological perspective points us in a promising direction, but without providing any further guidance as to how different national or local ideologies might have yielded differing results. Perhaps some of the seven explanations of "American exceptionalism," also introduced in Chapter 1, offer a more promising comparative perspective.

The long scholarly tradition, roughly as old as America itself, of searching for the origins of American distinctiveness is best viewed as a form of intellectual "stone soup." After all the research and analysis have been completed, we are probably best off if we jettison the original question altogether. The historian might reasonably ask how, and why, two cities and nations behaved differently in response to similar circumstances, but the assertion that one of the nations was somehow exceptional or distinctive is not really the stuff of historical analysis, particularly in the absence of a much broader comparative perspective. Still, the explanations for national distinctiveness can be recast as comparative questions.[5]

The first two approaches to American distinctiveness address aspects of political decision-making. In his journeys across the United States, Alexis de Tocqueville celebrated the important role of "Democracy in America" in shaping a national identity. Tocqueville, enamored with what he saw as a healthy rejection of European deference and hierarchy, identified a wealth of virtues in this new democracy, but much of his discussion emphasized the significance of America's political process and *political structure*, including the emphasis on participation, the nature of competing political parties, and the constitutional division of authority between the federal government and the states.[6] A second source of supposed cultural —and political—distinctiveness is nineteenth-century America's powerful and persistent *localism*. This localism has been described in various forms. In its most limited sense the term suggests a specific emphasis on local self-government.[7] Localism can also be understood more broadly as a traditional ideology or worldview grounded in a profound faith in the local community and a strong mistrust of outsiders and distant powers.[8]

Did these two sources of supposed national distinctiveness lead Philadelphians to behave differently from Liverpudlians? In the policy areas that we have examined, it is not at all clear that the political *process* pointed local officeholders or policymakers in different directions. But that may be because, in fact, political participation and the political process were not understood very differently in the two cities. Nor did Philadelphians have any particular monopoly on localism, at least in the abstract. True, residents of both port cities had greater contact with distant locales, and perhaps a more cosmopolitan perspective, than did the denizens of the rural hinterlands. Nonetheless, voters and officeholders commonly viewed social ills—such as poverty, disease, delinquency, and crime—through the lens of local concerns, especially when the solutions involved local taxes. Even in their hostility to outsiders, it is not clear that Philadelphians behaved more enthusiastically than their Liverpool counterparts. Thanks to the Act of Union, Irish migrants were already British subjects before venturing across the Irish Sea. Still, few English-born Liverpudlians confused the Irish newcomers with their own countrymen or women. Politicians, philanthropists, and doctors routinely spoke of distinctive Irish characteristics and problems. Public and private institutions commonly recorded the numbers of Irish-born residents as a separate category. Philadelphia's powerful nativist movement indicates a special hostility to outsiders, but the efforts to restrict citizenship reflected specific partisan agendas (immigrants commonly voted Democratic) and sectarian disputes as much as a pure rejection of newcomers.

The power of these two aspects of distinctiveness lies less in ideological abstraction than in political structures and jurisdictional assumptions. Although recent scholarship has pointed out the importance of local autonomy beneath the sweep of Chadwickian social reforms (and Liverpool has been offered as a crucial case in point), the fact remains that England's central government repeatedly played a crucial role in molding local decision-making. National investigations and legislation on workhouses, schools, reformatories, and penitentiaries all helped shape—if not absolutely dictate—policies and practices in Liverpool. Even where Chadwick's vision of centralized efficiency was not realized, the visits of government inspectors and the prospect of government grants prompted public and private officials to bend to the national will. The power of the central government in the public mind was most apparent in moments of crisis. Faced with overwhelming numbers of Irish immigrants, Liverpool sent desperate missives—and eventually an official delegation—to London in search of relief. When Parliament refused assistance, local outrage revealed a presumption that the national government had abdicated its appropriate role. Similarly, rumors of Chartist rioting in the city prompted urgent inquiries from the Home Office and the rapid deployment of national troops.

In contrast, Americans—and certainly Philadelphians—rarely looked beyond local government for assistance, or even guidance, in addressing urban social problems. (One of the rare exceptions was the passage of national legislation regulating passenger ships. These laws, which fell under Congress's constitutional authority to regulate commerce, had their direct counterparts in parliamentary legislation.)[9] In the meantime, the national government never addressed the rising urban problems of poverty, sanitation, crime, education, and the like. Even the state legislature rarely played a large role in confronting these social issues, generally limiting its activities to the incorporation of locally run institutions. The Eastern State Penitentiary in Philadelphia was a prominent state-run exception. In Liverpool, the Kirkdale Gaol—one of four Lancashire County prisons—played a similar role.[10]

The argument here is not one of absolutes. Local concerns and local autonomy were dear to the hearts of Liverpool's voters and elected officials. Crucial reforms, such as the 1846 Liverpool Sanitary Act, owed more to local initiatives than to pressures from London. And Philadelphians were not walled off from the outside world. National and international movements ranging from abolitionism, temperance, and nativism to the shifts within the Roman Catholic Church all affected local developments. But if we focus on the processes of decision-making and problem-solving, the differences between experiences in Liverpool and Philadelphia are stark. Although Liverpool officials might insist on local autonomy and perhaps claim a distinctive position as an incorporated city, a succession of national commissions and parliamentary reforms had given the central government a significant voice. Sometimes those reforms included regulatory sticks, often they involved monetary carrots. Other national reforms—a national education system or subsidized worker housing, for instance—had not evolved much beyond general discussions, but the very nature of the public discourse revealed a shared understanding that the national government might reasonably play a role in future developments. By midcentury Philadelphians and Liverpudlians had come to very different understandings of the role of the central government in their lives and their futures, and thus their shared commitment to localism took on very different forms.

A third source of purported American distinctiveness was the national commitment to *voluntarism*. This faith in voluntarism, and the enthusiasm for voluntary associations that Tocqueville found so compelling, are part of a constellation of values that are commonly identified with America's evolving republican ideology. By the mid-nineteenth century these values included not only a celebration of liberty and equality, and a suspicion of authority and corruption, but also a faith in the ethic of individualism and a belief in the protection of private property.[11] None of these beliefs were absolute. As William Novak—who rejects the "myth of American exceptionalism"—has pointed out, nineteenth-century Americans shared an English (and continental European) belief in the "well-regulated society," where individualism and private property routinely yielded to a plethora of government regulations and limitations.[12]

Absolute or not, Philadelphians repeatedly demonstrated a greater commitment to voluntarism—and its associated values—than their Liverpool counterparts. The most dramatic evidence of this voluntary spirit was the city's response to poverty and material need. Although contemporary commentary suggests that Philadelphia had less visible poverty than Liverpool, the City of Brotherly Love supported a greater and more diverse array of philanthropic societies and benevolent institutions. Their approaches and affiliations varied widely, making it difficult to propose any particular ideology or sectarian agenda underlying their origins. Rather, it appears that Philadelphians were more predisposed to form small—decentralized —private associations in the face of demonstrated need. The burning of the *Ocean Monarch* off the coast of Liverpool is a strong counterexample. Here the human need was too powerful, and too dramatically visible, to be ignored. Local citizens responded generously to these highly visible victims, but apparently without the American knack for organizing. Whereas

Philadelphians customarily answered newly recognized public needs by holding organizing meetings, electing officers, and staging fund-raisers, benevolent-minded Liverpudlians responded to this crisis by funneling their donations through a centralized committee of elected officials. Moreover, the subsequent waves of self-congratulation demonstrated how unusual such voluntaristic bursts were in Liverpool's normal routine.

Insofar as much of Philadelphia's voluntaristic spirit arose in response to specific social ills, this distinctive characteristic should be set alongside the previous discussion of local versus national political authority. In addition to assuming that the federal—and even state—government had little role in addressing local problems, Philadelphians customarily assumed that solutions lay at least partially in private action rather than unfettered government measures. Sometimes those private actions were taken in concert with local government regulation, as when Philadelphia's sanitary officials—unlike those in Liverpool—relied almost exclusively on reports of nuisances from private citizens. On other occasions Philadelphians revealed a deep commitment to voluntary collective activism, as when Southwark's citizens responded to the landing of the *Rappahannock* (with disease aboard) by declaring their intention of blocking future foreign vessels by force, or when participants in a mass meeting in Moyamensing resolved to form vigilante bodies to do battle with unruly gangs. In none of these cases, nor in Philadelphia's wide assortment of private organizations to assist the needy, do we find volunteers necessarily acting in the absence of government. But there is a recurring sense that Philadelphians, far more so than Liverpudlians, presumed that these new urban problems might well call for independent, or collective, voluntary responses.

The other side of this coin is that although government regulation was a regular part of life in both cities, there were periodic indications that Philadelphians clung more vigorously to the rights of private property. We saw this most clearly in the discussion of sanitary reforms. By mid-century health and sanitation authorities in both cities had substantial powers to remove nuisances and regulate sanitation. They each recognized a public interest in emptying overflowing privies, removing unsanitary nuisances, cleaning streets and alleys, and regulating slaughterhouses and factories. But there were substantial differences in how those powers were exercised. Liverpool's 1846 Sanitary Act created an administrative structure exceeding that of any antebellum American city. Under the direction of Dr. William Duncan and Thomas Fresh, Liverpool's sanitary agents prowled the streets in search of unsanitary nuisances. Philadelphia's Board of Health had the authority to order nuisances removed and fines levied, and they occasionally sent delegations into the city to inspect notorious homes, but the normal sanitary system depended on citizen complaints. When cholera threatened the city, the Philadelphia Board of Health — working with the city Council's emergency committee — added a handful of special agents and adopted a series of emergency measures including the forced cleaning of some residences and the closing of the city's most notorious houses. But these more dramatic measures were expressly limited to the duration of the emergency. Under normal circumstances, evictions by the Board of Health during these years were rare. The few reported episodes involved crowded lodging houses where the residents were — significantly — mostly African American. In contrast, Dr. Duncan wielded tremendous power to order widespread evictions. During the cholera epidemic (which admittedly struck Liverpool much harder than Philadelphia) these measures dwarfed any such actions in Philadelphia. The comparison is once again one of degree, not absolute rule. Both cultures acknowledged the importance of private property, as well as the countervailing weight of public interest, but their response to the midcentury sanitary challenges suggests that Philadelphians remained relatively more suspicious of the inroads of the government on private homes.[13]

Irish immigrants were participants in, as well as beneficiaries of, Philadelphia's associational culture. As we have seen, the newcomers entered a complex world of clubs, lodges, and benefit societies. Sam Bass Warner has described the city's midcentury explosion in associations as a search for sociability and community in a world of flux.[14] Perhaps most distinctive, at least compared with Liverpool, were Philadelphia's volunteer fire companies and their affiliated youth gangs. These bellicose groups provided male immigrants — and their enemies — with comradeship, recreation, and a sense of belonging in the new world. The violent hose companies and youth gangs, and the persistent public outcry against them, constitute perhaps the most visible difference between Philadelphia and Liverpool. In addition to underscoring the importance of voluntary associations at all levels of Philadelphia society, and perhaps illustrating the speed at which the newcomers assimilated into American life, these disruptive groups point to several other theories of American distinctiveness. One perspective contends that *violence* in American culture sets the United States apart from other nations. As we saw in the previous chapter, it is impossible to offer a systematic comparison of violent behavior in Philadelphia and Liverpool, but a wide range of evidence suggests that street violence was a much greater concern in the City of Brotherly Love. The famine migrants did not create this violence, but they contributed to its explosion in the late 1840s.

What factors, short of the invigorating Philadelphia climate, might explain a greater predisposition for collective violence? Perhaps part of the explanation lies in the city's demographic *diversity,* a fifth perspective on national distinctiveness. Certainly many of the competing gangs and hose companies were aligned with different ethnic or sectarian groups. Moreover, many of the city's most violent episodes involved attacks on African Americans. Of course, Liverpool had its own sectarian conflicts that played themselves out in very different ways, but the English city had little racial diversity with its accompanying tensions. Whatever their origins, the tendency toward voluntary associations, the diversity of the population, and the propensity toward violence were mutually reinforcing aspects of Philadelphia society by the 1840s. Members of all classes gathered in groups perhaps to form community in an unstable world, perhaps to address specific social, economic, and recreational needs. Some of these groups — notably the gangs and hose companies — regularly fought in the public streets. Their battle lines often reflected the city's demographic diversity, suggesting that groups fought for status in a world of unsettled social and economic hierarchies. The success of Liverpool's sectarian leaders in muffling anticipated July 12 and St. Patrick's Day disturbances might also point to differing levels of hierarchy and deference, but that difference also reflects the distinction between violent episodes connected to traditional parade days and street disturbances with no such predictable patterns.

Philadelphia's demographic diversity, and the way Philadelphians perceived that diversity, also affected the reception of the Irish migrants. In both Liverpool and Philadelphia the newcomers were associated with a comparable range of undesirable traits: disease, poverty, unsanitary habits, intemperance, and what English Protestants called "popery." The hostility to Irish Catholic immigrants — both before and during the famine — in the two cities was really more similar than different: witness, in both cities, the conflicts over religion in the schools, the creation of powerful Protestant associations, the persistent concern for keeping the newcomers off the public rolls, and the general climate of sectarian violence. Still, the Americans — with no Established Church — were more inclined to frame their hostility in different terms, assailing the newcomers as immigrants as well as Catholics. (Again, this is a matter of degree. Anti-Catholicism flourished in Philadelphia in the 1840s.) Thus, in May 1849 the General Assembly of the

Presbyterian Church could resolve "That we should make efforts to induce children of *emigrants* to attend our Sabbath Schools, and the adults our congregations; . . . that as soon as possible they may be Americanized in the language and feelings, and become evangelical in their religion."[15] In this sense citizenship and religious beliefs became conflated, and those evangelical efforts aimed at converting the immigrants were also understood as teaching them to be Americans. Liverpool's English natives saw the Irish as outsiders, but—presumably because of proximity and history—they did not generally speak of campaigns to make them more English. Of course, this difference provided little comfort to Philadelphia's Irish Catholics, and consequently Bishop Kenrick undertook an energetic campaign to establish a separate school system. But the language of "Americanization" did reflect a distinctly national perspective, suggesting that outsiders could— and should— *learn* to be Americans.

Philadelphia's greater racial diversity also ensured that Irish immigrants did not arrive at the lowest rung of the city's social ladder. That position was reserved for the city's substantial African American population. In the long run this racial hierarchy had important implications for the Irish immigrant's assimilation into the nineteenth-century American mainstream.[16] In the short term the American tradition of institutional segregation ensured that the impoverished Irish newcomers, whatever their unpopular characteristics, would receive better institutional care and material support than thousands of native-born Americans. But although the presence of African Americans guaranteed the newcomers a slightly elevated status, the fact that some blacks and Irish immigrants lived together in the same neighborhoods and lodging houses—particularly in Moyamensing to the south of the city—was not only a source of repeated violence, but also an excuse for those Philadelphians who wished to attack the "depravity" of the immigrants.

A sixth possible source of national distinctiveness is a variant on what Daniel Boorstin called the American *"booster spirit."* Boorstin described a cohort of "go-getters" who engineered the rapid growth of America's western cities, often competing with other communities for new residents and resources.[17] Stripped of its western frontier component, and setting aside any notion of a specific national booster mentality, this perspective may be useful in comparing how different cities behaved in response to urban challenges. In both Liverpool and Philadelphia it was commonplace for politicians, business leaders, and newspaper editors to express concern for their city's reputation, especially as it competed commercially with other cities. These discussions portrayed each city as a discrete entity, with an international reputation to be carefully cultivated. The level of boosterism was similar in the two port cities, but the specific concerns were quite different. Liverpool's officials worried about the city's ill fame as a disease-ridden "black spot on the Mersey"; Philadelphians chafed at their reputation as the nation's most riotous city. Both reputations were well earned, but the resulting reforms were not purely pragmatic responses to these specific problems. The sanitary reforms in Liverpool and the police reforms in Philadelphia were undertaken to combat damaging images and to reassure the international commercial world. In this version of city boosterism the participants were engaged not in building new cities, but in competing in a world of established commercial ports. The policy priorities were shaped by popular perception as well as measurable realities. (Sometimes, in fact, such as when commercial interests resisted potentially embarrassing quarantines, the booster spirit cut against the broader health of the city.) It was this shared commitment to boosterism, perhaps as much as the specific urban disamenities, that left Liverpool at midcentury with one of the western world's most sophisticated public health apparatuses while Philadelphia enjoyed one of the nation's best-organized police forces.

The final approach to American distinctiveness originated with the work of Frederick Jackson Turner. In his classic essay, "The Significance of the Frontier in American History," Turner posited that the presence of the American frontier was behind the distinctive American character.[18] Writing in the early 1890s, Turner was arguing for the significance of a physical frontier that had begun to close. More than a half century later, David M. Potter suggested that it was not the frontier itself, but America's "economic abundance," that made the American character distinct.[19] Perhaps a variation of this "frontier thesis" can help explain differences in decision-making in Philadelphia and Liverpool.

Rather than arguing that available land or material abundance created a distinctive national character, one might offer the more modest contention that environmental and material factors led Philadelphians to select different solutions to the same set of challenges. There are several ways in which this analysis helps explain different policies and approaches in Philadelphia and Liverpool. First, the physical distance between Philadelphia and Ireland—as opposed to Liverpool's proximity—affected the nature of the arriving migrants as well as the opportunities for quarantines. Although the transatlantic journey was exhausting and debilitating, the cost of that trip selected out many of the poorest and most sickly famine migrants, who ended up remaining—and often dying—in Liverpool. Moreover, the size of the transatlantic vessels and the limited number of ports of entry made it possible for North American cities to exercise somewhat greater controls on the physical condition of arrivals, enforcing quarantines and charging large bonds for those who were most liable to become drains on local resources.[20]

The advice to potential immigrants, both from earlier migrants and from printed brochures, indicates the importance of American abundance—and the western frontier—in shaping decisions. American cities were able to welcome healthy immigrants because unskilled work was available. As Patrick Gilligan explained to his brother Michael: "Some does well here and Some does bad but in general all has to work hard for their liv[ ]ing."[21] Where there were no friends, family, or jobs awaiting them, new arrivals were often encouraged to continue west, to rural areas in western Pennsylvania and New York; orphanages commonly apprenticed their charges to farms outside of the city. Philanthropists in Liverpool, lacking a hinterland full of available jobs, encouraged their able-bodied workers to head for North America (or perhaps Australia). Even those institutions formed to aid the poor in Philadelphia presumed a level of abundance that Liverpool did not share. It was in Philadelphia, not Liverpool, that we saw houses of industry cropping up across the city to provide emergency employment and assistance for able-bodied workers. The power of abundance also showed itself in the differing levels of support forthcoming from Philadelphia Catholics as opposed to their brethren in Liverpool. Whether or not abundance shaped a distinctive American character, certainly the access to western farmland, the ability to limit the arrival of those most likely to become dependent, and the availability of unskilled jobs all affected how Philadelphians addressed the problems of the Irish famine migration.

TIMING, CONTINGENCY, AND LEGACIES

The crux of this study has been a comparison of choices—as they were made at roughly the same time in two different cities. Much of this concluding comparison, both of the two cities and of their national cultures, has come down to an examination of the interplay of political institutions, cultural assumptions, and material conditions. Among a wide assortment of crucial variables and explanatory models, a few—interrelated—characteristics have recurred most consistently. First, the structure of government and attitudes toward the role of government in society sometimes led Liverpool and Philadelphia down different decision-making paths. Second, Philadelphians seemed relatively more committed to voluntarism and voluntary societies as a central solution to social problems. And third, the policy decisions in the two cities were shaped by different levels of material abundance and different options for controlling the flow of immigrants both into ports and out into the hinterlands.

These distinctive characteristics, as well as others noted above, help explain how and why these English and American cities periodically came to different decisions when faced with comparable problems and shared knowledge. Of course, it is equally important to note that the two cities generally behaved in similar ways in response to each of the midcentury's emerging urban problems. Time and again Philadelphia and Liverpool addressed shared challenges with the same set of ideological assumptions and similar policy tools. Even where policies did not evolve identically, they generally moved in parallel directions.

The fact that the two cities were ideologically and institutionally similar makes it particularly important to consider the timing of events. Had the Irish famine migration, and the related epidemics, occurred a few years earlier or later, the impact on each city might have been different. In the years immediately preceding the migration, for instance, Liverpool passed the revolutionary Sanitary Act, and the Select Vestry opened the new Kirkdale Industrial Schools and voted to expand the Brownlow Hill workhouse. An imprecise look at the city's history might conclude that the famine migration was an important catalyst for these reforms. In fact, the new arrivals limited Liverpool's ability to apply the principle of less eligibility with its intended rigor, and the sanitary and health emergency forced Dr. Duncan to postpone his more ambitious plans. Philadelphia responded to the 1849 cholera epidemic with limited emergency measures that had little long-term impact, but the new immigrants contributed to a growing concern about urban sanitation that would not yield substantial reforms until after the Civil War.[22] The 1844 nativist riots, rather than the famine migration a few years later, provided the crucial incentive for Philadelphia's police reforms. On the other hand, the pressure of the famine migrants contributed to the police reforms in 1850 and the eventual consolidation in 1854. Both cities suffered through sectarian conflicts over local schooling in the years shortly before the famine, thus providing a crucial context for the arrival of poor Irish Catholics. In Philadelphia, the energetic Bishop Kenrick had already overseen extensive institutional and educational expansion before the influx of new Catholic immigrants, although other new projects—such as the construction of St. Joseph's Hospital—were unquestionably undertaken in response to the new demands posed by the famine migrants.

If we shift our focus from years to decades (still a short span in the larger scheme of things), the importance of the migration's timing becomes more apparent. Twenty years earlier, England had yet to undergo most of the parliamentary reforms that would change the nature of government and establish the institutional context for the emergence of the welfare state. Twenty years later Americans had just ended a huge Civil War, which included as one of its legacies an expanded federal role (albeit modest) in the welfare of two citizen groups: freed slaves and military veterans.[23] At midcentury England and the United States were similar in many respects, but only the former had begun to conceive of a national governmental role in regulating—much less assisting—the social welfare of its citizens.

This last observation invites broader speculation. The timing of the famine migration certainly affected the nature of policy reactions in Liverpool and Philadelphia. Did that timing also play a role in shaping each nation's long-term patterns of response to social problems?

Those characteristics that separated Philadelphia and Liverpool at midcentury—voluntarism, localism, abundance—were largely matters of degree. In fact, I have maintained that on the eve of the famine the two cities were much more similar than different. One might argue, further, that at a particular moment in history the popular acceptance of intervention by the state (as opposed to reliance on voluntarism) and the acknowledged preference for centralized solutions (as opposed to local autonomy) are associated with levels of abundance. By 1847 Parliament had adopted measures that Congress would have found inconceivable. The differences say much about the nature of the two governmental structures and the physical size of the two nations, but they also reflect different understandings of the level of social and economic need in each country.

One might reasonably assert that in the century and a half since the famine migration, one of the most important changes in American public life has been the huge expansion in the role of the federal government. In fact, when I began this project I would probably have declared that— despite political rhetoric to the contrary—developments over the last six decades had established a crucial federal role in protecting social welfare and addressing many problems that had been of purely local concern in the mid-nineteenth century. But as I was well into the writing of this book, Congress enacted revolutionary legislation "reforming" the American welfare system and calling into question some of these most basic assumptions.

The 1996 Welfare Reform Bill did several things that have relevance to the questions posed by this study. Most important, it ended the federal guarantee of assistance to the nation's poorest families, especially those with dependent children. Under the new law, the individual states have far greater authority and autonomy. The bill also included dramatic shifts in the nature and amount of assistance available to immigrants (the most draconian cuts were subsequently restored). The bill's proponents celebrated its shift from federal to state responsibility and the concomitant opportunity for promoting creative localized responses to welfare demands.[24] They also endorsed the bill's implied market assumptions that the poor can—and will—find work if the material threat is sufficient. Critics worried that the lost guarantees would have disastrous effects on dependent children and legal immigrants. They also argued that the Welfare Reform Bill gave the states insufficient incentives to establish training and educational programs but ample reason to push the poor into other jurisdictions.[25]

Despite the controversy that accompanied this revolutionary legislation, the future historian studying these events from a sufficient distance might note how well the new bill fit with contemporary discourse. Within months of its passage, the president was leading a high-profile national summit on "voluntarism" (in Philadelphia, no less). Meanwhile, many middle-class parents and advocates of educational reform were abandoning their faith in the public schools and instead marching under the banner of "school choice."[26] All of these developments might support the thesis that the United States does, in fact, have a distinctive cultural commitment to localism, voluntarism, and market forces. Perhaps history will judge that those developments that began with the New Deal and expanded dramatically during the War on Poverty and beyond were no more than an extended— and hardly complete—federal aberration. But even if the future validates this perspective, there might still be value in revisiting the lessons from the second quarter of the nineteenth century.

In the late 1840s Philadelphia and other American cities faced a series of challenges accompanying the Irish famine migration. Those challenges, although substantial, did not require that the city or the nation rethink its fundamental faith in voluntarism and localism. Even the sectarian disputes that threatened the public schools were effectively diffused by the emergence of a separate parochial school system. By this point Liverpool, and England generally, had already begun moving toward an expanded reliance on centralized solutions to social problems. Perhaps the difference between England and the United States lay less in inherent national characteristics than in the material and institutional ability to weather new challenges in the context of traditional values and approaches. Perhaps a much greater set of urban challenges might have forced American cities to turn to expanded governmental solutions in these crucial decades.[27] Twentieth-century developments, including two world wars and the Great Depression, would eventually compel Americans to rethink the role of the federal government in everyday life. But in certain fundamental ways the die had been cast by the 1850s, establishing the presumption—for better or for worse—that social problems should, whenever possible, be addressed by state and local governments in conjunction with voluntary efforts.

Notes

ABBREVIATIONS

AMA	American Medical Association
ASSU	American Sunday School Union
CH	*Catholic Herald*
DMS	Domestic Mission Society
HSP	Historical Society of Pennsylvania, Philadelphia
LM	*Liverpool Mercury*
LCP	Library Company of Philadelphia
LRO	Liverpool Record Office
PCA	Philadelphia City Archives
PL	*Philadelphia Public Ledger*
PSEIP	Philadelphia Society for the Employment and Instruction of the Poor
SHC	Southern Historical Collection, Chapel Hill, N.C.
UBA	Union Benevolent Association

CHAPTER ONE

1. *Susquehanna,* voyage #41, 1847, ticket #1885, Box 17, and "Inward Steerage Passengers, 1844–50," Thomas P. Cope Papers, HSP. The tickets are stored in bundles in envelopes for each voyage. "Inward Steerage Passengers" is a ledger volume of transactions in Philadelphia listing—among other things—the date of the transaction, the person purchasing the ticket, the amount paid, and the person who the ticket was purchased for. The tickets were transferable. In this case the ticket was purchased for "Eliza Mallon," but the notation on the ticket says that Ann Murphy made the trip. Wilson's note is addressed to a third party, perhaps Elizabeth Mallon. The tickets were ripped in half (presumably on departure) and only the stub remains, often cutting a message in half. Harnden and Company were Cope's agents in Liverpool.

2. *Susquehanna*, voyage #43, 1848, ticket #2597, Box 17, and "Inward Steerage Passengers," ibid.

3. For an excellent survey of the migration placed in a broader context, see Kerby A. Miller, *Emigrants and Exiles: Ireland and the Irish Exodus to North America* (New York, 1985). See also Terry Coleman, *Going to America* (New York, 1972; reprint, Baltimore, 1987); Oliver MacDonagh, "Irish Famine Emigration to the United States," *Perspectives in American History* (Cambridge, Mass., 1976); Joel Mokyr, *Why Ireland Starved: A Quantitative and Analytical History of the Irish Economy, 1800–50* (London, 1983; rev. 1985); Cormac Ó Gráda, *Ireland before and after the Famine: Explorations in Economic History, 1800–1925*, rev. ed. (Manchester, England, 1993); Robert James Scally, *The End of Hidden Ireland* (New York, 1995); and Christine Kinealy, *The Great Calamity: The Irish Famine, 1845–1852* (1994; Boulder, Colo., 1995).

4. Ó Gráda, *Ireland before and after the Famine*, 102–4.

5. Miller, *Emigrants and Exiles*, 291–92.

6. Passenger Lists, Box 17, Cope Papers, HSP.

7. "Inward Steerage Passengers," ibid. Many of these tickets were for several people.

8. *Tuscarora*, voyage #1, 1848, ticket #2885, Box 23, and "Inward Steerage Passengers," Cope Papers, HSP. The last name may be "Gladden."

9. *Tonawanda*, voyage #3, 1851, ticket #5636, Box 17, ibid.

10. *Tuscarora*, voyage #4, 1849, ticket #4234, Box 23, ibid.

11. *Susquehanna*, voyage #47, 1847, ticket #3733, Box 17, ibid.

12. *Saranak*, voyage #14, 1849, ticket #3622, Box 11, ibid.

13. *Susquehanna*, voyage #42, 1847, ticket #2287, Box 17, ibid.

14. *Monongahela*, voyage #51, 1847, ticket #3030[?], Box 21, ibid. Either this ticket number is in error or the ticket was misfiled with this voyage.

15. *Tonawanda*, voyage #1, 1850, ticket #5229, Box 17, ibid.

16. Ó Gráda, *Ireland before and after the Famine*, 122, 125–33; Miller, *Emigrants and Exiles*, 280–86.

17. Ó Gráda, *Ireland before and after the Famine*, 137.

18. For excellent descriptions of the journey and the dangers in the port cities, see Coleman, *Going to America*, and Scally, *End of Hidden Ireland*, 159–229. The details of the journey and efforts to regulate it are discussed more fully in Chapter 2.

19. The literature on the experiences of Irish immigrants in the United States and England is enormous and is growing annually. Portions of that literature inform many of the chapters in this book, but many issues that are central to the study of the Irish immigrant experience are not addressed here. The best entrée to Irish immigration studies are the essays in the multivolume collection, *The Irish World Wide: History, Heritage, Identity*, edited by Patrick O'Sullivan. Two particularly useful historiographic surveys in this collection are Roger Swift, "The Historiography of the Irish in Nineteenth-Century Britain" (52–81), and Donald Harman Akenson, "The Historiography of the Irish in the United States" (99–127), both in O'Sullivan, ed., *The Irish World Wide: History, Heritage, Identity*, vol. 2, *The Irish in New Communities* (Leicester, 1992). For a classic urban case study that places the Irish immigrants at

center stage, see Lynn Hollen Lees, *Exiles of Erin: Irish Migrants in Victorian London* (Ithaca, N.Y., 1979).

20. My decision to focus on England and the United States reflects my own scholarly background and a belief that the two worlds were sufficiently similar to allow for strong comparisons. Certainly the findings in this book could be profitably compared with developments in other countries.

21. When I began this project I was particularly familiar with Lees's *Exiles of Erin.* Before long I discovered that the Irish in both Liverpool and Philadelphia have been the subject of extremely sophisticated demographic studies, many of which are cited below or in subsequent chapters. Had I not preferred an English city, Glasgow would have been another excellent alternative. For two recent comparative studies involving the Scottish port city, see Tom Gallagher, "A Tale of Two Cities: Communal Strife in Glasgow and Liverpool before 1914," in Roger Swift and Sheridan Gilley, eds., *The Irish in the Victorian City* (London, 1985), 106–29, and Tom Hart, "Urban Growth and Municipal Government: Glasgow in a Comparative Context, 1846–1914," in Anthony Slaven and Derek H. Aldcroft, eds., *Business, Banking and Urban History* (Edinburgh, 1982), 193–219.

22. Often the secondary literature on specific topics has enabled me to broaden my comparative analysis beyond these two cities.

23. Each city has a large historical literature. For general histories, see Russell F. Weigley, ed., *Philadelphia: A 300-Year History* (New York, 1982); J. Thomas Scharf and Thompson Westcott, *History of Philadelphia,* 3 vols. (Philadelphia, 1884); Brian D. White, *A History of the Corporation of Liverpool, 1835–1914* (Liverpool, 1951); and Ramsay Muir, *A History of Liverpool,* 2d ed. (London, 1907).

24. Colin Gilbert Pooley, "Migration, Mobility, and Residential Areas in Nineteenth-Century Liverpool" (Ph.D. diss., University of Liverpool, 1978), 29; Howard Gillette Jr., "The Emergence of the Modern Metropolis: Philadelphia in the Age of Its Consolidation," in William W. Cutler III and Howard Gillette Jr., eds., *Divided Metropolis: Social and Spatial Dimensions of Philadelphia, 1800–1975* (Westport, Conn., 1980), 15. The Philadelphia population figures are for 1830 and 1850. The geographic scope of the borough of Liverpool and Philadelphia County are discussed below.

25. John Papworth, "The Irish in Liverpool, 1835–1871: Segregation and Dispersal" (Ph.D. diss., University of Liverpool, 1981), 14; Dale B. Light Jr., "The Role of Irish-American Organisations in Assimilation and Community Formation," in P. J. Drudy, ed., *The Irish in America: Emigration, Assimilation, and Impact* (Cambridge, England, 1985), 118; Alan Nathan Burstein, "Residential Distribution and Mobility of Irish and German Immigrants in Philadelphia, 1850–1880" (Ph.D. diss., University of Pennsylvania, 1975), 77.

26. Elizabeth M. Geffen, "Industrial Development and Social Crisis, 1841–1854," in Weigley, *Philadelphia,* 309; Theodore Hershberg et al., "A Tale of Three Cities: Blacks, Immigrants, and Opportunity in Philadelphia, 1850–1880, 1930, 1970," in Hershberg, ed., *Philadelphia: Work, Space, Family and Group Experience in the 19th Century* (New York, 1981), 465 passim; Colin G. Pooley, "The Residential Seg-

regation of Migrant Communities in Mid-Victorian Liverpool," *Transactions of the Institute of British Geographers* (1977): 366.

27. See, e.g., *Statistics of Cholera: With the Sanitary Measures Adopted by the Board of Health . . .* (Philadelphia, 1849), and William H. Duncan, *Report to the Health Committee of the Borough of Liverpool, on the Health of the Town during the Years 1847–48–49–50, and on Other Matters within His Department* (Liverpool, 1851). This issue will be considered more fully in Chapter 4.

28. Herman Melville, *Redburn* (1849; New York, 1971), 161. Melville visited Liverpool in 1839.

29. On comparisons of Birkenhead with Brooklyn, see Nathaniel Fleming Bowe Diary, Oct. 2, 1846, SHC; *PL*, May 3, 1847. For further comments on the Liverpool docks, see John D. Twiggs Diary, May 22, 1846, SHC; *The Workingman's Friend and Family Instructor* 5 (Mar. 1, 1851), cited in James O'Donald Mays, *Mr. Hawthorne Goes to England: The Adventures of a Reluctant Consul* (New Forest Leaves, Burnley, England, 1983), 59.

30. See *Handbook to Liverpool, or, a Guide for the Stranger and Resident* (Liverpool, n.d.). This small volume was reprinted regularly throughout the mid-nineteenth century.

31. *PL*, May 3, 1847. John D Twiggs also noted the Nelson Monument. Diary, Sept. 2, 1846, SHC.

32. Twiggs Diary, May 27, 29, 1846, SHC; Nathaniel Fleming Bowe Diary, Oct. 4, 1846, SHC; *The Workingman's Friend and Family Instructor* v (Mar. 1, 1851), cited in Mays, *Mr. Hawthorne Goes to England*, 59; Lewis Family Papers, 1857 Travel Diary, July 1, 1857, SHC, author unknown (the diarist added "the docks" over the reference to a few impressive buildings); *PL*, May 3, 1847; Twiggs Diary, May 22, July 18, 1846, passim; Moncure D. Conway, *Life of Nathaniel Hawthorne* (New York, 1890), 151—letter dated Sept. 13, 1853, recipient unknown.

33. *PL*, May 3, 1847.

34. Nathaniel Hawthorne, *The English Notebooks* (New York, 1941), 13, 18; entries for Aug. 20, 25, 1853; Conway, *Life of Nathaniel Hawthorne*, 151 (last sentence quoting from Sept. 13, 1853, letter).

35. Melville also drew this connection between Liverpool and Boston.

36. Civic boosterism was a regular part of daily discourse in Philadelphia. See *PL*, Sept. 24, 1847.

37. *PL*, Sept. 11, 1849; reprinted from *Boston Traveler.*

38. W. I. Mann's Diary of a Trip to the USA, 1848–49, Jan. 26, 1849, LRO; Anne Holt Diary, May 10–12, 1851, LRO; Henry L. Cathell Diary, Mar. 2, 1856, SHC.

39. On Liverpool's economy and workforce, see M. J. Power, "The Growth of Liverpool," in John Belchem, ed., *Popular Politics, Riot, and Labour: Essays in Liverpool History, 1790–1940* (Liverpool, 1992), 21–39; P. J. Waller, *Democracy and Sectarianism: A Political and Social History of Liverpool, 1868–1939* (Liverpool, 1981), 2–5; Francis Hyde, "The Growth of Liverpool's Trade, 1700–1950," in Wilfred Smith, ed., *A Scientific Survey of Merseyside* (Liverpool, 1953), 148–63; Scally, *End of Hidden Ireland*, 184–200; and François Vigier, *Change and Apathy: Liverpool and Manchester during the Industrial Revolution* (Cambridge, Mass., 1970).

40. Bruce Laurie and Mark Schmitz, "Manufacture and Productivity: The Making of an Industrial Base, Philadelphia, 1850–1880" in Hershberg, *Philadelphia*, 43–92; Geffen, "Industrial Development and Social Crisis"; Cynthia J. Shelton, *The Mills of Manayunk: Industrialization and Social Conflict in the Philadelphia Region, 1787–1837* (Baltimore, 1986); Diane Lindstrom, *Economic Development in the Philadelphia Region, 1810–1850* (New York, 1978); Philip Scranton, *Proprietary Capitalism: The Textile Manufacture at Philadelphia, 1800–1885* (New York, 1983).

41. Bruce Laurie, Theodore Hershberg, and George Alter, "Immigrants and Industry: The Philadelphia Experience, 1850–1880," in Hershberg, *Philadelphia*, 93–126.

42. For a discussion of ghettoes, see Papworth, "The Irish in Liverpool." Burstein ("Residential Segregation and Mobility," 148) finds a similar level of Irish segregation in Philadelphia.

43. Burstein, "Residential Distribution and Mobility"; Emma Jones Lapsansky, "South Street Philadelphia, 1762–1854: 'A Haven for Those Low in the World'" (Ph.D. diss., University of Pennsylvania, 1975). See also John J. Kane, "The Irish Immigrant in Philadelphia, 1840–1880: A Study in Conflict and Accommodation" (Ph.D. diss., University of Pennsylvania, 1950), 67–71.

44. Papworth, "The Irish in Liverpool," 64–65.

45. See Chapter 5.

46. Liverpool had a town Council and a Select Vestry, which came to serve as the Board of Guardians after reform of the Poor Law; Philadelphia had a bicameral Council and a Board of Guardians. I have referred to Philadelphia's Council in the singular, although in fact the city had a Select Council and a Common Council.

47. On Philadelphia, see Gillette, "Emergence of the Modern Metropolis," 3–26; Edward P. Allinson and Boies Penrose, *Philadelphia, 1681–1887* (Philadelphia, 1887); and Michael P. McCarthy, "The Philadelphia Consolidation of 1854: A Reappraisal," *Pennsylvania Magazine of History and Biography* (October 1986): 531–48. On Liverpool, see White, *Corporation of Liverpool*, 1–99. Unless otherwise noted, references to Philadelphia will include the entire county and references to Liverpool will include the borough.

48. White, *Corporation of Liverpool*; Chris Cook and Brendan Keith, *British Historical Facts, 1830–1900* (New York, 1975), 132.

49. Geffen, "Industrial Development and Social Crisis," 348; Sam Bass Warner Jr., *The Private City: Philadelphia in Three Periods of Its Growth* (Philadelphia, 1968), 101. On Philadelphia's political structure, see Allinson and Penrose, *Philadelphia;* Scharf and Westcott, *History of Philadelphia;* and *PL,* Oct. 15, 1849.

50. On Liverpool's political history, see Neil Collins, *Politics and Elections in Nineteenth-Century Liverpool* (Cambridge, England, 1994); Derek Fraser, *Power and Authority in the Victorian City* (New York, 1979), 22–50; Waller, *Democracy and Sectarianism,* 12–19; Charles David Watkinson, "The Liberal Party on Merseyside in the Nineteenth Century" (Ph.D. diss., University of Liverpool, 1967); and Vigier, *Change and Apathy,* 36–61, 173–86.

51. Geffen, "Industrial Development and Social Crisis," 349–50; Leonard Ta-

bachnik, "Origins of the Know-Nothing Party: A Study of the Native American Party in Philadelphia, 1844–1852" (Ph.D. diss., Columbia University, 1973).

52. *PL,* Oct. 16, 1848.

53. Miller, *Emigrants and Exiles,* 297 passim. On Philadelphia's Catholics, see James F. Connelly, ed., *The History of the Archdiocese of Philadelphia* (Philadelphia, 1976). On Liverpool's Catholics, see Alina Janina Klapas, "Geographical Aspects of Religious Change in Victorian Liverpool, 1837–1901" (M.A. thesis, University of Liverpool, 1977), and Thomas Burke, *Catholic History of Liverpool* (Liverpool, 1910). See Chapter 6.

54. Light, "Role of Irish-American Organisations," 113–41. See also Kane, "The Irish Immigrant in Philadelphia."

55. John Belchem, "Liverpool in the Year of Revolution: The Political and Associational Culture of the Irish Immigrant Community in 1848," in Belchem, *Popular Politics, Riot, and Labour,* 68–97; Papworth, "The Irish in Liverpool." See Chapter 7. Most of these clubs and formal associations were composed of men. Recent scholarship has uncovered the distinct, and historically illusive, experiences of Irish women in these immigrant communities. For the pioneering study, see Hasia Diner, *Erin's Daughters in America: Irish Immigrant Women in the Nineteenth Century* (Baltimore, 1983). The most recent scholarship is represented in Patrick O'Sullivan, ed., *The Irish World Wide,* vol. 4, *Irish Women and Irish Migration* (Leicester, 1995). See especially the essays in this volume by Dennis Clark (on Philadelphia) and Lynda Letford and Colin G. Pooley (on Liverpool).

56. See Chapters 6–7.

57. Kane, "The Irish Immigrant in Philadelphia," 123–33; Tabachnik, "Origins of the Know-Nothing Party." See Papworth, "The Irish in Liverpool"; Klapas, "Geographical Aspects of Religious Change"; Frank Neal, *Sectarian Violence: The Liverpool Experience, 1819–1914* (Manchester, 1988); and Anne Bryson, "Riotous Liverpool, 1815–1860," in Belchem, *Popular Politics, Riot and Labour,* 98–134. See also Chapters 6–7.

58. Mary P. Ryan, *Civic Wars: Democracy and Public Life in the American City during the Nineteenth Century* (Berkeley, 1997).

59. William J. Novak's analysis of government regulation in nineteenth-century America, based on a close reading of more than a thousand court cases, presents a fascinating reinterpretation of America's commitment to a well-regulated society. Novak, *The People's Welfare: Law and Regulation in Nineteenth-Century America* (Chapel Hill, N.C., 1996).

60. Derek Fraser, *The Evolution of the British Welfare State: A History of Social Policy since the Industrial Revolution* (2d ed., London, 1984), xxi–xxx. Fraser sees virtue in each of the models, while arguing that no single interpretation can fully suffice. Nonetheless, he is most nearly persuaded by the pragmatic model.

61. See Oliver MacDonagh, "The Nineteenth-Century Revolution in Government: A Reappraisal," in Peter Stansky, ed., *The Victorian Revolution* (New York, 1973), reprinted from *Historical Journal* (1958), and Henry Parris, "The Nineteenth-Century Revolution in Government: A Reappraisal Reappraised," in Stansky, *Victorian Revolution.*

62. Eric Monkkonen, *America Becomes Urban: The Development of U.S. Cities and Towns, 1780–1980* (Berkeley, Calif., 1988), 162–64 passim.

63. Seymour Martin Lipset is perhaps the most prominent advocate of American exceptionalism. See, most recently, his *American Exceptionalism: A Double-Edged Sword* (New York, 1996). Lipset insists that his subtitle reflects a belief that America is different, but not necessarily superior or more blessed than other nations. On the other hand, he also declares that "there can be little question that the hand of providence has been on a nation which finds a Washington, a Lincoln, or a Roosevelt when it needs him" (p. 14). For a series of critical essays on the idea of American exceptionalism and on Lipset's book, see *American Historical Review* (June 1997): 748–74. On comparative history and the problems of American exceptionalism, see George M. Fredrickson, "From Exceptionalism to Variability: Recent Developments in Cross-National Comparative History," *Journal of American History* (September 1995): 587–604, and the essays by Ian Tyrrell and Michael McGerr in "AHR Forum," *American Historical Review* (October 1991): 1031–71.

64. Alexis de Tocqueville, *Democracy in America*, edited by J. P. Mayer, translated by George Lawrence (1839, 1848; New York, 1969). The Mayer edition consists of two volumes bound together in a single volume and paginated consecutively through both volumes. But they are clearly identified as separate volumes, with the chapters numbered separately (reflecting the original chapters and volumes). I used those volume numbers and page numbers in citations, although the Mayer edition has only one volume.

65. See William C. Lubenow, *The Politics of Government Growth: Early Victorian Attitudes toward State Intervention, 1833–1848* (Newton Abbot, England, 1971); Oliver MacDonagh, *Early Victorian Government, 1830–1870* (London, 1977); Stansky, *Victorian Revolution*.

66. Tocqueville, *Democracy in America*, 2:513; Warner, *Private City*, 61–62; Margaret B. Simey, *Charitable Effort in Liverpool in the Nineteenth Century* (Liverpool, 1951), 14. America's enduring voluntarism is at the heart of Lipset's (*American Exceptionalism*) discussion of contemporary national distinctiveness.

67. Frederick Jackson Turner, "The Significance of the Frontier in American History," *Proceedings of the Forty-first Annual Meeting of the State Historical Society of Wisconsin* (Madison, 1894), 79–112.

68. Daniel J. Boorstin, *The Americas: The National Experience* (New York, 1965), 113–68.

69. Elizabeth M. Geffen, "Violence in Philadelphia in the 1840's and 1850's," *Pennsylvania History* 36 (October 1969): 381–410.

70. Alan I. Marcus, *Plague of Strangers: Social Groups and the Origins of City Services in Cincinnati* (Columbus, Ohio, 1991). Some of the most lively discussions about American exceptionalism have concentrated on the relative lack of a socialist movement in U.S. history. One popular explanation has been the ethnic, religious, and racial diversity of the U.S. working classes.

71. In an analysis of the coming of the American Civil War, James McPherson turned the traditional discussion of Southern exceptionalism on its head, suggesting that the North was really more out of synch with international developments.

This fundamental insight can be applied to our comparison of Liverpool and Philadelphia. Whereas the analysis might uncover differences, it would be impossible to posit true "distinctiveness" or "exceptionalism" without a much broader comparison of many cultures. See McPherson, "Southern Exceptionalism: A New Look at an Old Question," *Civil War History* (September 1983): 230–44.

72. For a fascinating discussion and application of contingency theory, see David Hackett Fischer, *Paul Revere's Ride* (New York, 1994).

CHAPTER TWO

1. The Pike scheme and the dock-rating controversy were regular topics in the *Liverpool Mercury*. For election coverage, see *LM*, Nov. 3, 1848, Nov. 2, 1849, and Neil Collins, *Politics and Elections in Nineteenth-Century Liverpool* (Aldershot, England, 1994). For a published political speech illuminating the importance of these two issues, see Samuel Holme, *Speech of Samuel Holme, Esq., at the Music Hall, Liverpool, on the 15th of October, 1849* (Liverpool, 1849). The water controversy and the sanitation question are considered more fully in Chapter 5.

2. *PL*, Oct. 6, 8, 10, 1849. On Philadelphia politics emphasizing nativism, see Judith A. Hunter, "Before Pluralism: The Political Culture of Nativism in Antebellum Philadelphia" (Ph.D. diss., Yale University, 1991), and Leonard Tabachnik, "Origins of the Know-Nothing Party: A Study of the Native American Party in Philadelphia, 1844–1852" (Ph.D. diss., Columbia University, 1973).

3. See, e.g., *PL*, Apr. 27, July 28, 1849.

4. *LM*, Dec. 28, 1849; *PL*, Oct. 6, 1, 20, 1849. Letters and editorials about taxation and excessive expenditures appeared fairly regularly in the *Public Ledger*.

5. François Vigier, *Change and Apathy: Liverpool and Manchester during the Industrial Revolution* (Cambridge, Mass., 1970).

6. For an excellent overview of these parliamentary reforms, see Derek Fraser, *The Evolution of the British Welfare State: A History of Social Policy since the Industrial Revolution* (2d ed., London, 1984). Of course, this comparison of government regulation is relative and not absolute. For a discussion of state-level government regulation and an assault on what he terms the "myth of American statelessness," see William J. Novak, *The People's Welfare: Law and Regulation in Nineteenth-Century America* (Chapel Hill, N.C., 1996).

7. Kerby A. Miller, *Emigrants and Exiles: Ireland and the Irish Exodus to North America* (New York, 1985), 282–84.

8. *LM*, Jan. 1, 8, 22, 1847; Rev. Hugh M'Neile, *The Famine a Rod of God: Its Provoking Cause—Its Merciful Design* (Liverpool, 1847). This view was popular among Irish Protestant ministers, who were fond of pointing out that the famine struck disproportionately among (poorer) Irish Catholics. Miller, *Emigrants and Exiles*, 280.

9. James Martineau, *Ireland and Her Famine: A Discourse Preached in Paradise Street Chapel, Liverpool, on Sunday, January 31, 1847* (Liverpool, 1847); Miller, *Emigrants and Exiles*, 283; *LM*, Jan. 22, 1847.

10. *Report of the General Executive Committee of the City and County of Philadelphia Ap-*

pointed by the Town Meeting of February 17, 1847 to Provide Means to Relieve the Sufferings of Ireland (Philadelphia, 1847), 3, 35–36; *CH,* Feb. 4, 25, 1847; *PL,* Feb. 18, 1847.

11. Concern for Ireland's famine victims filled the city's newspapers, particularly in the first months of 1847. See, e.g., *PL,* Feb. 2–3, 8, 11, 23, 1847; *CH,* Jan. 14, Feb. 4, 25, 1847; *Pennsylvania Freeman;* and *Pennsylvanian.* See also Arthur Ritchie to Miss Harriet Murdock (of Columbus, Ga.), Mar. 25, 1847, SHC; Eliza Cope Harrison, ed., *Philadelphia Merchant: The Diary of Thomas P. Cope, 1800–1851* (South Bend, Ind., 1978), 526–29 (January–March 1847).

12. *Report of the General Executive Committee of . . . Philadelphia Appointed by the Town Meeting of February 17, 1847,* 36. On immigrant money mailed home to Ireland, see also *CH,* Jan. 14, 1847. Kerby Miller (*Emigrants and Exiles,* 284) estimates that Irish-Americans rushed millions of dollars and vast supplies of food to their starving relations.

13. Frank Neal, "Liverpool, the Irish Steamship Companies, and the Famine Irish," *Immigrants and Minorities* (1986): 28–61; W. J. Lowe, *The Irish in Mid-Victorian Lancashire: The Shaping of a Working Class Community* (New York, 1989), 21; Margaret W Thompson, "Irish Famine Migration to the United States, with Special Reference to Irish Emigration into Liverpool, 1846–1849" (Liverpool University, B.A. thesis, 1956), 16; Edward Rushton, Esq., to Sir George Grey, Apr. 21, 1849, HC 1849 (266) XLVII, reprinted in Irish University Press Series of British Parliamentary Papers, vol. 22: Emigration (Shannon, Ireland, 1970); *LM,* May 15, 1849; Neal, "Lancashire, the Famine Irish, and the Poor Laws: A Study in Crisis Management," *Irish Economic and Social History* (1995): 28–30. See also Neal, "Liverpool, the Irish Steamship Companies, and the Famine Irish," 34–35, and *Sectarian Violence: The Liverpool Experience, 1819–1914* (Manchester, 1988), 81–82; John Papworth, "The Irish in Liverpool, 1835–71: Segregation and Dispersal" (Ph.D., University of Liverpool, 1981), 44–50. Lowe (*The Irish in Mid-Victorian Lancashire,* 21) estimates that there were over 1.5 million steamer passages from Ireland to Liverpool between 1846 and 1851. The *Mercury* (July 6, 1849) reported that 62,680 emigrants sailed from Liverpool in the first six months of 1848 and 87,443 departed in the first six months of 1849.

14. *LM,* Dec. 8, 12, 1848, May 1, 29, June 19, Aug. 17, 1849; Neal, "Liverpool, the Irish Steamboat Companies, and the Famine Irish"; Lowe, *The Irish in Mid-Victorian Lancashire,* 21–22; Robert James Scally, *The End of Hidden Ireland: Rebellion, Famine and Emigration* (New York, 1995), 159–83.

15. *LM,* Jan. 1, 8, 22, 29, 1847.

16. *LM,* Feb. 12, 26, Mar. 12, 26, Apr. 2, 1847; Neal, "Lancashire, the Famine Irish, and the Poor Laws" and *Sectarian Violence,* 86–89; Lowe, *The Irish in Mid-Victorian Lancashire,* 24–25. The poor relief system is discussed more fully in Chapter 3.

17. *LM,* July 9, 16, Aug. 20, Nov. 23, 1847; B.P.P. (HC), *Fifth Report of the Select Committee on Settlement and Poor Removal,* 1847 (226), vol. 11, testimony of Edward Rushton; Neal, *Sectarian Violence,* 86–87, 95–97; Lowe, *The Irish in Mid-Victorian Lancashire,* 25.

18. *LM,* Jan. 7, 1848.

19. Lawrence Feehan, "Charitable Effort, Statutory Authorities, and the Poor in Liverpool, c1850–1914" (Ph.D. diss., University of Liverpool, 1987). See also Thompson, "Irish Famine Migration to the United States," 25; Neal, "Lancashire, the Famine Irish, and the Poor Laws." (Neal gives slightly different numbers.) In addition to the immigrants who were forcibly removed, others simply fled Liverpool into the hinterlands. See *LM* July 27, 1847.

20. *LM,* Apr. 20, May 7, 14, 1847, Feb. 11, 1848; Lowe, *The Irish in Mid-Victorian Lancashire,* 22–23; Neal, *Sectarian Violence,* 95.

21. *LM,* Feb. 11, 1848, Nov. 12, 19, 1847.

22. Rushton to Grey, Apr. 21, 1849; *LM,* May 15, 1849.

23. *LM,* May 18, June 26, 1849. This is a recurring theme in the *Mercury.*

24. U.S. Bureau of the Census, *Historical Statistics of the United States, 1789–1945* (Washington, D.C., 1949), 34, ser. B 304–30; John J. Kane, "The Irish Immigrant in Philadelphia, 1840–1880: A Study in Conflict and Accommodation" (Ph.D. diss., University of Pennsylvania, 1950), 66–67; *PL,* Sept. 11, 1849; Dale B. Light Jr., "The Role of Irish-American Organisations in Assimilation and Community Formation," in P. J. Drudy, ed., *The Irish in America: Emigration, Assimilation, and Impact,* (Cambridge, England, 1985), 116. See also Elizabeth M. Geffen, "Industrial Development and Social Crisis, 1841–1854," in Russell F. Weigley, ed., *Philadelphia: A 300-Year History* (New York, 1982), 309; Dennis Clark, *The Irish in Philadelphia: Ten Generations of Urban Experience* (Philadelphia, 1973).

25. Seventy-five percent of Irish passengers landing in New York City in 1846 were listed as either laborers or servants. Between 1851 and 1855 the proportion of laborers and servants among overseas Irish migrants ranged from 79 to 90 percent. Miller, *Emigrants and Exiles,* 295.

26. Ibid., 296.

27. *PL,* Apr. 9, 13, 16, 22, May 19, June 24, Sept. 20, Oct. 23, 1847, Apr. 6, July 10, 15, 24, 1848, Mar. 21, July 14, Sept. 11, 1849 (reports on the arrival of new ships); *PL,* June 24, 1847 (nearly all of 260 steerage passengers ill); *PL,* Sept. 20, 1847 (events aboard the *Swatara*).

28. *PL,* Jan. 30, 1849. For other stories of diseased passengers arriving in Philadelphia and other U.S. ports, see *PL,* Feb. 26, Apr. 6, May 8, 26, June 8, Sept. 26, 1847, Jan. 22, 24, 1848.

29. *LM,* May 28, June 18, 1847, Feb. 22, Nov. 10, 1848; *PL,* Mar. 22, 1848; Richard J. Purcell, "The New York Commissioners of Emigration and Irish Immigrants," *Studies: An Irish Quarterly Review* 37 (1948): 29–42; Terry Coleman, *Going to America* (1972; reprint, Baltimore, 1987), 100–118, 134–35, 213–17, 287–94.

30. *CH,* Feb. 24, 1847. The *Public Ledger* made similar observations about Liverpool on Mar. 23, 1847.

31. *PL,* Mar. 20, 1847. Although never a major concern as in Liverpool, the Philadelphia papers occasionally included stories about Irish immigrants starving on the streets of Philadelphia. See *PL,* May 20, 1847.

32. Eliza Cope Harrison, ed., *Philadelphia Merchant: The Diary of Thomas P. Cope, 1800–1851* (South Bend, Ind., 1978), 527 (entry of Feb. 2, 1847); Nicholas B. Wainwright, ed., *A Philadelphia Perspective: The Diary of Sidney George Fisher Covering the Years*

1834–1871 (Philadelphia, 1967), 195 (entry of May 2, 1847). Fisher was speaking of "not the Irish merely, but Germans, whole villages at once."

33. For regular evidence of concerns about health dangers, see Philadelphia Guardians of Poor, Minutes, PCA, and Philadelphia Board of Health, Minutes, PCA. On New York City's head taxes, see *PL,* Feb. 18, June 14, 1847; *LM,* June 18, 1847; and Purcell, "The New York Commissioners," 29–42.

34. Philadelphia Board of Trade, *Annual Reports* (Philadelphia, 1845, 1850); Guardians of the Poor, Minutes, Feb. 12, 19, 26, Apr. 2, 1849, PCA; Purcell, "The New York Commissioners," 33 passim; Coleman, *Going to America,* 231–33; Maldwyn Allen Jones, *American Immigration* (Chicago, 1960), 250. Philadelphia's concern over the potential costs of diseased immigrants prompted a public meeting in November 1849 that resulted in a memorial calling on Congress to authorize the states to pass new health taxes to fund quarantines and immigrant hospitals. See *PL,* Nov. 23–24, 26, 1849.

35. *PL,* Apr. 26–27, 29, 1848.

36. Philadelphia Guardians of the Poor, Minutes, Apr. 24, 1848, PCA; *PL,* Apr. 26, 1848. The Guardians also ordered "that the President and Secretary issue a proclamation . . . forthwith warning all persons of the penalties imposed by law for introducing or entertaining such Foreign Emigrants."

37. *PL,* May 13, 1848; *Pennsylvanian,* Apr. 29, 1848.

38. *PL,* Apr. 29, 1848. Of course, the *Provincialist* had been allowed to continue only after the head money had been paid to Wilmington's treasurer of the poor.

39. *PL,* May 22–23, 1848. It does not appear that the Board of Health actually enforced the 1802 act. But it was able to achieve similar results by "rigid enforcement of the quarantine laws," which were in effect by June 1. Still, the barriers by sea could not fully stem the tide. On June 16, 1848, the *Public Ledger* reported the arrival of a trainload of immigrants from Wilmington.

40. *Pennsylvanian,* Apr. 29, 1848; *PL,* May 11, Apr. 28, 1848.

41. Both the Guardians of the Poor and the Board of Health had jurisdictions extending beyond the city limits and encompassing the most populated adjoining districts. Both were "quasi-independent bodies" selected by local authorities but reporting directly to state authorities. The periodic friction between them is discussed in subsequent chapters. Edward P. Allinson and Boies Penrose, *Philadelphia, 1681–1887: A History of Municipal Development* (Philadelphia, 1887), 106–9, 112–13.

42. On fraud in port cities, see Coleman, *Going to America;* Scally, *End of Hidden Ireland;* and Purcell, "The New York Commissioners."

43. *Constitution and Address of the Temporary Home Association* (Philadelphia, 1850). For fraudulent practices, see *PL,* May 27, 1847, Feb. 24, 1848, and *LM,* Feb. 19, 1847. Liverpool's magistrates regularly fined ticket agents for such ruses.

44. *Constitution and Address of the Temporary Home Association* (Philadelphia, 1849).

45. See Chapter 3.

46. For a broader discussion of advice to emigrants, see Coleman, *Going to America,* 28–41, 164–65 passim.

47. Kane, "The Irish Immigrant in Philadelphia," 102–3, 96. Kane cites the *Catholic Herald,* Apr. 20, 1843.

48. *PL*, Mar. 18, 20, 1847. For a story calling on unemployed immigrants to move to Maryland, where farmers were complaining of a lack of labor, see *PL*, Dec. 11, 1849.

49. *PL*, Mar. 10, Apr. 6, 1848; *Pennsylvanian*, Mar. 1, May 30, 1848.

50. *Report of the Executive Committee to the Board of Directors of the Emigrant's Friend Society, Established, April, 1848* (Philadelphia, 1848).

51. Ibid., *PL*, May 26, 1849, May 18, 1850; Guardians of the Poor, Minutes, May 18, 1848, PCA.

52. Rev. D. R. Thomason, *Hints to Emigrants or to Those Who May Contemplate Emigrating to the United States* (Philadelphia, 1848).

53. *LM*, Mar. 24, May 9, Dec. 12, 1848, Oct. 9, 1849. The *Mercury* made the same call for a local society on Jan. 16, 1849.

54. PEFS, *Report of the Executive Committee* (1848); *PL*, May 26, 1849; *LM*, Sept. 4, 1849, Dec. 26, 1848 (quoting from "Address of the Emigrant Society of New York to the People of Ireland"), Jan. 16, 23, Sept. 11, Dec. 4, 1849.

55. *LM*, Dec. 4, 1849. See also *LM*, Nov. 10, 17, 1848. In a letter published as an introduction to Thomason's *Hints to Emigrants*, England's Rev. Thomas Timpson acknowledged the concern that emigration would drain Britain's labor pool, but he insisted that the nation was already overpopulated and that emigration would be a good thing.

56. Wainwright, *Philadelphia Perspective*, 195 (entry of May 2, 1847).

57. AEFS, *Annual Report* (1852).

58. PEFS, *Report of the Executive Committee* (1848); Alexis De Tocqueville, *Democracy in America*, edited by J. P. Mayer, translated by George Lawrence (1839, 1848; New York, 1969), 2:509–13 (for an explanation of volume and page numbers, see n. 64 in Chapter 1). See Chapter 3 of this text.

59. *PL*, June 8, 1850; AEFS, *Annual Report* (Philadelphia, 1852).

60. The 1848 *Report of the Executive Committee* of PEFS makes specific reference to the report of New York's commissioners of emigration. See also *PL*, Aug. 23, 1849, and AEFS, *Foreign Pauperism in Philadelphia: A Memorial to the Legislature of Pennsylvania Exhibiting Reasons for the Amendment of Certain Laws in Relation to the Poor and to Foreign Emigrants . . .* (Philadelphia, 1851). On New York's commissioners, see Purcell, "The New York Commissioners."

61. *American Emigrants' Friend Society: Origin, Design, Plan of Operations* (Philadelphia, 1851). The AEFS used the plural possessive ("Emigrants'") in their publications, whereas the PEFS used the singular.

62. AEFS, *Foreign Pauperism in Philadelphia*. A year later the society was pleased to have received a charter from the state legislature, but it still relied on donations to fund its activities. AEFS, *Annual Report* (1852).

63. *Report of the Delegation Appointed by the Philadelphia Emigrant Society to Enquire into the Nature and Operation of the Emigration Laws in the State of New York: Together with a Memorial to the Legislature of Pennsylvania . . .* (Philadelphia, 1854).

64. AEFS, *Annual Report* (1852); *Pennsylvanian*, May 30, 1848.

65. *Report of the Executive Committee . . .* (Philadelphia, 1848); *Report of the Delega-*

tion . . . (Philadelphia, 1854). Apparently the PEFS regarded the New York disturbance as a preview of future events.

66. Coleman, *Going to America,* 195–96.

67. Ibid., 214–15, 242–45. In a different context Mary P. Ryan has pointed out that American cities commonly provided services through some interweaving of public and private efforts. Ryan, *Civic Wars: Democracy and Public Life in the American City during the Nineteenth Century* (Berkeley, 1997), 101–2 passim. Michael Katz makes a similar argument about public and private cooperation. Katz, *In the Shadow of the Poorhouse: A Social History of Welfare in America,* rev. ed. (New York, 1996). The argument here is not that Liverpool had no such collaborations, but that the limitations of private voluntarism and the expectation of a *national* government solution kept Liverpool from providing such a solution.

68. For a discussion of the interplay between philanthropy and social control, see Paul Boyer, *Urban Masses and Moral Order in America, 1820–1920* (Cambridge, Mass., 1978).

CHAPTER THREE

1. For the early histories of public welfare in England and the United States, see Derek Fraser, *The Evolution of the British Welfare State: A History of Social Policy since the Industrial Revolution* (2d ed., London, 1984), 31–55; Michael Katz, *In the Shadow of the Poorhouse: A Social History of Welfare in America,* rev. ed. (New York, 1996), 13–21; William I. Trattner, *From Poor Law to Welfare State: A History of Social Welfare in America* (5th ed., New York, 1994), 1–28; and Benjamin Joseph Klebaner, *Public Poor Relief in America, 1790–1860* (New York, 1976). For a fascinating collection of essays on how the world's poor negotiated urban relief systems, see Peter Mandler, ed., *The Uses of Charity: The Poor on Relief in the Nineteenth-Century Metropolis* (Philadelphia, 1990).

2. *LM,* Jan. 28, 1848.

3. *PL,* Oct. 25, 1848.

4. Mathew Carey, "Essays on the Public Charities of Philadelphia" (1828), in David J. Rothman, ed., *The Jacksonians on the Poor: Collected Pamphlets* (New York, 1971); Katz, *In the Shadow of the Poorhouse,* 4–10. See also Klebaner, "Public Poor Relief in America," 14–15, and Alexander Keyssar, *Out of Work: The First Century of Unemployment in Massachusetts* (New York, 1986). On the seasonality of labor, see Stanley Engerman and Claudia Goldin, "Seasonality in Nineteenth-Century Labor Markets," in Thomas Weiss and Donald Schaeffer, eds., *American Economic Development in Historical Perspective* (Stanford, 1994), 99–126.

5. *PL,* Oct. 12, 1848.

6. *PL,* Jan. 30, 1847; David Ward, *Poverty, Ethnicity, and the American City, 1840–1925* (Cambridge, England, 1989), 14–15. For Melville and Hawthorne, see Chapter 1.

7. Fraser, *Evolution of the British Welfare State,* 38–48, 99–123.

8. For a good introduction to Jacksonian political ideology, see Harry L. Watson, *Liberty and Power: The Politics of Jacksonian America* (New York, 1990). On the interaction of religion and social change in one U.S. town, see Paul E. Johnson, *A Shopkeeper's Millennium: Society and Revivals in Rochester, New York, 1815–1837* (New York, 1978).

9. See David J. Rothman, *The Discovery of the Asylum: Social Order and Disorder in the New Republic* (Boston, 1971), and Katz, *In the Shadow of the Poorhouse*, 11.

10. Joseph Tuckerman, *On the Elevation of the Poor: A Selection from His Reports as Minister at Large in Boston* (Boston, 1874), reprinted in David J. Rothman, ed., *Poverty, USA: The Historical Record* (New York, 1971). On evangelical reform, see Ward, *Poverty, Ethnicity, and the American City,* 20–23; Paul Boyer, *Urban Masses and Moral Order in America, 1820–1920* (Cambridge, Mass., 1978); and Carroll Smith Rosenberg, *Religion and the Rise of the American City: The New York City Mission Movement, 1812–1870* (Ithaca, 1971). For a comparative study of Unitarian philanthropy and Tuckerman's influences, see Howard M. Wach, "Unitarian Philanthropy and Cultural Hegemony in Comparative Perspective: Manchester and Boston, 1827–1848," *Journal of Social History* 26 (Spring 1993): 539–57.

11. The Law of Settlement provided that a legal settlement could be gained through birth, marriage, or apprenticeship.

12. Fraser, *Evolution of the British Welfare State,* 30–55; Felix Driver, *Power and Pauperism: The Workhouse System, 1834–1884* (Cambridge, England, 1993), 32–57; William C. Lubenow, *The Politics of Government Growth: Early Victorian Attitudes toward State Intervention, 1833–1848* (Newton Abbot, England, 1971).

13. Eric C. Midwinter, *Social Administration in Liverpool* (Manchester, 1969), 7–62, and *Old Liverpool* (Newton Abbot, England, 1971), 67–84; Sheila Kelly, "Select Vestry of Liverpool and the Administration of the Poor Law, 1821–1871" (M.A. thesis, University of Liverpool, 1971); Lawrence Feehan, "Charitable Effort, Statutory Authorities, and the Poor in Liverpool, c1850–1914" (Ph.D. diss., University of Liverpool, 1987); Fraser, *Evolution of the British Welfare State,* 51; Driver, *Power and Pauperism,* 42–47.

14. Fraser, *Evolution of the British Welfare State,* 53–54; Driver, *Power and Pauperism,* 26–37; *LM,* Aug. 11, 1848.

15. Kelly, "Select Vestry of Liverpool," 73–78; Feehan, "Charitable Effort," 319–20; Midwinter, *Old Liverpool,* 80; M. A. Crowther, *The Workhouse System, 1834–1929* (Athens, Ga., 1982), 51–52. The point here is not that the Brownlow Hill workhouse could have accommodated every pauper in Liverpool, but that the parish had already committed to a major workhouse expansion before the famine migration began.

16. Trattner, *From Poor Law to Welfare State,* 17–23, 31–44; Katz, *In the Shadow of the Poorhouse,* 3, 19–20.

17. Trattner, *From Poor Law to Welfare State,* 47–73; Katz, *In the Shadow of the Poorhouse,* 13–21. Both Trattner and Katz draw links between the English and American discussions. Katz (p. 22) suggests that American motives—which included a humanitarian disdain for the practice of auctioning off the poor—may have been less "repressive" than their English counterparts.

18. Priscilla Ferguson Clement, *Welfare and the Poor in the Nineteenth-Century City: Philadelphia, 1800–1854* (Rutherford, N.J., 1985), 38–66; Benjamin J. Klebaner, "The Home Relief Controversy in Philadelphia," *Pennsylvania Magazine of History and Biography* 78 (October 1954): 413–23, and "Public Poor Relief in America"; *Report of the Committee Appointed by the Board of Guardians of the Poor* (Philadelphia, 1827), reprinted in David J. Rothman, *The Almshouse Experience* (New York, 1971).

19. See, e.g., *PL,* June 9, 1847.

20. Klebaner, "Public Poor Relief in America," 236. See also Ivan D. Steen, "Philadelphia in the 1850's as Described by British Travelers," *Pennsylvania History* (1966): 43, and *PL,* June 24, 1848.

21. Charles Lawrence, *History of the Philadelphia Almshouses and Hospitals* (1905; reprint, New York, 1976), 150–75; Klebaner, "Public Poor Relief in America," 141; Katz, *In the Shadow of the Poorhouse,* 25–40; Rothman, *Discovery of the Asylum.*

22. See F. K. Prochaska, *Women and Philanthropy in 19th-Century England* (Oxford, 1980), and Lori D. Ginzberg, *Women and the Work of Benevolence: Morality, Politics, and Class in the 19th-Century United States* (New Haven, 1990).

23. This section is intended to sketch the benevolent network in each city. Specific issues are best left for later discussion. Medical charities, e.g., are considered in Chapter 4. The religious tensions accompanying proselytizing charities are taken up in Chapter 6. The range of organizations dedicated to helping poor children is considered below. Benevolent organizations that did not attend to the needs of the poor (and were thus unlikely to be affected by the famine migration) will receive less attention.

24. Margaret B. Simey, *Charitable Effort in Liverpool in the Nineteenth Century* (Liverpool, 1951), 21; *Fifty-third Report of the Ladies' Charity, or Institution for the Relief of Poor Married Women in Child-Bed, Liverpool, From the 1st of January to the 31st of December, 1848* (Liverpool, 1849); Liverpool Female Penitentiary, Minutes, LRO; *LM,* Apr. 30, 1847; *LM,* Jan. 1, 1847; Simey, *Charitable Effort,* 21. In the year ending in April 1847 the Strangers' Friend Society visited 1,800 cases, more than half of them Irish. *LM,* Apr. 2, 1847. For a survey of Liverpool benevolence, see Simey, *Charitable Effort.* See also Feehan, "Charitable Effort," 46–79.

25. By 1845 the Night Asylum—now on Soho Street—provided berths to 14,846 people. Egerton Smith, *Some Account of the Liverpool Night Asylum for the Houseless Poor in Freemason's Row . . .* (Liverpool, 1832); *LM,* Jan. 15, 1847; Simey, *Charitable Effort,* 27.

26. *The Liverpool Foreigners' Mission* (Liverpool, 1847).

27. *LM,* Jan. 1, 15, Feb. 26, 1847, Feb. 11, 1848; Simey, *Charitable Effort,* 30. In 1845 the DPS reported relieving 6,646 cases.

28. *LM,* Jan. 1, 1848.

29. Liverpool City Mission, *Annual Reports* (1830–55), LRO; Liverpool City Mission, Minutes, May 25, 1829–June 6, 1859, Merseyside Record Office, Liverpool; Gordon Read and David Jebson, *A Voice in the City: 150 Years History of the Liverpool City Mission* (Liverpool, 1980). Quotation is from *Seventeenth Annual Report* (1846); 1829–54 data are summarized in *Twenty-sixth Annual Report* (1855). In 1844 the mission's 21 agents made nearly 80,000 visits and held 3,694 religious meetings but

distributed only £87 in relief to 785 particularly needy families. In fact, in its first twenty-five years the mission distributed only £706 in direct assistance to distressed families.

30. *Laws and Constitutions of the Liverpool Domestic Mission Society, with a Statement of Accounts for the Year Ending December, 1842* (1843); DMS, *Annual Reports,* LRO; Anne Holt, *A History of the Poor Being the History of the Liverpool Domestic Mission Society, 1836–1936* (Liverpool, 1936); Simey, *Charitable Effort,* 33–41. For references to Tuckerman, see *Third Annual Report* (1839) and *Sixteenth Annual Report* (1853) (quotation).

31. *Thirty-first Report of the Catholic Benevolent Society, Anno Domino* (Liverpool, 1840); Liverpool Catholic Benevolent Society, "Account Book, 1811–1848," and Catholic Benevolent Society, "Minute Book, December 1850–November 1858," both in County Record Office, Preston. See also Thomas Burke, *Catholic History of Liverpool* (Liverpool, 1910), and Chapter 6 of this text. Occasionally local Catholics staged public events to raise money for particular projects. In January 1847 they held a charity ball to aid the Female Orphan Asylum. *LM,* Jan. 22, 1847.

32. *LM,* Nov. 6, 1849. The society's members had visited 300 families by the end of the decade.

33. Abraham Hume, "Analysis of the Subscribers to the Various Liverpool charities" *Transactions of the Historic Society of Lancashire and Liverpool* 7 (1854–55): app. 22–27. Hume's detailed analysis also confirms that the District Provident Society was the only organization in Liverpool providing substantial nonmedical outdoor assistance to the poor. On the characteristics of Liverpool's benevolent men and women, see Simey, *Charitable Effort,* 13–14 passim.

34. Indigent Widows' and Single Women's Society, *Annual Reports* (Philadelphia, 1842, 1846, 1851, 1856); Magdalen Society, *Annual Reports* (Philadelphia, 1841–57). For a survey of benevolence in Philadelphia, see Clement, *Welfare and the Poor,* 141–64.

35. *The Tenth Annual Report of the Executive Board of the Union Benevolent Association, with the Treasurer's Account, Oct 1841* (Philadelphia, 1841) (quotation); UBA, *Annual Reports* (Philadelphia, 1840–60); Clement, *Welfare and the Poor,* 154–56, and "Nineteenth-Century Welfare Policy, Programs, and Poor Women: Philadelphia as a Case Study," *Feminist Studies* 18 (Spring 1992): 43–44; Klebaner, "Public Poor Relief in America," 37–48. In 1847 the UBA assisted 855 Philadelphia families. *PL,* Oct. 30, 1847.

36. In the winter of 1847–48 the HMA aided 1,800 families. *PL,* Apr. 22, 1848. The Philadelphia Society for Bettering the Condition of the Poor, established in 1830, was also modeled on Tuckerman's Boston ministry. Clement, *Welfare and the Poor,* 156.

37. *The Constitution and By-Laws of the Female Society of Philadelphia for the Relief and Employment of the Poor* (Philadelphia, 1836); *Report of the FSPREP with a List of the Managers of the Society* (Philadelphia, 1840); Northern Association for the Relief and Employment of Poor Women, *Eleventh Annual Report* (Philadelphia, 1855), and *Twelfth Annual Report* (Philadelphia, 1856).

38. Hugh Nolan, *The Most Reverend Francis Patrick Kenrick: Third Bishop of Phila-*

delphia, 1830–1851 (Philadelphia, 1948), 363–65, 385–87, 433–44; *CH,* Oct. 21, Nov. 11, 18, 1847, Dec. 16, 1847; Hibernia Society, Minutes, 1840–50, HSP; *Act of Incorporation, By-Laws, &c of the Hibernia Society, for the Relief of Emigrants from Ireland* (Philadelphia, 1845).

39. Clement, "Nineteenth-Century Welfare Policy," 35–58. Clement notes that, ironically, black women may have profited in this shift in emphasis away from cash assistance.

40. Policies toward children reoccur throughout this book, specifically in the discussions of religious education and crime in Chapters 6 and 7. For three recent histories of policies toward children, see Peter C. Holloran, *Boston's Wayward Children: Social Services for Homeless Children, 1830–1930* (1989; reprint, Boston, 1994); Joan Gittens, *Poor Relations: The Children of the State in Illinois, 1818–1990* (Urbana, Ill., 1994); and Priscilla Ferguson Clement, *Growing Pains: Children in the Industrial Age, 1850–1890* (New York, 1997).

41. Boards of Guardians, Liverpool Select Vestry, "Industrial Schools Committee Minute Book, 1845–1850," Nov. 10, 1846, LRO. Once they had been admitted to the workhouse, children with no diseases were eligible to be transferred to the Industrial School. An additional 300 children could be housed in the infirmary. In 1853, 1,560 children and 1,287 adults received indoor relief in the workhouse and the Industrial School. Kelly, "Select Vestry of Liverpool," 106.

42. Blue Coat Hospital, *Annual Reports* (Liverpool, 1840–50); Female Orphan Asylum, *Annual Reports,* (Liverpool, 1844, 1849, 1851); Liverpool Asylum for Boys, *Annual Reports* (Liverpool, 1851); *LM,* Mar. 5, 1847.

43. *Report of the Roman Catholic Society of St Joseph's for Educating and Maintaining Poor Orphan Children* (Philadelphia, 1851); Clement, *Welfare and the Poor,* 124; *Report of the Board of Managers of the St John's Orphan Asylum for the Year 1845* (Philadelphia, 1846). In 1848 St. John's housed just over 50 boys. *PL,* Feb. 25, 1848. On children and welfare, see Clement, *Welfare and the Poor,* 118–40.

44. Clement, *Welfare and the Poor,* 121.

45. Philadelphia House of Refuge, *Annual Reports* (Philadelphia, 1830–59); *The Design and Advantages of the House of Refuge with Acts of Incorporation, By-Laws, Rules, &c* (Philadelphia, 1851); *PL,* Apr. 24, 1847. In 1850 the House of Refuge opened a separate branch for black children. New York (1825) and Boston (1826) established similar "congregate municipal institutions" (privately run but working closely with city authorities) for juvenile offenders at roughly the same time. See Holloran, *Boston's Wayward Children,* 24.

46. *LM,* Jan. 8, 1847, Jan. 7, 1848.

47. The County Prison did maintain "vagrant cells" in the 1840s. *PL,* Apr. 3, 1849. By the end of the century it had become commonplace for America's police stations to provide informal, temporary housing for the homeless. See Eric H. Monkkonen, "Nineteenth-Century Institutions: Dealing with the Urban 'Underclass,'" in Michael B. Katz, ed., *The "Underclass" Debate: Views from History* (Princeton, 1993), 336, 349–52.

48. This was widely acknowledged by the mid-nineteenth century. See Clement, *Growing Pains,* 188.

49. In 1848, 546 of the 5,962 (9.2 percent) people admitted to Blockley were children. *Auditor's Report of the Accounts of the Blockley Alms-House for the Year 1848* (Philadelphia, 1849). Between 1820 and 1850 the share of Philadelphia's indoor relief given to children dropped from 24 percent to only 11 percent. Clement, *Welfare and the Poor*, 118–40. Admissions to the House of Refuge reached 276 in 1851. *25th Annual Report* (Philadelphia, 1853), 5. Girard College's population (discussed below) hovered around 300 throughout the early 1850s. *Annual Reports* (1850–56).

50. *LM,* Feb. 1, 1848, July 2, 9, 13, 1847. Concerns about the cost of poor relief was a regular theme in the *Mercury.* See Nov. 9, 1847, Apr. 13, May 29, June 26, 1849. Advocates of rating the dock estates used this concern to their advantage in 1849. See *LM,* Mar. 16, 1849. For appeals to Parliament for financial assistance, see Chapter 2.

51. *LM,* July 23, Sept. 3, 1847. W. J. Lowe, *The Irish in Mid-Victorian Lancashire: The Shaping of a Working Class Community* (New York, 1989), 29. In the fiscal year ending on Mar. 25, 1848, the Liverpool Poor Law Union spent £25,926—or 40 percent of its total expenditures—on Irish recipients. This figure was more than eight times the total of two years earlier and roughly twice the expenditure on the Irish-born in the previous year. For the next six years the Poor Law Union spent between £12,000 and £14,000 annually on the Irish-born, or between 24 and 28 percent of annual expenditures. Frank Neal, "Lancashire, the Famine Irish, and the Poor Laws: A Study in Crisis Management," *Irish Economic and Social History* (1995): 42.

52. George Holt Sr. Diary, Dec. 26, 1846, Jan. 1, 17, 31, 1847, Feb. 13, 1848, LRO.

53. Holt Diary, Jan. 31, 1847, LRO; *LM,* Jan. 15, Feb. 19, 1847, Oct. 17, 1848, Apr. 27, May 1, 1849; *LM,* Feb. 12, May 11, 1847. See also *LM,* July 16, 1847, Dec. 1, 5, 1848. DMS ministers also criticized beggar fraud and indiscriminate giving. DMS, *Tenth and Fourteenth Annual Reports* (Liverpool, 1847, 1851).

54. Lowe, *The Irish in Mid-Victorian Lancashire,* 29–30; Feehan, "Charitable Effort," 319–34; *LM,* July 14, Aug. 15, Oct. 27, 1848. In a sample of paupers admitted to Liverpool's workhouse between November 1846 and March 1848, 50 percent were listed as Irish. Liverpool Guardians of the Poor, Liverpool Workhouse Records, "Admission and Discharge A–Z, November 1846 to March 1848," LRO. This sample is based on all cases on every tenth page of a roughly 500-page register. For 118 cases (7.4 percent), no known place of birth was listed.

55. Kirkdale Industrial Schools, Classification Registers (Boys and Girls), LRO; Boards of Guardians, Select Vestry, "Industrial Schools Committee Minute Book, 1845–1850," Mar. 31, 1847, May 10, 1848, LRO.

56. The 1850 opening of the new Boys' Orphanage may indicate a rise in demand. *Report of the Liverpool Asylum for Orphan Boys, with the Statement of Account . . . 1851* (Liverpool, 1851).

57. *LM,* May 4, 1849; *LM,* Nov. 26, June 22, 1847; *Report of the Blue Coat Hospital* (Liverpool, 1848, 1852); *Report of the Female Orphan Asylum* (Liverpool, 1851). In 1851 the Blue Coat Hospital finally paid off its outstanding debts.

58. *LM,* Apr. 2, Feb. 26, May 21, 1847, Aug. 14, 1848, Feb. 9, 1849. See also *LM,* Jan. 15, 22, 1847, Jan. 9, 1849. The DPS's clients were disproportionately Irish-born

before the heavy migration. In the last six months of 1845, 3,567 of the society's 6,646 cases were Irish. *LM,* Feb. 11, 1848.

59. DMS, *Annual Reports* (Liverpool, 1846, 1847, 1851); Holt, *History of the Liverpool Domestic Mission Society;* Liverpool City Mission, *Annual Reports* (Liverpool, 1847, 1852, 1855); Liverpool City Mission, Minutes, May 5, 1851, Merseyside Record Office. For Protestant proselytizing and Catholic hostility, see Chapter 6.

60. *LM,* Jan. 22, Apr. 10, Oct. 22. 1847. For Catholic charity sermons, see *LM,* Mar. 6, 13, 1849.

61. *LM,* Jan. 22, 1847, Feb. 11, 1848, Feb. 20, 1849; Catholic Benevolent Society, "Minute Book, December 1850–November 1858," and *Annual Reports* (Liverpool, 1852, 1855, 1856); *LM,* Dec. 23, 1851. (The 1851 Annual Report was published in the *LM* and inserted in the Minute Book; the 1853 report is in manuscript in the Minute Book.) For more on the work of the Catholic Benevolent Society, see Chapter 6.

62. DMS, *Tenth Annual Report* (Liverpool, 1847). The following March the Select Vestry arranged to sell soup to the Strangers' Friend Society and the DPS at reduced prices. *LM,* Jan. 15, 29, June 25, Nov. 12, 1847, Jan. 21, Mar. 17, June 2, 1848.

63. *LM,* May 19, June 2, 20, 1848, May 22, 25, 1849.

64. Liverpool Ragged School Union, *Fourth Annual Report* (Liverpool, 1851); *LM,* Jan. 5, Mar. 19, 1847, Jan. 11, 1848; DMS, *Tenth Annual Report* (Liverpool, 1847); *Narrative of the Origin, Progress and Details of Industrial Ragged Schools, in Scotland and England* (Liverpool, 1848) (first quotation); Liverpool Industrial Ragged Schools, *Annual Reports,* (Liverpool, 1850–58) (second quotation); *LM,* Oct. 13, 1848. Chapter 4 takes up the issue of medical assistance to the poor.

65. This account is taken from the following sources: the *Mercury, Albion, Courier,* and *Journal*—all Liverpool newspapers; *An Authentic Account of the Destruction of the Ocean Monarch by Fire, off the Port of Liverpool, and Loss of 176 lives, with an engraving* (Liverpool, n.d.); James Henry Legg, *The Ocean Monarch: A Poetic Narrative, with an Original Authentic Account in Prose, of the Loss of the Ill-fated Vessel* (Liverpool, 1848); and *Destruction of an Emigrant Ship, the Ocean Monarch, by Fire* (n.p., n.d.) (a 22-page pamphlet with missing title page).

66. *Journal,* Aug. 26, 1848. The same account appears in *An Authentic Account . . .* and *Destruction of an Emigrant Ship . . .* The *Journal* reported that the "fearful catastrophe produced . . . the deepest gloom in the town."

67. *Journal,* Aug. 26, 1848; *Albion,* Aug. 28, 1848.

68. For this sort of impromptu benevolence, see *LM,* Aug. 25, 1848; *Journal,* Aug. 26, 1848; *Courier,* Aug. 30, 1848; and Legg, *Ocean Monarch.* Some accounts claimed that certain unscrupulous rescuers took the passengers' watches and valuables in exchange for warm clothing.

69. *Albion,* Aug. 28, 1848; *Courier,* Aug. 30, 1848. The police did their part by donating extra uniform coats to the cause. *Journal,* Aug. 26, 1848.

70. *Journal,* Aug. 26, 1848; *LM,* Aug. 29, 1848; *Courier,* Sept. 6, 1848; Legg, *Ocean Monarch; Journal,* Aug. 26, 1848; *LM,* Aug. 29, 1848; *Courier,* Aug. 30, 1848. The various accounts described the committee's charge in almost identical terms.

The committee included the mayor, the city magistrate, a government emigration agent, the Brazilian consul, and seven local merchants and brokers. A few of these men—including the owner of the boat that rescued the captain—were involved in the episode.

71. *Journal,* Aug. 26, Sept. 2, 6, 1848; *LM,* Aug. 29, 1848; Legg, *Ocean Monarch.*

72. *Courier,* Aug. 30, Sept. 6, 1848; *Journal,* Sept. 2, 9, 1848; *Albion,* Sept. 4, 1848; *An Authentic Account.* The *Mercury* (Sept. 8, 1848) and the *Albion* (Sept. 11, 1848) both reprinted this editorial, expressing hope that it would ease any incendiary spirit among the Irish.

73. See, e.g., *CH,* Sept. 23, 1847.

74. *PL,* Feb. 19, May 7, 20, Aug. 11, 1847 (describing New York City), Aug. 12, 1847.

75. See *PL,* Aug. 18, 27, 1847. Such comments may reflect the smaller, more manageable numbers in the American city.

76. *PL,* Feb. 1, Aug. 18, 27, 1847, Mar. 17, Aug. 7, 1848. See also *Pennsylvanian,* May 1, 1848.

77. *PL,* Aug. 20, Dec. 14, 1847.

78. *PL,* Aug. 6, 1849.

79. Guardians of the Poor, Minutes, August 1846–May 1849, and Committee on Alms House, Minutes, 1837–53, PCA. See also Clement, *Welfare and the Poor,* 60–61. After several years of fluctuation, Blockley's population fell to just over 2,000 in December 1852.

80. *Auditors' Report of the Accounts of the Blockley Alms-House* (Philadelphia, 1847–52); *PL,* Apr. 3, 1849. In 1850 Philadelphia County had a total population of 408,742.

81. Clement, *Welfare and the Poor,* 112; Guardians of the Poor, Almshouse, Register of White Male Children, January 1848–February 1849, PCA; Guardians of the Poor, Minutes, Jan. 29, 1849, and 1847, PCA; *Auditors' Report . . . Blockley Alms-House . . . Year Ending May 19, 1851* (Philadelphia, 1852). Between February and July 1847 the Guardians collected $9,542.50.

82. *PL,* May 24, 1849. See Chapter 6. The Magdalen Society's annual reports occasionally discussed the various forces responsible for prostitution without ever mentioning the rise in poor immigrants.

83. UBA, *Annual Reports* (Philadelphia, 1847–52). In 1851 the UBA reported visiting 238 "colored" families. *Pennsylvanian* Jan. 7, 1848; *PL,* Nov. 16, 1848.

84. Hibernia Society, Minutes, Mar. 10, Dec. 17, 1847, Dec. 18, 1848, HSP. In 1847 the Hibernia Society distributed $1,250 to the local Irish poor; in 1848 that figure rose slightly—to over $1,300.

85. *PL,* Jan. 13, 1847; *Ninth Annual Report of the Ladies' Union City Mission of Philadelphia* (Philadelphia, 1856); *PL,* Jan. 21, 25, Feb. 4, May 19, 1847, Oct. 4, Dec. 30, 1848, Jan. 1, 11, 1849; Clement, *Welfare and the Poor,* 156.

86. *PL,* Feb. 4, 1848; Western Association of Ladies for Relief and Employment of the Poor, *Annual Reports* (Philadelphia, 1848, 1849); *PL,* Feb. 5, 1847. Within three months the Northern Liberties House of Industry had aided 234 destitute persons and supplied 116 women with paid labor. *PL* Feb. 1, 22, Nov. 13, 1847.

87. The Provident Society provided work for 752 women in 1847. *PL*, Jan. 20, 1848.

88. *PL*, Mar. 23, 30, 1847; *Constitution of the Philadelphia Society for the Employment and Instruction of the Poor, with a Report of a Committee of the Board of Managers on the Erection and Organization of a House of Industry* (Philadelphia, 1847). See also *PL*, Mar. 29, 31, 1847.

89. PSEIP, *Annual Reports* (Philadelphia, 1848–56); *PL*, Dec. 30, 1848, Jan. 1, 13, Apr. 9, 11, 1849.

90. PSEIP, *Annual Reports* (1853, 1855, 1856).

91. *Constitution and Report of the Managers of the Rosine Association* (Philadelphia, 1848); Rosine Association, *Semi-Annual Report of the Managers . . .* (Philadelphia, 1848), *Semi-Annual Report* (Philadelphia, 1851), and *Annual Reports* (Philadelphia, 1852, 1854); *PL*, Apr. 6, 1847, Jan. 4, 1849.

92. *PL*, Dec. 7, 1849.

93. *PL*, July 9, Nov. 15, 17, 1849; *Constitution and Address of the Temporary Home Association* (Philadelphia, 1849); Temporary Home Association, *Annual Reports* (Philadelphia, 1852, 1857). In its first eighteen months the association aided 1,700 women.

94. *PL*, Jan. 2, 4, 1847, Jan. 6, 10, Apr. 9, 13, 1848, Jan. 1, 10, 1849; *CH*, Apr. 15, 1847; Guardians of the Poor, Minutes, Feb. 19, 1849, PCA.

95. *CH*, Oct. 27, 1847; *PL*, Feb. 3, 11, 1848; Clement, *Welfare and the Poor,* 157; Dennis Clark, *The Irish in Philadelphia: Ten Generations of Urban Experience* (Philadelphia, 1973), 99, 102. Clark notes that by 1857 branches of the Society of Saint Vincent de Paul were at work in seven other Philadelphia parishes. See Chapter 6.

96. House of Refuge, *Annual Reports* (Philadelphia, 1840–55); Philadelphia Orphan Society, *Annual Reports* (Philadelphia, 1840–60). Despite these increases in inmates the annual reports of the Presbyterian-run society drew no explicit links to the Irish migration.

97. *Report of the Roman Catholic Society of St. Joseph for Educating and Maintaining Poor Orphan Children* (Philadelphia, 1851, 1854); St. John's Orphan Asylum, *Annual Reports* (Philadelphia, 1846, 1851); Clement, *Welfare and the Poor,* 136.

98. Board of Directors of the Girard College for Orphans, *Annual Reports* (Philadelphia, 1849–60) (quotation from *First Annual Report*); Clement, *Welfare and the Poor,* 136 passim; *First Annual Report of the Northern Home for Friendless Children* (Philadelphia, 1854).

99. DMS, *Sixteenth Annual Report* (Liverpool, 1853); W. I. Mann Diary, Jan. 26, 1849, LRO; Anne Holt Travel Diary, May 12, 1851; Liverpool City Council, Gaol Committee, Minutes, Apr. 29, 1846.

100. See *PL*, Aug. 26, 1848.

101. William Rathbone Jr., *Social Duties Considered with Reference to the Organisation of Effort in Works of Benevolence and Public Utility* (London, 1867) (quotations, pp. 51, 60–61); "Liverpool Central Relief and Charity Organisation Society, 1861–1884," file of press clippings, LRO; Liverpool Central Relief Society, Minute Book, LRO. The London Society traced its intellectual roots to Edinburgh's Rev. Thomas Chalmers. See Boyer, *Urban Masses and Moral Order,* 145.

102. Tuckerman, *On the Elevation of the Poor,* 47; Trattner, *From Poor Law to Welfare State,* 94–105; Josephine Shaw Lowell, *Public Relief and Private Charity* (1884; reprint, David J. Rothman, ed., New York, 1971); Philadelphia Society for Organizing Charitable Relief and Repressing Mendicancy, *First Annual Report* (Philadelphia, 1879); "Liverpool Central Relief and Charity Organisation Society, 1861–1884," file, LRO; Liverpool Central Relief Society, Minute Book (quotation, Jan. 28, 1863). The two charity-organizing societies also differed in several ways. Liverpool's initially relied on male visitors, whereas Philadelphia's—like many such bodies in both England and the United States—had female visitors. See Prochaska, *Women and Philanthropy in 19th Century England.*

103. "Liverpool Central Relief and Charity Organisation Society" file, LRO: Jan. 22, 1862 clipping from unnamed newspaper; Feb. 7, 1863 clipping from *The Porcupine.* These discussions mirrored Hume's earlier observation that Liverpool's charities depended on the heavy participation of a relatively small number of donors.

104. See Boyer, *Urban Masses and Moral Order,* 147–48.

105. In fact, in 1863 a handful of benevolent Liverpool men created the Liverpool Central Relief Committee to organize in-kind assistance to locals suffering unusual economic hardships that were largely attributed to America's Civil War. Charitable Philadelphians launched no such citywide venture despite economic difficulties both at the beginning of the war and immediately following the peace. Liverpool Central Relief Committee, Minutes, LRO; J. Matthew Gallman, *Mastering Wartime: A Social History of Philadelphia during the Civil War* (New York, 1990).

CHAPTER FOUR

1. For surveys of the history of public health in England and the United States, see John Duffy, *The Sanitarians: A History of American Public Health* (Urbana, Ill., 1990), and Anthony S. Wohl, *Endangered Lives: Public Health in Victorian Britain* (London, 1983). Stuart Galishoff's *Newark: The Nation's Unhealthiest City, 1832–1895* (New Brunswick, N.J., 1988) is a particularly valuable case study. For a broad comparative analysis of nineteenth-century medicine, science, and public health in England, Europe, and the United States, see W. F. Bynum, *Science and the Practice of Medicine in the Nineteenth Century* (New York, 1994). This chapter emphasizes medical institutions and responses to epidemic diseases. The next chapter addresses sanitation reform more broadly.

2. For a general history of the responses to diseases and the "immigrant menace," see Alan M. Kraut, *Silent Travelers* (New York, 1994), esp. 31–49 on cholera and the Irish immigrants.

3. See Charles E. Rosenberg, *The Care of Strangers: The Rise of America's Hospital System* (New York, 1987), esp. 15–93. For a comparative discussion of hospital development, see Morris J. Vogel, "The Transformation of the American Hospital," in Norbert Finzsch and Robert Jutte, eds., *Institutions of Confinement: Hospitals, Asylums, and Prisons in Western Europe and North America, 1500–1950* (Washington, D.C., 1996), 39–54.

4. *Liverpool as It Is: A Picturesque Hand Book for the Resident & Stranger* (Liverpool,

n.d.), 99–100; *Ninety-second Annual Report, List of Subscribers, and Statement of Accounts of the Liverpool Infirmary, Lock Hospital, and Lunatic Asylum, Jan 1, 1840 to Jan 1, 1841* (Liverpool, 1841).

5. *Report of the Committee of the Liverpool Dispensaries for the Year 1849* (Liverpool, 1849).

6. Michael Cook, *Liverpool's Northern Hospital, 1834–1958* (Liverpool, 1981); Northern Hospital, Committee Meeting Books, 2 vols. (1833–73), LRO; Dr. Thomas H. Bickerston Scrapbook, LRO.

7. *Reports of the Liverpool Southern Hospital, 1842–61* (bound volume of printed annual reports), LRO; Charles J. Macalister, *The Origin and History of the Liverpool Royal Southern Hospital* (Liverpool, 1936).

8. *Fifty-third Report of the Ladies' Charity, or Institution for the Relief of Poor Married Women in Child-Bed, Liverpool, from the 1st of January to the 31st of December, 1848* (Liverpool, 1849); Records of the Liverpool Maternity Hospital, LRO.

9. In 1847, e.g., the Council voted to give the dispensaries £157, the Northern and Southern Hospitals £100 each, and the Ladies' Charity and the Ophthalmalic Institute £30 each. City Council, Minute Book, January 6, 1847, LRO; *LM,* Jan. 8, 1847. See also *LM,* Jan. 5, 1849.

10. For a detailed description of Philadelphia's medical institutions, see J. Thomas Scharf and Thompson Westcott, *History of Philadelphia, 1609–1884,* 3 vols. (Philadelphia, 1884), 2:1669–85 passim. See also Elizabeth Geffen, "Industrial Development and Social Crisis, 1841–1854," in Russell F. Weigley, ed., *Philadelphia: A 300-Year History* (New York, 1982), 319–22. For an interesting, although dated, history of Philadelphia medicine, see Richard H. Shryock, "A Century of Medical Progress in Philadelphia, 1750–1850," *Pennsylvania History* (January 1941): 7–28.

11. Rosenberg, *Care of Strangers,* 18, 22–23, 32, 109. Although independent, the Pennsylvania Hospital did work with local government, routinely transferring pauper patients to the almshouse hospital or seeking reimbursement from other governments for indigent patients who were not residents of Philadelphia. Ibid., 364 n. 38.

12. Rosenberg, *Care of Strangers,* 101; *State of the Accounts of the Pennsylvania Hospital* (Philadelphia, 1842–52).

13. *Report of the Southern and Toxteth Hospital* (1847).

14. David Lewis Northern Hospital, Committee Meeting Books, Jan. 12, 1847, LRO.

15. Scharf and Westcott, *History of Philadelphia,* 2:1685; *Rules, Regulations and By-Laws, of the Northern Dispensary, for the Medical Relief of the Poor* (Philadelphia, 1840).

16. Rosenberg, "From Almshouse to Hospital: The Shaping of Philadelphia General Hospital," *Health and Society* 60 (1982): 108–54, and *Care of Strangers,* 32, 364 n. 38; Scharf and Westcott, *History of Philadelphia,* 2:1676.

17. W. H. Duncan, *On the Physical Causes of High Mortality in Liverpool* (Liverpool, 1843). See also Paul Laxton and Gerry Kearns, "Statistics and the Management of Public Health: The Methods of W. H. Duncan M.D., 1805–1863" (paper delivered at the meetings of the Social Science History Association, 1993); Eric C. Midwinter, *Social Administration in Lancashire, 1830–1860* (Manchester, England, 1969).

18. On the national discussions of public health, see Wohl, *Endangered Lives,* and Margaret Pelling, *Cholera, Fever, and English Medicine, 1825–1865* (Oxford, 1978).

19. Edwin Chadwick, *Report on the Sanitary Condition of the Labouring Population of Great Britain* (1842; reprint, edited by M. W. Flinn, Edinburgh, 1965); Wohl, *Endangered Lives,* 147–48, 179–80; William C. Lubenow, *The Politics of Government Growth: Early Victorian Attitudes toward State Intervention, 1833–1848* (Newton Abbot, England, 1971), 71–80; *Report of the Proceedings at a Public Meeting of the Friends of the Liverpool Health of Towns' Association* (Liverpool, 1845).

20. Wohl, *Endangered Lives,* 122–25.

21. See ibid., 150 passim, and Lubenow, *Politics of Government Growth,* 69–106. On local responses to Lord Morpeth's bill, see *LM,* Apr. 2, 6, 13, 20, May 14, June 18, 1847, Apr. 4, May 9, 1848; quotation from May 12, 1848.

22. Derek Fraser, *Power and Authority in the Victorian City* (New York, 1979), 26–29; Midwinter, *Social Administration in Lancashire,* 63–85; Brian D. White, *A History of the Corporation of Liverpool, 1835–1914* (Liverpool, 1951), 30–47.

23. Laxton and Kearns, "Statistics and the Management of Public Health," 9 passim.

24. W. M. Frazer, *Duncan of Liverpool* (London, 1947); Laxton and Kearns, "Statistics and the Management of Public Health"; Wohl, *Endangered Lives,* 179–81. On the impact of the 1848 legislation on other Lancashire towns, see Eric Midwinter, "Local Boards of Health in Lancashire, 1848–1858," *Transactions of the Historic Society of Lancashire and Cheshire* 117 (1965): 167–80.

25. *LM,* Jan. 8, 15, Feb. 12, 26, Mar. 5, 12, 1847.

26. See, e.g., Duncan, *On the Physical Causes of High Mortality in Liverpool.*

27. Duncan's reports to the Health Committee (summarized in the daily newspapers) and his annual reports are an invaluable source for Liverpool's public health measures throughout this period. For the annual reports in their most accessible form, see William H. Duncan, *Report to the Health Committee of the Borough of Liverpool, on the Health of the Town during the Years 1847–48–49–50, and on Other Matters within His Department* (Liverpool, 1851).

28. *LM,* Feb. 12, Apr. 9, 16, 27, 30, May 11, 1847. In February 1847 Duncan (*Report to the Health Committee,* 6) stated that seven-eighths of the patients in the Fever Hospital were Irish, with the majority of them coming from the crowded lodging houses in the area between Scotland and Vauxhall Roads.

29. *LM,* May 4, 7, 11, 18, 25, 1847; Duncan, *Report to the Health Committee,* 8. For a short time the fever sheds became a political battleground when it became known that one of the vestrymen had rented a vacant building to the parish at a tidy profit. *LM,* Apr. 3, 1847.

30. Town Council, Minute Books, Mar. 5, 1847; *LM,* Feb. 26, Mar. 12, July 23, 1847.

31. *LM,* Jan. 1, 29, Mar. 5, 12, May 4, 28, June 1, 18, 25, July 6, 27, Aug. 31, Sept. 14, 1847; Duncan, *Report to the Health Committee,* 18.

32. As we have seen, the health threat was an important component in the city's appeal for national relief. See also *LM,* May 4, 1847.

33. Health Committee, General Purposes Sub-Committee, Minute Book, Janu-

ary 1847–October 1847, LRO, entries for Feb. 5, 9, 11, Mar. 12, July 2 (these are periodic reports by Thomas Fresh, the inspector of nuisances); *LM*, June 25, July 9, 13, 20, Sept. 24, Oct. 15, 26, 1847. Liverpool's housing dilemmas are considered more fully in the next chapter.

34. *LM*, Aug. 27, Sept. 27, Nov. 5 (quotation), 1847; Duncan, *Report to the Health Committee*, 10–15.

35. *LM*, Mar. 10, 1848. On the spread of cholera, see *LM*, Oct. 15, 19, 22, 1847.

36. Wohl, *Endangered Lives*, 118–25. See also Charles Rosenberg, *The Cholera Years: The United States in 1832, 1849, and 1866*, revised ed. (New York, 1987). Many people continued to see a higher power involved in epidemic deaths. See, e.g., Rev. J. Herbert Jones, *God's Voice in the Cholera, a Sermon, Preached in St. Augustine's Church, Liverpool, on Tuesday Morning, October 9, 1849, Being the Day Appointed for Public Humiliation in the Town* (Liverpool, 1849), and *Cholera: Form of Prayer to Be Used in All Churches and Chapels on Sunday 16, 1849* (Liverpool, 1849).

37. *LM*, Jan. 11, 18, 25, Feb. 1, 4, Aug. 22, Dec. 22, 1848, Jan. 2, Mar. 16, 1849. The Select Vestry debated the merits of Hawthorne's methods on several occasions. See *LM*, June 1, July 13, 1849.

38. *LM*, Dec. 24, 1847.

39. The larger sanitation question is considered in the next chapter. On the Health Committee's early discussions of cholera, see *LM* Jan. 14, Oct. 20, 1848.

40. *LM*, Aug. 11, 1848; Midwinter, *Old Liverpool*, 96–97. Forced removals back to Ireland continued in conjunction with cellar and lodging house evictions. *LM*, Feb. 20, Aug. 3, 1849.

41. *LM*, Oct. 24, 31, 1848; Thomas Fresh, *Report to the Health Committee of the Town Council of the Borough of Liverpool* (Liverpool, 1851). The Health Committee's weekly reports were printed in the *Mercury*. See, e.g., *LM*, Dec. 15, 22, 1848, Jan. 30, Feb. 2, 13, 20, 1849.

42. *LM*, Dec. 12, 15, 1848; June 1, 15, July 27, Aug. 3, Sept. 28, Nov. 30, 1849. In his reports to the Health Committee Duncan routinely linked the disease to the Irish poor. For his report on 1849, including a detailed analysis of the mortality figures, see Duncan, *Report to the Health Committee*, 25–56.

43. Health Committee, General Purposes Sub-Committee, Minute Book, May 28, 1847. As we have seen, things grew tense in 1847 when Duncan began ordering emergency cellar clearances without consulting parish authorities.

44. Health Committee, General Purposes Sub-Committee, Minute Book, Feb. 9, 1847; Watch Committee, Orders to the Head Constable, LRO, Nov. 20, 1847, Dec. 30, 1848, July 21, 1849, passim, and Standing Sub-Committees or Daily Board, Minute Book, October–December 1847, December 1848; LRO; *LM*, Dec. 3, 1847. Jurisdictional issues will come up again in Chapter 5.

45. *LM*, June 22, 29, Aug. 10, 31, Sept. 7, 18, 28, Nov. 30, 1849; Duncan, *Report to the Health Committee*, 43–47, 75–79.

46. See Wohl, *Endangered Lives*, 142–65, and Midwinter, *Local Boards of Health in Lancashire*.

47. Duncan, *Report to the Health Committee*, 42–43.

48. *LM*, Mar. 5, 13, 1847, Oct. 24, 1848, June 29, 1849. On June 22, 1849,

the *Mercury* applauded discussions of a complete removal of quarantines on the grounds that they were ineffectual and damaging to commerce.

49. *LM,* June 8, July 20, 1849.

50. Duncan, *Report to the Health Committee;* Liverpool Dispensaries, *Annual Report* (Liverpool, 1848); *LM,* Feb. 12, 19, 1847, Feb. 8 (quotation), July 7, 1848, Jan. 26, Mar. 23, 1849; *Report of the Committee of the Liverpool Dispensaries for the Year 1849* (Liverpool, 1849); Liverpool Infirmary, *Annual Reports* (Liverpool, 1840–50); Liverpool Northern Hospital, *Annual Reports* (Liverpool, 4 undated and 1852); *LM,* Jan. 14, 1848; Northern Hospital, Committee Meeting Books, Minutes, LRO. The share of Irish-born patients admitted per year was as follows: 1846: 874 of 2,503 = 34.9 percent; 1849: 916 of 2,809 = 32.6 percent; 1850: 1,149 of 3,138 = 36.6 percent; and 1851: 1,113 of 3,019 = 36.8 percent.

51. *LM,* Jan. 18, 1848. The number of patients dropped slightly in 1853 before rising dramatically in the mid-1850s. Southern Hospital, *Annual Reports* (Liverpool, 1847–54); *LM,* Jan. 22, 1847, Jan. 16, 1849.

52. *LM,* Dec. 28, 1848, Jan. 9, 12, 1849; Southern Hospital, *Annual Report* (1849); Macalister, *Royal Southern Hospital.*

53. *LM,* June 22, 26, Aug. 10, 14, 17, 1849; Anne Holt Diary, Aug. 9, 1849, LRO; Royal Infirmary, *Annual Report* (1850); Northern Hospital, Committee Meeting Books, Nov. 6, 1849; Southern Hospital, *Annual Report* (1850).

54. Dispensaries, *Annual Report* (1849); *LM,* Dec. 25, 1848; Ladies' Charity, *Annual Report* (1849); Southern Hospital, *Annual Report* (1851). The hospital managers asked the Select Vestry for financial assistance on the grounds that it would be cheaper to fund them than build a second workhouse at the southern end of the city. The report makes no reference to the ethnicity of the patients.

55. Rainhill Asylum, Minutes, Merseyside Record Office, Liverpool; Liverpool Royal Infirmary, *Annual Report* (1852). In 1851 the Infirmary was given the right to call itself the "Royal Infirmary."

56. Geffen, "Industrial Development and Social Crisis," 318–19. According to one scholar, the death rate in Philadelphia declined between 1825 and 1850. Shryock, "Medical Progress in Philadelphia," 10.

57. Rosenberg, *Cholera Years,* 13–98.

58. Edward P. Allinson and Boies Penrose, *Philadelphia, 1681–1887: A History of Municipal Development* (Philadelphia, 1887), 112–13.

59. Rosenberg, *Care of Strangers,* 42 (quotation); Philadelphia Guardians of the Poor, Minutes, August 1846–May 1849, May 5, 1847, Jan. 29, 1849, PCA; *Auditors' Report of the Accounts of the Blockley Alms-House for the Year Ending May 19, 1851* (Philadelphia, 1852) (2,358 patients were born in Ireland, and an additional 184 were born in the almshouse). See also Rosenberg, "From Almshouse to Hospital," 108–54.

60. *Journal of the Common Council of the City of Philadelphia, for 1846–1847* (Philadelphia, 1847), app. 21; *Journal of the Select Council of the City of Philadelphia for 1847–48* (Philadelphia, 1848), app. 11. By 1851 the proportion of Irish patients treated at the Wills Hospital had dropped slightly, to 78 out of 191. *Journal of the Select Council of the City of Philadelphia for 1851–52* (Philadelphia, 1852), app. 21.

61. Pennsylvania Hospital, *Statement of Accounts* (Philadelphia, 1855 and 1848). The 1855 report includes a tabular summary of patients treated from 1842 to 1855. The Pennsylvania Hospital accepted both paying and charity patients. The *Public Ledger* routinely reprinted the hospital's annual reports, including details on patient nativity.

62. *PL*, Dec. 2, 1848; *The Charter, By-Laws and Rules, of the St. Joseph Hospital* (Philadelphia, 1849); St. Joseph's Hospital, *Annual Reports* (Philadelphia, 1850–52, 1858); Gail Farr Casterline, "St. Joseph's and St. Mary's: The Origins of Catholic Hospitals in Philadelphia," *Pennsylvania Magazine of History and Biography* (July 1984): 289–314; Scharf and Westcott, *History of Philadelphia,* 2:1679. The original building was on Locust Street, but that was soon replaced with a new hospital at Girard and Schuylkill.

63. Episcopal Hospital, opened in 1852, was also designed to assist the poor of all creeds, but it offered neither the low rates nor the spiritual comfort to attract Irish immigrants away from St. Joseph's. Rosenberg, *Care of Strangers,* 109–21; Scharf and Westcott, *History of Philadelphia,* 2:1678–79.

64. *Rules, Regulations and By-Laws, of the Northern Dispensary, for the Medical Relief of the Poor* (Philadelphia, 1840); Northern Dispensary, *Annual Report* (Philadelphia, 1853); *PL*, Nov. 29, 1848; *Report of the Philadelphia Society for the Employment and Instruction of the Poor* (Philadelphia, 1852, 1855). In 1858–59 the City Dispensary treated nearly 10,000 patients, including 4,851 Irish born. *Pennsylvania Journal of Prison Discipline and Philanthropy* 14, no. 3 (July 1859): 141.

65. Board of Health, Minutes, June 1, Apr. 17, 28, 1847, PCA; Guardians of the Poor, Minutes, May 31, 1847, PCA; *PL*, Oct. 9, Apr. 23, 1847. For a similar story, see *PL*, Nov. 10, 1848.

66. Guardians of the Poor, Minutes, May 24, 31, June 14, 21, 1847, PCA; Board of Health, Minutes, June 3, 11, 16, 1847, PCA.

67. *PL*, Nov. 1–Dec. 13, 1847 (quotation, Dec. 4, 1847); Guardians of the Poor, Minutes, Nov. 8, 1847, PCA; *Report of the Philadelphia Society for the Employment and Instruction of the Poor, for the Seasons of 1847–1848* (Philadelphia, 1848).

68. Guardians of the Poor, Minutes, Apr. 24–June 26, 1848, PCA.

69. Rosenberg, *Cholera Years,* 101–5. See *Pennsylvanian,* Jan. 19, 1848; Eliza Cope Harrison, ed., *Philadelphia Merchant: The Diary of Thomas P. Cope, 1800–1851* (South Bend, Ind., 1978), Jan. 23 (p. 547), Aug. 30, 1848 (p. 564), Jan. 13, 1849 (p. 569); and *PL*, Aug. 24, 29, 1848.

70. *Report of the Sanitary Committee of the Board of Health of Philadelphia on the Subject of the Asiatic Cholera* (Philadelphia, 1848); *PL*, Nov. 20, 22, Dec. 2, 1848. See also *PL*, Dec. 11, 1848, Jan. 18, Feb. 16, Mar. 8, 1849.

71. Scharf and Westcott, *History of Philadelphia,* 1:690; Charles Lawrence, *History of the Philadelphia Almshouses and Hospitals* (1905; reprint, New York, 1976), 176; *PL*, Apr. 12, May 24, 1849; Rosenberg, *Cholera Years,* 106; Arthur Ritchie to Miss Harriet Murdock, May 18, 1849, Murdock-Wright Papers, SHC; *PL*, May 24–26, 1849.

72. The Board of Health's official report on the epidemic, prepared by the sanitary committee, was distributed in a 70-page pamphlet. Philadelphia Board of Health, *Statistics of Cholera* (Philadelphia, 1849). See also *PL*, May 31, June 28, 1849.

73. Philadelphia Board of Health, *Statistics of Cholera,* app. 4; Lawrence, *History of the Philadelphia Almshouses,* 176–78; *PL,* July 21, 1849 (the *Ledger* actually states that 100 almshouse residents died in a single week).

74. *PL,* June 1, July 6, 1849. As of August 11 the hospital had treated 96 cholera patients, including 25 who died. *PL,* Aug. 11, 1849.

75. *Report of the Managers of the Society for the Employment and Instruction of the Poor* (Philadelphia, 1851).

76. Philadelphia Board of Health, *Statistics of Cholera,* p. 42 and app. 5. The sanitary committee noted that this figure included several hundred cases that were not reported to the board until after the fact and presumably a few cholera victims who had died in the country but were buried within the county limits.

77. Rosenberg, *Cholera Years,* 133–72; *PL,* July 10, 12, 16, 1849.

78. Philadelphia Board of Health, *Statistics of Cholera,* 44 passim; Nicholas B. Wainwright, *A Philadelphia Perspective: The Diary of Sidney George Fisher Covering the Years 1834–1871* (Philadelphia, 1967), 224–25 (July 7, 19, 1849).

79. Arthur Ritchie to Miss Harriet Murdock, June 25, 1849, SHC; *PL,* Aug. 10, 1849.

80. On transatlantic medical discussions, see Rosenberg, *Care of Strangers,* 78–93, and *Cholera Years,* 151–72; Duffy, *The Sanitarians,* 95 passim. Rosenberg (*Cholera Years,* 135–36) suggests that the 1849 cholera epidemic fueled nativism in the United States.

81. It is interesting that hospitals—whether public or private—were generally reserved for the poor or the working classes. People with greater wealth would opt for treatment at home. Thus, the line drawn between the city hospital and the charity hospital approximated the line between the working poor and those suffering the ignominy of pauperdom.

82. See Rosenberg, *Cholera Years,* 111–20. By the turn of the century health reform had taken a much more central place in American urban political discourse. See Judith Walzer Leavitt, *The Healthiest City: Milwaukee and the Politics of Health Reform* (1982; reprint, Madison, Wis., 1986).

83. Lubenow, *Politics of Government Growth,* 72.

84. Dr. Wilson Jewell, *Annual Report of the Committee on Public Hygiene* (Philadelphia, 1851); Jewell, *Yellow or Malignant Bilious Fever in the Vicinity of South Street Wharf . . .* (Philadelphia, 1853); Duffy, *The Sanitarians,* 103–4.

CHAPTER FIVE

1. For general histories of mid-nineteenth–century urban sanitation and public health, see Anthony S. Wohl, *Endangered Lives: Public Health in Victorian Britain* (London, 1983); John Duffy, *The Sanitarians: A History of American Public Health* (Urbana, Ill., 1990); and Stanley K. Schultz, *Constructing Urban Culture: American Cities and City Planning, 1800–1920* (Philadelphia, 1989), 111–49. For an excellent urban case study, see Stuart Galishoff, *Newark: The Nation's Unhealthiest City, 1832–1895* (New Brunswick, N.J., 1988). Although dated, George Rosen's *A History of Public Health* (1958; expanded ed., Baltimore, 1993) is still useful; the 1993 edition includes a

lengthy bibliography. On the concern for the urban environment, see David Ward, *Poverty, Ethnicity, and the American City, 1840–1925* (New York, 1989), 28–31, and Paul Boyer, *Urban Masses and Moral Order in America, 1820–1920* (Cambridge, Mass., 1978), 85–107. W. F. Bynum's *Science and the Practice of Medicine in the Nineteenth Century* (New York, 1994) is an intriguing comparative study of medical science and institutional development in Europe, England, and the United States.

2. In his discussion of nineteenth-century America's "well-regulated society," William J. Novak comes to different conclusions, stressing the power of local regulation even in the face of concerns about private property. For his discussion of public health regulations, see Novak, *The People's Welfare: Law and Regulation in Nineteenth-Century America* (Chapel Hill, N.C., 1996), 191–233.

3. Mary Poovey, *Making a Social Body: British Cultural Formation, 1830–1864* (Chicago, 1995), 40 passim. In her discussion of James Phillips Kay's 1832 pamphlet, *The Moral and Physical Conditions of the Working Classes . . . in Manchester,* Poovey (pp. 55–72) points out that Kay perceived the Irish as inherently inhuman and thus antithetical to the healthy social body.

4. For histories of housing in Liverpool, see Iain C. Taylor, "The Insanitary Housing Question and Tenement Dwellings in Nineteenth-Century Liverpool," in Anthony Sutcliffe, ed., *Multi-Storey Living: The British Working-Class Experience* (London, 1974), 41–87; J. H. Treble, "Liverpool Working-Class Housing, 1801–1851," in Stanley D. Chapman, ed., *A History of Working-Class-Housing: A Symposium* (Totowa, N.J., 1971), 165–220; and W. Bate, "Sanitary Administration of Liverpool, 1847–1900" (M.A. thesis, University of Liverpool, 1955). For a broader survey of housing in England, see John Burnett, *A Social History of Housing, 1815–1985,* 2d ed. (London, 1986).

5. Eric C. Midwinter, *Social Administration in Lancashire, 1830–1860* (Manchester, England, 1969), 72.

6. John Finch Jr., *Statistics of Vauxhall Ward, Liverpool, Showing the Actual Condition of More Than Five Thousand Families . . .* (Liverpool, 1842), 12–13, 37–38. Finch's numbers are deceptive because he found 154 families "lodging" in cellars. I have included them as cellar dwellers.

7. William H. Duncan, *On the Physical Causes of High Mortality in Liverpool* (Liverpool, 1843), 10–11, 18, 57 passim—here and next two paragraphs. Taylor ("The Insanitary Housing Question," 43) estimates the cellar population at 32,000 in the early 1840s.

8. For further description of Liverpool's working class and poor housing, see Treble, "Liverpool Working-Class Housing," 176–87.

9. *Laws and Constitutions of the Liverpool Domestic Mission Society, with a Statement of Accounts for the Year Ending December, 1841* (Liverpool, 1843); DMS, *Annual Reports* (Liverpool, 1841, 1844, 1845, 1846).

10. *Report of the Proceedings at a Public Meeting of the Friends of the Liverpool Health of Towns' Association . . . September 29, 1845* (Liverpool, 1845).

11. Midwinter, *Social Administration in Lancashire,* 73–75; Derek Fraser, *The Evolution of the British Welfare State,* 2d ed. (London, 1984), 56–72; Poovey, *Making a Social Body,* 115–31. See Chapter 4.

12. Schultz, *Constructing Urban Culture*, 129–33; Duffy, *The Sanitarians*, 98–99.

13. In 1827 Philadelphia's Guardians of the Poor sent a delegation to investigate the conditions of the poor in several East Coast cities; ten years later Mathew Carey surveyed conditions in Philadelphia's poor neighborhoods. Philadelphia Board of Guardians, *Report of the Committee Appointed by the Board of Guardians of the Poor* (Philadelphia, 1827), reprinted in David J. Rothman, ed., *The Almshouse Experience* (New York, 1971); Mathew Carey, *A Plea for the Poor, Particularly Females* (Philadelphia, 1837), reprinted in David J. Rothman, ed., *The Jacksonians on the Poor: Collected Pamphlets* (New York, 1971). See also Schultz, *Constructing Urban Culture*, 130, 136.

14. For a typical discussion of Philadelphia's unusual cleanliness, see *PL*, Aug. 26, 1847. See also Chapter 1. In contrast to this view, Sam Alewitz, in his history of sanitation in late-nineteenth-century Philadelphia, argues that "Filthydelphia" actually had a long history of filthy conditions—and a reputation to match—that predated this period. This may simply be a matter of seeing the glass either "half clean" or "half dirty." The larger point is that Philadelphia's natural and structural conditions gave it advantages over Liverpool and many other cities. See Alewitz, *"Filthy Dirty": A Social History of Unsanitary Philadelphia in the Late Nineteenth Century* (New York, 1989), 1 passim.

15. Dennis Clark, *The Irish in Philadelphia* (Philadelphia, 1973), 40.

16. Alan Nathan Burstein, "Residential Distribution and Mobility of Irish and German Immigrants in Philadelphia, 1850–1880" (Ph.D. diss., University of Pennsylvania, 1975), 69–70, 84; Iain Cooper Taylor, "'Black Spot on the Mersey': A Study of Environment and Society in Eighteenth- and Nineteenth-Century Liverpool" (Ph.D. diss., University of Liverpool, 1976), table 7.6. Burstein found that Philadelphia had 6.6 individuals per dwelling in 1850; Taylor found that Liverpool had 6.64 individuals per house in 1851. (In the same years Philadelphia had 1.18 households per dwelling and Liverpool 1.28 households per house.)

17. *PL*, Nov. 1, 6, 9, 12, 18, Dec. 4, 1847. See Chapter 4 for a discussion of this episode. The following June health officials carried a deceased African American man from a 7th and Baker cellar and removed two dying African American women to the almshouse. *PL*, June 22, 1848.

18. *Report of the Philadelphia Society for the Employment and Instruction of the Poor, for the Seasons of 1850–51* (Philadelphia, 1851). These quotations were describing the conditions in 1847, when the PSEIP began operations.

19. *Report of a Joint Special Committee of Select and Common Councils (Appointed on the 7th December, 1848), to Whom Was Referred Certain Queries Contained in a Circular Letter from the American Medical Association on the Subject of Public Hygiene* (Philadelphia, 1849), 35–36 passim, reprinted in Select Council, *Journal for 1848–49* (Philadelphia, 1849), 170–99. For a history of the Bedford-Baker Street neighborhood, see Emma Jones Lapsansky, "South Street Philadelphia, 1762–1854: 'A Haven for Those Low in the World'" (Ph.D. diss., University of Pennsylvania, 1975), 141–50 passim.

20. Isaac Parrish, "Report on the Sanitary Condition of Philadelphia," in AMA, *Transactions* (1849), 2:459–86 (quotations, 460, 464).

21. Ibid., 466. Parrish cites the special committee's report.

22. Ibid., 467–68.

23. Wilson Jewell, *Annual Report of the Committee on Public Hygiene, Read before the Northern Medical Association of Philadelphia, November 20th, 1851* (Philadelphia, 1851[?]), 4, 6.

24. Wilson Jewell, *Yellow or Malignant Bilious Fever in the Vicinity of South Street Wharf, Philadelphia, 1853* (Philadelphia, 1853). See Chapter 4.

25. *The Mysteries and Miseries of Philadelphia as Exhibited and Illustrated by a Late Presentment of the Grand Jury, and by a Sketch of the Condition of the Most Degraded Classes in the City Dedicated to the Citizens of Philadelphia* (Philadelphia, 1853), 7.

26. Ibid., 12–19. Souder made several references to the seemingly indiscriminate mingling of blacks and whites in this area of Moyamensing. Whereas some commentators claimed that the Irish had unusually unsanitary habits, none made similar racial judgments.

27. Midwinter, *Social Administration in Lancashire,* 78, 84; Wohl, *Endangered Lives,* 142–65. See also Chapter 4.

28. In addition to the sources cited below, the *Mercury* kept up a steady barrage of editorials, letters, and articles underscoring the city's sanitation problems.

29. *The Liverpool Health of Towns' Advocate, Published under the Sanction of the Committee of the Liverpool Health of Towns' Association* (Liverpool, 1845–47). The LRO has a bound volume of nineteen issues published between Sept. 1, 1845, and May 1, 1847. *First-Third Addresses of the Committee of the Liverpool Health of Towns' Association* (Liverpool, 1847). See also *LM,* passim. Volume 1 of the *Advocate* listed W. H. Duncan, S. Holme, Rev. J. Johns, Harmood Banner, J. A. Picton, H. G. Harbored, and W. Rathbone among its members. It also named (by title) the mayor, senior rector, senior churchwarden, stipendiary magistrate, and "Presidents and Senior Physicians and Surgeons" of all Liverpool's major medical institutions.

30. *Second Addresses of the Committee of the Liverpool Health of Towns' Association to the Working Classes* (Liverpool, 1847), 2; *First Addresses of the Committee of the Liverpool Health of Towns' Association to the Working Classes* (Liverpool, 1847); *LM,* Nov. 12, May 18, 1847, Feb. 22, 1848; DMS, *Annual Reports* (Liverpool, 1847, 1849). On May 18, 1847, the *Mercury* described a sermon on cleanliness delivered at St. Joseph's Catholic Church; on Feb. 22, 1848, "A Protestant" correspondent related a similar message delivered at St. Mary's Catholic Church. See Chapter 6.

31. In 1851 the medical officer of health, the inspector of nuisances, and the borough engineer all delivered published *Reports to the Health Committee* covering their actions since 1847. Their activities were also routinely reported in the *Mercury.*

32. Thomas Fresh, *Report to the Health Committee of the Town Council of the Borough of Liverpool, Comprising a Detail of the Sanitary Operations in the Nuisance Department, from 1st Jan., 1847, to 31st March, 1851* (Liverpool, 1851), 22–29; Taylor, "The Insanitary Housing Question," 48; Fresh, *Report to the Health Committee,* 29–39. For one of the first cases against an unregistered lodging house owner, see *LM,* Sept. 24, 1847.

33. W. H. Duncan, *Report to the Health Committee of the Borough of Liverpool on the Health of the Town during the Years 1847–48–49–50* (Liverpool, 1851), 6. As we have seen, Duncan's reports regularly linked the Irish immigrants with epidemic disease and heavy mortality.

34. Fresh, *Report to the Health Committee,* 29–39. Duncan (*Report to the Health Com-*

mittee, app. F) estimated that nine-tenths of the registered lodging house keepers were Irish.

35. Duncan, *Report to the Health Committee,* 20. W. F. Bynum (*Science and the Practice of Medicine,* 78) suggests that the cholera epidemic "was a mixed blessing for Chadwick's plans" because it "focused the nation's attention on public health, [but] it deflected to the crisis at hand what should have been the Board's long-term concerns with housing, sanitation, and poverty."

36. Fresh, *Report to the Health Committee.* See also Health Committee, General Purposes Sub-Committee, Minute Book, January 1847–October 1847, LRO. This subcommittee heard regular reports from Inspector Fresh. Knackers' yards disposed of unwanted animals.

37. Fresh, *Report to the Health Committee,* 9–15 passim; Wohl, *Endangered Lives,* 89–91. The *Mercury* regularly reported on the inspector of nuisances's actions and on complaints about overflowing middens. On Apr. 20, 1847, e.g., the paper printed a lengthy account of such a complaint filed by Rev. Thoms against a neighboring property owner. Between 1847 and early 1851 the borough's contractors emptied over 200,000 middens and cesspools, with the costs distributed to the specific townships and parishes.

38. Duncan, *Report to the Health Committee,* 38–42. See Chapter 5 for a discussion of Duncan's methods for fighting the disease once it arrived.

39. Fresh, *Report to the Health Committee,* 20–21.

40. Watch Committee, Orders to the Head Constable, LRO; Watch Committee, Standing Sub-Committees or Daily Board, Minute Book, LRO. See Chapter 4.

41. Fresh, *Report to the Health Committee,* 52–53; Health Committee, General Purposes Sub-Committee, Minute Book, January 1847–October 1847, May 28, 1847; *LM,* Feb. 29, 1848; Bate, "Sanitary Administration of Liverpool."

42. *LM,* Sept. 17, 1847. The magistrate's rulings appeared regularly in the *Mercury*—e.g., see *LM,* Sept. 24 and Oct. 1, 1847.

43. *LM,* Apr. 11, 1848. The *Mercury* reported that Rushton once again declared his intention of supporting Fresh and the Health Committee.

44. *LM,* Aug. 3, 17, 1849; Health Committee, General Purposes Sub-Committee, Minute Book, Feb. 9, 1847; Watch Committee, Orders to the Head Constable, LRO, Nov. 20, 1847, passim; Watch Committee, Standing Sub-Committees or Daily Board, Minute Book, LRO, October–December 1847. See Chapter 4.

45. Duncan, *Report to the Health Committee,* 99–100; Fresh, *Report to the Health Committee,* 22–29; Treble, "Liverpool Working-Class Housing," 171–72, 196–99.

46. See Board of Health, "Rough" Minutes, 1846–47 passim, PCA; *Rules of the Government of the Board of Health, Its Officers and Committees,* pamphlet (penciled date is 1853), HSP; Edward P. Allinson and Boies Penrose, *Philadelphia, 1681–1887* (Philadelphia, 1887), 112–13, 215.

47. Board of Health, Complaints of Nuisances (July 1847) and General Correspondence (1809–58), PCA. The Complaints of Nuisances file includes fifty-eight letters received during the month. The PCA files include similar bundles of letters for other years. The *Public Ledger* periodically published letters or editorials com-

plaining about specific nuisances and calling on the Board of Health to respond. See *PL*, Aug. 21, Dec. 10, 1847, June 21, 23, Sept. 9, 1848. On June 28, 1848, the paper informed its readers that it would be more efficient for them to write directly to the board. The board also issued permits to applicants seeking to remove bodies or empty their privies and fined those who deposited "privy filth in other places than those designated by the Board." On Mar. 10, 1847, the newly elected board discussed an appeal to the state legislature for greater authority to arrest violators of these regulations. Board of Health, "Rough" Minutes.

48. Allinson and Penrose, *Philadelphia, 1681–1887*, 71–75. For examples of petitions directed to the councils and passed on to the subcommittees, see *PL*, Feb. 26, Mar. 26, Apr. 4, 1847, passim. See also *Journal of the Select Council* (Philadelphia, 1847 and throughout period). The activities of the district commissioners are best traced in the regular reports in the *Public Ledger*. See, e.g., *PL*, Nov. 4, 1847. See also *A Digest of Acts of Assembly Relating to the Incorporated District of the Northern Liberties and of the Ordinances for the Government of the District Published by Authority of the Board of Commissioners* (Philadelphia, 1847); *Digest of Acts of Assembly Relating to the Kensington District of the Northern Liberties and of the Ordinances of the Corporation* (Philadelphia, 1847); and *A Digest of the Acts of Assembly and Ordinances of the District of Moyamensing* (Moyamensing, 1848).

49. *PL*, Aug. 18, Sept. 4, 7, Nov. 30, Dec. 1, 1848. The board had made a similar request to the city Council the previous summer. See *PL*, July 20, 1847, also June 23, 1848.

50. *PL*, Sept. 22, 1848. The local police were occasionally called in to capture animals in the streets. For an account of hogs in Southwark, see *PL*, June 26, 1847.

51. *PL*, Aug. 24, 1848; *Report of the Sanitary Committee of the Board of Health of Philadelphia on the Subject of the Asiatic Cholera Embracing Certain Sanitary Suggestions and Recommendations* (Philadelphia, 1848); *PL*, Nov. 20, 22, 1848.

52. *Statistics of Cholera: With the Sanitary Measures Adopted by the Board of Health, prior to, and during the Prevalence of the Epidemic in Philadelphia, in the Summer of 1849: Chronologically Arranged* (Philadelphia 1849); *PL*, Dec. 7, 2, 9, 1848. During this period the *Ledger* published numerous articles, editorials, and letters linking sanitation and cleanliness to the cholera epidemic. Many of these drew on the experiences of other American or English cities. See, e.g., *PL*, Dec. 11, 1848, Jan. 18, 26, Feb. 16, 1849.

53. *Statistics of Cholera*, 10 passim; *PL*, Dec. 13–14, 18, 21, 1848, Jan. 3, Feb. 1, Mar. 21, 1849.

54. *PL*, May 24, 1849; Select Council, *Journal for 1848–49*, app. L, "Report of the Committee on Cleansing the Street"; *PL*, June 4, 7, 1849; *Report of the Sanitary Committee of the Councils of Philadelphia, Made to Councils, September 27, 1849* (Philadelphia, 1849—a three-page unbound report); *PL*, May 24, 28, June 2, 6–7, 1849. Southwark's commissioners each agreed to take responsibility for inspecting one of the district's wards. *PL*, June 1, 1849.

55. *Statistics of Cholera*, 19; *PL*, June 6, 11, 1849.

56. In June 1849 the commissioners of Spring Garden resolved that "wherever

nuisances may be found to exist in cellars or other places over which they may have authority, that the Board of Health be immediately applied to for authority to remove them." *PL,* June 6, 1849.

57. *PL,* June 6, 13, 1849.

58. *Statistics of Cholera,* 10–13, 44.

59. This dependence on citizen initiative was similar to that associated with Philadelphia's criminal justice system. As Allen Steinberg has noted, before the 1854 consolidation, "private prosecutions" dominated the local court dockets. Steinberg, *The Transformation of Criminal Justice: Philadelphia, 1800–1880* (Chapel Hill, N.C., 1989).

60. Midwinter, *Social Administration in Lancashire,* 102, 114; *Report of Evidence Taken before a Special Committee of the Highway Board in the Year 1845, on the Alleged Dearness & Insufficiency of the Supply of Water in Liverpool* (Liverpool, 1845); Harmood Banner, *Water: A Pamphlet* (Liverpool, 1845) and *Water, as Supplied to Liverpool: A Second Pamphlet* (Liverpool, 1845); *Abstract of Proceedings before the Committee of the House of Commons, on the Liverpool and Harrington Water Works Bill, 1846* (1846); *Extracts from Proceedings before the House of Commons, on the Liverpool Corporation Water Works Bill, 1847* (Liverpool, 1847); Samuel Holme, *Speech of Samuel Holme, Esq., at the Music Hall, Liverpool, on the 15th of October, 1849* (Liverpool, 1849). Throughout this period debates about the water supply appeared regularly in the *Liverpool Mercury.* For one criticism of the *Mercury's* anti-Pikist stance, see George Holt Sr., Diary, June 5, 1849, LRO.

61. Midwinter, *Social Administration in Lancashire,* 108, 114; *Reports to the Health Committee of the Borough of Liverpool, by the Borough Engineer, Inspector of Nuisances, and Medical Officer of Health* (Liverpool, 1851), 3–51.

62. Ivan D. Steen, "Philadelphia in the 1850s as Described by British Travelers," *Pennsylvania History* 33 (January 1966): 46 Elizabeth M. Geffen, "Industrial Development and Social Crisis, 1841–1854," in Russell Weigley, ed., *Philadelphia: A 300-Year History* (New York, 1982), 317; Parrish, "Report on the Sanitary Condition of Philadelphia," 459–60, 477–78. The *Public Ledger* ran regular accounts of minor battles over water access. See, e.g., *PL,* Oct. 8, Nov. 4, 1847, Jan. 6, 13, Feb. 2–3, 9, Mar. 7, 1848, Mar. 2, May 19, June 11, 1849.

63. Parrish, "Report on the Sanitary Condition of Philadelphia," 471–72; Jewell, *Annual Report of the Committee on Public Hygiene* and *Sanitary, Meteorological Mortuary Report of the Philadelphia County Medical Society, for 1855* (Philadelphia, 1856); Samuel H. Kneass, *Report of the Drainage and Sewerage, Made to the Select and Common Councils of the City of Philadelphia, May 9, 1853, by Samuel H. Kneass, City Surveyor and Regulator* (Philadelphia, 1853).

64. See *LM,* Oct. 19, 1847, Aug. 18, 1848. Most of the reports listed above stressed the importance of water access to good public health.

65. *LM,* July 16, 1847. Two years later Holme explained his support of the Pike scheme as a positive measure for public sanitation and the city's poor. See Holme, *Speech . . . at the Music Hall.*

66. For an excellent overview of water and sewage reform, see Schultz, *Constructing Urban Culture,* 162–75.

67. See Marilyn Thornton Williams, *Washing "The Great Unwashed": Public Baths in Urban America, 1840–1920* (Columbus, Ohio, 1995), 1–16.

68. Ibid., 7; Herbert R. Rathbone, ed., *Memoir of Kitty Wilkinson of Liverpool, 1786–1860* (Liverpool, 1927).

69. Wohl, *Endangered Lives*, 73; Rathbone, *Memoir of Kitty Wilkinson;* Brian D. White, *A History of the Corporation of Liverpool* (Liverpool, 1951), 46–47; *Third Address of the Committee of the Liverpool Health of Towns' Association* (Liverpool, June 1847); *LM,* Jan. 8, 15, Feb. 26, Mar. 5, Oct. 8, Dec. 3, 1847, Jan. 4, 21, Feb. 4, 29, May 2, June 6, 9, Aug. 4, 1848, Sept. 11, 14, Oct. 26, 1849. The *Memoir of Kitty Wilkinson* says that the Frederick Street baths opened in 1846, but the *Mercury* indicates that they opened in 1848.

70. *LM,* Feb. 26, July 16, Aug. 6, 1847. For six months in mid-1848 the Paul Street bathhouse accepted 20,650 free bathers. *LM,* Sept. 1, 1848.

71. Williams, *Washing "The Great Unwashed,"* 12–14; PSEIP, *Annual Reports* (Philadelphia, 1848, 1852); *PL,* July 7, Sept. 15, 1848, June 11, Aug. 21, 1849. Those bathers who could afford it were charged five cents apiece, *PL,* June 11, 1849. By 1851–52 Moyamensing's PSEIP was furnishing "about 3,450 baths" annually, "mostly to persons of color."

72. PSEIP, *Second Annual Report; PL,* July 7, Sept. 15, 1848; Jewell, *Annual Report of the Committee on Public Hygiene.* Jewell (*Sanitary, Meteorological Mortuary Report*) made the identical point to the County Medical Society in 1855, stressing that this was the easiest solution to the lack of running water in the city's cheapest housing.

73. Kneass, *Report of the Drainage and Sewerage.*

74. Williams, *Washing "The Great Unwashed,"* 15–16.

75. *LM,* May 4, 1847; Taylor, "The Insanitary Housing Question," 55–60. On the Birkenhead Dock Company housing, see Burnett, *Social History of Housing,* 86.

76. *LM,* Feb. 29, Mar. 3, 7, 14, 28–29, 1848, Aug. 7, 1849 (quotation). See also Nov. 9, 1847.

77. Francis Bishop, *Report Addressed to the Committee of the Domestic Mission Society, by Their Minister to the Poor, and Presented at the Seventeenth Annual General Meeting of the Society* (Liverpool, 1854); Taylor, "The Insanitary Housing Question," 55–61; Treble, "Liverpool Working-Class Housing," 171–72 passim.

78. Duncan, *Report to the Health Committee,* 102; Bishop, *Report to . . . the Domestic Mission Society;* White, *Corporation of Liverpool,* 64; Taylor, "The Insanitary Housing Question," 63–69; W. Bate, "Sanitary Administration of Liverpool, 1847–1900" (M.A. thesis, University of Liverpool, 1955), 63–66; Burnett, *Social History of Housing,* 185.

79. *PL,* Jan. 16, 23, May 14, Sept. 29, 1847. Two years later the *Ledger* wrote approvingly of efforts in Boston to keep the poor out of unhealthy cellars. *PL,* Oct. 1, 1849.

80. Jewell, *Sanitary, Meteorological Mortuary Report.*

81. John F. Sutherland, "Housing the Poor in the City of Homes: Philadelphia at the Turn of the Century," in Allen F. Davis and Mark H. Haller, eds., *The Peoples of Philadelphia: A History of Ethnic Groups and Lower-Class Life, 1790–1940* (Philadelphia, 1973), 175–202; John F. Bauman, "Public Housing in the Depression: Slum

Reform in Philadelphia Neighborhoods in the 1930s," in William W. Cutler III and Howard Gillette Jr., eds., *The Divided Metropolis: Social and Spatial Dimensions of Philadelphia, 1800–1975* (Westport, Conn., 1980), 227–48; Carroll Smith Rosenberg, *Religion and the Rise of the American City: The New York City Mission Movement, 1812–1870* (Ithaca, N.Y., 1971), 262–273; Howard P. Chudacoff and Judith E. Smith, *The Evolution of American Urban Society,* 4th ed. (Englewood Cliffs, N.J., 1994), 125.

82. Gerry Kearns, "Private Property and Public Health Reform in England, 1830–1870," *Social Science and Medicine* 26 (1988): 187–99.

83. On local resistance to centralization, see Robert M. Gutchen, "Local Improvements and Centralization in Nineteenth-Century England," *Historical Journal* 4 (1961): 85–96.

84. For excellent surveys of two American cities, see Galishoff, *Newark,* and Alan I. Marcus, *Plague of Strangers: Social Groups and the Origins of City Services in Cincinnati* (Columbus, Ohio, 1991).

85. In his analysis of nineteenth-century America's "well-regulated society," Novak (*The People's Welfare*) emphasizes the underrecognized power of local government regulation. But a comparison with English practice suggests that those regulations were really quite modest, particularly before the Civil War.

CHAPTER SIX

1. Kerby A. Miller, *Immigrants and Exiles: Ireland and the Irish Exodus to North America* (New York, 1985), 293–300, 331–34.

2. The secondary literature on mid-nineteenth–century Catholics in each city is extensive. The most useful sources on Liverpool include Thomas Burke, *Catholic History of Liverpool* (Liverpool, 1910); John Papworth, "The Irish in Liverpool, 1835–71: Segregation and Dispersal" (Ph.D. diss., University of Liverpool, 1981); W. J. Lowe, *The Irish in Mid-Victorian Lancashire: The Shaping of a Working Class Community* (New York, 1989); Janina Alina Klapas, "Geographical Aspects of Religious Change in Victorian Liverpool, 1837–1901," (M.A., University of Liverpool, 1977); and R. B. Walker, "Religious Changes in Liverpool in the Nineteenth Century," *Journal of Ecclesiastical History* 19 (October 1968): 195–211. On Philadelphia, see Dale B. Light Jr., *Rome and the New Republic: Conflict and Community in Philadelphia Catholicism between the Revolution & the Civil War* (South Bend, Ind., 1996); Hugh Nolan, *The Most Reverend Francis Patrick Kenrick Third Bishop of Philadelphia, 1830–1851* (Philadelphia, 1948); James F. Connelly, ed., *The History of the Archdiocese of Philadelphia* (Philadelphia, 1976); and Dennis Clark, *The Irish in Philadelphia: Ten Generations of Urban Experience* (Philadelphia, 1973).

3. Klapas, "Geographic Aspects of Religious Change," 58–59; Janina A. Lasek, "Liverpool and the 1851 Census of Religious Worship," *University of Liverpool Geography Society Journal* (October 1972): 42–56. Lasek (née Klapas?) includes tables derived from the original returns in both essays.

4. Frank Neal discovered two more surveys of religious attendance in the *Liverpool Mercury.* On Feb. 25, 1853, the *Mercury* reported an average attendance of

43,380 Catholics at churches with a total seat room of 15,300. Two years later the paper found that 46,130 Catholics attended churches seating 15,900. Neal, *Sectarian Violence: The Liverpool Experience, 1819–1914* (Manchester, England, 1988), 127. Papworth ("The Irish in Liverpool," 161), citing Burke, gives a slightly different version of what appears to be the same 1855 survey.

5. Roger Swift and Sheridan Gilley, Introduction to Swift and Gilley, eds., *The Irish in the Victorian City* (London, 1985), 9–10.

6. "Statistics of the Diocese of Liverpool," RCLv, Box 17, Lancashire Record Office, Preston. This estimate is based on 1850 baptisms using a multiplier of 20. The table appears to have been constructed in the 1870s. It offers no explanation for the multiplier.

7. Abraham Hume, *Condition of Liverpool, Religious and Social* (Liverpool, 1858); Lowe, *The Irish in Mid-Victorian Lancashire*, 112–13. Hume assumed that Liverpool's relatively few non-Irish Catholics were equal to the number of non-Catholic Irish.

8. Papworth, "The Irish in Liverpool," 141–46; Burke, *Catholic History*, 13–75; Neil Collins, *Politics and Elections in Nineteenth-Century Liverpool* (Aldershot, England, 1994), 19–21; Lowe, *The Irish in Mid-Victorian Lancashire*, 113.

9. Papworth, "The Irish in Liverpool," 142–46; Lowe, *The Irish in Mid-Victorian Lancashire*, 109–38; Raphael Samuel, "The Roman Catholic Church and the Irish Poor," in Swift and Gilley, *The Irish in the Victorian City*, 277–79 passim. Liverpool's Irish organizations included the Hibernia Society, Benevolent Society of St. Patrick, Ancient Order of Hibernians, and Catholic Young Men's Society. Their actions are discussed more fully in the next chapter. On the importance of parish priests among Irish immigrants to the United States, see Jay P. Dolan, *The American Catholic Experience* (Garden City, New York, 1985), 164–66.

10. Account Book, 1811–48, Liverpool Catholic Benevolent Society, and Minute Book, December 1850–November 1858, Catholic Benevolent Society, Lancashire County Record Office; *LM*, Dec. 23, 1851 (this *Mercury* story is affixed to the Minute Book). See also the previous discussion of poverty and benevolence. Burke (*Catholic History*, 79–81) makes some reference to fund-raising but does not address the Benevolent Society's death and rebirth.

11. Burke, *Catholic History*, 94; Lowe, *The Irish in Mid-Victorian Lancashire*, 130. Apparently, this club's records do not survive and its activities during the famine years went unreported in the *Mercury*. Lowe, citing Canon John Bennett's *Father Nugent of Liverpool* (Liverpool, 1949), says that the club was initially called the Irish Catholic Club and then in 1860 changed its name to the Catholic Club. Burke uses the latter name in describing its founding, and the *Mercury* used that name in describing the 1851 effort to reinvigorate the Catholic Benevolent Society.

12. *LM*, July 25, 1848, Aug. 10, Nov. 11, 1849; Burke, *Catholic History*, 73. The *Mercury* (Mar. 5, 1847) reported that the Catholic Orphan Asylum housed 40–50 children annually, or roughly a third of the capacity of Philadelphia's two Catholic orphanages. Burke states that the Sisters of Charity began working with eighteen blind pupils in 1843, and later newspaper reports refer to a Catholic Blind Asylum.

13. Lowe, *The Irish in Mid-Victorian Lancashire*, 134; Burke, *Catholic History*, 110. One could reasonably make the case that the founding of three Catholic news-

papers suggests a vibrant local community, or that the swift failure of all three is evidence of the weakness of that community. The prominence of Philadelphia's *Catholic Herald* is an interesting contrast.

14. Nolan, *Francis Patrick Kenrick,* 105–6; Hugh J. Nolan, "Francis Patrick Kenrick," in Connelly, *History of the Archdiocese of Philadelphia,* 140–42. On Kenrick's background and appointment to the Philadelphia diocese, see Light, *Rome and the New Republic,* 247–53 passim. On his beliefs and activities particularly in the years prior to the famine migration, see Judith Amanda Hunter, "Before Pluralism: The Political Culture of Nativism in Antebellum Philadelphia" (Ph.D. diss., Yale University, 1991), 62–103. On the diversity of nineteenth-century American Catholicism, see Dolan, *American Catholic Experience,* 158–94.

15. Nolan, *Francis Patrick Kenrick,* 433–34 passim, and "Francis Patrick Kenrick," 113–208; Dennis Clark, "A Pattern of Urban Growth: Residential Development and Church Location in Philadelphia," *Records of the American Catholic Historical Society* 82 (September 1971): 159–70; Light, *Rome and the New Republic,* 272–79; Nicholas B. Wainwright, "The Age of Nicholas Biddle, 1825–1841," in Russell F. Weigley, ed., *Philadelphia: A 300-Year History* (New York, 1982), 296; J. Thomas Scharf and Thompson Westcott, *History of Philadelphia, 1609–1884,* 3 vols. (Philadelphia, 1884), 2: 1375–92.

16. *Address of the Catholic Lay Citizens of the City and County of Philadelphia to Their Fellow-Citizens in Reply to the Presentment of the Grand Jury of the Court of Quarter Sessions of May Term, 1844, in Regard to the Causes of the Late Riots in Philadelphia* (Philadelphia, 1844), 4; *CH,* Jan. 14, 1847.

17. Nolan, *Francis Patrick Kenrick,* 363–65, 385–87, 433–34; *CH,* Oct. 21, Nov. 11, 18, 1847. The clothing societies included the St. Philip De Neri's Benevolent Society and Dorcas Societies from St. John's, St. Mary's, and St. Phillip's. For a case study in institution building, see Gail Farr Casterline, "St. Joseph's and St. Mary's: The Origins of Catholic Hospitals in Philadelphia," *Pennsylvania Magazine of History and Biography* 108 (1984): 198–223. Catholic benevolence is discussed more fully in Chapter 3.

18. Light, *Rome and the New Republic,* 253–59. For Light's discussion of the crucial role of wealthy Philadelphia Catholics in funding the midcentury building, see 274–76.

19. Neal, *Sectarian Violence,* 38. Neal's book is a detailed history of sectarian violence in Liverpool that highlights the actions of the Orange Lodges. For his discussion of the period 1800–1844, see 37–79. For the moment we will concentrate on the conflicts in party politics and from competing pulpits, leaving street violence for the next chapter.

20. Neal, *Sectarian Violence,* 15–16; Burke, *Catholic History,* 42–43.

21. Collins, *Politics and Elections,* 13–22. Voters had to be up-to-date in their tax payments and not have received parochial relief in the previous year.

22. Collins, *Politics and Elections,* 25–28; Neal, *Sectarian Violence,* 44.

23. Neal, *Sectarian Violence,* 44–45; James Murphy, *The Religious Problem in English Education: The Crucial Experiment* (Liverpool, 1959); Burke, *Catholic History,* 50–51; Brian D. White, *A History of the Corporation of Liverpool, 1835–1914* (Liverpool, 1951),

21–24. Despite its deceptive title, Murphy's book is a detailed study of the sectarian battle over schooling in Liverpool.

24. Burke, *Catholic History*, 44. White (*Corporation of Liverpool*, 21) suggests that the education reforms were also intended as a means of social control.

25. Neal, *Sectarian Violence*, 45–54; Collins, *Politics and Elections*, 29–42.

26. Neal, *Sectarian Violence*, 63; Klapas, "Geographic Aspects of Religious Change," 48–49; White, *Corporation of Liverpool*, 24.

27. For the classic history of nativism, see Ray Allen Billington, *The Protestant Crusade, 1800–1860* (New York, 1938). See also Dale T. Knobel, *Paddy and the Republic: Ethnicity and Nationality in Antebellum America* (Middletown, Conn., 1986); Jay P. Dolan, *The Immigrant Church: New York's Irish and German Catholics, 1815–1865* (Baltimore, 1975); and Tyler Anbinder, *Nativism and Slavery: The Northern Know Nothings and the Politics of the 1850s* (New York, 1992).

28. On Philadelphia nativism, see Leonard Tabachnik, "Origins of the Know-Nothing Party: A Study of the Native American Party in Philadelphia, 1844–1852" (Ph.D. diss., Columbia University, 1973), and Hunter, "Before Pluralism." On Philadelphia Catholics, see Light, *Rome and the New Republic*. See also Clark, *The Irish in Philadelphia*. On the strong links between Irish Catholics and the Democratic Party, see Miller, *Emigrants and Exiles*, 328–30.

29. Billington, *Protestant Crusade*, 168, 170, 183–84 passim; Elizabeth Geffen, "Industrial Development and Social Crisis, 1841–1854," in Weigley, *Philadelphia*, 356; Tabachnik, "Origins of the Know-Nothing Party," 20–22.

30. ASSU, *Nineteenth Annual Report* (Philadelphia, 1843), 9; ASSU, *Considerations Touching the Principles and Objects of the American Sunday-School Union: Addressed to Evangelical Churches and Other Benevolent Citizens of the United States* (Philadelphia, 1845), 4. On the history of the ASSU, see Paul Boyer, *Urban Masses and Moral Order in America, 1820–1920* (Cambridge, Mass., 1978), 34–53.

31. Billington, *Protestant Crusade*, 142–65; Anbinder, *Nativism and Slavery*, 10–11; Carl E. Kaestle, *Pillars of the Republic: Common Schools and American Society, 1780–1860* (New York, 1983), 167–68. For a complete history of the conflicts over New York City's public schools, see Diane Ravitch, *The Great School Wars: New York City, 1805–1973* (New York, 1974).

32. For a full history of the 1844 riots, see Michael Feldberg, *The Philadelphia Riots of 1844: A Study in Ethnic Conflict* (Westport, Conn., 1975). Feldberg offers an abbreviated version in *The Turbulent Era: Riot and Disorder in Jacksonian America* (New York, 1980), 9–32. See also David Montgomery, "The Shuttle and the Cross: Weavers and Artisans in the Kensington Riots of 1844," *Journal of Social History* 5 (1972): 411–46; Mary Ann Meyers, "The Children's Crusade: Philadelphia Catholics and the Public Schools," *Records of the American Catholic Historical Society* 75 (June 1964): 103–27; Nolan, "Francis Patrick Kenrick," 172–86; Billington, *Protestant Crusade*, 220–37.

33. *Address of the Catholic Lay Citizens;* Light, *Rome and the New Republic*, 291–92.

34. Eliza Cope Harrison, ed., *Philadelphia Merchant: The Diary of Thomas P. Cope, 1800–1851* (South Bend, Ind., 1978), 437, 441. Entries for May 7, 22, 1844.

35. Philip English Mackey, ed., *A Gentleman of Much Promise: The Diary of Isaac*

Mickle, 2 vols. (Philadelphia 1977), 2:459. Entry for July 7, 1844. Mickle's diary includes lengthy accounts of both riots.

36. Light, *Rome and the New Republic*, 296–99.

37. Clark (*The Irish in Philadelphia*, 21) saw the 1844 riots as "essentially a clash between Irish Protestants and Irish Catholics, at least in their inception."

38. Burke, *Catholic History*, 85; *LM*, Jan. 29, Feb. 19, Sept. 7, 1847. The *Mercury* routinely ridiculed M'Neile for his anti-Catholic stances.

39. The Catholic voters withheld their votes until late on election day and then voted for the leading two vote getters (returns were announced hourly), both Liberal candidates. *LM*, July 23, 27, 1847; Burke, *Catholic History*, 91–92; Collins, *Politics and Elections*, 53–54.

40. Burke, *Catholic History*, 97; Collins, *Politics and Elections*, 67–68; George Holt Sr., Diary, Nov. 24, 1850, LRO; Rev. Verner M. White, AB, *Popish Intolerance: Is the Imposition of Salutary Restrictions upon Popery Inconsistent with the Principles of Religious Toleration?* (Liverpool, 1851).

41. *LM*, Jan. 15, 22, 1847; Burke, *Catholic History*, 85–86.

42. On May 21, 1847, the *Mercury* addressed local Protestant ministers, pointing out that "the Roman Catholic priests were very assiduous and attentive to their people, and they should follow so good an example." The deaths of Catholic clergymen received heavy attention in the pages of the pro-Catholic *Mercury*. Eighteen of Liverpool's 24 priests contracted typhus ministering to the Irish immigrants, 10 of whom eventually died. *LM* May 15, 1849; Burke, *Catholic History*, 86–87; Lowe, *The Irish in Mid-Victorian Lancashire*, 115; Neal, *Sectarian Violence*, 94. News of the martyr priests even reached Philadelphia. See *PL* July 31, 1847; *CH*, July 23, 1847; and *Pennsylvania Freeman*, July 15, 1847.

43. *LM*, Nov. 26, 30, 1847, Feb. 15, 18, Oct. 13, 1848, Sept. 11, 1849. See also Burke, *Catholic History*, 95–96.

44. *LM*, Feb. 15, 1848, Mar. 29, 1849; Burke, *Catholic History*, 94–96 passim. For the 1851 census, see "The Religious Landscape" earlier in this chapter.

45. *LM*, Nov. 12, May 18, 1847, Feb. 22, 1848; *CH*, July 23, 1847 (quoting *LM* of June 25, 1847). Lowe (*The Irish in Mid-Victorian Lancashire*, 120–21) suggests that Lancashire clergymen routinely included lessons on citizenship in their sermons. Neal points out that the clergy cooperated with Dr. Duncan and the health authorities in encouraging Irish parishioners to bury diseased corpses immediately rather than waiting for wakes. *Sectarian Violence*, 93.

46. *LM*, Jan. 22, May 11, 1847, Jan. 18, Feb. 11, 1848, Mar. 20, 1849. The quotation is from 1848 but the language used each year was nearly identical. The *Mercury*'s accounts never identified the "other" Catholic charities. For charges of indiscriminate giving, see Chapter 3.

47. *LM*, Mar. 5, 1847. The orphan asylum also received assistance from charity sermons. See *LM*, Dec. 14, 1849.

48. *LM*, July 25, 1848, Nov. 6, 1849.

49. Catholic Benevolent Society, *Annual Reports* (Liverpool, 1852, 1855, 1856), and Minute Book, December 1850–November 1858, and Account Book, 1811–48,

Lancashire Record Office. Where the annual reports were not printed they appear in the Minute Book.

50. Both the Female Orphan Asylum (founded in 1844) and the Asylum for Orphan Boys (1851) catered to resident Protestants. *Report of the Female Orphan Asylum, with the Statement of Accounts, and Lists of Donations, Church Collections, and Annual Subscriptions 26th February, 1844* (Liverpool, 1844); *Report of the Liverpool Asylum for Orphan Boys, with the Statement of Accounts . . . 1851* (Liverpool, 1851). The reports from many local benevolent institutions stressed their affiliation with the Established Church. See *Report of the Liverpool Sailor's Home, Registry, and Savings' Bank for the Year 1849* (Liverpool, 1850), and *Report of the Liverpool School for the Deaf and Dumb for the Year 1848* (damaged copy in the British Library, London). In 1848 the Lying-In Hospital only received donations from two churches, one of which was Roman Catholic. Nonetheless, the hospital was adamant in refusing assistance to Irish newcomers. *LM,* Dec. 15, 1848. These institutions are discussed in Chapter 3.

51. Southern and Toxteth Hospital, *Annual Report . . . 1846* (Liverpool, 1846) (first quotation); *LM,* Jan. 18, 1847 (second quotation); Liverpool Female Penitentiary, Minutes, LRO. Printed rules are attached to the final page of the first volume of minutes. The minutes for 1850–51 reveal a conflict over the appropriateness of religious tracts distributed by one minister. Unfortunately, the minutes do not indicate the messages in these tracts.

52. *Report of the Investigations of the Treatment of Roman Catholics in the Liverpool School for the Blind* (Liverpool, 1841); Liverpool City Mission, *Seventeenth Annual Reports* (Liverpool, 1846, 1851–52), and Minutes, 1850–52, Merseyside Record Office (first quotation); Journal of Robert Day, Aug. 2, 1848, LRO (filed under Mersey Mission to Seamen).

53. DMS, *Annual Reports* (Liverpool, 1841, 1850, 1856).

54. Burke, *Catholic History,* 78. Burke says that an investigation sustained the charges but the master received only a minor censure.

55. Burke, *Catholic History,* 78–79; Collins, *Politics and Elections,* 52.

56. *LM,* Jan. 15, 29 (first quotation), Dec. 7 (second quotation), 1847, June 2, 16, 1848; Burke, *Catholic History,* 119, 133–34.

57. In November 1851 the workhouse register began recording the religion of the inmates. A sample of every twentieth page between November 1851 and June 1853 yielded 864 names, including 435 Protestants, 425 Catholics, and 1 unknown. Liverpool Workhouse, Admissions and Discharges Register, LRO. For a demographic discussion of the workhouse, see Chapter 3. Conflicts over workhouse chaplains, either concerning costs or sectarian disagreements, were commonplace in England. See M. A. Crowther, *The Workhouse System, 1834–1929* (Athens, Ga., 1981), 128–30.

58. In his study of anti-Irish stereotypes, Knobel (*Paddy and the Republic,* 75–76 passim) suggests that the magnitude of the famine migration, and the extreme poverty of many of the migrants, might have "magnified the apparent distinctiveness" perceived by the dominant culture.

59. *PL,* May 24, 1849. For general discussions of nativism and anti-Catholicism, see the sources cited in notes 27–28 above. Even while reporting local examples of anti-Catholicism, the Philadelphia press also kept abreast of international developments. On Feb. 11, 1847, e.g., the *Catholic Herald* reported the publication of a new pamphlet by Liverpool's Rev. Hugh M'Neile on "The State in Danger," which assailed the Roman Catholic Relief Bill of 1829.

60. As Tabachnik ("Origins of the Know-Nothing Party," 182–83, 270–71 passim) has demonstrated, between 1844 and 1854 nativists in Philadelphia maintained a strong political voice under various guises. From 1844 to 1847 they ran under their own banner, from 1848 through 1850 they formed a powerful fusion ticket with local Whigs, and in the early 1850s they reestablished a separate ticket but with strong Whig support.

61. William E. Gienapp, *The Origins of the Republican Party, 1852–1856* (New York, 1987), 100–101; Anbinder, *Nativism and Slavery,* 53–55; Tabachnik, "Origins of the Know-Nothing Party," 251–69; Light, *Rome and the New Republic,* 258.

62. Clark, "A Pattern of Urban Growth," 162–69; *PL,* Apr. 24, 1849; *CH,* Dec. 2, 23, 1847. The *Ledger* (Apr. 5, 1847) called on its Protestant readers to make donations to the "afflicted congregation" of St. Michael's Church, ravaged by the 1844 riots. The Kensington churches eventually won a settlement from the city to help pay for rebuilding.

63. Nolan, *Francis Patrick Kenrick,* 385–89. For the importance of nuns to the immigrants, particularly Irish women, see Hasia R. Diner, *Erin's daughters in America* (Baltimore, 1983), 130–37.

64. Nolan, *Francis Patrick Kenrick,* 363–65. For fund-raising efforts, see *CH,* Jan. 14, 1847, and *PL,* Jan. 1, 1847, Feb. 25, 1848.

65. In early 1847 the committee charged with funding the new cathedral appealed to wealthier Catholics, insisting that there must be 10,000–20,000 churchgoers who could donate $5 to the project. This committee apparently assumed that for the vast majority of Philadelphia's estimated 60,000 Catholics, such a figure was too much to ask. *CH,* Jan. 14, 1847.

66. *CH,* Jan. 14, Feb. 4, 25, Apr. 22, 1847. Word of the famine and local fund-raising efforts appeared regularly in both the *Herald* and the other local newspapers. On the citywide meeting sponsored by local Quakers, see *PL,* Feb. 15, 18, 1847.

67. See Chapter 3.

68. *CH,* Oct. 21, Nov. 11, 18, 1847. In late 1847 St. John's Church had special collections for the orphan asylum and the Ladies' Benevolent Charity Society. *CH,* Aug. 5, Dec. 16, 1847.

69. *Act of Incorporation, By-Laws, and Terms of Admission of St Anne's Widow's Asylum Incorporated 1849* (Philadelphia, 1850); St. John's Orphan Asylum, *Annual Report* (Philadelphia, 1851); Clark, *The Irish in Philadelphia,* 99, 102; Priscilla Clement, *Welfare and the Poor in the Nineteenth-Century City* (Rutherford, N.J., 1985), 157.

70. Clement (*Welfare and the Poor,* 157) suggests that the proselytizing of evangelical charities stimulated the concomitant expansion of Philadelphia's Catholic charities. For Catholic charities and Protestant proselytizing nationwide and

in certain cities, see Dolan, *American Catholic Experience*, 321–26; Michael Katz, *In the Shadow of the Poorhouse* (New York, 1986), 61–63; Raymond Ralph, "The City and the Church: Catholic Beginnings in Newark, 1840–1870," *New Jersey History* 96 (1978): 105–18; Susan S. Walton, "To Preserve the Faith: Catholic Charities in Boston, 1870–1930," in Robert Sullivan and James M. O'Toole, eds., *Catholic Boston: Studies in Religion and Community, 1870–1970* (Boston, 1985), 67–119; and Dolan, *The Immigrant Church*.

71. *PL*, Feb. 3, 11, Dec. 2, 1848, July 27, 1849; *The Charter, By-Laws and Rules, of the St. Joseph Hospital* (Philadelphia, 1849); *First Annual Report of the Managers of St. Joseph's Hospital* (Philadelphia, 1850); Alan M. Kraut, *Silent Travelers: Germs, Genes, and the "Immigrant Menace"* (New York, 1994), 43–48; Christopher Kauffman, *Ministry and Meaning: A Religious History of Catholic Health Care in the United States* (New York, 1995), 63–73; Gail Farr Casterline, "St. Joseph's and St. Mary's." The hospital's *Annual Reports* routinely pointed out that patients of all creeds and nationalities were welcome. See Chapter 4.

72. UBA, *Annual Reports* (Philadelphia, 1840–60); PSEIP, *Annual Reports* (Philadelphia, 1847–58). Several reports in the 1850s mentioned diverse religious services, but the only specific reference, in 1858, just mentioned Methodists, Episcopalians, and the YMCA. Clement, *Welfare and the Poor*, 156. The Rosine Association for reforming prostitutes stressed religious education and regularly took in large numbers of Catholic women, but the association's annual reports do not discuss the nature of religious services or any sort of sectarian conflict. *Constitution and Report of the Managers of the Rosine Association, with a List of the Annual Subscribers and Contributors* (Philadelphia, 1848); Rosine Association, *Annual Reports* (Philadelphia, 1849–54).

73. *Constitution and By-Laws of the Evangelical Home Mission Society of Kensington* (Philadelphia, 1852). The society's directors included Presbyterians, Baptists, Episcopalians, Lutherans, and Methodists.

74. *Second Annual Report of the Young Christians' Missionary Association, Laboring in Bedford, Baker and Spafford Sts.* (Philadelphia, 1854). Several other local missionaries' societies were dedicated to bringing evangelical messages to the poor. Even where the reports do not mention resistance, one could well imagine Irish Catholics responding as they did to the YCMA. See, e.g., Ladies' Union City Mission of Philadelphia, *Ninth Annual Report* (Philadelphia, 1856).

75. For New York City's mission movement, see Carroll Smith-Rosenberg, *Religion and the Rise of the American City: The New York City Mission Movement, 1812–1870* (Ithaca, 1971).

76. House of Refuge, *Annual Reports* (Philadelphia, 1830–59); Northern Home for Friendless Children, *Seventh Annual Report* (Philadelphia, 1860); Girard College for Orphans, *First Annual Report* (Philadelphia, 1848); *CH*, July 1, 1847; Clement, *Welfare and the Poor*, 136. See also Scharf and Westcott, *History of Philadelphia*, 3:1944–49, and Chapter 3.

77. Philadelphia Guardians of the Poor, Minutes, May 29, 1848, PCA. Following the first vote, which was 9 to 6 in favor of postponement, the secretary took the highly unusual step of recording the roll call in the minutes.

78. Philadelphia Guardians of the Poor, Committee on Almshouse, Minutes, Dec. 29, 1848, PCA. The committee addressed the problem by ordering alternating worship at the men's and women's sections of the almshouse, with periodic worship at the lunatic asylum and the hospital.

79. Board of Guardians, Minutes, Feb. 26, 1849, and Almshouse Committee, Minutes, Mar. 9, 1849; *PL,* Apr. 10, 12, 1849.

80. *PL,* June 3, 1848.

81. *LM,* Sept. 21, 1847, *LM,* Feb. 13, 1849. This story followed reports of a survey of education in the St. John's district conducted by Rev. W. M. Falloon, a well-known Protestant minister. For more on Falloon's efforts, see *LM,* Feb. 23, 1849.

82. Here I am using the term "public school" in the American sense of schools funded and administered by the government at some level.

83. Rev. Abraham Hume was perhaps Liverpool's most persistent advocate for educational reform for the poor. His various pamphlets and reports include descriptions of available schooling and estimates of the shortfall in educational coverage. See *LM,* Jan. 11, 1848; Hume, *Missions at Home* (Liverpool, 1850), "On the Education of the Poor in Liverpool," *Proceedings of the British Association for the Advancement of Science* (1853), and *Suggestions for the Advancement of Literature and Learning in Liverpool* (Liverpool, 1851). The Education Committee regularly reported to the town Council. For numbers of pupils, see *LM* Apr. 7, 1847, Apr. 7, 1848, Jan. 9, 1949.

84. Liverpool Ragged School Union, *Annual Reports* (Liverpool, 1849, 1851); *LM,* Dec. 28, Mar. 19, 1847, Jan. 11, Apr. 25, 1848. Burke (*Catholic History,* 108) suggests that the "proselytisers" in ragged schools used food and clothing to tempt children into "abandoning the 'errors of Rome.'"

85. *LM,* Dec. 5, 1848; Liverpool Industrial Ragged Schools, *Annual Reports* (Liverpool, 1850–52); DMS, The First Minute Book of the Committee of the Ragged Schools, Feb. 17, 1848, microfilm, LRO. See Chapter 3 for a broader discussion of ragged schools and Industrial Ragged Schools.

86. The minutes do not explain what Rev. Fisher had requested.

87. When the motion came up a third time it was withdrawn "after some discussion."

88. Board of Guardians, Select Vestry, Industrial Schools Committee Minute Book, 1845–50, entries for July 2, 1845, Oct. 19, 1846, June 3, July 15, 1848, Sept. 24, Oct. 8, 22, 1851, Oct. 24, 1852, LRO. See also Bennett, *Father Nugent,* 39–40.

89. Burke, *Catholic History,* 118, 120; Industrial Schools Committee Minute Book," entry for July 26, 1854, LRO. The controversies over the treatment of Catholic children in the Kirkdale schools did not disappear at this point. See Burke, *Catholic History,* 130–31.

90. Papworth, "The Irish in Liverpool," 146–48; Burke, *Catholic History,* 44–45, 72–75, 100–110; Klapas, "Geographical Aspects of Religious Change," 48; Hume, "On the Education of the Poor in Liverpool," and *Condition of Liverpool; LM,* Mar. 5, Nov. 26, 1847, Feb. 15, 18, May 16, 1848, Mar. 6, 13, 23, Oct. 9, 1849; Bennett, *Father Nugent,* 26–27. The link between the famine migration, the administration of

the Corporation schools, and the building of Catholic schools is evident in many accounts in the *Mercury*. For a lucid example, see the report of the new church and school in St. Mary's District in *LM*, Feb. 18, 1848. This pattern of school building in Irish areas was common across England. See Samuel, "Roman Catholic Church," 273–74.

91. Derek Fraser, *The Evolution of the British Welfare State*, 2d ed. (London, 1984), 78–84; D. G. Paz, *The Politics of Working-Class Education in Britain, 1830–50* (Manchester, England, 1980); Richard Johnson, "Educational Policy and Social Control in Early Victorian England," in Peter Stansky, ed., *The Victorian Revolution* (New York, 1973), 199–227.

92. *LM*, Apr. 13, 23, 27, 30, 1847, Feb. 29, 1848; Paz, *Politics of Working-Class Education*, 134–36; Burke, *Catholic History*, 93.

93. *LM*, Sept. 25, 1849; Burke, *Catholic History*, 93, 107. The Sept. 25, 1849, article in the *Mercury* reprinted a May 22, 1849, letter from a member of the Catholic Poor School Committee to the Privy Council committee and the Aug. 9, 1849, reply. The Holy Cross parish opened a new school in 1854 funded by voluntary donations. See Burke, *Catholic History*, 107, and *LM*, Oct. 9, 1849.

94. Hibernia Schools, *Annual Report* (Liverpool, 1836, 1839), and Committee Minute Book, 1831–73, esp. entries for Feb. 2, July 13, Dec. 30, 1842, LRO; Murphy, *Religious Problem in Education*, 19–20. The comment about the Corporation was handwritten on the back of the copy of the 1839 *Annual Report* on file at the LRO. The public notice was attached to the minutes.

95. Hibernia Schools, Minutes, Oct. 30, 1847, Feb. 13, 1848, and *Annual Reports* (1849–54), LRO (quotation from 1852); *LM*, Jan. 14, 1848, Jan. 16, 1849.

96. On the Lancashire Public School Association, see *LM*, Oct. 24, 1848, Feb. 27, Nov. 27, 1849; Charlton Hall, *The Duty of the Legislature to Provide for the Education of the People* (Liverpool, 1850). On calls for national schools under the Established Church, see Church of England Education Series, *Proceedings of a Public Meeting Held in the Royal Amphitheatre, Liverpool, on Thursday, June 23, 1853* (Liverpool, 1853); James Gillespie, *Liverpool and Its Educational Wants, or, a Plea for the Erection of National Schools in Connection with St. Peter's and St. George's Churches* (Liverpool, 1855).

97. Anne Holt, Travel Diary, May 12, 1851, LRO.

98. J. Thomas Scharf and Thompson Westcott, *History of Philadelphia, 1609–1884,* 3 vols. (Philadelphia, 1884), 3:1921–36; Kaestle, *Pillars of the Republic*, 58–59; Edgar P. Richardson, "The Athens of America, 1800–1825," in Weigley, *Philadelphia*, 225–26. By midcentury Philadelphia had taken some modest steps toward providing African Americans with separate—and unequal—schooling. The sources in this note offer some discussion of black schooling. See also *PL*, Jan. 20, 1849.

99. Scharf and Westcott, *History of Philadelphia*, 3:1949–55; Nolan, "Francis Patrick Kenrick," 131, 170–86; Clark, *The Irish in Philadelphia*, 94. Nolan provides the Catholic perspective on the riots. For other sources on the riots, see note 32 above.

100. Nolan, "Francis Patrick Kenrick," 167–86; Nolan, *Francis Patrick Kenrick*, 385–90; Alfred C. Rush, "The Saintly John Neumann and his Coadjutor Archbishop Wood," in Connelly, *History of the Archdiocese of Philadelphia*, 209, 225–29; Clark, *The Irish in Philadelphia*, 97; Meyers, "Children's Crusade," 126.

101. For contemporary reports on public schooling in Philadelphia, see *PL*, Feb. 9, 1847, Apr. 3, Oct. 15, 1849.

102. Kaestle, *Pillars of the Republic*, 161–71; Dolan, *The Immigrant Church*, 99–120; James W. Sanders, "Boston Catholics and the School Question, 1825–1907," in Brian C. Mitchell, *Building the American Catholic City* (New York, 1988), 151–83 (originally published in *From Common School to Magnet School* [Boston, 1979], 43–75).

103. *PL*, Oct. 19–20, 1849. For Philadelphia's ragged schools and houses of industry, see *PL*, Mar. 30, 1847, Jan. 1, June 18, 1849. On the evening school movement, see *PL*, Nov. 3, 30, Dec. 4–5, 12–13, 21, 28, 1849. See also Chapter 3. Clark (*The Irish in Philadelphia*, 95) mentions complaints about efforts to convert Catholics, although the organization's records (unlike those in Liverpool) do not refer to such controversies.

104. See Miller, *Emigrants and Exiles*, 331–34.

105. See Boyer, *Urban Masses and Moral Order*, 85–86. On Irish education, see Robert James Scally, *The End of Hidden Ireland* (New York, 1995), 133–58.

106. Papworth, "The Irish in Liverpool," 148; Clark, *The Irish in Philadelphia*, 97. Of course, such comparisons are of limited value without complete information on the total number of students.

107. Hume, *Condition of Liverpool*, 19; Scharf and Westcott, *History of Philadelphia*, 3:1936; Clark, *The Irish in Philadelphia*, 97.

CHAPTER SEVEN

1. The literature on nineteenth-century policing and crime is vast. On England, see Stanley G. Palmer, *Police and Protest in England and Ireland, 1789–1850* (New York, 1988), and Clive Emsley, *The English Police: A Political and Social History* (New York, 1991). On the United States, see Roger Lane, "Urban Police and Crime in Nineteenth-Century America," *Crime and Justice: An Annual Review of Research* 2 (1980): 438–480; Lane, *Policing the City: Boston, 1822–1885* (New York, 1975); David R. Johnson, *Policing the Urban Underworld: The Impact of Crime on the Development of the American Police, 1800–1887* (Philadelphia, 1979); and Eric Monkkonen, *Police in Urban America, 1860–1920* (New York, 1981). For a comparative study, see Wilbur R. Miller, *Cops and Bobbies: Police Authority in New York and London, 1830–1970* (Chicago, 1971).

2. Roger Swift has explored the evolution of policing in several English communities. For an excellent comparative overview, see Swift, "Urban Policing in Early Victorian England, 1835–86: A Reappraisal," *History* 73 (June 1988): 211–37. For several explanatory models, see Monkkonen, *Police in Urban America*, 49–64.

3. On both the real and perceived roles of the Irish in nineteenth-century crime, see Roger Swift, "Crime and the Irish in Nineteenth-Century Britain," in Swift and Sheridan Gilley, eds., *The Irish in Britain, 1815–1939* (Savage, Md., 1989), 163–82, and Swift, "Heroes or Villains?: The Irish, Crime, and Disorder in Victorian England," *Albion* 29 (Fall 1997): 399–421.

4. Emsley, *The English Police*, 36–40. For the *Constabulary Report's* findings for

Liverpool and Lancashire presented from a Chadwickian perspective, see Eric Midwinter, *Social Administration in Lancashire* (Manchester, England, 1969), 124–35.

5. W. R. Cockcroft, "The Liverpool Police Force, 1836–1902," in S. P. Bell, ed., *Victorian Lancashire* (Newton Abbot, England, 1974), 150–52; Eric Midwinter, *Old Liverpool* (Newton Abbot, England, 1971), 61–64; Anne Bryson, "Riotous Liverpool, 1815–1860," in John Belchem, ed., *Popular Politics, Riot and Labour: Essays in Liverpool History 1790–1940* (Liverpool, 1992), 113; Brian D. White, *A History of the Corporation of Liverpool, 1835–1914* (Liverpool, 1951), 11, 16, 19–20. For a detailed history of Liverpool's police force, summarized in Cockcroft's article, see W. R. Cockcroft, "The Rise and Growth of the Liverpool Police Force" (M.A. thesis, University College, Bangor, 1969). Midwinter's *Social Administration in Lancashire* places Liverpool's police developments in the context of neighboring Lancashire communities.

6. Midwinter, *Old Liverpool*, 62–63; Emsley, *The English Police*, 35; White, *Corporation of Liverpool*, 19.

7. Bryson, "Riotous Liverpool," 113–14. The papers of the Watch Committee in the LRO include Minutes; Daily Board, Minutes; Orders to the Head Constable; and Head Constable, *Annual Reports*.

8. Bryson, "Riotous Liverpool," 119; Frank Neal, *Sectarian Violence: The Liverpool Experience, 1819–1914* (Manchester, England, 1988), 61; W. J. Lowe, *The Irish in Mid-Victorian Lancashire* (New York, 1989), 152; Thomas Burke, *Catholic History of Liverpool* (Liverpool, 1910), 76–77.

9. Watch Committee, Daily Board, Apr. 24, 1847, LRO; Cockcroft, "Liverpool Police Force," 151, 162–63; Bryson, "Riotous Liverpool," 115.

10. Bryson, "Riotous Liverpool," 104–34. The reforms implemented in 1836 were not necessarily aimed at addressing street rioting. As Bryson points out, the magistrates and the mayor—not the new Watch Committee—were chiefly responsible for anticipating and suppressing major riots.

11. Bryson, "Riotous Liverpool," 117–19. Bryson divides her data into two periods: 1815–35 and 1836–60. Her tables do not allow for a comparison of the years before and during the famine migration, but her narrative seems to indicate relative calm in all categories between 1836 and 1846. For the importance of sectarian tensions before the famine (and during the 1841–42 violence), see Neal, *Sectarian Violence*, 37–79. In his study of popular politics, Kevin Moore contends that Neal overstated the number of local Orangemen and the power of sectarian tensions. Moore, "'This Whig and Tory Ridden Town': Popular Politics in Liverpool in the Chartist Era," in Belchem, *Popular Politics, Riot and Labour*, 52–60.

12. *LM*, Mar. 5, 19, 1847. On St. Patrick's Day disturbances, see Bryson, "Riotous Liverpool," 118–20; Neal, *Sectarian Violence*, 117–18, 128–29, 134; Lowe, *The Irish in Mid-Victorian Lancashire*, 132–34. On the clergy's efforts to maintain calm in 1845, see Burke, *Catholic History*, 77.

13. *LM*, Feb. 12, 1847. These arrest figures do not necessarily indicate an increase in crimes committed; instead, they may show an increase in police activity.

14. Several historians have addressed disorder in Liverpool, particularly in 1848. Unless otherwise noted, the following account of events in 1848 has been taken from manuscript sources and local newspapers. For other analyses of these events,

some of which rely on additional materials, see especially John Belchem, "Liverpool in the Year of Revolution: The Political and Associational Culture of the Irish Immigrant Community in 1848," in Belchem, *Popular Politics, Riot and Labour,* 68–97. See also Louis R. Bisceglia, "The Threat of Violence: Irish Confederates and Chartists in Liverpool in 1848," *Irish Sword* 14 (1981): 207–15; W. J. Lowe, "The Chartists and the Irish Confederates: Lancashire 1848," *Irish Historical Studies* 24 (November 1984): 172–96; Bryson, "Riotous Liverpool," 98–134; and Neal, *Sectarian Violence,* 115–21. A brief discussion of the historiographical debates will follow.

15. *LM,* Jan. 4, 1848. Watch Committee records indicate that the mayor called for fifty extra men to address the "recent outrages." Watch Committee, Orders to the Head Constable, Dec. 30, 1847, and Daily Board Minute Book, Dec. 30, 1847, LRO. Whatever the cause, these assaults were apparently atypical and did not last long. The *Mercury* reported unusual violence on the outskirts of town on Jan. 4 and 7, 1848, but there were no reports of note before or after that week in either the newspaper or the various Watch Committee records.

16. *LM,* Mar. 14, 1848; Proceedings of Magistrates, Town Council, Special and Sub-Committees Minute Book, 332–46: "Apprehending Riots," Mar. 12, 1848, LRO.

17. *LM,* Mar. 16, 1848; Proceedings of Magistrates, "Apprehending Riots," Mar. 12–16, 1848.

18. *LM,* Mar. 14, 17, 1848; Proceedings of Magistrates, "Apprehending Riots," Mar. 15–16, 1848; George Holt Sr., Diary, Mar. 16, 1848, LRO.

19. *LM,* Mar. 21, 1848.

20. Ibid. Belchem ("Liverpool in the Year of Revolution," 81) credits the magistrates, "supported by the Catholic Church," with not allowing the annual processions.

21. *LM,* Mar. 24, 28, Apr. 4, 7, 11, 1848; Belchem, "Liverpool in the Year of Revolution," 80, 83–86. Belchem shows evidence of ongoing Confederate activity and strong rhetoric while also noting that Liverpool authorities were more concerned about reported Chartist activities.

22. *LM,* Apr. 7, 11, 25, 1848; Holt Diary, Apr. 9, 1948, LRO. Published reports routinely lumped together the Repealers, Irish Confederates, and Chartists as threats to local order. See, e.g., *LM,* Mar. 24, 28, Apr. 4, 1848. Belchem ("Liverpool in the Year of Revolution," 74, 79–80, 85–89) describes Reynolds as a leading Confederate who was engaged in spurring on the Chartists.

23. *LM,* May 30, June 9, 1848. This is the first report of a court case or news story found in the *Mercury* involving Irish-Orangemen violence.

24. *LM,* July 21, 25, 1848. The police had begun gathering reports about the clubs from infiltrators and informants by late June. Belchem ("Liverpool in the Year of Revolution," 88–91) estimates that there were between 30 and 40 clubs with 2,000 to 4,000 members in July.

25. *LM,* June 16, 20, July 11, 21, 25, 28, Aug. 1, 1848; A. Melly to George Melly, July 20, 1848, George Melly Papers, LRO; Belchem, "Liverpool in the Year of Revolution," 92. The June references are to Council meetings ordering the swearing in of special constables.

26. *LM,* July 25, 1848.

27. Belchem, "Liverpool in the Year of Revolution," 92–95; *LM,* Aug. 1, 11, 1848.

28. Holt Diary, Mar. 22, 1848, and Louisa Melly to George Melly, July 25, 1848, Melly Papers, LRO.

29. Bisceglia, "Threat of Violence" 215 passim; Moore, "'This Whig and Tory Ridden Town,'" 38–67; Belchem, "Liverpool in the Year of Revolution," 68 passim. See also John Belchem, "English Working-Class Radicalism and the Irish, 1815–50," in *Eire-Ireland* (1984): 78–93.

30. Lowe, *The Irish in Mid-Victorian Lancashire,* 188. See also Lowe, "The Chartists and the Irish Confederates: Lancashire, 1848," in *Irish Historical Studies* (November 1984): 172–96.

31. Neal, *Sectarian Violence,* 119–120. In his 1992 article Belchem, whose research on the Irish Confederates has been extensive, notes his disagreements with Bisceglia, Lowe, and Neal in several footnotes. See "Liverpool in the Year of Revolution," 69 n. 5, 74 n. 23, 82 n. 58.

32. *LM,* Mar. 16, 20, 1849; Justice Sessions, Gaol and House of Corrections, Records of the Borough Gaol and Walton's Prison, Mar. 7, 1850, LRO; Lowe, *The Irish in Mid-Victorian Lancashire,* 132; Neal, *Sectarian Violence,* 128–29. Lowe described a calm celebration in 1850 and apparently found no reference to the 1849 procession.

33. Neal, *Sectarian Violence,* 129–30. For slightly different accounts, see Lowe, *The Irish in Mid-Victorian Lancashire,* 154, and Bryson, "Riotous Liverpool," 119.

34. See Chapter 6.

35. *A Full Report of the Speech of Mr. Roebuck, Q.C., M.P., in Defence of the Birkenhead Catholics Delivered at Chester Assizes, on Monday, 7th April, 1851* (Liverpool, 1851); Neal, *Sectarian Violence,* 131–33.

36. *A Full Report of the Speech of Mr. Roebuck;* Neal, *Sectarian Violence,* 133; Bryson, "Riotous Liverpool," 115, 119; Lowe, *The Irish in Mid-Victorian Lancashire,* 157.

37. Neal, *Sectarian Violence,* 134–37; Lowe, *The Irish in Mid-Victorian Lancashire,* 154–56; Bryson, "Riotous Liverpool," 119. According to Lowe, more than one hundred people, mostly Irish, were arrested.

38. Burke, *Catholic History,* 109–10; Neal, *Sectarian Violence,* 137–46; Bryson, "Riotous Liverpool," 116, 119–20, 129; Lowe, *The Irish in Mid-Victorian Lancashire,* 132, 156–58; Orders of the Watch Committee to the Head Constable, Nov. 27, 1852, LRO.

39. Belchem, "Liverpool in the Year of Revolution," 74–79 passim; Lowe, *The Irish in Mid-Victorian Lancashire,* 180–81. In his comparison of "communal strife" in Liverpool and Glasgow, Tom Gallagher concluded that the Lancashire city's heavier famine migration produced a more divisive sectarian world than that of Glasgow. Gallagher, "A Tale of Two Cities: Communal Strife in Glasgow and Liverpool before 1914," in Roger Swift and Sheridan Gilley, eds., *The Irish in the Victorian City* (London, 1985), 107–229.

40. Swift, "Crime and the Irish," 163–79. See also Swift, "Heroes or Villains?"

41. Watch Committee, Minutes, Apr. 24, 1847, LRO. For Irish arrests in Liver-

pool and Lancashire, see also Neal, *Sectarian Violence,* 110–13, and Lowe, *The Irish in Mid-Victorian Lancashire,* 36–37.

42. Watch Committee, Daily Board, May 25, 1848, LRO. The head constable made the same point about the famine migrants in his report the following year. See also *LM,* June 9, 1848, and Cockcroft, "Liverpool Police Force," 163. The *Mercury*'s regular "Police Court" column routinely noted that Irish "imposters" had been charged with illegally seeking relief or simply dishonest begging practices. See, e.g., *LM,* Apr. 4, May 4, 11, July 6, 13, 1847.

43. *LM,* Nov. 19, 1847. In a single day the following January Rushton saw 145 prisoners, 70 of whom were Irish immigrants charged with begging or petty theft; only 3 of the 70 accepted his offer of warm clothes and a free passage back to Ireland. *LM,* Feb. 1, 1848.

44. Bryson, "Riotous Liverpool," 124–25. Bryson offers little details on these "private battles," but she found only thirty-three for the twenty-five years between 1835 and 1860. For more on these "intracommunal disorders," see Swift, "Heroes or Villains?," 412–13.

45. Watch Committee, Daily Board, July 28, 1849, LRO. This report was also quoted almost verbatim in *LM,* Sept. 7, 1849. This comment would seem to confirm Bryson's view that the predominantly Irish neighborhoods were the scenes of many unrecorded "private battles." For a case of an "Irish row," see *LM,* June 2, 1847. For a case against the police, see *LM,* Nov. 30, 1847.

46: *LM,* Jan. 16, 1849. The next month the Finance Committee reported the same data to the Select Vestry along with a table of total prisoners for the entire decade. *LM,* Feb. 23, 1849. Previous reports had not listed the prisoners' nativity. This large share of Irish arrests—well beyond their roughly 22 percent of the population—provided a ready explanation for the year's sudden jump in total arrests from 19,719 the previous year.

47. Edward Rushton, Esq., to Sir George Grey, Apr. 21, 1849, HC 1849 (266) XLVII, reprinted in *Irish University Press Series of British Parliamentary Papers,* vol. 22: *Emigration* (Shannon, Ireland, 1970). This letter was also published in the local newspapers—see *LM,* May 15, 1849. The 1848 arrest statistics were routinely cited in petitions to Parliament and in local letters, editorials, and political discussions. See Rector Campbell's report to the Select Vestry on his special delegation's meeting with Sir Grey, *LM,* May 15, 1849. See also *LM,* June 26, 1849. Rushton's letter and Liverpool's broader campaign for relief are discussed in Chapter 2.

48. *Report of the State of the Liverpool Police Force by the Head Constable, 1852* (Liverpool, 1853), table 5; Lawrence Feehan, "Charitable Effort, Statutory Authorities and the Poor in Liverpool, c1850–1914" (Ph.D. diss., University of Liverpool, 1987), and see Chapter 2 of this book; David Jones, *Crime, Protest, Community and Police in Nineteenth-Century Britain* (London, 1982), 178–84; *LM,* Feb. 23, 1849. Jones (*Crime, Protest, Community and Police,* 183) found that the Irish made up as much as 40 percent of midcentury arrests for vagrancy and that women fluctuated between a sixth and a quarter of vagrancy arrests.

49. Watch Committee, Head Constable's Police Statistical Returns for the Year 1848, Minutes, Apr. 28, 1849, LRO, reprinted in *LM,* May 4, 1849; Watch Com-

mittee, Report of Special Committee on the Increase of the Police Force, Minutes, Sept. 21, 1848, LRO. In 1848 the Watch Committee and the Dock Estate spent nearly £26,000 for "extra expenses consequent on the increase of the police force in anticipation of the Riots in 1848." The government covered £396 of these unusual expenses. Watch Committee, Miscellaneous Sub-Committee Minutes, Apr. 20, 1850. Dowling's report on the 1848 statistics noted the July 1848 jump in the police force.

50. *LM*, Dec. 3, 1847 (Holme), May 16, 1848 ("Old Police-Officer"); Watch Committee, Minutes, May 25, 1848, LRO. For letters criticizing the local police force, see *LM*, Nov. 5, 9, 1847, Jan. 18, Mar. 21, Apr. 25, May 16, July 11, 1848. Many of these letters are quite long and detailed. The "Old Police-Officer," the most persistent writer, apparently found his mark. In March 1847 Constable Dowling sent a letter to the Watch Committee complaining about the public correspondence and calling on the *Mercury* for equal coverage. Watch Committee, Daily Board, Minutes, Mar. 20, 1847, LRO.

51. *LM*, Dec. 3, 1847; Watch Committee, Minutes, Nov. 27, 1847, LRO. The proposal did not pass, but the Watch Committee's daily board stopped meeting, effectively shifting more power to the constable.

52. *LM*, Feb. 9, 16, June 15, 19, 1849; Watch Committee, Orders to the Head Constable, July 7, 1849, Statement from Head Constable Dowling, Minutes, July 28, 1849, Daily Board, July 28, 1849, and Miscellaneous Sub-Committee Minutes, Mar. 2–Apr. 19, 1850, LRO; *LM*, Sept. 7, 1849. The figures on staff include the dock police, which increased from 311 men in 1849 to 314 in 1850 and then remained constant for the next six years. J. J. Greig, *Report on the State of the Liverpool Police Force by the Head Constable, 1857* (Liverpool, 1858), 8. Of course, this ratio was greatly exceeded during the emergency months in late 1848.

53. Johnson, *Policing the Urban Underworld*, 7–9; Monkkonen, *Police in Urban America*, 30–64, and *America Becomes Urban: The Development of U.S. Cities & Towns, 1780–1980* (Berkeley, 1988), 98–100. In his 1988 book Monkkonen dissents from the common view that nineteenth-century police reforms were prompted by specific disorderly episodes rather than "deeper, underlying pressures [which had] little to do with rising crime or class or ethnic conflict" (p. 100). See also Miller, *Cops and Bobbies*.

54. Howard O. Sprogle, *The Philadelphia Police, Past and Present* (Philadelphia, 1887; reprint, New York, 1971), 70–76; Johnson, *Policing the Urban Underworld*, 16–17; Edward P. Allinson and Boies Penrose, *Philadelphia, 1681–1887: A History of Municipal Development* (Philadelphia, 1887), 34–36, 98–101.

55. Allinson and Penrose, *Philadelphia*, 102–3; Sprogle, *Philadelphia Police*, 75–76; Johnson, *Policing the Urban Underworld*, 17–18, 21. As Johnson (p. 18) points out, in 1833 London had 1 officer for every 434 inhabitants, whereas Philadelphia had 1 officer for every 3,352 inhabitants.

56. Johnson, *Policing the Urban Underworld*, 12–15, 21, 25; Sprogle, *Philadelphia Police*, 26.

57. Johnson, *Policing the Urban Underworld*, 78. For general studies of Philadelphia's violence, see Elizabeth M. Geffen, "Violence in Philadelphia in the 1840's

and 1850's," *Pennsylvania Magazine of History and Biography* 36 (October 1969): 381–410; Michael Feldberg, "Urbanization as a Cause of Violence: Philadelphia as a Test Case," in Allen F. Davis and Mark H. Haller, eds., *The Peoples of Philadelphia* (Philadelphia, 1973), 53–69; and David R. Johnson, "Crime Patterns in Philadelphia, 1840–1870," in Davis and Haller, *Peoples of Philadelphia,* 89–110. On racial tensions, see Noel Ignatiev, *How the Irish Became White* (New York, 1995), 124–44. On violence in Philadelphia's heterogenous Cedar Street neighborhood, with a particular emphasis on racial conflicts, see Emma Jones Lapsansky, "South Street Philadelphia, 1762–1854: 'A Haven for Those Low in the World' " (Ph.D. diss., University of Pennsylvania, 1975), 206–22 passim.

58. Bruce Laurie, "Fire Companies and Gangs in Southwark: The 1840s," in Davis and Haller, *Peoples of Philadelphia,* 71–87; Johnson, *Policing the Urban Underworld,* 84–89. For the perspective of one fire company, see Hibernia Fire Company, Minutes, 1839–49, HSP (see, e.g., entry of Oct. 18, 1844). Accounts of fire company violence also appeared regularly in the daily newspapers.

59. Johnson, *Policing the Urban Underworld,* app. 1.

60. For fuller histories of the events surrounding the riots (discussed more fully in Chapter 6), see Michael Feldberg, *The Philadelphia Riots of 1844: A Study in Ethnic Conflict* (Westport, Conn., 1975), and *The Turbulent Era: Riot and Disorder in Jacksonian America* (New York, 1980), 9–32; David Montgomery, "The Shuttle and the Cross: Weavers and Artisans in the Kensington Riots of 1844," *Journal of Social History* 5 (1972): 411–46; Johnson, *Policing the Urban Underworld,* 25–27; and Sprogle, *Philadelphia Police,* 80–84.

61. Johnson, *Policing the Urban Underworld,* 26–28; Sprogle, *Philadelphia Police,* 84–88. On New York City, see James Richardson, *The New York Police: Colonial Times to 1901* (New York, 1970).

62. *PL,* Jan. 5, 1847. Judge Kelley offered similar praise of local law enforcement in his charge to the court of quarter sessions that May. *PL,* May 4, 1847.

63. *PL,* Jan. 5, 11–12, 1847. Such reports appeared in the *Ledger* several times a week. See, e.g., *PL,* Feb. 24, Aug. 2, 6, 1847, Feb. 21, 1848. Similar accounts were rare in the *Liverpool Mercury.*

64. *PL,* Nov. 9, 1847.

65. On Council discussions, see *Journal of the Select Council of the City of Philadelphia for 1846–47* (Philadelphia, 1847), 53–55 (February 11, 1847); *Journal of the Common Council for 1846–47* (Philadelphia, 1847), 33–35; *PL,* Jan. 1, 29, Feb. 12, June 18, Nov. 27, 1847, Jan. 7, 1848. On Northern Liberties, see *PL,* July 8, Nov. 4, Dec. 9, 1847; on Spring Gardens, see Feb. 24, 1847. Johnson (*Policing the Urban Underworld,* 29) found a peak in gang activities between 1845 and 1849.

66. *PL,* May 4, Sept. 14, Nov. 27, Dec. 6, 9, 1847, Jan. 26, Feb. 1, 4, 1848; *Journal of the Select Council* (Philadelphia 1848), app. 24, Report of the Special Committee of Councils on "Remodeling the Police Department," 146–98. See also J. Thomas Scharf and Thompson Westcott, *History of Philadelphia, 1609–1884,* 3 vols. (Philadelphia, 1884), 1:689. On the Councils' continuing discussions, see *PL,* Jan. 7, 21, 1848.

67. *PL*, Feb. 4, Mar. 3, Apr. 17, May 4, 6, 1848; *Journal of the Select Council,* "Report of the Special Committee of Councils on 'Remodeling the Police Department,'" 146–98; *A Digest of the Laws in Force Relating to the Police of the City of Philadelphia* . . . (Philadelphia, 1851), 11–14. Oddly enough, at roughly the same time the Southwark commissioners reduced their police force from 45 to 40 men. *PL,* May 26, 1848.

68. Scharf and Westcott, *History of Philadelphia,* 1:689. Earlier efforts by the state legislature to control the worst fire company offenders had been met with angry petitions from local companies but widespread popular support. *PL,* Jan. 18, 22, 1847.

69. *PL,* July 12 (Spring Garden), 25, Aug. 1 (Northern Liberties), 5 (Kensington), Oct. 3, 9, 13, Nov. 15, 25, 1848. On Moyamensing's disorders, see Johnson, *Police in Urban America,* 29–30, and Scharf and Westcott, *History of Philadelphia,* 1:691–92.

70. *PL,* Feb. 6, 1849. A new trial involving the Kensington's Hibernia and Taylor Hose Companies appeared in the same issue of the *PL.*

71. *PL,* Apr. 3, 1849.

72. See *PL,* May 9, 16, June 4, 18, 1849.

73. *PL,* June 18, 1849. The paper expressed similar booster sentiments on July 17, 1849.

74. *PL,* June 18, 1849; Sprogle, *Philadelphia Police,* 90.

75. *PL,* June 19, July 12, 1849.

76. *PL,* June 20, 1849.

77. *PL,* Aug. 20, 1849. Two days later the newspaper reported another incident a few blocks away. *PL,* Aug. 22, 1849.

78. *PL,* Oct. 10, 1849. See extensive coverage of this riot in the next several issues of the *Ledger.* For a colorful contemporary account of the riot, emphasizing the role of the central gang leader, see *Life and Adventures of Charles Anderson Chester, the Notorious Leader of the Philadelphia "Killers"* (Philadelphia, 1850). See also Lapsansky, "South Street Philadelphia," 221–22, and Scharf and Westcott, *History of Philadelphia,* 1:692–93.

79. *PL,* Oct. 1, 6, 10, 13, 1849.

80. *PL,* Oct. 18, 23, Nov. 4, 9, 16–17, 1849. In November 1849 an episode in Northern Liberties seemed to be the last straw. After reports that a gang had attacked an elderly man, the local police committee petitioned the state legislature for a "uniform police establishment for the City of Philadelphia and adjacent districts." Johnson, *Policing the Urban Underworld,* 32. On the Councils' worries about rioting, see *Journal of the Select Council* (Philadelphia, 1850), app. 3.

81. *Rules for the Government of the Board of Police of the Philadelphia Police District* (Philadelphia, 1850); *Report of the Marshal of Police of the Philadelphia Police District* (Philadelphia, 1851); *A Digest of the Laws in Force Relating to the Police of the City of Philadelphia* . . . (Philadelphia, 1851); *Pennsylvania Journal of Prison Discipline and Philanthropy* (January 1851): 87; Sprogle, *Philadelphia Police,* 93–95; Johnson, *Police in Urban America,* 33–34.

82. *Pennsylvania Journal of Prison Discipline* (April 1849): 70–72, (October 1850): 209–20. In 1844, 17 of 143 (12 percent) prisoners were Irish. *Pennsylvania Journal of Prison Discipline* (April, 1846): 147.

83. *Annual Report of the Inspectors of the Philadelphia County Prison, made to the Legislature* . . . (Philadelphia, 1848–1857). Between 1853 and 1854 the figure hovered around a quarter of all prisoners, before dropping back to 18 percent in 1855.

84. Ignatiev, *How the Irish Became White.*

85. *PL,* Apr. 3, 1849; *Pennsylvania Journal of Prison Discipline and Philanthropy* (July 1849): 151–52. The *Journal* seemed unconcerned that it was comparing data that were clearly not comparable.

86. *Pennsylvania Journal of Prison Discipline and Philanthropy* (April 1856): 126; In 1858, 9,925 of 22,367 arrests were of Irish-born people; the following year they totaled 15,003 of 32,225. *Annual Messages of Mayor Alexander Henry* (Philadelphia, 1859, 1860). Once again, Roger Swift has offered valuable observations about the implications of such arrest patterns in an English context. See his "Crime and the Irish" and "Heroes or Villains?".

87. Johnson, *Police in Urban America,* 80–89; Feldberg, *Turbulent Era;* Dale B. Light, *Rome and the New Republic: Conflict and Community in Philadelphia Catholicism between the Revolution and the Civil War* (Notre Dame, Ind., 1996), 282. For the minutes of one Irish hose company, see Hibernia Fire Company, Minutes, 1839–49, HSP.

88. Johnson, *Police in Urban America,* 87; Feldberg, *Philadelphia Riots,* 169. William McMullen, the Moyamensing-born son of an Irish father, cut his political teeth with the Killers and the Moyamensing Hose Company before going on to become a leading local Democrat. See Ignatiev, *How the Irish Became White,* 160–64; Harry C. Silcox, *Philadelphia Politics from the Bottom Up: The Life of Irishman William McMullen, 1824–1901* (Philadelphia, 1989).

89. *Report of a Committee Appointed at a Meeting Held on Friday Evening, December 3rd, 1852, to Consider the Propriety of Organising a Paid Fire Department* (Philadelphia, 1853); *The Character of the Fire Companies of Philadelphia as Exhibited by the Dockets of the Criminal Courts of That County* (Philadelphia, n.d.) (a single printed sheet on file in the Library Company of Philadelphia, probably 1853); *Report of the Committee Appointed to Devise a Plan for the Better Organization of the Fire Department* (Philadelphia, n.d.) (Library Company dates as 1853); *Paid Fire Department: Letters of the Judges of the Court of Quarter Sessions, and the Marshal of Police, and Report of the Board of Trade* (Philadelphia, 1853). A contemporary pamphlet about Charles Anderson Chester, reputed leader of "the Killers," included a detailed discussion of the California House riot and its aftermath without ever mentioning the nativity of the rioters. *Life and Adventures of Charles Anderson Chester.* Thomas P. Cope described the October 1849 riot, and several other instances of fire company violence, without noting the ethnicity of the participants. *Philadelphia Merchant: The Diary of Thomas P. Cope* (South Bend, Ind., 1978), 580–81.

90. Dale B. Light Jr., "The Role of Irish-American Organisations in Assimilation and Community Formation," in P. J. Drudy, ed., *The Irish in America: Emigration, Assimilation and Impact* (New York, 1985), 113–41; Light, "Class, Ethnicity and

the Urban Ecology in a Nineteenth-Century City: Philadelphia's Irish, 1840–1890" (Ph.D. diss., University of Pennsylvania, 1979); Dennis Clark, *The Irish in Philadelphia* (Philadelphia, 1973), 106–11; Hibernia Society, Minutes, HSP. The most famous political society, the secret Fenian Brotherhood, did not emerge until the decade after the famine migration.

91. Hibernia Society, Minutes, Mar. 10, 1847, passim, HSP. See Dennis Clark, "Saint Patrick's Day Observed," in Clark, *The Irish Relations: Trials of an Immigrant Tradition* (Rutherford, N.J., 1982), 193–204. Susan G. Davis reports that nervous officials periodically tried to discourage St. Patrick's Day parading and that burning "Paddies" in effigy on St. Patrick's Day eve "was a venerable nativist tradition." But she cites evidence only from 1819 and 1823. Davis, *Parades and Power: Street Theater in Nineteenth-Century Philadelphia* (Philadelphia, 1986), 47, 190 n. 82. In 1849 the *Public Ledger* merely noted that St. Patrick's Day was "celebrated in an appropriate manner" with a dinner and a high mass. *PL*, Mar. 19, 1849. On the role of St. Patrick's Day celebrations in nineteenth-century America, with an emphasis on New York City, see Kenneth Moss, "St. Patrick's Day Celebrations and the Formation of Irish-American Identity, 1845–1875," *Journal of Social History* 29 (Fall 1995): 125–48.

92. Scharf and Westcott, *History of Philadelphia*, 1:713–16; Sprogle, *Philadelphia Police*, 96–99; Russell F. Weigley, "The Border City in Civil War, 1854–1865," in Weigley, ed., *Philadelphia: A 300-Year History* (New York, 1982), 368–69; Johnson, *Policing the Urban Underworld*, 34–40.

93. Sprogle, *Philadelphia Police*, 103; Johnson, *Policing the Urban Underworld*, 38–40, 97–99; Lane, *Policing the City*, 104–5; Monkkonen, *Police in Urban America*, 45–46; Midwinter, *Old Liverpool*, 63.

94. Sprogle, *Philadelphia Police*, 101–2; Johnson, *Policing the Urban Underworld*, 96. Sprogle indicated that Conrad's rule "certainly was not long enforced." Johnson suggests that this partisan pattern stopped with the election of Alexander Henry in 1858.

95. See Johnson, *Policing the Urban Underworld*, 102–3, 140–41, 184–85; *PL*, Sept. 29, Oct. 4, 13, 1848.

96. Monkkonen, *Police in Urban America*, 55–64. The adoption of badges and uniforms is recognized as an important benchmark in the development of a police force.

97. One might reasonably argue that most of the measures addressed in the previous chapters—quarantines, poor relief, sanitary reform, education, etc.—were undertaken in the pursuit of order.

98. Light, *Rome and the New Republic*, 285–94; Cockcroft, "Liverpool Police Force," 155–57; Burke, *Catholic History*, 115–16; *LM*, May 22, 1849; *PL*, Dec. 4, 1849; Paul E. Johnson, *A Shopkeeper's Millennium: Society and Revivals in Rochester, New York, 1815–1837* (New York, 1978), and *Policing the Urban Underworld*, 125–29; Swift, "Crime and the Irish." See also Chapter 2. In 1845 the Liverpool police made 16,743 arrests, including 9,791 for drunk and disorderly. Watch Committee, *Report on the Police Establishment . . . 1845* (Liverpool, 1846), table 13. In 1848 the mayor

of Philadelphia heard 2,793 cases, including 1,044 for intoxication, 244 for disorderly conduct, 202 for vagrancy, and 85 for either disturbing the peace, fighting, or being "deranged." *PL,* Mar. 19, 1849.

99. See David Rothman, *The Discovery of the Asylum: Social Order and Disorder in the New Republic* (New York, 1971, 1990). For an excellent collection of essays placing the history of prisons into a broad comparative and theoretical framework, see Norbert Finzsch and Robert Jutte, eds., *Institutions of Confinement: Hospitals, Asylums, and Prisons in Western Europe and North America, 1500–1950* (New York, 1996).

100. Scharf and Westcott, *History of Philadelphia,* 3:1834–38; Rothman, *Discovery of the Asylum,* 79–108. The Philadelphia Society for Alleviating the Miseries of Public Prisons, publishers of the *Pennsylvania Journal of Prison Discipline,* were particularly engaged in this international dialogue. For evidence of local pride in Pennsylvania's innovative penitentiary system, see *PL,* Feb. 15, 1847. For the number of inmates in the state penitentiary and the county prison annually, see *PL,* Apr. 3, 1849.

101. Committee of Councils, Gaol Committee Book, Nov. 30, 1847, July 19, 1848, LRO; *LM,* July 9, Nov. 19, Dec. 3, 1847; Justice Sessions, Gaol and House of Correction, Jan. 14 1851, LRO; *Liverpool As It Is* (Liverpool, n.d. [early 1850s]), 58, 140; Midwinter, *Social Administration in Lancashire,* 131; Margaret DeLacy, *Prison Reform in Lancashire, 1780–1850* (Stanford, Calif., 1986), 12, 20, 205–23 passim; Midwinter, *Old Liverpool,* 66. The Chaplain of Lancashire County's Kirkdale Gaol also reported unusual strains in 1848, which he linked to the recent Chartist scare and the general "scarcity of employment." *Annual Reports of the Chaplain of Kirkdale Gaol* (Preston, England, 1849).

102. Hibernia Schools, Minute Book, Dec. 30, 1842, LRO; Anne Holt Diary, Sept. 10, 1848, LRO; *LM,* Apr. 20, 27, 1847; House of Refuge, *Second and Fifth Annual Reports* (Philadelphia, 1830, 1833). Boston's House of Reformation opened in 1822; New York City's followed three years later. Holloran, *Boston's Wayward Children,* 24–25. The literature on nineteenth-century juveniles is vast, particularly in the United States. For a recent introduction to the American literature, see Priscilla Clement, *Growing Pains: Children in the Industrial Age, 1850–1890* (New York, 1997). For an important local study, see Peter C. Holloran, *Boston's Wayward Children: Social Services for Homeless Children, 1830–1930* (Boston, 1989). On British policies and attitudes, see Martin J. Wiener, *Reconstructing the Criminal: Culture, Law, and Policy in England, 1830–1914* (New York, 1990), 131–41. For charitable responses to poor children, including the ragged schools and industrial schools, see Chapter 3; for the evolving public school systems and sectarian conflicts, see Chapter 6.

103. On similar concerns in Boston, see Holloran, *Boston's Wayward Children,* 32–33.

104. House of Refuge, *Annual Reports* (Philadelphia, 1847–56); *The Design and Advantages of the House of Refuge with Acts of Incorporation, By-Laws, Rules, &c* (Philadelphia, 1851); *PL,* Apr. 3, Oct. 1, 30, Nov. 3, Dec. 4, 1849; *First Annual Report of the Board of Directors of the Girard life College for Orphans* (Philadelphia, 1848). In 1853 the House of Refuge received 295 children, including 63 Irish born and 119 of Irish parentage.

105. *Narrative of the Origin, Progress and Details of Industrial Ragged Schools* (Liver-

pool, 1848); Liverpool Industrial Ragged Schools, *First Annual Report* (Liverpool, 1850); *PL*, Nov. 30, Dec. 4, 28, 1849.

106. Board of Guardians, Liverpool Select Vestry, Industrial Schools Committee Minute Book, 1845–50, Nov. 10, 1846, LRO; Minutes of the Juvenile Offenders Committee (June 1850–June 1852) and the Juvenile Reformatories Special Committee (October 1854–February 1855), LRO (these two sets of minutes are in the same bound volume); Derek Fraser, *The Evolution of the British Welfare State*, 2d ed. (London, 1984), 96–98; Cockcroft, "Liverpool Police Force," 154.

107. Liverpool Catholic Reformatory Association, Reformatory (Fund) Committee, Minute Book, 1856–60, LRO. See also Canon John Bennett, *Father Nugent of Liverpool* (Liverpool, 1949), 50–53.

108. In fact, both cities' policing histories support all seven of Derek Fraser's historiographic models presented in Chapter 1.

109. In a slightly different historical context, Norbert Finzsch points out that comparative analysis can undercut a theoretical analysis of institution building. An American reform that fits the model of an emerging "young republic" or Jacksonian ideas about individualism must be reconsidered when it also appears in an English or a European context. Finzsch, " 'Comparing Apples and Oranges?': The History of Early Prisons in Germany and the United States, 1800–1860," in Finzsch and Jutte, *Institutions of Confinement*, 213–33. Even if the Philadelphia system had distinct intellectual roots in American individualism, the theoretical assumptions about the potential for rehabilitation and the utility of separation found a receptive audience in England.

110. Ignatiev, *How the Irish Became White*. In his study of America's Jacksonian rioting, Feldberg (*Turbulent Era*) identified certain categories of violence, including "preservationist riots" (such as those against blacks and immigrants), "expressive riots" (which demonstrate ethnic, racial, social or political cohesiveness), and "recreational riots" (involving gangs, volunteer fire companies, etc.).

111. Watch Committee, Daily Board, July 28, 1849, LRO. In his summary of the possible origins of Jacksonian violence, Feldberg (*Turbulent Era*, 91) suggests that if the United States does not have a commonly respected "culture of violence," its history does include the "sporadic *practice* of violence that derives from its ideology of popular, direct-action democracy."

112. This differs from Feldberg's (*Turbulent Era*, 99–100) suggestion that Irish immigrants were "predisposed" to violence.

CONCLUSION

1. Derek Fraser, *The Evolution of the British Welfare State*, 2d ed. (London, 1973, 1984), xxi–xxx. I have rearranged Fraser's order somewhat, saving the ideological model for last.

2. This study has had relatively little to say about Jacksonian Party politics. For analyses of Jacksonian politics and ideology, see Harry L. Watson, *Liberty and Power: The Politics of Jacksonian America* (New York, 1990), and Lawrence Frederick Kohl,

The Politics of Individualism: Parties and the American Character in the Jacksonian Era (New York, 1980).

3. This was actually the fourth on his list.

4. Fraser, *Evolution of the British Welfare State*, xxv.

5. For a recent discussion of American Exceptionalism, see Seymour Martin Lipset, *American Exceptionalism: A Double-Edged Sword* (New York, 1996), and essays on Lipset's book by H. V. Nelles, J. Victor Koschmann, and Mary Nolan in *American Historical Review* (June 1997): 749–74. See also Chapter 1.

6. Alexis de Tocqueville, *Democracy in America*, edited by J. P. Mayer, translated by George Lawrence (1848; New York, 1969), esp. 1:196–230.

7. See William J. Novak, *The People's Welfare: Law and Regulation in Nineteenth-Century America* (Chapel Hill, N.C., 1996), 10 passim.

8. See Kohl, *Politics of Individualism*, 59. In his comprehensive study of public life in late-nineteenth–century America, Morton Keller argues that Americans continued to cling to certain fundamental values: localism, racism, and limited government. Keller, *Affairs of State: Public Life in Late Nineteenth Century America* (Cambridge, Mass., 1977).

9. See Terry Coleman, *Going to America* (1972; reprint, Baltimore, 1987), app. A, 287–94.

10. Even the history of penitentiaries reveals important national differences. Despite a modicum of county autonomy, prison reform in Lancashire owed much to a series of nineteenth-century parliamentary reforms. See Margaret DeLacy, *Prison Reform in Lancashire, 1700–1850: A Study in Local Administration* (Stanford, Calif., 1986), 171–94.

11. Seymour Martin Lipset (*American Exceptionalism*) sees an ongoing connection between American voluntarism and individualism.

12. Novak, *People's Welfare*. On Jacksonian ideology, see Watson, *Liberty and Power;* on individualism, see Kohl, *Politics of Individualism.* Sam Bass Warner described a similar set of ideas as part of a national culture of "privatism." Warner, *The Private City: Philadelphia in Three Periods of Its Growth* (Philadelphia, 1968).

13. Novak (*People's Welfare*, 194–204 passim) points out that mid-nineteenth–century American law actually gave the "medical police" far more power over private property than has commonly been supposed. Nonetheless, Liverpool's sanitary authorities exercised far more power than contemporary American public health officials.

14. Warner, *Private City*, 61.

15. *PL*, May 24, 1849. See Chapter 6.

16. See Noel Ignatiev, *How the Irish Became White* (New York, 1995).

17. Daniel J. Boorstin, *The Americas: The National Experience* (New York, 1965), 113–68.

18. Frederick Jackson Turner, "The Significance of the Frontier in American History," *Proceedings of the Forty-first Annual Meeting of the State Historical Society of Wisconsin* (Madison, 1894), 79–112.

19. David M. Potter, *People of Plenty: Economic Abundance and the American Character* (Chicago, 1954).

20. Of course, the proximity argument cuts both ways, as over 60,000 Irish paupers were "removed" from Liverpool in the decade beginning in 1845. See Chapter 2.

21. Patrick Gilligan to Michael Gilligan, 42d voyage of the *Susquehanna*, ticket #1956, 1847, folder B 17, H & A Cope Papers, HSP.

22. In fact, the cholera epidemic of 1866 would be met with far more lasting health reforms in the United States. See Charles E. Rosenberg, *The Cholera Years* (Chicago, 1961, 1987), 175–234.

23. On the importance of Civil War pensions, see Theda Skocpol, *Protecting Soldiers and Mothers: The Political Origins of Social Policy in the United States* (Cambridge, Mass., 1992).

24. Having grown up in the slowly, and grudgingly, desegregating American South, I am perhaps not the best person to explain this enthusiasm for state autonomy, particularly in regard to the distribution of assistance to the politically disenfranchised.

25. For an analysis of recent events in the context of the broader history of American welfare reform, see Michael B. Katz, *In the Shadow of the Poorhouse: A Social History of Welfare in America*, rev. (New York, 1996), 300–334.

26. For an enlightening discussion of the state of American schools, see Jonathan Kozol, *Savage Inequalities: Children in American Schools* (New York, 1991).

27. Elsewhere I have argued that even the challenges of the Civil War, a decade after the famine migration, did not shock Philadelphia out of its traditional patterns. See Gallman, *Mastering Wartime: A Social History of Philadelphia during the Civil War* (New York, 1990).

Index

117, 118, 127–28, 130, 138, 220, 225, 261 (n. 52); neighborhoods, 118; and water, 132; and public baths, 134

Christian Home Missionary Society, 76, 160

Church of St. Augustine, 153

City Hospital (Philadelphia), 33, 106, 107

Class issues: and ethnic ghettos, 10; and contact between classes, 83–84; and cholera, 108–9; and Irish famine emigrants, 116, 175; and sanitation, 120, 132; and Catholic Church, 144; and violence, 179–80; and public order, 184, 204

Clay, John, 205

Clement, Priscilla, 55–56, 62, 74–75, 160

Commerce
—of Liverpool: prominence of, 6, 7; and docks, 9–10; and Council, 12, 214; and dock-rating controversy, 24; emphasis on, 25; and Irish famine emigrants, 31; and quarantines, 46, 99, 110, 223, 254 (n. 48); and health conditions, 99–100, 102; and sanitation, 117, 140; and policing, 174, 180, 181, 182, 184; and public order, 208; and boosterism, 222
—of Philadelphia: prominence of, 6; and Council, 12–13; and bonds on immigrants, 34; and head taxes, 34; and disease, 36; and quarantines, 46, 110; and cholera, 108, 109; and policing, 174; and disorder, 197; and public order, 208; and boosterism, 222

Congress, U.S., 81, 112, 217, 227

Conrad, Robert Taylor, 14, 158, 202

Conspiratorial model, 16, 47, 212, 213

Constantinople, 96

Cope, Thomas P., 34, 150

Crime: patterns of, 15; and Irish famine emigrants, 23, 174; and children, 151; and alcohol, 204
—in Liverpool: and Irish famine emigrants, 4, 187–90, 199, 278 (n. 46); and public policy, 32; and emigrants' friends organizations, 39–41, 44; and children, 81, 205, 206–7, 208; and policing, 175, 176; and removals, 189
—in Philadelphia: and emigrants' friends organizations, 37, 38, 40–41, 43; and children, 63–64, 195, 205–8; and benevolent societies, 76; and policing, 191, 193–94; rate of, 195, 199; and Irish famine emigrants, 199–200

Day, Robert, 155–56

Delaware, 36

Democracy, 51, 203, 215–16

Democratic model, 16, 212, 214

Democrats, 12, 14, 24, 158, 196–97, 202

Dietrich, Dr., 35, 36

Disease: and potato famine, 2; and Irish famine emigrants, 4, 17, 23, 33–36, 46–47, 100, 105, 123; and urban development, 5; epidemics, 15, 20, 55, 86, 100, 105, 134; in Liverpool, 32, 33, 100, 123, 136; in Philadelphia, 33, 34, 35, 36, 46–47, 55, 105; theories on, 86, 87, 110, 112, 212; and sanitation, 113. See also specific diseases

Disorder: and urban development, 5, 15; and ideology, 200, 208; and conspiratorial model, 213. See also Sectarian conflict; Violence
—in Liverpool: and violence, 177–86; and policing, 179, 208; and Irish famine emigrants, 187–91, 210
—in Philadelphia: and violence, 19, 24; and political conflicts, 26; and policing, 191, 193–98, 200, 208; reputation for, 192, 194; and commerce,

197; and Irish famine emigrants,
198–201, 210; and sectarian conflict,
200, 209

Dissenters, 26, 146, 147, 156, 165, 166

District Provident Society (DPS): religious support of, 27, 69; and poor
relief, 59, 61, 64–65; and indiscriminate giving, 66; and Irish famine
emigrants, 68, 246–47 (n. 58); and
Central Relief Society, 83; and outdoor relief, 244 (n. 33)

Diversity, demographic: of Philadelphia, 6–7, 19, 21–22, 209, 221–22;
of Liverpool, 7, 19, 143; and national
characteristics, 19–21, 209; and
"otherness," 20, 22; and policing,
175; and violence, 221

Docks, 7, 9–10, 12, 23–24, 176, 180,
214

Domestic Mission Society (DMS): and
Tuckerman, 52; and moral reform,
59–60; and Unitarians, 61; and Irish
famine emigrants, 68–69, 156; and
U.S. tour, 81; and sanitation, 116,
122; and housing, 136; and education, 164

Dorcas Societies, 62, 159

Dowling, M. G., 177, 180, 185, 186,
188, 190, 210

Dublin, Ireland, 180

Duffy, Patrick, 120, 121

Duncan, William H.: and health,
90–91; and housing, 91, 95, 96, 98,
111, 114, 115, 118, 123, 124, 126,
129, 130, 131, 136, 220, 253 (n. 43);
and sanitation, 92, 115, 117, 119,
123–24, 138, 139, 219, 225, 268
(n. 45); as medical officer of health,
93, 110; and Irish famine emigrants,
94, 100, 116, 122–23, 259 (n. 33);
reports of, 96, 97, 98, 252 (n. 27),
253 (n. 42); and cholera, 97, 121;
and medical relief, 98–99, 102; and
environmental causes, 112–13

Dysentery, 2, 33

Eastern Penitentiary, 204, 217

Ecclesiastical Titles Act, 152

Education: and religion, 13–14, 15,
141, 147–51, 163–70; and children,
62; choice of, 227

—in Liverpool: and religion, 13–14,
70, 146–47, 164, 221; and Catholic
Church, 14, 147, 153, 163–66, 170–
72; and ragged schools, 70, 77, 81,
82, 133, 163, 205; and sectarian conflict, 146–47, 163, 165, 168, 186,
225; and poverty, 163, 166–67, 205,
206, 272 (n. 83); and national government, 165–66, 172, 218; and conspiratorial model, 213–14

—in Philadelphia: and sectarian conflict, 14, 141, 148, 149–51, 163, 168–
72, 225, 227; and orphanages, 80;
and Catholic Church, 163, 168–72,
222, 225–26; and poverty, 168–69,
206; and Irish famine emigrants,
169; and conspiratorial model, 213–
14; and religion, 221

Education Act of 1870, 168

Emigrants' friends societies, 23, 37–45

Emigrants' Protection Society, 40

Employment: and public works, 26, 27;
in Philadelphia, 38–40, 42, 43, 45,
47, 50, 56, 61–62, 64, 76–78, 82;
and Irish famine emigrants, 41; and
labor requirements, 52, 56, 78; and
outdoor relief, 53; and auctioning of
labor, 55; and benevolent societies,
58, 61–62, 76–78, 82; in Liverpool,
70, 224

England: Irish emigration to, 2, 104;
public policy in, 5, 16, 81, 176; voter
access in, 18, 214; national administrative state of, 18, 228; and Act of
Union, 19, 143, 179; responds to
potato famine, 26–27; employment
in, 41; poor relief in, 49, 52, 57, 81;
state-sponsored reform in, 51; benevolent societies in, 58; organizing
charities movement in, 84; sanitation

in, 91–92, 114, 139; health in, 93;
religion in, 142–43, 152; and Catholic Church, 143, 185; policing in,
174, 191; disorder in, 204
Episcopal Church, 28, 168
Equalitarianism, 51
Established Church: dominance of, 13;
and "otherness," 20; and sectarian
conflict, 26, 147, 152; and benevolent societies, 59, 155, 269 (n. 50);
and children, 63; and workhouse,
156, 157; and education, 163, 172;
and Irish famine emigrants, 221
Ethnicity
—in Liverpool: and Irish famine emigrants, 4, 13; and Act of Union,
19–20; and sanitation, 116, 140; and
sectarian conflict, 141, 151, 184; and
education, 167; and disorder, 175,
209; and policing, 202; and alcohol,
204
—in Philadelphia: and neighborhoods,
10–11; and Irish famine emigrants,
13; and demographic diversity, 19,
22; and almshouses, 64; and benevolent societies, 78; and hospitals,
104–5; and health, 109; and sanitation, 140; and sectarian conflict, 141,
151; and disorder, 175, 200, 209,
210; and crime, 199; and alcohol,
204; and violence, 221
Europe, 15, 74, 96, 103, 179, 183
Evangelical Home Missionary Society,
160

Fairmount Waterworks, 9, 131–32
Female Orphan Asylum (Liverpool),
63, 68, 69, 269 (n. 50)
Female Society of Philadelphia for the
Relief and Employment of the Poor,
61
Ferry operators, 4, 23, 29, 31
Fever Hospital (Liverpool), 123
Finch, John, 114–15
Fisher, Rev. George, 164

Fisher, Sidney George, 34, 41, 109
Five Years' Residence Act, 30
Foucault, Michel, 213
France, 144, 179
Fraser, Derek, 16, 18, 46, 212–14
Free market principles, 50, 53, 126,
212, 227
Fresh, Thomas, 98, 122–23, 124, 138,
219
Friendly societies, 13
Friendly Sons of St. Patrick, 62
Frontier, 19, 26, 46, 82, 223–24

General Board of Health, 91, 98, 99,
102, 112, 121, 125
General Colporteur Association, 76
Germans, 6, 10, 13, 32, 41, 75, 109,
144, 145
Germantown, Pennsylvania, 10, 148
Gilligan, Michael, 224
Gilligan, Patrick, 224
Girard, Stephen, 79–80, 161, 191,
192
Girard College for Orphans, 9, 65,
79–80, 81, 161, 206
Glasgow, Scotland, 6, 19, 33, 59, 61,
180, 277 (n. 39)
Goss, Bishop, 207
Graham, Sylvester, 134
Great Britain. See England; Ireland
Greig, J. J., 186
Grey, George, 31, 44
Griscom, John H., 117, 120

H & A Cope Company, 1–2, 3, 34,
43–44
Harnden and Company, 71, 72
Hawthorne, George Stuart, 96
Hawthorne, Nathaniel, 8, 50, 73
Health
—of Liverpool: and Council, 11, 92–93,
94, 97, 98; and epidemics, 15; and
Irish famine emigrants, 29, 33, 87,
94–95, 102; and jurisdiction, 46,
111, 125; and public policy, 87, 92,

Lancashire Public School Association, 168

Lane, Rev., 154

Law of Settlement (1662), 52

Lees, Lynn Hollen, 6

Legg, James Henry, 72

Legislation: and transatlantic passage, 4, 33, 41; and jurisdictional dilemmas, 11; regarding settlement, 52, 55, 56; and poor relief, 52–53, 56; and benevolent societies, 78; and health conditions, 91–92, 117; and sanitation, 128, 129, 139; and public baths, 133; and housing, 136, 137; and education, 168; and policing, 176, 177; and violence, 194

Less eligibility, principle of, 3, 53, 54, 67, 80, 225

Liberals: and Liverpool Council, 12, 214; and education, 13–14, 147, 151; and Rivington Pike scheme, 24; and municipal reforms, 25; and health, 92; and Catholic Church, 148, 153; and workhouse, 156–57; and policing, 178

Light, Dale B., Jr., 145–46, 158, 201

Lind, Jenny, 101

Lindsay, John, 127

Liverpool, England: Irish famine emigrants in, 4, 17, 19, 28–32, 33, 45–46; Irish famine emigrants traveling to, 4, 17, 28; during famine years, 5, 6–14; Irish in, 6, 8; characteristics of, 7–8; manufacturing sector, 10; local/municipal government, 12, 25, 30, 31, 32, 121, 139; urban development, 14–22; dock-rating controversy, 23–24

—and national government: municipal government's relationship with, 26, 30, 31, 32, 54; and Irish famine emigrants, 44; and poor relief, 47, 81, 226; and medical relief, 87; and health conditions, 91, 98, 111–12; and public policy, 102, 217–18; and

sanitation, 139; and education, 165–66, 172, 218; and crime, 207; and voluntarism, 241 (n. 67)

Liverpool Asylum for Boys, 63

Liverpool Board of Guardians, 11, 54, 65, 164

Liverpool Charitable Society, 59

Liverpool City Mission, 59, 69, 155

Liverpool Corporation Waterworks Act of 1847, 131

Liverpool Council: and health, 11, 92–93, 94, 97, 98; and sanitation, 11, 92–93, 121; and policing, 11, 176, 177, 179; and bureaucratic structure, 11–12; and Liberals, 12, 214; and Catholic Church, 14, 146; and Rivington Pike scheme, 24; and Irish famine emigrants, 32; and benevolent societies, 64; and hospitals, 88, 89; and public baths, 133; and housing, 136; and education, 146–47, 163, 172; and prisons, 205; and juvenile delinquency, 207

Liverpool Female Penitentiary, 58, 155

Liverpool Foreigners' Mission, 59

Liverpool Infirmary, 88, 89, 100, 101, 102

Liverpool-Manchester railroad, 10

Liverpool Maternity Hospital, 89

Liverpool Night Asylum for the Houseless Poor, 58–59, 64, 69–70

Liverpool Sanitary Act: as model, 92–93; and MOH, 93, 111; and localism, 94, 117, 217; and sanitation, 121, 123, 219–20; and housing, 122; efficiency of, 125; and reform, 177; and boosterism, 193; timing of, 225

Liverpool School for the Blind, 155

Liverpool Select Vestry: and Irish famine emigrants, 29, 31; and forced removal, 30, 65–66, 95; and poor relief, 53–54, 65–66, 92, 105; and workhouses, 54–55, 67; and children, 63, 67; and Vagrant Ward, 69–70; and medical relief, 93,

94–95, 98–99, 102; and cholera, 96–97

Localism: and potato famine, 3; national characteristics of, 18, 216–18; American emphasis on, 36, 227; and Irish famine emigrants, 46; and poor relief, 57; and health, 94; and sanitation, 117, 139, 140, 217; and policing, 203, 209; and political culture, 212; and voluntarism, 219

Logan Evening School, 206

London, England, 6, 74, 77, 121, 137, 174–76, 191, 197, 203

London Society for Organizing Charitable Relief and Repressing Mendacity, 83

Lowe, W. J., 143, 184

Lunatic Asylum, 102

Lying-In Hospital (Liverpool), 101

Mackworth, Digby, 152

Magdalen Society, 60, 77

Malthusian theories, 53, 55

Manayunk, Pennsylvania, 10

Manchester, England, 6, 50, 166, 176, 180, 190

Mann, W. I., 9, 81

Marcus, Alan I., 19

Marshall's Police, 197, 198

Martineau, Harriet, 56

Martineau, James, 27

Material conditions, 4, 5, 20, 21, 211–12, 224–25

Mathew, Theobald, 204

Measles, 33, 96

Medical officer of health (MOH), 92, 93, 103, 111, 121

Medical relief: in Philadelphia, 55, 58, 60, 77, 79, 89; and benevolent societies, 58, 60, 77, 79, 101, 105; in Liverpool, 58, 87, 89, 94–95, 98–99, 101–2, 105; public/private roles in, 86, 87, 89, 101–2, 105; and disease, 110

Medical schools, 102

Melly, George, 181

Melly, Louisa, 183

Melville, Herman, 7, 50

Mersey Mission to Seamen, 155–56

Merton, Samuel Holland, 153

Mickle, Isaac, 150–51

Mill, John Stuart, 51

Miller, Kerby A., 27, 33

Milwaukee, Wisconsin, 134

Ministry at Large, 52

Missions to the Poor, 81

M'Neile, Hugh, 27, 147, 152, 178

Monkkonen, Eric, 16, 203

Moore, John Bramley, 44, 101

Moore, Kevin, 183–84

Moral reform: and alcohol, 49; and poor relief, 52, 56, 80, 204; and benevolent societies, 52, 58, 59, 61, 76, 161; and disease, 86–87, 88, 110; and hospitals, 89; and cholera, 103, 109; and sanitation, 113, 116, 132; and housing, 137; and education, 163, 170; and children, 206

Morpeth, Lord, 91, 92, 93, 94, 117

Moyamensing, Pennsylvania: poverty in, 10–11; health in, 74, 105, 106, 108, 109, 118; religion in, 76; soup kitchens, 78; sanitation, 120–21, 128, 129, 130; water, 132; public baths, 134; violence, 194, 195–96, 197, 200, 203, 219, 222; prisons, 204

Moyamensing House of Industry, 108

Mullen, William J., 105

Municipal Corporations Act (1835), 146, 176, 178

Municipal Reform Act (1835), 12, 25, 214

National characteristics: and comparative history, 17–19, 20, 21, 215, 228; and political structure, 18, 25–26, 36; and voluntarism, 18–19, 28, 65, 172, 212, 228; and violence, 19, 210, 220, 285 (n. 111); and boosterism, 19, 222; and demographic diversity,

societies, 58, 78; and hospitals, 110; and religion, 156

Poor Law Board, 54, 165

Poor Law Commission, 25, 29, 30, 53, 54, 91

Poor Law Removal Act, 30

Poor Law Report, 53, 54, 57

Poor Law Unions, 11, 53, 54

Poor relief: and public policy, 16, 51, 212; and ideology, 48, 51; costs of, 52, 53, 56, 57; and moral reform, 52, 56, 80, 204; and children, 151

—in Liverpool: and dock-rating controversy, 24; and policing, 29, 32, 65, 72, 177; and Irish famine emigrants, 29, 65–73; reforms in, 31, 81, 122; and taxation, 34, 65, 72; jurisdiction, 46, 47, 57; and public/private roles, 52–55, 58–60, 63, 64–73, 82, 83; and forced removal, 65–66, 67, 81; and indiscriminate giving, 66–67, 82, 83, 154; and health conditions, 92, 93, 95; and sanitation, 124; and conspiratorial model, 213–14

—in Philadelphia: demand for, 24; jurisdiction, 46, 57; and benevolent societies, 48, 55, 60–62, 79; and public/private roles, 55–56, 60–62, 63, 64–65, 82; and indiscriminate giving, 61, 73–74, 77, 82; compared to Liverpool, 64, 81; and Irish famine emigrants, 73–80; and conspiratorial model, 213–14

Poovey, Mary, 114

Population density: and urban development, 5, 14; and local government, 12; and Malthusian theories, 53, 55; and sanitation, 113, 131; and policing, 174, 175, 203, 208; and crime, 188, 199

Ports, 6, 10, 32, 87

Potato famine, 2, 3–4, 26–28, 211. *See also* Irish famine emigrants

Potter, David M., 223

Poverty: and Irish famine emigrants, 4, 13, 14, 17, 23, 110, 141; and urban development, 5; and worthy/unworthy, 47, 49, 55, 57, 58, 61, 65, 73–74, 87–88, 160; and ideology, 48, 49–51; and alcohol, 49–50, 80, 204; and hospitals, 50, 87, 256 (n. 81); and disease, 110; and sanitation, 113; and public baths, 132–34

—in Liverpool: pervasiveness of, 8, 50; and forced removal, 30; and public policy, 32; and sanitation, 49, 116; and public baths, 133–34; and housing, 136; and Catholic Church, 144, 154–55; and education, 163, 166–67, 205, 206, 272 (n. 83); and crime, 188

—in Philadelphia: and children, 50; and benevolent societies, 60, 76, 218; rate of, 73; compared to New York, 74; and housing, 136, 137; and education, 168–69, 170, 206; and incarceration, 199; and voluntarism, 218

Pragmatic model, 16, 212–13

Presbyterian Church, 75, 158, 222

Preston Gaol, 205

Prisons: and urban development, 15; reform, 17, 205, 207, 208, 285 (n. 109); in Liverpool, 30, 58, 205, 208; and poverty, 50, 52; and rehabilitation, 51, 204, 205; and religion, 162; in Philadelphia, 198–99, 204–5, 208; design, 212

Private enterprise, 140

Private property: in Philadelphia, 21, 111, 114, 130, 139, 203, 218, 219–20, 286 (n. 13); and health concerns, 86, 91; and sanitation, 114, 130, 139, 219–20; and housing, 137; in Liverpool, 140; and policing, 174, 203

Prostitution, 50, 58, 60, 77

Protestant Association, 147, 151

Protestant Church: and Irish emigration, 13, 141, 171; and "otherness," 20; and poor relief, 51; work ethic,

55; and benevolent societies, 58; political power, 152; and alcohol, 204
—in Liverpool: and education, 13–14; and benevolent societies, 27, 59, 155; and children, 63; and Catholic Church, 142, 178, 221; and typhus, 153; and sectarian conflict, 185
—in Philadelphia: and sectarian conflict, 14, 200; and orphanages, 63; and benevolent societies, 76, 160–61; and Catholic Church, 142, 148, 149, 151, 193; and Irish famine emigrants, 148, 160

Protestant Crusade, 148
Protestant Institute, 148
Providence, Rhode Island, 206
Provincialist (ship), 35, 106, 107
Public Health Act, 91, 94, 117, 121
Public order, 174–75, 184, 204. *See also* Disorder; Policing
Public policy: English, 5, 16, 81, 176; and Irish famine emigrants, 14, 21, 22, 23; government's role in, 15–16, 151–52, 224–25, 226, 228; local versus national, 16, 17, 18, 21, 26, 30, 31, 32, 54, 55; historiographic models of, 16, 18, 46, 47, 212–15; and poor relief, 16, 51, 212; and national characteristics, 20, 25; on packet ships, 23; and benevolent societies, 58; on health, 86; and sanitation, 114, 132–33; and religion, 151–52
—in Liverpool: and Irish emigration, 5; development, 16, 18; issues, 23–24, 25; and Irish famine emigrants, 25, 30–32, 46; and sanitation, 32, 92, 99; and poor relief, 48, 65, 73; and benevolent society cooperation, 69; compared to Philadelphia, 80, 212, 216–18, 223–24; and health, 87, 92, 99; and national government, 102, 217; and education, 166–67; and policing, 176
—in Philadelphia: and Irish emigra-

tion, 5; development, 16, 18; issues, 24, 25; and Irish famine emigrants, 25, 46; and potato famine response, 27–28; and disease, 36; and poor relief, 48; and children, 65; compared to Liverpool, 80, 212, 216–18, 223–24; and health, 87, 103; and housing, 137; and frontier, 223

Public School Society, 149

Quakers, 55, 60, 61, 76, 136, 159, 160, 161, 168
Quarantines: of Irish famine emigrants, 4, 35–37, 46, 105, 110, 223–24; and epidemics, 15, 86, 113; in Liverpool, 46, 92, 94, 99, 110, 223, 223–24, 254 (n. 48); in Philadelphia, 46, 105, 107, 110, 126, 223–24; and cholera, 103, 107
Quebec, Canada, 6
Quigley, Patrick, 162
Quinn, Jemmy, 121

Ragged Schools, 70, 82, 164, 170, 206
Ragged School Union, 164
Railroads, 10
Rainhill Asylum, 102
Rappahannock (ship), 35–36, 46, 219
Rathbone, William, 24, 59, 83, 133, 167
Reform Act (1835), 18
Religion: and education, 13–14, 15, 141, 147–51, 163–70; and children, 62, 151, 162–63; in Philadelphia, 76, 162–63; and public policy, 151–52. *See also* Catholic Church; Protestant Church; Sectarian conflict; *specific churches*
—in Liverpool: and education, 13–14, 70, 146–47, 164, 221; and Irish famine emigrants, 27, 152–53; and emigrants' friends organizations, 40; and hospitals, 89; census of, 142; and workhouses, 156–57, 164, 269 (n. 57)

Repealers, 179, 180, 181, 184
Reynolds, Lawrence, 181
Ribbonism, 187, 190, 201
Ricardo, David, 53
Richmond, Pennsylvania, 130
Ritchie, Arthur, 107, 109
Rivington Pike scheme, 23, 24, 131
Roebuck, Mr., 185
Rosenberg, Charles, 103
Rosine Association, 77
Runners, 4, 40
Rural Constabulary Act, 176
Rushton, Edward, 28–31, 66, 125, 157,
    177, 181, 188–89, 206–7
Russell, John, 27, 176
Ryan, Mary, 15

St. Anne's Widows Asylum, 79, 159
St. John's Orphan Asylum, 63, 79, 159
St. Joseph's Catholic Church, 79, 104
St. Joseph's Female Orphanage, 79
St. Joseph's Hospital, 79, 104–5, 110,
    112, 145, 160, 172, 226
St. Joseph's Society for the Relief of Dis-
    tressed Emigrants from Ireland, 79,
    160
St. Mary's Church, 153
St. Patrick's Day, 178, 180–81, 183–86,
    201, 210, 221, 283 (n. 91)
St. Philip de Neri's Catholic Church,
    150
Sanders, James W., 170
San Francisco, California, 15
Sanitation: and ferry operators, 4,
    29; and ideological traditions, 17;
    and Irish famine emigrants, 23, 113–
    14, 142; urban reform in, 86; in
    England, 91; specialists in, 112; and
    population density, 113, 131; and
    cholera, 121; and public baths,
    132–33; and model housing, 135–37
—in Liverpool: and Irish famine emi-
    grants, 4, 29, 139; compared to Phil-
    adelphia, 7, 8–9; and Council, 11,
    92–93, 121; innovations in, 15, 21;

and reputation, 24, 25, 139–40, 223;
    and jurisdiction, 32, 46; and public
    policy, 32, 92, 99; and poverty, 49,
    116; and benevolent societies, 60;
    and health conditions, 91, 94, 111;
    and Duncan, 92, 115, 117, 119, 123–
    24, 138, 139, 219, 225, 268 (n. 45);
    and cholera, 97, 130, 134; serious-
    ness of, 113; and housing, 114–15,
    122, 125, 126, 135–36, 137, 138–39;
    reform of, 121–26, 138; and Catholic
    Church, 122, 154, 268 (n. 45); and
    waters and sewers, 131, 132, 138–39;
    and public baths, 133–34, 138–39
—in Philadelphia: compared to Liver-
    pool, 7, 8–9; and Council, 11; inno-
    vations in, 15; demand for, 24; and
    jurisdiction, 46; and cholera, 103,
    107, 109–10, 117, 127–28, 138, 261
    (n. 52); and spotted fever, 106–7;
    and health, 111; and private prop-
    erty, 114, 130, 139, 219–20; and rep-
    utation, 117, 126, 258 (n. 14); and
    housing, 117–20, 128, 130–31, 136–
    37, 138, 139, 220; reform in, 126–31,
    138; and water and sewers, 131–32,
    138; and public baths, 134, 138, 139
Schiffler Association, 200
Schuylkill River, 132
Scotland, 7, 70
Sectarian conflict
—and Irish famine emigrants, 15, 23,
    141
—in Liverpool: and education, 13–14,
    141, 146–47, 151, 163, 165, 170, 172,
    186, 225; violence, 14, 148, 175, 178,
    179, 184, 185–86, 221; and Catholic
    Church, 26, 146–47, 183, 185–86;
    and Established Church, 26, 147,
    152; and benevolent societies, 27;
    and public policy, 32; and Irish
    famine emigrants, 148, 152–53, 187,
    277 (n. 39); compared to Philadel-
    phia, 151, 221; policing, 177, 179,
    183–86, 209; disorder, 209

—in Philadelphia: and Catholic
Church, 14, 25, 145, 150, 200; and
education, 14, 141, 148, 149–51,
163, 168–72, 225, 227; violence, 14,
149–50, 169, 172–73, 193, 221; and
Protestant Church, 14, 200; and Irish
famine emigrants, 148, 150, 158;
compared to Liverpool, 151, 221;
and Board of Guardians, 161–62;
disorder, 200, 209

Settlement laws, 52, 55, 56

Shelter for Colored Orphans, 63, 80

Simey, Margaret, 18–19

Simon, John, 93

Simpson, John, 162

Smallpox, 36, 95, 96, 106, 107, 118

Smith, Adam, 50, 53, 212

Smith, Southwood, 137

Societies of Naturalized Citizens, 42

Society for Organizing Charitable
Relief and Repressing Mendicancy,
84

Society for the Employment and
Instruction of the Poor, 108

Society for the Employment and Relief
of the Poor, 106

Society for the Promotion of the Religious Instruction of the Poor, 59

Society of Friends, 27, 63–64

Society of Saint Vincent de Paul, 60,
79, 144, 154, 159, 249 (n. 95)

Souder, Casper, Jr., 120–21

Soup kitchens, 60, 69, 70, 76, 78–79,
81, 82–83

South Dispensary, 88, 100

Southern Home for Destitute Children, 80

Southern Hospital, 88–89, 90, 100–
101, 154, 155

Southwark, Pennsylvania: ethnicity,
11; blocking foreign vessels, 35, 36,
46–47, 219; soup kitchens, 78; sanitation, 109, 130; water, 132; sectarian
conflict, 150, 173; policing, 195, 196;
violence, 200

Spotted fever, 106

Spring Garden, Pennsylvania, 78–79,
128, 129, 132

Spring Garden Soup Society, 79

Sprogle, Howard, 197

State government: and municipal government, 26; bonds, 34; autonomy,
36; and Castle Garden, 45; and poor
relief, 81, 227; and health, 103; and
education, 168–69; and policing,
193, 197, 281 (n. 80); and public
policy, 217

Stokes, S. Nasmyth, 166

Strangers: and Irish famine emigrants,
2–3, 4, 40, 41, 171; and demographic diversity, 19–20; and emigrants' friends, 38, 40; and poor
relief, 49; and legal settlement, 53;
and benevolent societies, 58, 76; and
violence, 180

Strangers' Friend Society, 58, 66, 68,
83

Street, John, 61

Supreme Court, U.S., 34

Susquehanna (ship), 1

Swatara (ship), 33

Swift, John, 27, 36

Swift, Roger, 187

Systematic Beneficence Society (SBS),
84

Taxation: in Liverpool, 24, 25, 29, 34,
46, 65, 72, 81, 135, 140, 168; in Philadelphia, 25, 34, 35, 43, 46, 75, 81,
103, 134, 168, 239 (n. 34); and poor
relief, 34, 57, 65, 72, 80, 81; and Castle Garden, 45; and poverty, 50, 55;
skepticism of, 212; and localism, 216

Temperance reformers, 17, 52, 61, 62,
217

Temperance Society, 42

Temporary Home Association, 37, 42,
78

Tenement House Law, 137

Thom, John, 59

Voter access, 12, 18, 25, 34, 41, 146, 214

Wales, 7, 142, 152, 176, 185
Walmsley, Rev., 154
Walnut Street Prison, 204
Walton's Prison, 205
Warner, Sam Bass, 18, 220
War on Poverty, 227
Watch Committee. *See* Policing—Liverpool
Water supply, 9, 24, 131–32, 138–39
Welfare Reform Bill (1996), 227
Western Association of Ladies for Relief and Employment of the Poor, 76
Western lands, 19, 21, 34, 39, 50, 81–82
Western Penitentiary, 204
West Philadelphia, Pennsylvania, 79
Whig model, 16, 47, 212
Whigs, 12, 24, 26–27, 158, 197, 202, 214, 270 (n. 60)
White, Verner M., 153
Whitty, Michael James, 176, 177
Wilkinson, Kitty, 133

William III (king of England), 178
Williams, Justice, 185
Wills Hospital for the Indigent Lame and Blind, 104
Wilmington, Delaware, 35, 36
Wohl, Anthony, 96
Women: of Philadelphia, 12, 76–78, 79, 82, 134, 199; and labor system, 50; and poor relief, 56, 62, 74; and benevolent societies, 58, 61–62, 76–78, 79, 82; of Liverpool, 58, 89, 101, 189, 191
Woolson, John, 162
Workhouses
—and poverty, 51, 52, 57
—in Liverpool: and forced removal, 30; and indoor relief, 53–55, 64, 67; and children, 63, 245 (n. 41); and typhus, 94, 95; and cholera, 100; and medical relief, 102, 110; and religion, 156–57, 164, 171, 269 (n. 57)

Yellow fever, 15, 112, 120
Young Christians' Missionary Association (YCMA), 160–61
Youthful Offenders Act, 206